Indigenous Education

Indigenous Education

New Directions in Theory and Practice

HUIA TOMLINS-JAHNKE,
SANDRA STYRES,
SPENCER LILLEY &
DAWN ZINGA, *Editors*

UNIVERSITY *of* **ALBERTA** PRESS

Published by

The University of Alberta Press
Ring House 2
Edmonton, Alberta, Canada T6G 2E1
www.uap.ualberta.ca

Copyright © 2019 The University of
Alberta Press

LIBRARY AND ARCHIVES CANADA
CATALOGUING IN PUBLICATION

Title: Indigenous education : new directions
  in theory and practice / Huia Tomlins-
  Jahnke, Sandra Styres, Spencer Lilley,
  and Dawn Zinga, editors.
Names: Tomlins-Jahnke, Huia, editor.
  | Styres, Sandra D., 1961- editor. | Lilley,
  Spencer, 1963- editor. | Zinga, Dawn, editor.
Description: Includes bibliographical
  references.
Identifiers: Canadiana (print) 20190094281 |
  Canadiana (ebook) 20190094338 |
  ISBN 9781772124149 (softcover) |
  ISBN 9781772124453 (EPUB) |
  ISBN 9781772124477 (PDF) |
  ISBN 9781772124460 (Kindle)
Subjects: LCSH: Indigenous peoples—
  Education—North America. | LCSH:
  Indigenous peoples—Education—
  Islands of the Pacific. | LCSH: Culturally
  relevant pedagogy.
Classification: LCC LC1099.515.C85 I53 2019 |
  DDC 370.117—dc23

First edition, first printing, 2019.
First printed and bound in Canada by
Houghton Boston Printers, Saskatoon,
Saskatchewan.
Copyediting and proofreading by The Editing
Company, Toronto.

All rights reserved. No part of this publication may be reproduced, stored in a retrieval system, or transmitted in any form or by any means (electronic, mechanical, photocopying, recording, or otherwise) without prior written consent. Contact University of Alberta Press for further details.

University of Alberta Press supports copyright. Copyright fuels creativity, encourages diverse voices, promotes free speech, and creates a vibrant culture. Thank you for buying an authorized edition of this book and for complying with the copyright laws by not reproducing, scanning, or distributing any part of it in any form without permission. You are supporting writers and allowing University of Alberta Press to continue to publish books for every reader.

University of Alberta Press is committed to protecting our natural environment. As part of our efforts, this book is printed on Enviro Paper: it contains 100% post-consumer recycled fibres and is acid- and chlorine-free.

University of Alberta Press gratefully acknowledges the support received for its publishing program from the Government of Canada, the Canada Council for the Arts, and the Government of Alberta through the Alberta Media Fund.

Contents

Expanding the Indigenous Education Agenda IX
A Foreword
LINDA TUHIWAI SMITH

Opening XIII
Contested Spaces and Expanding the Indigenous Education Agenda
SANDRA STYRES, DAWN ZINGA, SPENCER LILLEY, & HUIA TOMLINS-JAHNKE

I Vision
Theoretical Approaches to Indigenous Education

1 Education Through Paideia 3
The Contested Space of the Indigenous Psyche
MARGARET J. MAAKA

2 Pathways for Remembering and (Re)cognizing Indigenous Thought in Education 39
Indigenizing Teacher Education and the Academy
SANDRA STYRES

3 Kaupapa Māori within the Academy 63
Negotiating Sites of Struggle
LEONIE PIHAMA

4 Contested Spaces 83
Indigeneity and Epistemologies of Ignorance
HUIA TOMLINS-JAHNKE

5 *Homo Economicus* and Forgetful Curriculum 103
Remembering Other Ways to Be a Human Being
DWAYNE DONALD

II Relationships
Negotiating Contested Spaces

6 Contested Places in Education 129
The Radical Potential for "Being Māori"
WALLY PENETITO

7 He Pelapela anei ka 'Ōlelo a ka Hawai'i? 149
Contested Values in Language Revitalization
K. LAIANA WONG & SAM L. NO'EAU WARNER

8 Wisdom Maps 171
Metaphors as Maps
KATRINA-ANN R. KAPĀ'ANAOKALĀOKEOLA NĀKOA OLIVEIRA

9 What's in a Name? 189
Contested Eponyms
SPENCER LILLEY

10 Contested Spaces of Indigenization in Canadian Higher Education 205
Reciprocal Relationships and Institutional Responsibilities
MICHELLE PIDGEON

III Knowledge
Practice and Pedagogy

11 Confronting Indigenous Identities in Transcultural Contexts 233
FRANK DEER

12 Preparing Teachers for Indigenous Language Immersion Classrooms 255
MARGIE HOHEPA & NGAREWA HAWERA

13 Teaching as the Creation of Ethical Space 277
Indigenous Student Learning in the Academy/University
DAWN ZINGA

14 Exploring Teacher Candidate Resistance to Indigenous Content in a Teacher Education Program 311
JEAN-PAUL RESTOULE & ANGELA NARDOZI

15 Kia Mahi Hei Waewae Mo Te Atawhai 339
MARI ROPATA-TE HEI

IV Action
New Directions in Indigenous Education

16 Improving Special Needs Education for Māori Children 365
Concepts, Principles, and a Promising Program
JILL BEVAN-BROWN

17 Maintaining Indigeneity within Education and Broader Contexts 405
WIREMU DOHERTY

18 Essentially Māori 427
A Māori Art Paradigm
ROBERT JAHNKE

19 **Indigenous Knowledge Systems as the Missing Link in Scientific Worldviews** 453
A Discussion on Western Science as a Contested Space
DANIEL LIPE

20 **Is "Space" the Final Frontier?** 483
Talking Forward Indigenous Frameworks in Education
PATRICIA MARINGI G. JOHNSTON

Closing 513
Drawing the Threads of Contested Spaces
SPENCER LILLEY, HUIA TOMLINS-JAHNKE, SANDRA STYRES, & DAWN ZINGA

Contributors 521

Expanding the Indigenous Education Agenda
A Foreword

LINDA TUHIWAI SMITH

THERE IS SOMETHING IMPORTANT to be gained in reading works by Indigenous educators from different contexts, writing about aspects of Indigenous education all together in one book. A whole book on Indigenous education: that is both an accomplishment and a testimony to the scholarship that has emerged about Indigenous education and the diverse topics now being addressed by Indigenous scholars. I recall those texts where Native or Indigenous education referred either to the "traditional" practices as observed by non-Native scholars or to the deficits and failings of Native communities. I also remember those texts where there was one chapter on Indigenous education buried in among other chapters. It is a pleasure to read a book all about aspects of Indigenous education that are told from different perspectives by Indigenous authors.

There is an interesting discussion to be had about the positioning of different Indigenous experiences alongside each other. At one level all the chapters resonate an idea about Indigenous education while at the same time casting more light on how particular aspects of Indigenous education are understood against a different historical, cultural, and social context. The places people write from add something deeply authentic to the stories they tell. I know that I gain new insights about my context when I read what others have said about their context and their experiences. Is it serendipitous that scholars write about matters that are shared by other Indigenous Peoples across different jurisdictions, or do we indeed have a shared experience and a shared struggle in Indigenous education?

The four sections of this book capture the work being done in theory, knowledge, practice, and the future, while also capturing the growing Indigenous expertise and leadership being gained in specific areas of education, from special education to teacher education, from curriculum to higher education. These and other topics addressed in the book are specializations and subject fields within the broader study of education. The book provides a multidisciplinary set of perspectives across different arenas of Indigenous education, and that makes the book interesting but also relevant to students of education and especially useful to Indigenous educators who are practitioners, researchers, and policy makers.

The book demonstrates the expanded nature of our Indigenous interest in education and our expertise in many aspects of education. The kind of issues being raised demonstrate a deeper knowledge and reflection about our own initiatives. The best example of this is in the field of language revitalization where we have expertise and authority over what we know about the revitalization of Indigenous languages. Some issues raised here would not be seen as a concern for outsiders, perhaps, that intersection of language, culture, and identity within the nation state. What we know is intimate, is experienced, and is researched. We know something about pedagogy, about initial teacher education, about curriculum, about identity and meanings, and about the implications of our own success in some areas.

Clearly, the chapters address the continuing challenge for Indigenous knowledges, values, languages, and peoples to be included in public education systems. What strikes me, however, is how expert we have become at recognizing, naming, and then calling to account the specific barriers we encounter. Some of these barriers, like denialism, dominant language cultures, and institutional accreditation practices, work at different levels or layers and are often unseen; they are the less obvious barriers that continue to challenge Indigenous educational ideas and practices. The examples within the book of positive initiatives, of strong Indigenous analysis, and of the message of hopefulness and determination tell us that education is worth our collective efforts.

Opening
Contested Spaces and Expanding the Indigenous Education Agenda

SANDRA STYRES, DAWN ZINGA, SPENCER LILLEY,
& HUIA TOMLINS-JAHNKE

WE WOULD LIKE TO BEGIN our journey by acknowledging not only the complex histories of those on whose traditional lands we collaboratively worked as an editorial team to bring this text together but also the lands of each of the contributing authors. We acknowledge our Elders past and present as well as the ancestors who have shared teachings that guided each of us through the creation of this book. While as authors we may be geographically, culturally, and linguistically distinct, we all wrote on the ancestral lands of our own people or of other Indigenous Peoples (not our own), were conscious of land and its stories, and were thankful that conversations about the book occurred in Aotearoa, Hawai'i, and Turtle Island.[1] If you are on another's land as you read this volume, we ask that you be mindful of and acknowledge the lands on which you are located.

As a research team, we considered what to name this opening chapter of the book and explored what words might be appropriate. Given the cultural and linguistic diversity of voices represented in this text, not only across the research team but also among the contributing authors, the choice of a name for this section raised questions of whose words, lands, stories, and ancestors would become privileged in the naming of the opening and closing sections of this text. Out of respect for the rich and diverse socio-cultural and socio-linguistic distinctiveness represented throughout this text, we return to the teachings of our Elders. In discussions as an editorial team, we have chosen to draw upon the wisdom of Elders who have counselled that when faced with a context of plurality and distinctiveness, in order to bring everyone together with good minds and good hearts, it is critically important not only to acknowledge that diversity among ourselves but also to open the process in ways that, as much as is possible, represent everyone present and are as inclusive as possible. Following those wise words, we have chosen to name this first section of the book, "Opening."

It is important to recognize that the rich and diverse socio-cultural and socio-linguistic distinctiveness represented in the voices throughout this text offer unique place-specific perspectives, which we have purposefully combined in sections so that themes are considered from diverse perspectives and positionalities. It would have been simpler to organize the chapters according to the three geographical areas represented in this text. However, we would have lost the richness of exploring how contestation is taken up in similar ways related to shared overarching experiences, as well as the nuanced complexities of place-specific engagement with colonialism. While colonization is in many ways a shared experience, its expression is unique and shaped by differing histories of colonization and settler relationships. The authors in this text speak from their own particular cultural locations and positionalities to explore both shared and unique issues of pressing concern. While there are some shared experiences, this text in no way is an expression of pan-Indigeneity that essentializes Indigenous colonial experiences; rather, it highlights the uniqueness of place in engaging contestation and addressing concerns related to different histories of colonization, land dispossession, and treaty relationships, as well as assimilationist policies and practices.

An example of this is that, while acknowledging the linguistic richness of the Hawai'ian and Māori languages, conversations concerning linguistic diversity are of particular importance within the context of Turtle Island (North America). While Hawai'i and Aotearoa each benefit from their own unique and rich language, culture, and identity, Turtle Island (North America) has a vast cultural and linguistic plurality. The Canada/United States border represents a colonial construct that has introduced legislative and political complexities. Therefore, when thinking about linguistic plurality across Turtle Island we must also consider it in terms of the colonial representation of two distinct countries. Canada currently has approximately 60 Indigenous languages being spoken, which are grouped into about nine overarching language families. Similarly, in the United States there are approximately 132 Indigenous languages being spoken today, which can be grouped into about 10 overarching language families. A linguistic element shared by the authors representing Hawai'i, Aotearoa, and Turtle Island is that English became the dominant language of colonization.

While the use of English is problematic in that it is the language of conquest and a reminder of colonial relations of power and privilege, and is therefore contested space, it is the language that, of necessity, this book is written in. At present, the English language unifies each of our culturally and linguistically diverse traditions and allows us to share, for a wider audience, understandings of our own realities and truths, particularly where individual authors have chosen to use their own languages (at times with English translations following) to inform key parts of their writings. Four Arrows (2006, 274) writes that "communication is a sacred release of power. Words can literally sing things into existence. A language of conquest has the power to bring about destruction. A language of truth has the power of renew." One of the shared truths among Indigenous Peoples transnationally is that understandings of spirituality and relationships are of paramount importance in daily socio-cultural and socio-political interactions. In this context, the concept of *opening*, as we use it here, suggests the ways one sets about preparing for and beginning a journey. As well, many of our contributing authors have chosen to represent their truths and to disrupt and challenge the language of conquest by using concepts, values, and beliefs derived from their own specific language and traditions of philosophical thought.

Drawing on the philosophical approaches to Indigenous thought from Aotearoa, Hawai'i, and Turtle Island, we collectively examine both theoretical and applied approaches to Indigenous education practice and pedagogy. The theoretical approaches explore the way spiritual understandings concerning relationships and knowledges between Indigenous communities, government sectors, and educational institutions and, more particularly, the ways we prepare teachers to be teachers, must take seriously the historical and contemporary understandings of Indigeneity both within education and across broader contexts. All those who are involved as stakeholders in education make policy and practice decisions that impact the lives of Indigenous children and their families. In the chapters that follow, the authors not only provide insights to assist those stakeholders in reflecting on their policy and practice decisions but also explore the contested places in which those decisions are made. In addressing contested places, we focus on how relationships inform the ways we educate Indigenous students to participate effectively in local, national, and global arenas. Drawing on those arenas, the authors offer insight into the ways practice and pedagogy need to be re-conceptualized and challenged to create safe and inclusive learning environments for the benefit of all students. They also provide insights into new directions being explored within Indigenous education by offering grounded examples of programs and research across Turtle Island, Hawai'i, and Aotearoa. Woven throughout the book is the concept that, for many Indigenous educators and students, education occurs in contested places.

While we need to define contested space in some general terms, it is important to note that the authors have defined contested spaces in their own unique ways. In general terms, contestation occurs in the shared spaces where disparate worldviews collide. In educational contexts where education is provided through mainstream curriculum that does not include or value Indigenous ways of knowing, contested spaces are constantly triggered, engaged, enacted, and maintained to the detriment of Indigenous learners and educators. This also acts to the detriment of non-Indigenous learners and educators, who continue to be trapped in these patterns of colonial relations and are not provided with opportunities to recognize and explore contestation in respectful and meaningful ways. Those non-Indigenous individuals who have begun to explore and challenge these relations have to choose to either engage or disengage the contestation and accept the consequences associated with either decision. Those learners and educators who see themselves reflected in the mainstream have the privilege of being able to choose to be unaware of the contested spaces and their role in maintaining those spaces, while Indigenous learners and educators have no choice but to be aware of and constantly negotiate those spaces. Thus, education can be considered one of the key sites of conflict and resistance, but we frequently do not discuss it as such. Contestation is also about spaces of loss, as Indigenous voices and knowledges are more often than not erased from the conversation, and may be framed in deficit-theorizing models by mainstream lenses and represented back as something unrecognizable and stripped of cultural and linguistic integrity. The authors call attention to these aspects of educational contexts as we need to be aware of, acknowledge, and engage these contestations.

The purpose of this book is to open up dialogue so that contestation in education contexts can be acknowledged and engaged in relevant, respectful, and meaningful ways. While as authors we may choose to do this in different ways, we are collectively joined in our efforts to bring these contested spaces into view. One might ask why education is an important site and question the importance of examining contestation within education. It is important to start with the idea that education as a site of resistance is not a new idea, and is one that will be visited often by the authors in their chapters. However, while education is widely understood as a site of resistance, it is not conceptualized or commonly talked about as a place of contestation. While other types of contestation exist within education, we are specifically and explicitly examining contestation as it applies to Indigenous education. Education is seen to be critical to issues relating to sovereignty, governance, and self-determination in moving forward in a shared future. Unrecognized and unresolved contestation within education can influence relations between Indigenous and non-Indigenous stakeholders such that it perpetuates tangled colonial relations and undermines our collective ability to develop partnerships and support new directions for change that can serve to realize that future.

By engaging contestation in relevant, respectful, and meaningful ways, we can begin to understand how we might untangle some of these colonial relations so that we can forge new relationships based on mutual respect and egalitarianism that eliminate the unilateral assumption that dominant Western perspectives are the only lens from which we should operate. Contested spaces and the assumptions embedded within that contestation must be acknowledged in order to be critically examined and explored effectively. For example, in higher education we can consider how Western views and assumptions of authorship collide and frequently dominate Indigenous worldviews related to knowledges and the sharing of knowledge. As outlined by Zinga and Styres (2011; see also Styres and Zinga 2013), authorship is an interesting and important contestation within mainstream academia that is assumed but not often talked about—rarely, if ever, do we venture outside our comfort zones created by assumed hierarchicality to have the important conversations around it. It is often said that actions speak louder than words. It is important that we do not just write about contestation but live it—in all its discomfort and in its many expressions. It is important, in having these conversations, that we address what the assumed conventions around authorship are really saying. Authorship offers a way for each of us to live with and engage contestation by exploring the types of conversations and issues that are evoked concerning authorship, in order to challenge and disrupt the ways these assumptions become normalized and remain unchallenged. These normalized assumptions privilege the power structures embedded in mainstream understandings of authorship and de-centre Indigenous ways of knowing and sharing knowledge.

As an editorial collective, we have each reflected deeply and meaningfully about authorship and its role in both our vision for this book and the ways it informs and influences our relationships with one another. At the outset of the book project, we agreed that it would be inappropriate for a non-Indigenous author to be the first editor for a wide variety of reasons, not the least of which being that to do so would reinforce and maintain the contested spaces we have challenged and disrupted. Furthermore, we wanted to communicate clearly that, as articulated by Graham Smith (2012), there are some conversations that Indigenous people must have among themselves, and other conversations that non-Indigenous people may, if they are fortunate enough to be invited, take part in.

This book is about having those conversations that serve to disrupt networks and relations of power, and is a space to privilege and centre Indigenous voices and perspectives. In light of Graham Smith's and this editorial team's assertions, this book was a mindful and purposeful choice to engage in these conversations among ourselves first as Indigenous scholars—in other words, what are we saying about issues of concern related to education and contestation to us as Indigenous people? That said, we have chosen to include two chapters that offer particular non-Indigenous perspectives, which speak to the tensions and challenges that arise when non-Indigenous people engage with and make meaningful attempts to include Indigenous content within learning environments, while mindfully and purposefully challenging the associated contestations. Another area of contestation that this editorial team has actively chosen to engage with is related to issues concerning authorship and positioning within mainstream publishing contexts. While Western conventions of authorship are tied to one's position in terms of being junior or senior as well as to the division of labour, these conventions do not apply to the collective work that we have done in this volume. As editors, we all agreed that it would be inappropriate for a non-Indigenous person to assume the role of first editor, as such an action would undermine the premise of this book. We are actively engaging the contestation that positions junior and senior scholars in linear and hierarchical relationships to one another, and privileges division of labour as a method of determining authorship. While such hierarchical relations were not involved in the conceptualization of this book, we did come to the process with diverse socio-cultural and socio-political normalized assumptions that, while having some shared themes, required negotiation to establish specific and nuanced understandings. Our order of editorship has been consciously chosen to uncover, disrupt, and challenge Western conventions, while privileging Indigenous ways of knowing and sharing knowledge.

One of the aspects of Indigenous knowledges shared across multiple cultural contexts and landscapes is the understanding of circles and placing things within circles as a conceptual framework for making meaning (see Fixico 2003; Graveline 1998; Black Elk in Neihardt 2008; Stewart-Harawira 2005; Styres 2017). As an editorial team, we agreed to use Styres's (2017) framework to structure the sections of this volume. As previously mentioned, we consciously chose not to organize the chapters according to place but rather thematically. While on a surface level organizing the voices of the authors by nationality makes sense, it actually takes away from the depth of each author's critical engagement in contestation. We have organized the chapters thematically around the following elements: Vision, Relationships, Knowledge, and Action. Organizing the chapters in this way allows for the clustering of synergies that lend themselves to the transnationality of the text. Furthermore, it highlights the various ways the authors examine the complex and nuanced multiplicities associated with inhabiting their places, as well as the ways in which they are complicit in the very contestation they are critiquing. The order of the chapters within each of the sections has been carefully thought out to ensure creative flow and to balance content, geographic location, and cultural positioning (connections to place).

Vision

Visioning is the process whereby one imagines or conceptualizes desired goals, outcomes, and/or objectives for an envisioned future; it also informs theorizing. Theorizing is abstract thinking and refers to particular ways of framing, thinking about, and coming to understand relevant issues, as well as proposing ways of moving forward in realizing the vision. In this way the theoretical section of the book frames the context and opens a dialogue for the other sections, and focuses on visioning for education and the related concepts and contested spaces. The authors theorize education from various Indigenous philosophical understandings to explore the complexities of contestation in its varied expressions, which challenge Indigenous intellectualism within mainstream academia and other educational contexts.

We begin with Maaka, who offers an insider commentary of a particular perspective on an Indigenous psyche and the impacts of colonial education on individuals. She leaves us asking what role public education has played and continues to play in stripping away the fundamental markers of Māori identity. She challenges readers to consider the long-term repercussions of this cultural stripping. It is important to note that for those readers not familiar with the Māori context and history Maaka provides an important background and orientation that will be essential for other chapters related to the Māori context. Styres then explores the importance of taking Indigenous thought seriously in education by examining issues related to tokenism, voyeurism, and cultural tourism—gesturing to particular ideologies that privilege networks and relations of power. Styres's chapter opens a critical dialogue on appropriation and the ethics of protocol, as well as considering the various tensions and challenges concerning the ways we think about and do teacher education in the academy. She concludes with a consideration of the ways we might move forward in respectful relations. Pihama discusses the historical evolution of *kaupapa Māori* philosophy and theory as applied to research. Kaupapa Māori is a theoretical framework grounded in Māori philosophies, knowledges, and experiences. She offers a broad discussion of the contested spaces within academia and the ways these spaces are created and maintained through the imposition of colonial knowledge and the devaluing of Māori philosophies. Tomlins-Jahnke looks further into the oppressive nature of mainstream universities, where she argues complex layers of ignorance are enacted and replicated in order to maintain oppressive institutional systems and structures. Her examples of how these complex layers are enacted and impact Indigenous faculty and students help disrobe (peel away the coverings and divest of authority) the contested spaces within academia, as well as the ways such networks and relations of power can be disrupted and resisted. We conclude the visioning and theoretical section with Donald, who discusses deep-seated concerns about how the settler dream has permeated and become mythologized within curriculum such that it is taken to be the dominant way of understanding and measuring the ways human beings are to live and relate to one another.

Relationships

Within the context of this book, relationships are critical and grounded in Indigenous understandings of our roles and responsibilities to our kinship and community ties, to our places, to one another cross-culturally, and to all of creation. Relationships refer to all of the tangled and complex interplay of interactions that inform and impact visioning. This section on negotiating contested spaces highlights the role of relationships in both maintaining and challenging contestation, while also framing the resistances that push back from both Indigenous and mainstream responses to contestation. What is unique about this section is the variety and complexity of the education contexts addressed, as the authors include physical classrooms as well as the ways landscapes and language inform our understandings of self-in-relationship to space and place.

Penetito focuses on the interaction and interplay between human beings in relationship within three contested spaces specific to relationships between Māori and mainstream. In addressing the question, "Can a mainstream education system truly deliver an education to fulfill the aspirations of a non-dominant cultural group (Māori) intent on maintaining and developing its own educational futures?" Penetito explores the complexities of these relationships and their impacts on understandings of what it means to be Māori. Similarly, Wong and Warner explore the ways in which language revitalization that includes using words and phrases that might be deemed inappropriate from a mainstream perspective is tangled within colonial relations. They explore the larger issues and speak to the importance of language in informing one's worldviews and sense of self. Wong and Warner make the argument that the failure to revitalize all aspects of their language imposes mainstream values and worldviews that shift and limit Native Hawaiians' ability to determine for themselves the ways they understand and shape their own identities. In the next chapter, Oliveira explores tensions between Native Hawaiian practices and mainstream mapping practices. She focuses on understandings of positionality and identity relative to place, with a particular emphasis on the wisdom contained within the Hawaiian language and the ways language frames Hawaiian worldviews and infuses meaning into places. Lilley then offers insight into the connection between Māori identity and land. Drawing upon his own understanding of his places, Lilley identifies the ways contact and subsequent colonization have led to the separation of the relationships between Māori and their landscapes, as well as the suppression of traditional knowledges. In this section, Pidgeon brings us full circle by focusing on contested spaces within mainstream education, in particular higher educational contexts, in different but related ways. Drawing on the relationships involved in supporting practice and pedagogy through the Office of Aboriginal Student Services, she identifies the complex ways this vital service historically and contemporarily navigates these contested spaces. Pidgeon also speaks to the competing relationships that are shaped by the broader forces of colonization, neo-liberalism, and internationalization. These forces continually influence and inform mainstream institutions' conceptualization of Indigenous education in terms of how they understand and frame commitment, responsibility, and accountability, as well as translate these into practice.

Knowledge

This section refers to all of the knowledges that are found within the complex interplay of interactions informing the visioning and relationship processes. In this section we explore contested spaces related to diverse knowledges that inform practices and pedagogies situated across educational contexts. The authors take us on a journey through geographically, culturally, and linguistically distinct classrooms that illustrate some of the parallels, intersections, and diversity within the contestation found in those spaces.

Deer opens this section by focusing on the importance of Indigenous identity within schools that do not offer instruction in an Indigenous language medium. He discusses the multiple aspects of localized Indigenous identity that can and should be acknowledged and understood in mainstream Canadian schools to facilitate identity awareness in educational programming. Deer stresses the importance of conceptualizing culture as systems of behaviour, attitudes, and values that comprise personal and collective continuity and assist educators in providing learners with more supportive and inclusive learning environments. Following, Hohepa and Hawera offer a broad perspective on Māori-medium schooling and the critical role it has been playing in the regeneration and development of Māori language, knowledge, and cultural practices. They argue that a commitment to producing teachers who can successfully teach in Māori-medium classrooms is an essential component to ensuring the educational success of Indigenous Māori learners in New Zealand schools. As a non-Indigenous educator, Zinga turns her attention to the contested spaces associated with creating learning environments within higher education that are supportive and inclusive of Indigenous ways of learning and knowing. By exploring the dynamics of these contested spaces, she discusses what it means as a non-Indigenous instructor to teach Indigenous and non-Indigenous students within and about these contested spaces by moving beyond the myth of good intentions, becoming aware of Indigenous student realities, and co-creating safe ethical spaces for learning. Restoule and Nardozi explore a similar theme in their discussion of the Deepening Knowledge Project and the associated contested spaces that they encounter in its design and implementation. This project is a resource designed to assist educators and teacher candidates in embedding Indigenous perspectives throughout all areas of teacher education. It has encountered spaces of contestation within the university around notions of privilege and settler identities that have resulted in taken-for-granted narratives of the Canadian state and resistances to negotiating the amount of time and space dedicated to teaching topics that challenge these narratives. Ropata-Te Hei, in related but very specific contexts, brings us back to a focus on language and identity as she speaks to her own experiences growing up immersed in Māori language and traditions. She shares the ways these core aspirations, instilled in her by her Elders, have influenced and continue to influence her practices as an educator within multiple contexts. In particular, she explores the various tensions and challenges of teaching in a unique Māori-immersion initial teacher education program situated within a mainstream academic institution.

Action

This final section is essentially a call to action, bringing us full circle in order to explore the ways visioning and theorizing may shift practices to create spaces for new directions in education. Each author shares a unique approach or conceptualization applied to a specific contestation within broad educational contexts. In so doing, the authors expose and address contestation in its multiple expressions and suggest possible new directions in the ways we think about and do education.

Bevan-Brown addresses issues related to student services and challenges the ways educational services are delivered to Indigenous students with special needs. She identifies the problematic influences of the majority culture on the ways these education services are defined and provided, resulting in disproportionate representation and inadequate and alienating provisions for these students. Bevan-Brown suggests alternative ways of addressing these issues by training professionals to provide a culturally responsive education to Māori and other ethnic minority children with special education needs. Doherty brings forth the idea that context is a critical component that must be understood in a teaching and learning environment. In his discussion related to understanding the importance of maintaining traditional connections to space and place, he shares lessons that can be learned from the ancestral processes employed by the early settlers into the Eastern Bay of Plenty from the outer Cook Islands, which can be used today as learners are confronted with multiple new experiences. Jahnke addresses the broader contexts of contested spaces as revealed in the medium of Māori visual arts. He argues that the ethnic labelling of Māori art is an essentialist act imposed by other cultures' worldviews, and identifies the centre of the contestation as revolving around the critical importance of form, content, and genealogy being named in the language of the culture and from a Māori worldview. Lipe discusses contested space and the clash of worldviews within the context of science. While science can be viewed through multiple lenses, he suggests there is a Western scientific domination over the ways Indigenous knowledges conceptualize the natural world that makes talking about complex ideas and issues related to the natural world a confusing, difficult, and painstaking process, especially for those who want to utilize multiple knowledge systems.

Johnston brings us full circle in her discussion of place and space as it is associated with Indigenous students and faculty working in dominant educational contexts, and she pushes us to consider the implications of other alternatives. Johnston engages key questions, such as: Does a completely Indigenous context make the journey for Indigenous education less difficult and more successful? What exactly does success look like, and are there other challenges created by the Indigenous context that need consideration? These questions and the questions posed by the other authors in these chapters identify critical areas of contestation and open up opportunities to engage these spaces to move education, in its broadest context, forward in positive and relevant ways. It is the responsibility of each of us to decide how we are going take up these questions, in order to engage them in meaningful and respectful ways that will open up dialogue and result in positive action that recognizes the complexity of contestation. This will allow us to become catalysts for change leading to more supportive and inclusive learning environments, for the benefit of all learners, educators, and professional practitioners.

Words for the Journey

The creation of this book was a journey, and anyone who engages with this book embarks on their own journey of engaging contestation and discovery. As you begin the journey through this book we would ask that you be open to what each of the authors is sharing. Be mindful of your own resistances and places of resonance, considering what each means in your specific context. Every individual has a role to play in the revisioning of education. Anyone can have a vision, but to successfully realize that vision it is essential to conceive of all the relationships that you need to achieve the vision. As we move forward in education, it is important to be aware that the relationships we will call upon may be grounded in these contested spaces and may shift in unexpected ways to inform/influence these visions. The vision can only be realized through changes in practice and pedagogy that offer new directions for moving forward. This brings us full circle to action, where we evaluate if the actions taken are realizing the vision or if we need to move back to revisioning. Throughout this journey, we challenge you to examine and shift your own assumptions about and conceptualizations of education in all its forms. Consider what lessons and challenges each of the authors has to offer and how you might take those up in your own work. Education is a pervasive influence in society in all of its many levels, and it is essential that we challenge the assumptions that inform how we think about and do education by exploring the complexities of contested spaces in their varied expressions within mainstream education that challenge Indigenous intellectualism.

Battiste (2013, 186) argues that "in order to effect change, educators must help students understand the Eurocentric assumption of superiority within the context of history and to recognize the continued dominance of these assumptions in all forms of contemporary knowledge." The chapters in this text bring together relevant research and experiences related to the complexities of contestation, to foster an understanding of the pertinent issues related to education (in its broadest contexts) and to assist all those involved in education and educational practices to engage with some of the realities facing learners and educators across Aotearoa, Hawai'i, and Turtle Island. Both implicitly and explicitly, many of the authors address issues of change and/or lack of change in moving forward and transforming the landscape of Indigenous education. Collectively, these scholars bring together a variety of approaches to understanding the contexts of teaching and learning within spaces of contestation in order to envision more inclusive, fulfilling, and culturally relevant learning environments.

Notes

1. Turtle Island is a self-defining term for what is understood to be North America, going back to the origin stories of many First Nations such as Anishinaabe, Haudenosaunee, and Lenape Peoples. It has also been adopted as a descriptor by many other First Nations Peoples. We recognize the distinctiveness of origin

stories among First Nation, Métis, and Inuit Peoples and the ways that they define how their places were created. It is not possible within the confines of this volume to address the complexities around origin stories, and we cannot speak to other Nations' creation stories; therefore, we have chosen to use the defining term used by many of the Indigenous Peoples represented in this edited volume.

References

Battiste, Marie. 2013. *Decolonizing Education: Nourishing the Learning Spirit*. Saskatoon, SK: Purich Publishing.

Fixico, Donald. 2003. *The American Indian Mind in a Linear World: American Indian Studies and Traditional Knowledge*. New York: Routledge.

Four Arrows (Don Trent Jacobs). 2006. "Epilogue." In *Unlearning the Language of Conquest: Scholars Expose the Anti-Indianism in America*, edited by Four Arrows (Don Trent Jacobs), 273-4. Austin: University of Texas Press.

Graveline, Fyre Jean. 1998. *Circle Works: Transforming Eurocentric Consciousness*. Halifax, NS: Fernwood Publishing.

Neihardt, John G. 2008. *Black Elk Speaks: Being the Life Story of a Holy Man of the Oglala Sioux, the Premier Edition*. 2nd ed. New York: State University of New York Press.

Smith, Graham. 2012. "Kumu 'Ula'ula: Who Are We and Where Are We Heading Symposium." Opening remarks presented at the 2012 Annual Meeting of the American Educational Research Association, Vancouver, British Columbia.

Stewart-Harawira, Makere. 2005. *The New Imperial Order: Indigenous Responses to Globalization*. New York: Zed Books.

Styres, Sandra. 2017. *Pathways for Remembering and Recognizing Indigenous Thought in Education: Philosophies of Iethi'nihsténha Ohwentsia'kékha (Land)*. Toronto: University of Toronto Press.

Styres, Sandra, and Dawn Zinga. 2013. "The Community-First Land-Centred Theoretical Framework: Bringing a 'Good Mind' to Indigenous Education Research?" *Canadian Journal of Education* 36 (2): 284-313.

Zinga, Dawn, and Sandra Styres. 2011. "Pedagogy of the Land: Tensions, Challenges and Contradictions." *First Nations Perspectives: The Journal of the Manitoba First Nations Resource Centre* 4: 59-83.

1 **Vision**
Theoretical Approaches to Indigenous Education

1 | Education Through Paideia
The Contested Space of the Indigenous Psyche

MARGARET J. MAAKA

Introduction

When I first mapped out this chapter, I called it "Education Through Paideia: The Contested Space of Indigenous Schooling."[1] My plan was to write a commentary on the damage caused to Māori children in the contested space of public education, with specific reference to the political and social context of New Zealand in the 1950s and 1960s. In particular, I was interested in examining the education system's preoccupation with the assimilation of Māori children into the broader culture of the New Zealand democratic state and the impact of this "program" on the Māori psyche. Initially, I planned to use a formal writing style that would divorce my own schooling experiences and me from the discussion. I was hung up on embracing an "academic" genre that would position me as an outside commentator rather than as an individual intimately involved in the experience. Most probably, I had bought into the mindset of the Western academy that a detached stance is more credible than accounts of firsthand experiences.[2] In truth, this plan would have resulted in a chapter completely devoid of life force.

The deviation from my initial writing plan took place at the beginning of the section that I call "Small Savages on the Road to Civilization." At first, I intended to use archival documents to examine the direction of public schooling for Māori children over the years in question. My idea for this section was to hook the reader with a poignant anecdote from my own school days and segue him or her into a full-blown treatise on the attempt to transform small Māori savages into "Brown Britons" (Simon and Smith 2001, ix). But as I wrote this piece, I experienced a flood of memories conjuring a wide range of emotions that propelled my writing into several pages of personal reflection. I was sometimes moved to laughter, sometimes tears, sometimes anger, sometimes nostalgia, but most times to a stoic contemplation. As I peeled my memories away, I became more and more aware of the "trauma" that can be brought to young children through their schooling. What follows are snapshots of the psychological journey of a small child through the politics of public education in New Zealand, a journey that began in a very small Māori school in the country, ventured through a large urban intermediate school, and ended up at a large urban high school. I believe these snapshots speak volumes about the disruptive force of public schooling.

Personal stories like the ones I tell in this chapter and storytelling in general are integral parts of Indigenous lives—they document our lived experiences. Smith (1999, 144) explains: "Each individual story is powerful. But the point about the stories is not that they simply tell a story, or tell a story simply. These new stories contribute to a collective story in which every indigenous person has a place." On one level, my recollections (albeit through an adult lens) describe the struggles of a young Māori child in public education caught in a lopsided tug-of-war between two cultures. But on another level, my recollections illustrate acts of racism suffered by many Indigenous Peoples, especially in public education systems. Stuart Rintoul (cited in Smith 1999, 144) talks about the importance of "stories handed down in the homes of Black Australians, told to new generations, taught in explanation of racism and mistreatment, recited with rage and dignity and sorrow." For many Indigenous Peoples, stories are the vehicle by which knowledge—accounts of love, death, sadness, revenge, family, childhood, work, laughter, oppression, and the like—are passed from one person to another and from one generation to another. As such, this chapter has evolved into an insider commentary on the contested space of the Indigenous psyche as a result of the process of education through paideia. This commentary and similar commentaries from other children-now-adults will tell and retell Indigenous experiences. The unplanned evolution of my lived experiences has made the writing of this chapter a very personal and emotional experience.

The Democratic State

> I would maintain that the questions we need to raise about education are among the most important questions that can be raised in our society, particularly at this juncture in history. What knowledge should "we the people" hold in common? What values? What skills? What sensibilities? When we ask such questions, we are getting at the heart of the kind of society we want to live in and the kind of society we want our children to live in. We are getting at the heart of the kind of public we would like to bring into being and the qualities we would like that public to display. We are getting at the heart of the kind of community we need for our multifarious individualities to flourish.
> —L.A. CREMIN, "Public Education and the Education of the Public"

New Zealand has been a democracy since the mid-1800s, with the beginning of representative government. Atkinson (2003) provides a unique overview of the evolution of New Zealand's interpretation of democracy from that time and how this interpretation reflects a determined quest to develop an identity as a nation. Although there are many interpretations of democracy throughout the nations of the world, Stevick and Levinson (2007) raise the critical argument that there is a distinct cultural dimension in the quest for democracy, particularly democracy in education:

Democracy is not an abstract system that can be dropped into any new context and be expected to function, nor is it a set of institutional arrangements that can be evaluated satisfactorily simply by examining a flowchart in a document. Democracy is rather the product of interaction, the interaction of a system and its institutions with the cultural context and the people who make them real. (2)

New Zealand's democracy, like many others, prides itself on having checks and balances that prevent people of privilege from abusing the power inherent in that privilege. There are also expectations that individual rights are protected; that minority voices are heard, as well as those of the majority; and that the "system" accords everyone the right to be treated equally. But how do these translate into real life? If the history of Māori disenfranchisement in New Zealand is brought under scrutiny, it is definitely arguable that the tenets of democracy are no more than platitudinous affirmations of a system of governance that reads well on paper, but does not translate to real life. The Waitangi Tribunal, a commission of inquiry established under the Treaty of Waitangi Act of 1975,[3] was charged with making recommendations on claims brought by Māori relating to actions or omissions of the Crown that breach the promises made in the Treaty. This acknowledged that people of privilege abused their power over Māori, that Māori rights were not protected, that the Māori voice was not heard, and that Māori were not accorded the right to equal treatment.

The problematic nature of democracy is not new. Commentaries by writers, wits, intellectuals, scholars, critics, and the like—those who reflect the thoughts of their day—clearly register concern that democracy as a form of government has significant shortcomings. Two critiques of democracy pervade—one registering the ignorance of the individual voter and the other registering the tyranny of the majority. Winston Churchill (1874-1965), former prime minister of the United Kingdom and legendary wit, allegedly made the following quip when registering concern about "everyman's" capacity to make sound decisions with his or her vote: "The best argument against democracy is a five-minute conversation with the average voter."[4] This sentiment was echoed by American satirist H. L. Mencken (1880-1956), who said (1926), "Democracy is a pathetic belief in the collective wisdom of individual ignorance," and British playwright George Bernard Shaw (1856-1950), who said (1903), "Democracy substitutes election by the incompetent many for appointment by the corrupt few." The idea of democracy as a tool of tyranny for the majority is reflected in the words attributed to Thomas Jefferson (1743-1826),[5] an American Founding Father, the principal author of the Declaration of Independence, and the third president of the United States: "A democracy is nothing more than mob rule, where fifty-one percent of the people may take away the rights of the other forty-nine." Writer Ray Bradbury (1920-2012) picked up this theme in his depiction of anti-intellectualism within a degraded democratic idea (1953): "Most dangerous enemy to truth and freedom, the solid unmoving cattle of the majority. Oh God, the terrible tyranny of the majority." And British playwright Oscar Wilde (1854-1900), in his reflections on the many forms of failed government, stated (1891), "High hopes were once formed of democracy, but democracy means simply the bludgeoning of the people by the people for the people."

In pondering what he refers to as the closely knit relationship between democracy and colonialism, Gordon (2010, 1) contends that colonialism has served a significant role in creating and sustaining modern democracies and that, more often than not, the indoctrination of people for the citizenry has come about through violent forms of exclusion:

> Moreover, the series of exclusions that colonialism produces are, I claim, part of democracy's very logic and can operate in tandem with democracy's basic principles. Insofar as this is the case, the democracy/colonial relationship can teach us something important about democracy for it reveals, using Michael Mann's phrase, one of the dark sides of the so-called best possible regime. It underscores, for example, how democracy's universalist and inclusionary claims are always

bound up in colonial exclusionary practices that are implemented through the deployment of violence. (1, referring to Mann 2005)

Gordon's (2010) assertion that colonialism is a strategy employed by democracies to achieve geopolitical and economic goals is evidenced by the "violent exclusion" of Māori from our traditional lands and resources through confiscation and other shady means. Similarly, the achievement of socio-political goals by democracies through colonial muscle is evidenced by the "violent exclusion" of Māori from our traditional knowledge and practices as a result of our assimilation into the broader culture of the New Zealand democratic state. We are left asking, then, What role has public education played in stripping away the fundamental markers of Māori identity—sovereignty, ancestral lands, language, and cultural knowledge? And what has been the impact of this cultural stripping on the Māori psyche?

Education Through Paideia

So, what about schooling in New Zealand over the years? What roles have schools and schooling played, and what roles do they continue to play, in preparing the New Zealand populace for citizenship in its democracy? The ancient Greeks used the term paideia to refer to the educational act of moulding an "ideal" citizen who has a mature, broad outlook on life. This act involved the training of physical and mental faculties within a particular cultural context through disciplines such as rhetoric, grammar, philosophy, arithmetic, gymnastics, music, and poetry. In the 21st century, Goodlad, Mantle-Bromley, and Goodlad (2004) use a more succinct definition: education by, in, and for the culture. Specifically, they talk about the

> educational agenda for enculturating the members of the group, tribe, or community and the probable need for some kinds of mechanism for ensuring universal attention to that agenda. Implicit in the well-being

of the collective—not just of the individual—is an awareness that we, the people, however diverse we are, must live in a considerable degree of harmony with everybody and everybody's children, or else the group, the tribe, the community dissipates, disperses, or perishes. (2)

It is obvious, then, that schooling for a democracy through paideia is a political act as much as it is an educational act. And it is also obvious that this process has its supporters. There is a plethora of literature promoting the benefits of democracy for education and the need for a cohesive and unified citizenry of people sharing a common physical space—regardless of the diverse cultures of the peoples contained therein. But education for a democracy through paideia, especially in a colonial context in lands such as New Zealand, also has its critics. And this criticism is the line of thought that I explore in this chapter through reflections on my experiences in the New Zealand education system.

Hunter and Milofsky's (2007, 77) commentary on socialization for civility and the coercive control exercised by those in positions of authority to use institutions to "threaten, coerce, or bribe" disadvantaged people (they reference, particularly, the poor), holds significance for the schooling of Māori. It is noteworthy that this coercion also involves undermining the efforts of disadvantaged people to engage in collective political and economic action. Schools, Hunter and Milofsky argue, serve the purpose of creating competitive psychological environments that establish the legitimacy of social inequality. They argue that disadvantaged children are constantly exposed to school experiences that reinforce the fact that they are inferior because the curriculum, the teaching approaches, the school environment, and all other aspects of schooling are more congenial to the culture of the middle class (in New Zealand, the Pākehā middle class). Thus, the rewards of schooling go to the wealthy and not the poor—and especially not the "brown poor." For Māori, the coercive control exercised by schools has been taken one step further—the stripping away of the fundamental markers of Māori identity, coupled with a curriculum designed to privilege Pākehā, middle-class New Zealanders, has resulted in the devastation of the Māori people. In his examination of the reconstruction of Māori identity through colonization, Mason Durie (1998) explains the process and its far-reaching consequences:

> The new constructions of a Māori identity were accompanied by the promotion of a range of stories, "legends," and traditions, based on various tribal accounts but amalgamated to form new pan-Māori versions which frequently also drew heavily on both European tradition and the Old Testament. It was part of the colonizing process which not only led to alienation of land and other resources but also brought Māori history and culture into a regimented framework so that it could readily be understood and controlled by the colonizers. In the process, new myths were created and a new type of Māori identity was forged. (54)

The forging of a new type of Māori identity has taken place in multiple contexts. Fanon (1963) presents a compelling argument that colonialism, which includes the context of public education, is not simply content to impose its rule upon the present and the future of a dominated country (like New Zealand). For him, colonialism "is not satisfied merely with holding a people in its grip and emptying the native's brain of all form and content. By a kind of perverted logic, it turns to the past of the oppressed people, and distorts, disfigures, and destroys it" (210).

The Indigenous Psyche

I have chosen to use the term "psyche" in this chapter, but I need to clarify that I perceive it to refer to the essence of an individual, not just the mind in isolation. Most definitions of psyche talk about the mind and associate this solely with the function of the brain. I prefer to perceive the psyche as spirituality, the soul, the life force—the intangible self. In Māori culture, the concept of mauri signifies this same essential quality and vitality of an individual. Durie (1998) explains the critical nature of mauri:

> In Māori terms all living things, including natural and physical resources, possess mauri, a life principle or life essence. Distinctions between inanimate and animate objects are therefore blurred, because each is afforded a spiritual existence which complements the physical state. Nothing is lifeless. Damage to a resource not only creates physical impairment but also causes spiritual damage and in the process impinges on the mauri of other objects, including people. (23)

Damage to the psyche is the result of a severely distressing event or series of events. In simple terms, traumatic stress to the psyche is equivalent to the amount of stress that exceeds an individual's ability to cope. Trauma-induced stress manifests itself in many different ways—some symptoms are immediate and some percolate over time to emerge years later, even generations later. Although there are multiple causes of trauma-induced stress, they all have one primary outcome— the individual feeling that his or her world and the rights associated with that world are violated. The experiences of extreme fear, insecurity, confusion, anger, angst, betrayal, violation, hopelessness (and other discombobulating emotions) cause the individual to respond in many different ways—most often in depression, substance abuse, violence, dependency, poor health, criminal behaviour, failed opportunities in life, and the like.

Burke Harris (2014) describes how trauma-induced stress affects brain development, the immune system, hormonal system, and even more interesting and important, the way human DNA is read and transcribed. She contends (0:41) that individuals exposed to very high doses of stress have "triple the lifetime risk of heart disease and lung cancer and a 20-year difference in life expectancy." Dovetailing with the thrust of my chapter is Burke Harris's claim (1:16) that childhood traumas (for example, abuse or neglect, growing up with a parent who struggles with mental illness or substance dependence, or homelessness) are often so "severe or pervasive that they literally get under our skin and change our physiology." In making her point, Burke Harris cites the Adverse Childhood Experiences Study (Felitti et al. 1998), which gathered data from nearly 14,000 adults in the United States about their histories of "adverse childhood experiences." These experiences included physical, emotional, or sexual abuse; physical or emotional neglect; parental mental illness, substance dependence, or incarceration; parental separation or divorce; domestic violence; and emotional and physical neglect. Their study found a direct link between childhood trauma and adult onset of chronic disease, as well as mental illness, doing time in prison, and work issues, such as absenteeism. They also found that the adverse childhood experiences resulted in higher risk of medical, mental, and social problems in adulthood.

Closer to home, Arohia Durie (1997) argues that the trauma that Māori have experienced through the dislocation of everything familiar accounts for the many challenges we now face. Her argument is simple and makes complete sense—an essential determinant of the social and economic well-being of any group is its connectedness. When a group is connected, it flourishes. Conversely, when the shared meanings, values, and beliefs that identify group membership are broken down, so does the group break down. Could this "group breakdown" explain the fact that life expectancy for Māori is around seven years less than for non-Māori?[6] Farrelly, Rudegeair, and Rickard (2006) also advance the argument that the social and health problems that have befallen Māori are the result of the trauma of colonization and that this trauma has manifested itself as an intergenerational phenomenon. Their research advances the credible argument that New Zealand needs to acknowledge the prevalence of traumatic stress among its population and develop ways to address it.

However, in spite of these compelling findings, the medical field and society in general do not acknowledge that stress is probably the greatest unaddressed public health threat today, especially for Māori.

The racist side of New Zealand society has always seen this "Māori predicament" as one of uselessness on the part of Māori. In other words, Māori are responsible for the reduced circumstances in which we find ourselves. Māori heart disease, diabetes, mental health, and numerous perceived social failings are often attributed to lack of good judgement, lack of character, lack of fortitude, and lack of getting our act together— these are ailments that, apparently, Māori have brought on ourselves. The term "useless bloody Māori" has been used freely by Pākehā to instill this belief in the general populace, as well as in Māori, and to deflect any responsibility from themselves for the significant challenges that Māori have faced since their arrival to our lands. Fanon (1963) best explains the situation:

> When we consider the efforts made to carry out the cultural estrangement so characteristic of the colonial epoch, we realize that nothing has been left to chance and that the total result looked for by colonial domination was indeed to convince the natives that colonialism came to lighten their darkness. The effect consciously sought by colonialism was to drive into the natives' heads the idea that if the settlers were to leave, they would at once fall back into barbarism, degradation, and bestiality. (21)

There is no question New Zealand public schools and other public institutions have played a central role in undermining the health and well-being of our Māori people.

Growing Up in Godzone

> Give me, give me God's own country! there to live and there to die,
> God's own country! fairest region resting 'neath the southern sky,
> God's own country! framed by Nature in her grandest, noblest mould;
> Land of peace and land of plenty, land of wool and corn and gold!

> Oh! the mountains of New Zealand! wild and rugged though they be,
> They are types of highest manhood, landmarks of a nation free.
> Pleasure-ground of the Pacific! brightest region on the main!
> Land of many a rushing river, verdant valley, fertile plain!
> —T. BRACKEN, "God's Own Country," 1890[7]

Pākehā have a long history of claiming the New Zealand land base through all manner of vehicles, especially patriotic verse and song. In particular, the theme of "Give me, give me God's own country!" reflects the nature of the Crown's acquisition of huge tracts of land originally held under the stewardship of Māori. Even New Zealand's national anthem, to this day, celebrates the idea that New Zealand was there for the taking by the newcomers: "Hear our voices, we entreat, God defend our free land." Indeed, through many means, including the breached Treaty of Waitangi, the Crown managed to acquire a lot of "free land" from Māori. But running parallel with this push to acquire land and resources was a greater imperative—an all-out effort to create a national identity that would secure the roles, rights, and acquisitions of the newcomers. The creation of a national identity hinged on the calculated structuring of a collective consciousness or communal psyche.

Fast forward to the 1950s! New Zealand's post–Second World War era was viewed by many as one of national prosperity, achievement, pride, and celebration. War rationing had ended; unemployment was dramatically reduced; new industries, farming, and exports flourished; Edmund Hillary had excelled as the first person to scale Mt. Everest—followed by a rarely named brown person (for ages, kids at my school thought his name was Sherpa); game show host Selwyn Toogood was entertaining the nation by asking whether a contestant should take the "money or the bag, by hokey!"; somebody invented jandals; accomplishments in sports and the arts extended into the international arena; the Auckland Harbour Bridge opened; the expected fare for teatime was meat and three veg; a New Zealand housewife baked the first pavlova (she was not living in Australia at the time); and the standard of living saw more and more New Zealanders building homes on their quarter-acre sections. Life was blissful in Paradise!

On the surface, the 1950s saw a huge surge in national identity that promoted the idea of equality in the New Zealand population, especially for the two main races—Māori and Pākehā. It was believed that because of their bravery and sacrifice in the Second World War, Māori had earned an elevated standing in New Zealand society. This new standing spilled over into other places of accomplishment such as the sports arena, the entertainment world, and some jobs. Many Pākehā and some Māori at the time believed that New Zealand had good race relations and that both races shared equally in the enjoyment of the fruits of Godzone.

But was this true? A more logical explanation for the semblance of harmony is that Pākehā were mostly urban with opportunities, Māori were mostly rural without opportunities, and the two groups rarely came into contact. In reality, the opportunities afforded by Godzone were not available to many Māori; in fact, the opposite was the case. During this time, for example, the Ngāti Whātua people had been evicted from their last remaining land in Auckland and their marae and homes burned by the Crown because they were deemed an eyesore. Under the 1953 Māori Affairs Act (http://www.trc.org.nz/Māori_Affairs), Māori land could be alienated from its owners if the land in question was deemed unproductive, or had noxious weeds or unpaid taxes. Compared with Pākehā, Māori performed less well in school and had poorer health. The mortality rate for infants was much higher for Māori than for Pākehā. And Māori were overrepresented as a group receiving long stretches of incarceration, courtesy of Mt. Eden Prison, other prison establishments, and Her Majesty the Queen. For many Māori, poverty was a lived experience.

When the rural-to-urban drift of Māori kicked into full swing, it was clear that Māori had the potential to become a major social problem, particularly so with our alienation from iwi and hapū and the associated cultural history and life that anchored our people. It was clear that the efforts to assimilate Māori into the broader New Zealand citizenry needed to be kicked up a notch. What was needed was an emptying of the native's brain of all form and content (Fanon 1963) and a refilling with civility and conformity. Enter a renewed thrust through public schooling!

Small Savages on the Road to Civilization

Primary School

Māori Schools have become an episode in the history of Māori education. The Māori Schools system was a solution of its time, a mixture of Māori aspirations for our own future and government designs for building a nation dominated by British culture, language, laws, and institutions. Probably, neither side was totally satisfied with what they achieved, but both played out a charade of pretending that was the best we could achieve at that time.
—H.M. MEAD, cited in J. Simon, *Ngā Kura Māori: The Native School System, 1867–1969*

I attended Te Hāroto Māori School,[8] located in a small Māori community in rural Hawkes Bay, Aotearoa New Zealand. Our two-room school had a roll of about 40 kids, with 80% Māori. On days of a tangi or on days of other important events on the marae, attendance dropped to a handful. Although my class level changed each year, my classmates remained the same—Kimi, Willie, Peter, and my cousin Canna. Other kids came and went, but we were the five mainstays throughout the years.

From the first day of school we learned order, discipline, and cleanliness. Cleanliness, in particular, was important for a people considered devoid of hygiene. Every morning we assembled in rows at the front of the school: junior kids at the front, senior kids at the back. A senior boy conducted the assembly in a manner that, on the surface, would impress the most formidable of drill sergeants. The exercise began with an inspection of hands and fingernails. And heaven help anyone who

FIGURE 1.1 Margaret Maaka at Te Hāroto Māori School, 1963.

had a snotty nose and no handkerchief (shirt sleeves were deemed an unacceptable substitute). Dirty anything was rewarded with a light slap across the hands to denote a grubby person. Sometimes, however, we knew our tuakana had to slap harder if the Pākehā headmaster was watching. But we really didn't mind being chastised by the senior boy because it was his job to look after us. Later, he would give us extra attention to let us know that all was well. In spite of the fact that the Pākehā headmaster had assigned him the role of disciplinarian, our tuakana's responsibility to us was etched far deeper in a cultural understanding that the senior kids had to look after us little kids. It was his job to teach us about ways to behave and it was our job to help him become a strong and caring leader. Through his care of us we also learned that, in time, we would take on the mantle of caring for our younger schoolmates. We would not be tēina forever.

"Ma te tuakana ka totika te teina, ma te teina ka totika te tuakana."⁹

In the afternoon, our schooling started with a massive teeth-cleaning marathon that required us to keep a toilet bag with toothbrush and toothpaste at school. On occasion, the Pākehā headmaster conducted a public kutu inspection. Sometimes, he did an elaborate performance of pretending to catch a kootie and squash it, all the while uncaring about the humiliation of the person whose head served as his theatrical prop. On completion of the afternoon ablutions, our tuakana marched us inside to resume our lessons.

"Feet together jump, turn, forward!"

Every Friday afternoon, we cleaned the school. Girls were responsible for cleaning the classrooms, toilets, and staffroom. We were also responsible for polishing the wood floors. For the little kids, a hair-raising ride on top of the electric floor polisher was one of the highlights of the week and there was always a long line of primers begging for a go. Boys were responsible for gardening, cleaning and repairing the exterior of the school, and mowing lawns. But most important, this weekly cleaning marathon served another purpose that was not obvious to the Pākehā headmaster. It was a chance for the senior kids to take temperature checks on how all the kids were feeling about school and who needed support. It was a therapy and cleaning session rolled into one!

Primer One to Standard One

Our first teacher was Māori and from the community. She and her husband were friends of my parents, so there was an understanding that, while at school, she took on the dual role of teacher/parent. This was so for all the children, many of whom belonged to her extended family. In this role, she exuded a warm, no-nonsense teaching style that drew on strong cultural underpinnings. Her desk was the place where she administered hugs in the morning when we arrived at school, hugs in the afternoon when we left, and, sometimes, telling-offs in between. She fashioned makeshift hats for us if we had to walk home when it was snowing, and she taught us popular Māori action songs, the words of which she adapted to reflect the community (to this day, I sing the wrong words when these songs come up in broader Māori contexts). She scolded us when we were naughty and then bear-hugged us soon afterwards to make us feel better, and she regaled us with stories of Rangi and Papa, Māui, Kupe, and other famous tīpuna. I remember being annoyed later in my schooling when a Pākehā teacher had the gall to claim that Captain Cook discovered the very place that Māui fished up and that Kupe from Hawaiki later visited!

Captain Cook discovered our lands? Not even!

Best of all, if we ever needed to fart, our teacher made us raise our hands and ask for permission to go outside. Once outside, we had to complete the act and spin three times in a circle while swishing our hands back and forth like an agitator washing machine. After that, we were allowed to return odourless to the classroom. The toilet roll on our teacher's desk was for those kids with snotty noses who didn't own handkerchiefs and there was an unspoken rule in her classroom that we all helped each other—the big kids especially were responsible for the little kids. It is hard to explain, but we felt a deep and abiding connection to her that we did not feel for the Pākehā headmaster.

In spite of this connection to our Māori teacher, the core curriculum for the junior classroom kept us disconnected from things that were familiar. The daily offerings relied heavily on basal textbooks in reading and arithmetic. Janet and John readers, which depicted the exploits of a Pākehā middle-class family, subjected us to the purgatory of reciting mindless statements about Janet's watering can, John's wheelbarrow, mother's flower garden, father's lawnmower, and Spot's doggy behaviours (although I suspect that, in reality, "See Spot run" was referencing the dog's desperate attempt to escape from this ridiculous family and head off down to the pā for a feed). The day I completed the final Janet and John book in the series was one of great elation but, shortly after, one of greater despair—momentary elation because I thought I would never have to read the books again, but great despair when I found that I had to teach the younger kids to read them!

"Look, John look, I see two Māori kids bored shitless reading about us!" said Janet.

When the Janet and John readers were finally purged from the New Zealand public-school curriculum in the 1970s, thousands of Māori children were no longer forced to experience the bafflement of trying to learn to read from books about strange, sanitized Pākehā family values. Girls, too, learned that life held more for them than being useless twits—it was okay, after all, to run faster, jump higher, and yell louder than boys.

And, as for the arithmetic problems we had to solve in our basal textbook—it was puzzling to us why we would want to go to the store and buy 60 apples, 40 bananas, and 20 oranges. Our local store never stocked that much fruit in the first place.

Standard Two to Standard Four

The senior classroom at Te Hāroto Māori School was quite different. The teacher was Pākehā, and he was also the headmaster. I have two significant memories from the three years that I was in his classroom. He taught us a lot of new and interesting things about the world (although not about the Māori world), and he utilized the leather strap on a regular basis. Corporal punishment was meted out to both boys and girls. I don't recall many of the infractions but I doubt whether any of them was so egregious as to warrant the physical beatings we received. When not in use, the leather strap sat coiled in the front corner of the Pākehā headmaster's desk as a reminder that there were consequences for stepping out of line. Being called up to his desk held a fearful possibility, and there was always relief if the strap remained coiled for the duration.

"Six-of-the-best" was the worst sentence handed down and all beatings took place in front of the class. Pain and public humiliation were thought to ensure control and obedience in the Pākehā classroom. On freezing winter days, the pain from the strap was excruciating. Sometimes we would cup our hands so that the brunt of the blow was taken on the balls of our palms and on our fingertips. But that was bloody painful too. And if the Pākehā headmaster caught on, he would straighten our hands out and strap us again. Sometimes, if we took the punishment and defiantly refused to cry, he would strap us again for that too.

On one occasion, one of the girls rubbed a raw onion on her hands after receiving "four-of-the-best" for taking extra milk[10] in the morning because she was hungry. She had heard that onion juice would make her hands swell. Her plan was to go home with swollen hands that would invoke the wrath of her parents, who would then give the teacher a hiding. All the kids waited with bated breath for her hands to swell to elephantine proportions, but sadly, this did not occur. The best day, though, was when Johnny Boy's nanny marched from the pā to yell at the Pākehā headmaster for scrubbing her grandson's mouth out with soap used to clean the toilets. He had caught Johnny Boy swearing. After a heated exchange, Johnny Boy's nanny slapped the Pākehā headmaster's glasses right off his face. The cheering inside our heads was deafening. Nanny was our heroine. Violence for violence is what we wanted and what we learned.

Sometimes we got strapped for not doing a good job with our learning. Not being able to understand a lesson was perceived as our failing rather than the Pākehā headmaster's failing. I was eight when I was first strapped. I can't remember why. Imagine, a little kid taking the full force of a hunk of leather wielded in an overarm swing by an adult male. Rather than feeling deep remorse, I felt an emotion new to me— searing resentment. I refused to cry, even though my hand hurt like hell. I remember the other kids sitting at their desks with their shoulders hunched and their eyes looking down at the floor. I knew they would comfort me later when the Pākehā headmaster was not looking and that made me feel better about being singled out.

Apart from about an hour every Wednesday with Auntie Connie[11] who taught us Māori, our Pākehā headmaster made us learn other stuff—civics (structure of the British Parliament), grammar (Woe is I), poetry ("Ozymandias"), and songs ("The British Grenadiers" and "Land of Hope and Glory").

> Land of Hope and Glory, Mother of the Free
> How shall we extol thee, who are born of thee?
> Wider still and wider shall thy bounds be set;
> God, who made thee mighty, make thee mightier yet
> God, who made thee mighty, make thee mightier yet. [12]

While we sang our little hearts out, we were unaware of the tensions in our own backyard. Right from birth, we had it drilled into us that we had to help God save the queen. For years, New Zealand held the status of a Dominion. This accorded New Zealand the right to home government while retaining the British monarch as head of state, represented by a governor-general appointed in consultation with the New Zealand government. Because of this status, successive New Zealand governments went to great pains to ensure that New Zealanders paid homage to an entity that was thousands of miles away. We literally ate, drank, read, and sang "dominion-ness." While eating Dominion sausage, New Zealanders drank Dominion beer and read the Dominion newspaper. One of the first songs we learned to sing at Te Hāroto Māori School was "God Save the Queen," and every major event, including the movies, began with an upstanding observance of Queen Elizabeth's rule. The only place that we did not pay homage to the queen in this manner was at the picture nights at Te Hāroto pā. I am not sure whether this was because the local iwi did not have a copy of the coronation film or whether it was because of a stance of resistance. I want to believe the latter.

In the summer of 1963, the kids from Te Hāroto Māori School were jammed on a bus and taken to Napier city to see Queen Elizabeth.[13] The queen's visit commemorated the 10th anniversary of her ascension to the throne. It was also the 123rd anniversary of the signing of the Treaty of Waitangi, although we were not told about this. For several weeks leading up to the royal visit, we learned about the important role of the monarchy and its relationship to New Zealand. We were also apprised of civilized dress and behaviour—what to wear, how to cheer and wave our flags, how to walk in orderly file, how to eat our lunch nicely (which included not cadging any food from the lunch boxes of the Pākehā kids from the city), and how to bow and curtsy should the queen select us for special attention over the thousands of other flag-waving kids. I don't remember anything about the queen, but I do remember the excitement of visiting the beach on the way home. Many of the children from Te Hāroto had not ventured into the city before and so a swim at the beach was an exciting whoop-it-up experience that saw 40 little savages on the loose! So much for the hours put into practising curtseying, bowing, and "I'm honoured to meet you, Your Majesty!"

> Māori kid, Māori kid, where have you been?
> I've been to Napier to visit the queen.
> Māori kid, Māori kid, what did you there?
> Eh! I had a swim at the beach. Churr![14]

When the Pākehā headmaster taught us about Māori, he focused on ancient societies and legends (as he called them). As far as the curriculum was concerned, modern-day Māori did not exist—apparently, we had neither events, nor people, nor accomplishments worthy of learning.[15] No one taught us about the Treaty of Waitangi—the defining document that shaped the modern-day building of the New Zealand nation. I would have liked to learn that there are two versions of the Treaty, each with widely different provisions. I would have liked to learn that the Māori version of Article Two of the Treaty guaranteed chieftainship over lands, villages, and all treasured things, and that the Crown had the right to engage with Māori in land transactions. And I would have liked to learn that the English version of the Treaty, which few Māori signed, gave Māori "exclusive and undisturbed possession" of lands, forests, fisheries, and other properties, but, very sinisterly, it also gave the Crown the exclusive right to deal with Māori over buying land (see http://www.teara.govt.nz/en/treaty-of-waitangi). And, in this absence of learning about anything Māori, bit-by-bit, piece-by-piece, our language and culture, our accomplishments, our aspirations, and our well-being were being supplanted by an English-only mindset. And we sang on!

W-i-der still and w--i--der shall thy bounds be set;
God, who made thee mighty, make thee m-i-g-h-t-i-e-r yet,
Indeed, small savages on the road to civilization!

Form One and Form Two

At the end of Standard Four, I experienced the great rural-to-urban migration. When my family moved from Te Hāroto to the city, it was an indescribable culture shock. I was anxious about going to an intermediate school with hardly any Māori kids. I remember throwing up on my first day. I think that in my class of 39 kids, four were Māori, but they never spoke about it. Nothing was familiar and there were no older kids to turn to. No one did things the same way or thought the same way. Nothing at my new school was Māori. It was as if I had landed on an alien planet. For months, when anybody asked where I lived, I gave my Te Hāroto address. That is, until my homeroom teacher told me off: "You don't live there anymore! Te Hāroto is not your home," he said. And I cried.

In some ways, my time at intermediate school turned out to be a strangely successful experience. I made friends and had great teachers who stuffed my little pumpkin head with exciting new things. But I did not learn one thing about Māori—no songs, no language, no visits to marae, no distinguished Māori visitors to our class…Nothing. It was as if the Māori people and our ways had fallen off the face of the earth—our earth! The only things Māori at the school were the names of our school houses—Rātā House, Rimu House, Pūruri House, and Tōtara House. That was it! In my second year, I was placed in the "gifted and talented" class, where I found myself being prepared for stunning success in life. The number of Māori kids in that class dropped to two. My teacher was strict, knowledgeable, inspiring, and Pākehā. And I liked her. I remember getting quite proficient in English literature and French under her guidance. And, all the while, Te Hāroto was slipping further and further away.

Je ne vais pas très bien!

High School

At the end of my first year of high school, my homeroom teacher took me aside and, with a beaming smile on her face, informed me that I had won the prize for the "Most Promising Māori Pupil."[16] When I asked her who had won the prize for the "Most Promising Pākehā Pupil," she looked at me as if I had sprouted two heads (both brown) and said, "There is no such prize!" Being a facetious 13-year-old of both Māori and Pākehā ancestry, I wondered out loud whether, if in fact there had been a prize for the "Most Promising Pākehā Pupil," I would have won that as well. My homeroom teacher looked at me askance and then replied, "Don't be so silly!"

For being "a brown person of promise," I was taken to the school's hallowed prize room to select my reward. Inside was an awesome sight to behold—piles and piles of books that seemed to reach from floor to ceiling. And best of all, I was told that I could choose any two books! My consternation from carrying the mantle of "person of promise" for the Māori nation was momentarily forgotten as I set about the delicious task of hunting out the two books that would feed my passion—a love of horses, fuelled by a love for my own horse. Bred at Te Hāroto, she was my only connection to a life I had to put behind me. When I moved to the city, I made sure she came with me.

And, so, in the room of prizes, I allowed myself to get lost in books, especially books about horses. I could have stayed there all day! About an hour or so later, I emerged from the tomes and took my treasured selections to the teacher in charge of prize-giving—a pasty-hued dowager with a career-long commitment to civilizing savages to the ways of the British Empire through her English literature classes. As she flicked through the large glossy pages of equinity, her "wrinkled lip and sneer of cold command" (Shelley 1818) told that my passions well she could not read! In my choice, I had clearly screwed up! Without pause, she thrust the books into my chest and snapped, "Go back and choose books that set a better example for others like you!"

"Get stuffed! You bloody stupid old cow!"

No longer impassioned, I returned to the meaningless stacks and picked up the first two books within my reach—*Le Petit Prince* (French version) and *A Book of New Zealand* (with 54 photographs). As I watched her clutch her pen with her cloven hoof and print my name on the flyleaves of the books, I vowed that I would never read them. Ever!

Which yet survive, stamped on these lifeless things... (Shelley 1818).

The Girding on of Amulets and Spears

The old men told us, study your descent lines, as numerous as the hairs upon your head. When you have gathered them together as a treasure for your mind, you may wear the three plumes, *"te iho makawerau," "te pareraukura,"* and *"te raukura"* on your head. The men of learning said, understand the learning of your ancestors, so you can talk in the gatherings of the people. Hold fast to the knowledge of your kinship, and unite in the knot of mankind.

—ERUERA STIRLING, cited in A. Salmond, *Between Worlds*

Hold fast to the knowledge of our kinship, and unite in our knot of mankind? My schooling, like the schooling of thousands of other Māori children, was designed to do the exact opposite. It was designed to assimilate me, at all cost, into the dominant culture through a dominant language and a dominant mindset, English. It was a civilizing experience and it was done, as my stories illustrate, at the expense of my mana and of the mana of generations of my people gone before and yet to come. Mine are the schooling experiences that, for countless decades, have bound Māori children together in a perpetual state of dislocation from anything and everything that should be familiar. Simon and Smith (2001) argue that the Native Schools system, in particular, had been established in accordance with the "civilising" agenda of the nineteenth-century state, specifically to facilitate the "Europeanizing" of Māori. The Native School thus was intended as a structured interface between Māori culture and European culture—a site where the two cultures would be brought into organized collision, as it were—with one culture being confronted by the other in a systematic way. Pākehā teachers appointed to these schools were expected to engage with Māori in specific ways designed to systematically undermine their culture and replace it with that of Pākehā. (3)

And for those of us who endured the great rural-to-urban drift—the transition from our familiar, rural Native Schools to faceless, urban Pākehā public schools—the experience was gut-wrenching.

What, then, are the outcomes of this civilizing mission? Māori children as a group have rates of school absenteeism and referral for special education services that are far above average. Māori teenagers are more likely to drop out of high school without qualifications and have one of the highest suicide rates in the world. Our adults are overrepresented in prisons, have the poorest health records, and are underrepresented as students and faculty in higher education. Chronic homelessness is a Māori phenomenon (Bishop et al. 2009; Education Review Office 2006; Farrelly, Rudegeair, and Rickard 2006; Marriott and Sim 2014). Thus, it appears that upward mobility for Māori through the public-school hegemony of things English (at the expense of things Māori) is a myth.

Apple (1996) sheds light on this phenomenon. He argues that education is deeply implicated in the politics of culture. The curriculum is

never simply a neutral assemblage of knowledge, somehow appearing in the texts and classrooms of a nation. It is always part of a selective tradition, someone's selection, some group's vision of legitimate knowledge. It is produced out of the cultural, political, and economic conflicts, tensions, and compromises that organize and disorganize a people. (22)

Māori educator Wally Penetito (2011, 29) brings Apple's argument to life in his account of his own school days: "The most frustrating aspect of schooling for me was the relationship between me and the curriculum (perceived as what one was at school to learn). At least at primary school virtually everything we learned had a novelty appeal, but apart from being taught to read, little else we were force-fed appeared to have meaning." Penetito describes his school experiences as remote, detached, separate from reality, and institutionalized.[17] Schooling at Te Hāroto Māori School was a similar experience.

Why, then, are Māori like Penetito and me different from many Māori children? Why are we among the few who "succeeded" in an education system rife with discriminatory attitudes and practices? There are several reasons—some complex and some simple. Penetito (2011) explains that his experiences of school taught him many things. He learned that it was wise to choose teachers who liked him because this enhanced his chances of succeeding. He also learned that school (or academic success) was contingent upon behaving well, making every effort to be liked, and regurgitating what he was taught. However, while the art of sycophantic regurgitation was perfected by many of us, so too was the art of simmering resistance. From the earliest days of my schooling, I learned how to play the game without losing my mana. I learned how to be "nice" to teachers when I had nothing to lose and how to befriend without trust. And I learned how to hide my anger and frustration every time those who held sway over my educational well-being let me down with their artful acts of bigotry. But, most important, I refused to learn how to wiggle my hips and clap my hands when a "performance" was the order of the day.

> Tamariki Māori hei ha hei
> E poi rere nei hei ha hei
> Hei mātakitaki
> Mo te iwi haere mai
> Whati whati to hope hei
> Whati whati to hope hei.[18]

FIGURE 1.2 *New Zealand tourist industry photograph of very young Māori children. "A Haka for a Penny," circa early 1910s. [Photograph by W. Beattie & Co.]*

These are the amulets and the spears that I carry to this day. For those of us who are successful in maneuvering our ways through the hegemony of public education, we have paid (and continue to pay) steep prices. Our successes come with layers upon layers of deep cuts administered by those of a privileged mainstream who saw no wrong in their perspectives, policies, and practices. In this 21st century, very little has changed in public education for Māori or for Indigenous Peoples across the globe.

Conclusion

Haere ra Matahine, e huna i a koe
Haere ra te whenua, te ora o te tangata
Haere ra te whenua, te pono o te tangata
ki nga tira haere

Kauaka te mahara e rangirangi mai
He mea ka ronaki ki te nui raorao
Na te kapo o te ringa, nana i whatoro
To te tangata hemonga, he moni e

E tama ma e, ka mahue i a koutou
Nga kai a Toi, i waiho i muri ra
Te aruhe, te mamaku, te pono o te tangata e

E hine ma, e aku ki waho ra
ki nga kai o Kuini e kohete mai nei
ki ona tamariki
Tikina ake ra he tami riwai
Pae ana te huka o te pia i te waha e

Moumou hanga noa te taru nei te tikanga
Te whakatautia ki runga ki te whenua
Apopo koutou, e tama ma, pae noa ai i te rori e
— ARITAKU MAAKA, cited in Haami, *Dr. Golan Maaka: Māori Doctor*

Previously, I wrote about my grandfather Aritaku Maaka, who died long before I was born (Maaka 2004). Aritaku was raised in a small rural community of Aotearoa New Zealand and his first language was Māori. He spoke only a little English. When his son, and my father, Inia Whangataua Maaka, was born, Aritaku was well into his 50s. My father remembered him with great affection—a loving older parent who was well-respected, very spiritual, and a little stern. Every day, my father would read the English newspaper to Aritaku and they would discuss the day's events in English. This was Aritaku's way of learning the language of his son. When I asked my father if Aritaku taught him Māori, he paused for some time and then replied wistfully, "No."

Aritaku was a prolific writer in the Māori language. He had copperplate writing, as well as a command of many genres—whakapapa, maps, legal papers, committee reports, waiata, poetry, and stories, to name some.[19] Only in recent years, I learned that Aritaku was actively involved in the fight for the retention of Māori lands and that he expressed his views on this through writing waiata.[20] In 1889, Aritaku wrote about the loss of Māori lands—the sustainer of the Māori people for generations—through confiscation and sale. His waiata here not only laments this loss, it also chastises Māori for contributing to their dispossession by turning their backs on Māori ways (living off and caring for the land)[21] and embracing Pākehā ways (desiring money and drinking too much beer). The last two lines of Aritaku's waiata predict the fate of Māori—to be left on the side of the road with nothing.

There is irony in Aritaku's prophetic writing. Although his children's legacy included our ancestral lands, it did not include our ancestral language and the knowledge contained therein. For many good reasons—and this was not an uncommon position at that time—Aritaku, a caring and loving father, felt that his 10 children, especially his youngest children (including my father, who was number nine in the family line-up), would fare better in their lives if they set aside the language and culture of our ancestors and embraced the language and culture of the Pākehā. When Aritaku's youngest children were attending school, he moved his family from the country to the city. This move was in the late 1920s, well over 30 years after he wrote his cautionary waiata. I believe that in the time that had passed between the writing of his waiata and moving his family to the city, Aritaku was forced to realize that the English language had become pervasive, especially in the cities and especially in the domain of public education. Schooling for democracy through paideia had become Aritaku's reality and it was in this English-only context that he made the choice to do what he thought was best for his children—prioritize the English language and all its trappings. When I look at Aritaku's beautiful command of the Māori language, I can only wonder at the devastation he might have felt in making this decision. Or perhaps, like other Māori Elders of the time, he felt that the decision had already been made for him. He saw the writing on the wall—and none of it was

Māori! The legacy of Aritaku's children became the legacy of his grandchildren. This tragic loss, coupled with a public education system that had as its primary goal the assimilation of Māori into the broader culture of the New Zealand democratic state, ensured that within the span of two generations much of the knowledge of a thousand years could be accessed only with difficulty and always through the hazy lens of colonization.

I conclude my chapter by returning to my title, "Education Through Paideia: The Contested Space of the Indigenous Psyche." Like a Hollywood movie with a happy ending, commentaries such as mine are usually expected to offer up hopeful thoughts on the solution to the trauma that has been visited upon Māori by public education and other similar public institutions, political mandates, social attitudes, and the like for the past 150 or so years. But where do I start? Any attempts to find solutions promise to be extremely complicated, especially if I embrace the commentary by Burke Harris (2014) and the study by Felitti et al. (1998) that purport that trauma-induced stress affects brain development, the immune system, hormonal system, and human DNA. Have Māori been rewired for the worse over years of traumatic dislocation from everything that is familiar to us? And, if so, how do we even begin to think about "re-rewiring"? And what about non-Māori New Zealanders who have grown up on a healthy diet (also through the education system) of devaluing anything Māori, particularly our language and our culture? What trauma-induced stress has affected their physiological functioning, especially as this relates to their prioritization of Māori well-being? Farrelly, Rudegeair, and Rickard (2006) rightly argue that New Zealand needs to acknowledge the prevalence of traumatic stress plaguing its population and develop ways to address it. But where to begin?

Having painted this grim picture, it might be fitting, after all, to end with hopeful words saying that the world of subjugation (whether through a democracy or any other form of government) need not be perceived as one from which there is no exit. Rather, it should be perceived as one that can be transformed. Noam Chomsky (Democracy

Now 2012, 57:48), an American philosopher and social justice activist, says as much: "Under the worst conditions, horrendous conditions, people still, you know, fight for their rights and don't just succumb." The Māori spirit of endurance in the New Zealand democratic state has definitely brought reality to Chomsky's words, but what has been the cost? And, most importantly, what is needed for Māori to become whole again—to "hold fast to the knowledge of our kinship, and unite in the knot of mankind"?

What, indeed?

Notes

1. *Author's Note*: It is an important step in the process of decolonization that Indigenous writers work to Indigenize the precepts of compositional writing. As we strive to produce an Indigenous body of literature, including one that utilizes English as the matrix language, we should strive to elevate ways of writing that serve to honour our Indigenous worldviews. The author has chosen to honour Māori words by normalizing their use in the text (i.e., by not marking them in italics and not providing English glosses). It is, in effect, a way to utilize compositional resource to effect a counter-hegemonic attack on an otherwise dominant mindset, one that is uncompromising for the very fact that its norms seem so normal. This chapter represents the author's attempt to contest a space that comes with preconceived notions of normalcy that subordinate native desires for recognition in our own right. In doing so, the author recognizes that Indigenous ways of knowing, and of presenting that knowledge, cannot be confined to a single style, as we all have unique ways of expressing ideas and various responses to their presentation. The idea that one size fits all stifles our individuality, levels the differences that identify our different peoples, and limits our creativity whether individually or collectively.

2. Wong (personal conversation, January 27, 2015) observed that this mindset is not surprising. He argues that an Indigenous scholar recounting his or her own stories is accorded little credibility in Western academies. However, if a Pākehā scholar interviews an Indigenous scholar on the same subject and publishes the exchange, the Pākehā scholar is heralded as an expert on Indigenous Peoples. Wong notes that there is a long history of outsiders researching Indigenous

Peoples, reconstituting Indigenous identity through this process, and passing their results off as truth.

3. The Treaty of Waitangi was a written agreement first signed in 1840 between the British Crown (the monarch) and more than 500 Māori chiefs. In essence, the treaty gave the Crown rights to govern and develop British settlement, while the Crown guaranteed Māori full protection of their interests and status and full citizenship rights. There are two versions of the treaty—one in English and one in Māori. It is the (mis)interpretation of the two versions that has led to significant conflicts since the signing (see http://www.justice.govt.nz/tribunals/waitangi-tribunal/treaty-of-waitangi).

4. There is debate over the origin of this comment, although it is widely attributed to Churchill.

5. There is debate over the origin of this comment, although it is widely attributed to Jefferson.

6. See https://www.health.govt.nz/our-work/populations/maori-health/tatau-kahukura-maori-health-statistics/nga-mana-hauora-tutohu-health-status-indicators/life-expectancy. These statistics illustrate a long history of inequality in the health and well-being of Māori and non-Maori. In 1952, for example, the life expectancy for Māori was approximately 14 years less than for non-Māori. See historical statistics at http://www.stats.govt.nz.

7. "Godzone" is the New Zealand vernacular for God's Own Country. It is taken from the title of Thomas Bracken's poem (1890). Bracken also penned the New Zealand national anthem, "God Defend New Zealand" (1876). Both works embody a sense of pride in New Zealand that is predicated on the possession of land and what that land affords and on a strong belief in Christianity.

8. Te Hāroto Māori School was established under the Native Schools Act of 1867. Native Schools were state-controlled and, primarily, state-funded primary schools set up in small rural Māori communities. The curriculum was taught in English and was designed to assimilate Māori children into the broader context of urban New Zealand. In many communities, Māori parents took active roles in establishing these schools because they wanted their children to benefit from European educations (Simon and Smith 2001). Te Hāroto Māori School went from Primer One to Standard Six. The United States equivalent is an elementary school from kindergarten to sixth grade.

9. This is a pēpeha or wise saying. Pēpeha are not just proverbs—"the term includes charms, witticisms, figures of speech and boasts, and other sayings" (Mead and Grove 2001, 9). There are many explanations of the tuakana/teina

relationship—this pēpeha reflects the reciprocal relationship between the younger and older children at Te Hāroto Māori School. While the tuakana/teina relationship is gender-specific, the reference here was used more generically to denote the relationship between younger children and older children.

10. Free milk was given to New Zealand children from 1937 to 1967 as an effort by the Labour government to grow healthy New Zealanders. For many children from poor families, the daily half-pint bottle of milk served as their breakfast and lunch.

11. In the Māori culture, the references "Auntie" and "Uncle" are used as forms of respect to address persons from older generations (regardless of familial connection).

12. "Land of Hope and Glory" is a British patriotic song, with music by Edward Elgar and lyrics by A. C. Benson. It was written in 1902. This and other songs, like "Rule, Britannia," "Jerusalem," and "Onward, Christian Soldiers," were designed to supplement what children learned in the classroom about the British Empire and boost pride in the far-off motherland of England.

13. Not at any time during my schooling was the fanfare, pomp, and ceremony accorded to Queen Elizabeth ever accorded to any of our revered Māori leaders.

14. This rhyme from my childhood is a parody of "Pussy Cat, Pussy Cat," an English nursery rhyme circa 1805.

15. Our learning about other Indigenous Peoples also came through a Pākehā lens. We learned, for example, that "red Indians" were marauding savages who impeded the settlement of America; that Australian Aborigines were primitive, ate only witchetty grubs, and could throw a boomerang and make it come back; and that the Eskimos of Alaska lived in igloos, chewed on whales, and paddled around all day in kayaks.

16. The 1960s saw a governmental push to urbanize Māori, with the intent of assimilating us into the broader fabric of New Zealand. Education, in particular, was seen as a vehicle to accomplish this. The Department of Māori Affairs sponsored the Most Promising Māori Pupil Award to encourage Māori to value education and, as a result, do well in school (see Hunn 1960). It is important to note that the school awarded academic prizes for each class level, including Dux of the school. It is not surprising that Māori were rarely the recipients of these academic prizes. The value of the Most Promising Māori Pupil Award may be assessed in this context.

17. In a lighthearted email conversation (February 21, 2015) with Penetito about the Janet and John readers, he suggested that Māori children would have been

far more interested if the text had read more like, "Spot ran to the tree and he cocked his leg and did a mimi." Penetito's comment reflects the difference between Māori and Pākehā worldviews—the uptight Victorian abhorrence for public acknowledgement of sexual activity, bodily functions, and the like was not shared by Māori and other Indigenous Peoples of the Pacific.

18. Old children's song—loosely translated it refers to Māori children dancing in circles/wiggling their hips for tourists.
19. In 1969, I remember seeing boxes and boxes of my grandfather's papers in storage at our family homestead in Takapau. Sadly, the bulk of my grandfather's writings was lost when the family homestead burned to the ground shortly after.
20. I am grateful to my cousin Bradford Haami (1995) for the research he conducted in writing his book, *Dr Golan Maaka: Māori Doctor*. My grandfather's waiata is cited on p. 59 of Haami's book.
21. Eddie Durie (as cited in Mead 2003, 273) describes the unique relationship of Māori to the land: "In the beginning land was not something that could be owned or traded. Māoris did not seek to own or possess anything, but to belong. One belonged to a family, that belonged to a hapu, that belonged to a tribe."

References

Apple, Michael W. 1996. *Cultural Politics and Education*. New York: Teachers College Press.

Atkinson, Neill. 2003. *Adventures in Democracy: A History of the Vote in New Zealand*. Dunedin, NZ: Otago University Press.

Bishop, Russell, Mere Berryman, Tom Cavanagh, and Lani Teddy. 2009. "Te Kotahitanga: Addressing Educational Disparities Facing Māori Students in New Zealand." *Teaching and Teacher Education* 25 (5): 734-42. https://doi.org/10.1016/j.tate.2009.01.009

Bradbury, Ray. 1953. *Fahrenheit 451*. New York: Ballantine Books.

Burke Harris, Nadine. 2014. "How Childhood Trauma Affects Health Across a Lifetime." TEDMED video, 15:59. September 2014. http://www.ted.com/talks/nadine_burke_harris_how_childhood_trauma_affects_health_across_a_lifetime

Cremin, Lawrence A. 1975. "Public Education and the Education of the Public." *Teachers College Record* 77: 1-12.

Democracy Now. 2012. "Noam Chomsky on Gaza, and the 2 Positives of Election 2012: The Worst Didn't Happen—and It's Over." Democracy Now: Independent Global News video, 58:56. November 14, 2012. https://www.democracynow.org/2012/11/14/noam_chomsky_on_gaza_and_the

de Saint-Exupéry, Antoine. 1943. *Le Petit Prince*. New York: Reynal & Hitchcock.

Durie, Arohia E. 1997. "Te Aka Matua: Keeping a Māori Identity." In *Mai i Rangiātea: Māori Wellbeing and Development*, edited by P. Te Whāiti, M. McCarthy, and A. Durie, 142–62. Auckland, NZ: Auckland University Press.

Durie, Mason H. 1998. *Te Mana, Te Kāwanatanga: The Politics of Māori Self-Determination*. Auckland, NZ: Oxford University Press.

Education Review Office. 2006. *The Achievement of Māori Students*. Wellington, NZ: Education Review Office.

Fanon, Frantz. 1963. *The Wretched of the Earth*. New York: Grove Press.

Farrelly, Susan, Thomas Rudegeair, and Sharon Rickard. 2006. "Trauma and Dislocation in Aotearoa (New Zealand): The Psyche of a Society." *Journal of Trauma Practice* 4 (3–4): 202–20. https://doi.org/10.1300/J189v04n03_02

Felitti, Vincent J., Robert F. Anda, Dale Nordenberg, David F. Williamson, Alison M. Spitz, Valerie J. Edwards, Mary P. Koss, and James S. Marks. 1998. "Relationship of Childhood Abuse and Household Dysfunction to Many of the Leading Causes of Death in Adults: The Adverse Childhood Experiences (ACE) Study." *American Journal of Preventive Medicine* 14 (4): 245–58.

Goodlad, John I., Corinne Mantle-Bromley, and Stephen John Goodlad. 2004. *Education for Everyone: Agenda for Education in a Democracy*. San Francisco, CA: Jossey-Bass.

Gordon, Neve. 2010. "Democracy and Colonialism." *Theory & Event* 13 (2). https://doi.org/10.1353/tae.0.0138

Haami, Bradford. 1995. *Dr. Golan Maaka: Māori Doctor*. Auckland, NZ: Tandem Press.

Hunn, Jack K. 1960. *Report on Department of Māori Affairs*. Wellington, NZ: Government Printer.

Hunter, Albert, and Carl Milofsky. 2007. *Pragmatic Liberalism: Constructing a Civil Society*. New York: Palgrave Macmillan.

Maaka, Margaret J. 2004. "E Kua Takoto te Mānuka Tūtahi: Decolonization, Self-Determination, and Education." *Educational Perspectives* 37 (1): 3–13.

Mann, Michael. 2005. *The Dark Side of Democracy: Explaining Ethnic Cleansing*. Cambridge: Cambridge University Press.

Marriott, Lisa, and Dalice Sim. 2014. *Indicators of Inequality for Māori and Pacific People*. Wellington, NZ: Victoria University.

Mead, Hirini M. 1998. "Foreword." In *Ngā Kura Māori: The Native Schools System, 1867–1969*, edited by J. Simon, viii–xi. Auckland, NZ: Auckland University Press.

———. 2003. *Tikanga Māori: Living by Māori Values*. Wellington, NZ: Huia Publishers.

Mead, Hirini M., and Neil Grove. 2001. *Ngā Pēpeha a Ngā Tīpuna*. Wellington, NZ: Victoria University Press.

Mencken, Henry Louis. 1926. *Notes on Democracy*. New York: Alfred A. Knopf.

Penetito, Wally. 2011. *What's Māori About Māori Education?* Wellington, NZ: Victoria University Press.

Salmond, Anne. 1997. *Between Worlds: Early Exchanges Between Māori and Europeans 1773-1815*. Honolulu: University of Hawai'i Press.

Shaw, George Bernard. 1903. *Man and Superman: Maxims for Revolutionists*. Westminster, UK: Archibald & Co.

Shelley, Percy Bysshe. 1818. "Ozymandias." *The Examiner* (London), January 11, 1918.

Simon, Judith, and Linda Tuhiwai Smith, eds. 2001. *A Civilizing Mission: Perceptions and Representations of the New Zealand Native Schools System*. Auckland, NZ: Auckland University Press.

Smith, Linda Tuhiwai. 1999. *Decolonizing Methodologies: Research and Indigenous Peoples*. London: Zed Books.

Stevick, Doyle, and Bradley A. Levinson, eds. 2007. *Reimaging Civic Education: How Diverse Societies Form Democratic Citizens*. New York: Rowman & Littlefield.

Wilde, Oscar. 1891. "The Soul of Man Under Socialism." *Fortnightly Review*, 49 (290): 292–319.

2 | Pathways for Remembering and (Re)cognizing Indigenous Thought in Education
Indigenizing Teacher Education and the Academy

SANDRA STYRES

LOCATING ONESELF in relation to everything one does is one of the key foundational principles in Indigeneity. The only place from which any of us can write or speak with any degree of certainty is from the position of who we are in relation to what we know—in this way, I am accountable for my own cultural location, which situates me in relation to my community, at home and at large, as well as within the pages of this chapter. Acknowledging my positionality peels back the layers, uncovering motives, intentions, and subjectivities while identifying particular epistemic perspectives informing and guiding this chapter. Last, but certainly not least, positioning and locating myself culturally and geographically is a relational, respectful, and reciprocal process that is a key element of Indigenous philosophies. In so doing, I acknowledge the multiple shifting identities that comprise my reality and sense of becoming in relation to all that I do.

My First Nations heritage comes from my connection to my ancestors through my father's lineage (Mohawk and French). My mother's lineage connects me to my English ancestors from Europe. I currently reside on

Six Nations of the Grand River Territory, a First Nations community located in Southern Ontario, in Canada. Six Nations is a unique community comprised of six distinct Nations (Mohawk, Oneida, Onondaga, Cayuga, Seneca, and Tuscarora), with each Nation having its own unique cultural traditions and language. Six Nations is generally considered to be one of the largest and most urbanized First Nations communities in Canada, and we have danced with the idea of taking over control of our own education for many years. Astronomical systemic complexities and serious financial implications ensured the idea was always, in the end, rejected. In light of current contexts, the conversation has once again been resurrected. Many First Nations communities across Canada have been very outspoken in responding to and rejecting the imposition of former prime minister Stephen Harper's proposed First Nations Education Act. First Nations people are not opposed to a First Nations-specific Education Act, but it is our assertion that the conversations around such an important piece of legislation needs to begin with us, as first and host Peoples of this land, and not the government—otherwise it remains another imposed colonial construct and a tool for assimilation.

Education has long been identified as a contested, albeit crucial, site for acknowledging, resisting, and disrupting colonial relations. This chapter focuses on articulating pathways for (re)membering and (re)cognizing Indigenous thought in education based on shared themes from community, national, and international relationships. Indigenous thought is crucial in education, as it decentres dominant Western[1] notions of what constitutes legitimate knowledges and knowledge creation, while centring Indigenous thought as a distinct knowledge system with its own understanding of rational thought and the ways one is deeply, intimately, and spiritually connected to lands and to all of creation (human and non-human/animate and non-animate). The point is not to replace dominant Western thought, but that the two can coexist in mutually egalitarian and sovereign relationships. This chapter explores the importance of taking Indigenous thought seriously in education; examines issues relating to tokenism, voyeurism, and cultural tourism, as well as opening a dialogue on appropriation and the ethics of protocol; looks at the various tensions and challenges of doing this work within academia; and concludes with a consideration of ways of moving forward in respectful relations.

Why Now in This Time?

There are many historical and contemporary systemic factors contributing to the current crisis in Indigenous education and the importance of why there should be a focus on Indigenous thought now. In using the term crisis, I want to be clear that I am not placing blame on First Nations, Métis, and Inuit people in Canada, or indeed Indigenous people globally, for an education system steeped in Eurocentrism and imperialistic intellectualism that fails so many of our children. Rather, I am using the term crisis to indicate that Indigenous education is (and has been for quite some time) experiencing intense struggles and challenges requiring important decisions to be made in collaboration with Indigenous communities, invested persons/parties, and, of course, universities. Kuhn (1962) writes that crises, particularly in academia, shake loose taken-for-granted assumptions and stereotypes to provide the foundation for shifting long-held and, at times, outdated and ineffective paradigms. As many scholars have written, Indigenous education has indeed reached a critical fork in the road, if you will, and we all need to work together to decide how we will move forward from here.

In 2008, New Democrat MP Charlie Angus challenged the Conservative government in the House of Commons by describing Indigenous education as a "third world" form of education and the schools themselves as "holding pens for cattle." Further, he said, "too many Aboriginal children are being denied the fundamental right to be educated in a school that gives them hope" (cited in Bailey 2008, 16). Again in 2012, Angus stated that many First Nations children in other communities across Canada are educated in substandard or even dangerous conditions, while some communities do not even have schools. Further, he is quoted as saying that "if these were public schools (off-reserve) there would be charges laid. These children have been dealt a rotten hand and nobody cares" (Ball 2012, n.p.). The Assembly of First Nations (AFN) states that there are approximately 70,000 First Nations children and youth living in their communities and attending community schools across Canada who do not have access to the same standard and quality of educational programs and services that are available to other children.

The results of a 2011 AFN school survey show that 47% of First Nations communities say they need a new school. Of those, 60% say they have waited longer than five years with unanswered requests; 10% have waited more than 20 years. More than 70% of those First Nations communities that have schools in their communities stated that they were substandard, hazardous, and in need of major repairs and upgrades to bring them up to minimum national standards. Seventy-two per cent said that health and safety were serious concerns. According to the Fraser Institute 2013 report (Milke 2013), the average provincial government in 2011–12 spent about $10,000 per capita to educate children, while the federal government only spent $7,000 per First Nations student, representing a shortfall of approximately $3,000. The funding gap continues to widen. In 2016 the Parliamentary Budget Officer reported that the high education gap was estimated at $665 million (cited in Morin, 2017). This funding shortfall means that much-needed supports for closing the educational gap and bringing First Nations community schools up to national standards are not being addressed by the federal government's current funding model.

Statistics tell us that the Indigenous population in Canada is not only younger than the national average, but is growing at a rate approximately 1.5 times higher than the mainstream, and Statistics Canada projects that this rate of growth will continue (Demosim Team 2011). One third of the Indigenous population is aged 14 or under, and the Assembly of First Nations (Chiefs Assembly on Education 2012) currently reports that approximately 36% of First Nations students who reside within their communities attend school in urban centres outside that community— these children will find their ways into K-12 classrooms in Canada.

Most distressing and heartbreaking is that suicide among Indigenous youth (ages 15-24) for both males and females is respectively five and eight times higher than the general national rate. According to the Mental Health Commission of Canada, the general national rate of suicide in Canada is approximately 4,000 suicides annually (Mental Health Commission of Canada 2012, 13)—that means that the annual suicide figures for young Indigenous men are 20,000, and 32,000 for women, each year!

The costs of the current Eurocentric-based education system have been socially astronomical, as evidenced by well-documented issues such as suicides, chronic underachievement, and the high dropout rates of Indigenous children. In 1996, only 12% of Indigenous youth completed high school (Royal Commission on Aboriginal Peoples 1996). In the 2002-03 school year, national statistics reveal that only 29% of the small group of Indigenous students who even made it into Grade 12 graduated (Mendelson 2008). The AFN and Fraser Institute report that across Canada approximately 60% of First Nations youth dropped out and did not complete high school, compared with 10% of the general Canadian population. These and other well-documented statistics reveal that the current Eurocentric system of education is failing First Nations, Métis, and Inuit children (indeed, all our children) and, therefore, we cannot continue to do education as we have been. In other words, we need to disrupt and shift current ways of thinking about and doing education—particularly the ways we train teachers to be teachers. There is a quote usually attributed to Albert Einstein that says, "The definition of insanity is doing the same thing over and over and expecting a different result."

Indigenous thought in education has significance for all teachers and students, particularly those seeking to become teachers—it is not just an Indigenous thing. Developing an understanding of the contemporary and historical connections Indigenous people have to their places, and the ways Indigenous Peoples have existed and continue to exist first and foremost in deeply intimate, spiritual, and respectful relationships to their lands, one another, and indeed all relations (animate and inanimate/human and non-human), is the key to success for all students as active and respectful participants, first in their own places, as well as in the wider global arena. It is important in building good, balanced, and equitable relationships to bring educators and learners together as culturally located individuals having the knowledge and abilities to bring relevant understandings of Indigenous knowledges into their pedagogies and practices in ways that are respectful and appropriate—always being mindful of cultural contexts and ethical protocols.

In order to reduce hegemonic ideologies that serve to perpetuate and inform dominant Western practices within education, the concept of bringing Indigenous thought into current educational contexts must take seriously the diverse ecological, epistemic, historical, and contemporary realities of Indigenous communities as the basis for its central tenets. Philosophical approaches to Indigenous education underpin administration and infrastructure; networks and relations of power; the ways knowledge is constructed and legitimized within the dominating epistemology; policies, pedagogies, and classroom practices; and the complex issues relating to literacies and evaluative strategies. First Nations, Métis, and Inuit children have the right to have an education system that values, legitimizes, and centres their knowledge, values, and ways of understanding their realities in classrooms.

In order for this goal to become a reality, I believe it is crucial to simultaneously focus on two aspects of education: (1) initial teacher education (ITE)—in other words, how we are training teachers to become teachers—because, by the time any teacher arrives in their own classroom, they have generally had 25-plus years of observing teaching modelled for them; and (2) in-service teacher development (ISTD). We cannot ignore the teachers who are already teaching our children in their classrooms, as many of these children are our future educators. By taking in-service teacher development seriously, we can disrupt the status quo of current teaching models for those educators teaching in both urban and rural classrooms, including those who teach in First Nations community schools—whether they are First Nations, Métis, and Inuit teachers or not. To do this, I will draw upon my own pedagogical experiences in various ITE and ISTD contexts and the impacts of those experiences on teacher candidates, in-service teachers (IST), and their respective classrooms. The moment we begin to engage the status quo, we intersect and disrupt taken-for-granted assumptions and long-held biases, as well as issues pertaining to power and privilege—in other words, we confront the historical and contemporary realities of Indigenous education on contentious ground—and we do so by Indigenizing education. Indigenizing education focuses on our role as Indigenous educators within academia and the ways we redefine what it means to think about and do education. Indigenizing education is not a toolbox, a list of best practices, or a checklist of items that can be crossed off—it is an active process of engagement, activism, patience, and unwavering persistence. The challenge for us as Indigenous educators is that we work in environments and institutions that are built upon and prosper on "stolen lands,"[2] having core systemic foundations of assimilationist agendas and colonialist ideologies. These environments are contested spaces that foster and perpetuate institutionalized racism, oppression, and violence. The violence arises out of the resistance and pushback from those seeking to maintain the status quo against those seeking to Indigenize and decolonize various spaces within the academy.

Decolonizing and Indigenizing

The term "decolonization" has always been like a needle in my brain—a sharp pain deep within the recesses of my thought processes. For a great many of us, depending on our positionality, the term "decolonization" can take on many different perspectives, with subtle nuances of meaning. While colonization practices have been a reoccurring and shifting part of human history, Loomba (2005) writes that modern understandings of colonization came into practice during the industrialization era with the movement of Europeans into permanent settlements and the organization of formal colonies in other lands. The term colonize refers to the systemic dismantling and reconstructing of another place into an economically and politically dependent relationship with the colonizing nation—the conquest and control of the lands and resources of one culture-sharing group by another. Colonialism, particularly as it relates to modernity, (re)frames the conquered by drawing the colonized into complex, exploitative, and tangled social, economic, and political relationships with the colonizers. Colonization and decolonization, as means to an end, serve to erase the histories and stories of the people living in the conquered lands by focusing colonial discourses and relations of power on the colonizers.

The notion of decolonizing is an active process whereby a colonized group makes attempts to return to a pre-colonial state of independence and sovereignty. It is also generally understood to be the process of eliminating colonial influences by freeing a colonized group of its colonial status. There are two concepts at play here: (1) decolonizing as the active process that engages colonialism in multiple ways; and (2) decolonization as the end result of the process of decolonizing. Freedom from colonial status may be granted either through the colonizers completely withdrawing from the colonized territory, or the colonizers remaining in the colonized territory but conferring sovereignty, self-determination, and the rights of self-governance to the colonized. Decolonization can also be achieved by active resistance and revolution, leading to the forcible removal of the colonizers. In the first two scenarios, the decolonizing process is based on relations of power and privilege and the granting of freedom and status by the colonizing forces. In these instances, the colonized are considered dominated bodies awaiting their fate. In the third instance, relations of power are resisted, engaged, and exercised.

Each of these decolonizing practices, no matter how well-intentioned or deserved, re-engages and re-centres colonial relations, thereby perpetuating and maintaining the very colonial practices it sought to remove. Alfred (2005, 22) argues that "whatever the specific means or rationale, violent, legalist, and economic revolutions have never been successful in producing peaceful coexistence between peoples; in fact, they always reproduce the exact set of power relations they seek to change, rearranging only the outward face of power." Linda Tuhiwai Smith (2012, 101) writes that decolonization in contemporary understandings "is recognized as a long-term process involving the bureaucratic, cultural, linguistic and psychological divesting of colonial power." While decolonizing is seen to be at the heart of social and political sovereignty and desired in principle, it is a process that, by its very nature, is and will always continuously be (re)centring colonial relations in a continuous cycle of repetition and replication.

The current context of colonialism is that the histories and contemporary realities of Indigenous Peoples and colonial settlers within Canada and indeed across all of Turtle Island are now inextricably connected—we have a shared and tangled history on this land; no one is leaving, no one is returning to their country of origin. Nor is such an outcome desirable. Colonialism is, however, the unfinished business that we have all inherited. Each of us remains inextricably woven in complex and shifting relationships and none of us who reside within colonized lands can erase colonial relations from our narratives—they are inextricably woven into our stories of struggle, resistance, assertions of sovereignty, and the reclamation of inherent rights embedded in our lands and territories. The term "decolonizing" has initially been useful for Indigenous Peoples in negotiating, working through, and articulating ancient deeply rooted rights based on self-in-relationship to lands upon which they have existed since time immemorial and continue to exist; however, I would suggest that Indigenous philosophies, particularly as they relate to understandings of land and self-in-relationship, might work better as conceptual approaches that acknowledge colonial relations, but do not centre or place emphasis on those relationships. I would also add that perhaps it is one of the ways we might all move forward in good, respectful, and egalitarian relationships for the benefit of all, particularly in education and the ways we train teachers to be teachers. There are two current and popular models for bringing Indigenous knowledges into ITE programs: infusion and integration. These two terms have, at times, been used interchangeably by educators. However, I believe that they are, in fact, distinct in their approaches to bringing Indigenous content into the classroom.

In biological or medical terms, infusion is the introduction of a fluid solution, such as saline, into a vein. The fluid then becomes an indistinguishable and inseparable part of the blood in the vein, moving fluidly and easily becoming part of the whole. In cooking terms, infusion is a process that involves immersing or steeping a substance, such as herbs or teas, in liquid, such as water or oil, to extract the flavour of the substance. The liquid then becomes infused with the flavour of whatever item is being steeped in it. Therefore, following this line of thinking, infusing Indigenous content in pedagogies would mean that these knowledges become seamlessly infused into every aspect of the classroom, pedagogical content, and practices, so that the whole system takes on the flavour, if you will, of Indigenous knowledges. While desirable in principle, this model poses some serious challenges and points of contestation. The very act of infusing these knowledges could have one of two outcomes: either the infusion model could drastically influence and alter both dominant Western thought and Indigenous thought until they are no longer distinct knowledge systems, but become a hybrid; or, because dominant Western thought is typically so pervasive and all-consuming—having a pattern of domination, assimilation, and appropriation—it could eventually consume the Indigenous knowledges that have been infused and appropriate their content as its own. Many times and for a variety of reasons, ITE infusion models are taught by non-Indigenous instructors who, while well-intentioned, are largely unaware of the influence and imposition of their positionalities in relation to the content they are infusing and the ways this positionality informs the infusion of these knowledges. The challenge and contestation is in maintaining the integrity and distinctive nature of both knowledge systems.

The second model for bringing Indigenous content into the classroom is accomplished through integration. Integration refers to the bringing together of two distinct parts that are kept distinct, but make up the whole larger unit. Kanu (2011) writes that teachers generally understand and practice integration approaches in one of three ways: contribution, addition, and transformation. The contributions approach focuses on the contributions of each separate culture-sharing group to the overall knowledge base. In the addition approach, content and concepts from other cultures are sporadically peppered throughout the "real" curriculum. I have seen these two approaches used primarily within multicultural educational contexts, and they offer students, at best, a superficial glimpse of perspectives from other culture-sharing groups, but do so in light of the "real" or "actual" curriculum that teachers are trained to believe they are supposed to deliver. In the transformational approach, course content is taught from the perspective of the culture-sharing group. I find this approach particularly disturbing and problematic when non-Indigenous instructors are teaching Indigenous courses or when they are integrating or infusing Indigenous course content. Another point of contestation is that one quite simply cannot teach Indigenous knowledges from an Indigenous perspective from outside the lived experiences of that particular culture-sharing group, no matter how hard one tries or how well one is intentioned—this is why it is particularly crucial for Indigenizing the academy and maintaining deep reflexivity for both educators and students in ITE programs.

Because of all of these complex tangled and contested issues, both infusion and integration models continue to reinforce colonial relations of power and privilege and centrally position dominant Western thought as the legitimate foundational perspective from which to educate our children, while all else are add-ins. Further, both these models can easily lead to tokenism, voyeurism, and cultural tourism. In this context, these isms are particular ideologies grounded in dominant Western thought that are perpetuated and maintained through networks and relations of power and privilege within education—they are often found in the hidden curriculum within the "real or actual" curriculum, as previously discussed. Tokenism arises out of integration models that superficially gesture to the inclusion of decontextualized Indigenous content without any real depth of critical reflection and engagement or attempt at understanding—thus giving the illusion of inclusivity and equality. Voyeurism is the process of observing, talking, or writing about people engaged in deeply intimate and spiritual cultural behaviours and practices without active engagement or connection to the observed. An example of this is found in a story a colleague shared with me where a non-Indigenous student attended a cultural social ceremony as one of the requirements of a course offered in one particular ITE program. At the end of the ceremony, there was an informal sharing circle and individuals were asked to say why they chose to participate in the ceremony. The student said that they were just there to get a grade for a course. This student was completely unaware that they had not only just invalidated the experience for him/herself, but also deeply offended the Elder who was overseeing the ceremony and the Indigenous participants. Cultural tourism, in this particular context, is defined as educators continuously engaging in cultural practices that are not their own. Educators engaged in cultural tourism are constantly seeking out information from various Elders and other cultural experts, asking them to attend their classes and "share" cultural information. Cultural tourism is a means by which educators gather and take information for the purposes of integrating Indigenous content in their courses or for passing the responsibility of integration to others—in this case Elders and Knowledge Holders. Cultural tourism is used to satisfy personal self-interests without regard or respect for cultural teachings, contexts, or local protocols, and can also be a way for educators to abdicate the responsibility for inclusion of Indigenous content, passing it onto someone else.

As an educator in ITE programs and IST development, I have experienced students and in-service teachers who only want the toolbox or checklist they can take into their classrooms and check off to show that they have integrated Indigenous content into their courses, but resist and push back against the requirement to critically reflect on and engage with those knowledges. These are individuals who already are or are going to be teaching our children—they are the ones who will model teaching for the next generation of children going through the education system. We, as educators, must actively seek ways of disrupting the stasis concerning critical and reflexive thinking in teacher education. One should never attempt to engage with Indigenous knowledges, or any culture-sharing group's knowledges, without the appropriate context, without respectfully being mindful of and adhering to local protocols, and without always demonstrating a genuine interest in learning and expanding one's understanding of self-in-relationship—otherwise, these actions are nothing more than token gestures, voyeuristic behaviours, and culture shopping.

Having said this, I do not want to leave the impression that there are not any non-Indigenous instructors in ITE and ISTD doing good work in appropriate and respectful ways. I have personally met and worked with several non-Indigenous educators who are actively engaged with the experiences of bringing Indigenous knowledges into their pedagogies and are effectively and meaningfully transcending the walls of the academy in bringing Indigenous thought into their teaching practices. The difference is in the ways these educators think about, engage with, and do education.

As I have argued elsewhere (Styres, 2017), Indigenous knowledges are distinct and egalitarian knowledge systems with their own practices of rational thought and ways of understanding and interacting with the world. It is not my position that we should negate the use of dominant Western knowledges, but that Indigenous education should be offered in ways that centre and privilege Indigenous thought, while keeping dominant Western knowledges in perspective. Indigenizing ITE programs and IST development would necessitate Indigenizing the academy. Without a doubt, universities built on dominant Western ideologies are spaces of contestation for Indigeneity. Therefore, Indigenizing the academy is an ongoing process in which the institution, as a network of relations of power and privilege, takes the position that it will be both responsive to and responsible for moving the self-determining interests of Indigenous communities forward. One of the ways of moving this goal forward is for universities to recognize that they need to hire more Indigenous faculty and seconded teachers to teach in ITE and IST development programs—and more; that is, not just to acknowledge, but also put that acknowledgement into action. Universities need to establish and maintain a visible, active, and engaged Indigenous presence across all disciplines and in every facet of education, particularly as it relates to Indigenous education.

Tokenism, voyeurism, and cultural tourism can also easily lead to cultural appropriation—that is, the unauthorized taking of something that belongs to a culture-sharing group other than one's own and adopting it as one's own. Appropriation can include material aspects of culture and the adoption of iconographic symbols such as sports teams and mascots, fashion and adornments, and artifacts and cultural/spiritual representations; however, it can also include spiritual and ceremonial practices such as dance and music, philosophies and political structures, and knowledges and stories. Appropriation is not just unauthorized taking (also known as theft, pursuant to s. 322(1) of the Criminal Code of Canada, 1985), but also refers to decontextualization—that is to say, in the unauthorized taking one is also stripping something of its cultural context/significance, in essence converting it from what it was. Similarly, Haig-Brown (2010) refers to appropriation as cultural theft.

Appropriation as normalized practice not only brings into question the importance of considering the appropriateness of bringing Indigenous knowledges into the academy, but also raises serious concerns relating to intellectual property rights and the ways these knowledges can easily be appropriated and decontextualized, and therefore must be conscientiously protected. Indigenous people have the self-determining right to control all aspects of Indigenous knowledges, including placing guidelines around the ways others may or may not have access to and use of those knowledges and traditional teachings. Article 31 of the 2007 United Nations Declaration on the Rights of Indigenous Peoples (United Nations 2007) stipulates that:

Indigenous peoples have the right to maintain, control, protect and develop their cultural heritage, traditional knowledge and traditional cultural expressions, as well as the manifestations of their sciences, technologies and cultures, including human and genetic resources, seeds, medicines, knowledge of the properties of fauna and flora, oral traditions, literatures, designs, sports and traditional games and visual and performing arts. They also have the right to maintain, control, protect and develop their intellectual property over such cultural heritage, traditional knowledge, and traditional cultural expressions. (11)

When cultural elements are removed from their Indigenous contexts, they are twisted, changed, and neutralized, and then subsequently represented back, imitated in misshapen ways, and reimposed on Indigenous people and indeed society as a whole as authentic. That is not to say that cultures existing in close proximity do not have cultural exchanges and in some ways influence one another. Cultural exchanges are based on the principles of relationship, respect, relevance, reciprocity, and responsibility (see Styres and Zinga 2013, for a more detailed discussion on the Five Rs). But when a dominant culture, grounded in its own sense of power and privilege, appropriates and exploits cultural elements of another minoritized culture-sharing group, it is nothing less than acculturation and assimilation.

We have seen this in magazines where non-Indigenous models are wearing hegemonic war bonnets and native fashion, as well as in the application of cultural symbols in body art without consideration or regard for cultural protocols or spiritual understandings of the significance of the symbolism. Recently in the news, at the time of this writing, there was a series of images and articles concerning the offensive nature of certain team names and trademarks, as well as the wearing of war bonnets and face paint by spectators at certain athletic games. These practices are really offensive to Indigenous people, not only across Turtle Island, but anywhere in the world. Shamanism and the use of Indigenous medicines and spiritual practices by non-Indigenous people without regard for the cultural teachings and/or appropriate guidance of Elders are also forms of cultural appropriation. We can also talk about the myriad ways various forms of media perpetuate offensive, stereotypical, and hegemonic representations and consistently engage in cultural appropriation, but for the purposes of this chapter I want to focus on the particular ways Indigenous knowledges are, at times, appropriated in teacher education.

Coyote as Trickster

Drawing from one of the many possible teachings found in a particular version of the Coyote and his Two Eyes story, I offer the following cautionary note concerning the potential consequences of decontextualized knowledge. Coyote is one of the trickster characters in Native American storytelling, and is a metamorph. The concept of morphing reflects the process of change, transformation, or transition from one form or image to another. Coyote's metamorphosis occurs through various storied contexts—humour, farce, sarcasm, self-ridicule, and the nonsensical. Trickster characters are constantly journeying, making mistakes, struggling, transforming, and journeying again. Coyote as a trickster carries the lessons that teach us about life and the ways of being in relationship with one another and all of creation (human/non-human, animate/inanimate). Thomas King (2003, 32) writes that "the truth about stories is that that's all we are...you can't understand the world without telling a story." Indigenous stories are circular, having many entry points into the story, with many other stories layered within and between.

In this particular story, Coyote requests that Rabbit, a metaphoric Elder, teach him how to use Indigenous knowledge in a particular way. Subsequently, Coyote misuses the knowledge he was taught by Rabbit, resulting in grave consequences for Coyote. Because of his flagrant disregard for the contextualized traditional teachings around the appropriate use of the knowledge he was taught, Coyote is out of balance and must now stumble awkwardly forward in life with two mismatched eyes that provide only a twisted and distorted perspective on the world—he no longer interacts with the world with a balanced clarity. One of the lessons or cautionary notes that can be drawn from this story is that decontextualized knowledge can be dangerous.

One example of this is when I observed a mathematics lesson plan created by an in-service teacher using wampum as an example of one of the many world currencies. This immediately caught my attention and alarmed me, because wampum use predates contact and was an ancient recording device invented by Aiionwatha (Hiawatha). Wampum, when strung into strings or woven into belts, was used to record important events, communicate important information, serve as a badge of office, and legitimize a nation's legal standing. Wampum is also used in ceremonies to bring forward and recall ancient knowledges that are passed down from generation to generation. The Peacemaker[3] used the wampum created by Aiionwatha to record the raising of the Tree of Peace and creation of the Confederacy, which is one of the reasons wampum is considered to be sacred. Due to its sacred and spiritual significance, wampum was never, as has been assumed by some, used as currency. However, because the particular shells that were used to make wampum came from coastal communities (dentalia shells on the west coast and quahog on the east coast), many of the interior nations would trade with the coastal nations for the highly valued shells from which they would then fashion wampum beads.

The early European settlers came to realize the high value that First Nations people placed on wampum, and due to the shortage of minted coins in the colonies, the settlers did, for a time, mass-produce wampum beads and used them to trade for furs with the Hauodenosaunee and Algonquin people. What the European settlers failed to realize is that the value placed on wampum beads had nothing to do with market value, but rather reflected the deep spiritual significance that wampum held for the Haudenosaunee and Algonquin people. The marketization and mass production of wampum as a method of exchange is a prime example of some of the ways colonial relations have shifted and continue to alter deep and sacred understandings of relationality and reciprocity for First Nations peoples across Turtle Island by imposing capitalist ideologies and the commodification of resources over sacred responsibilities. This is merely one example of knowledge decontextualized, misappropriated, and being represented back to First Nations, Métis, and Inuit children, and it continues to be taught to our children in schools today.

That is not to say that this or any other teacher does not have good intentions in integrating or infusing Indigenous course content. But if we are going to take seriously and effectively implement infusion and/or integration in good, balanced, and meaningful ways that honour, respect, and legitimize the egalitarian distinctiveness of Indigenous knowledges within our classrooms—indeed, throughout all places where education occurs—then we must look beyond the self-protective veil of *good intentions* and get on with the business of decolonizing (here is that word again) our curricula and practices, and Indigenizing initial teacher education. There are many tensions and challenges in doing this work within academia, even more so for the Indigenous academic. Specifically, the Indigenous academic must constantly and effectively work with and bridge two distinct knowledge systems. There are two forms of systemic contestations existing within academia for anyone doing this work in good, meaningful, and respectful ways: the first relates to dominant Western paradigms and ways of conceptualizing systems and doing the work; the second is the long-established concept of what constitutes legitimized knowledge. Tensions arise when Indigenous philosophies grounded in ancient knowledges are brought within the walls of the academy, informing particular ways of knowing, being, and relating in the world, as well as introducing knowledges that have their legitimacy in place-specific ancient roots and understandings of self-in-relationship. In so doing the status quo is shifted—disrupting the comfort of long-established taken-for-granted assumptions about ways of being, doing, and relating. Further, for all academics, but particularly for Indigenous intellectuals, there are complex issues concerning what knowledge can appropriately be shared, as well as educating other academics and students on the ethics of local protocols.

Moving Forward

It is we, as Indigenous scholars, who must set the standards by which Indigenous thought in education will be protected and, further, define the ways it can/cannot be used and by whom. Self-determination is a crucial aspect in Indigenizing ITE and ISTD—it is we who must take up the call to establish ethical guidelines for the positioning of Indigenous knowledges in the academy, and it is the university's responsibility to respect the limitations placed on access to and the sharing of these knowledges by Indigenous faculty and community members. It must also be understood that the fullness of Indigenous knowledges can only be known from the lived experiences of Indigenous people who have existed and continue to exist on and with these lands since time immemorial—time before there was time. I clearly remember the words of Graham Smith (2012) when he addressed conference attendees who had gathered to hear a panel of Indigenous scholars discussing issues relating to teacher education—he said that "there are some conversations that we, as Indigenous people, need to have among ourselves first. If you are non-Indigenous you are privileged to be sitting here—now sit quietly and listen while we converse." Similarly, Marie Battiste (2013, 73) writes that the "acknowledgement for Indigenous knowledge must begin with Indigenous people themselves." Non-Indigenous scholars and educators need to learn how to sit in on the conversation without "appropriating their new knowledge and experience for their own ends" (69).

As we have discussed throughout this chapter, education remains a contested, but critical, space for acknowledging, resisting, and disrupting colonial relations by way of (re)membering, (re)cognizing, and (re)centring Indigenous thought within education. I do not advocate replacing dominant Western thought, but rather centring and privileging Indigenous thought within Indigenous educational contexts—while always keeping Western thought in perspective. We have explored the importance of taking Indigenous thought seriously now and in this time, and how easily one can bring Indigenous knowledges into classrooms in ways that perpetuate tokenism, voyeurism, and cultural tourism. We have examined the implications of integration and infusion models that call into question issues around appropriation and the need for an ethics of protocol. We have also considered the various tensions and challenges of doing this work and the necessity of Indigenizing the academy. In looking at ways of moving forward, we must also give some consideration to the roles of non-Indigenous community stakeholders, faculty, scholars, administrative personnel, and educators who advocate for and are supportive of Indigenous education.

There is a new buzzword that is making its rounds—settler allies. When self-appointed allies join themselves with Indigenous people, they do so from a position of power and privilege. Self-appointed allies are more concerned with their own self-interests and what they are getting out of the process—they speak for Indigenous people rather than standing back and listening; they project their own emotions of guilt and outrage and come into the process with taken-for-granted assumptions, rather than stepping back and respecting the self-determining interests of Indigenous intellectuals and communities and, above all, learning to know that they do not know what they do not know. Fyre Jean Graveline (2002) writes:

> Transforming educational contexts requires
> daring thoughts
> challenging what we know
> thought we knew
> need to know to face the dawning of a new day.
> If people can be acculturated to hold dominant views
> people can also be un-acculturated
> reculturated to Traditional views. (13)

One cannot claim allyship as an inherent right; rather, genuine allyship is born from the development of respectful and meaningful relationships. It is to stand in solidarity along with Indigenous Peoples on the issues of pressing concern to them and to their communities, even in the face of severe oppression. One cannot claim to be an ally to fulfill a saviour complex or to place upon oneself a veil of presumed innocence (see also Tuck and Yang 2012) that only serves to entrench colonial relations of power and privilege. Those individuals from settler societies who wish to stand in solidarity with Indigenous Peoples must begin the hard work of troubling their own positionalities and journey down the challenging road of deep introspection and self-examination—that is, to theorize their own experiences, regardless of their arrival stories, as a settler on Indigenous lands and engage in the process of decolonizing one's biases, behaviours, and taken-for-granted assumptions. To be in good relationship with one another requires a move from purposeful ignorance and a veil of presumed innocence towards a critical conscious awareness and an acknowledgement of whose traditional lands we are now on, as well as the historical and contemporary realities of those relationships. Trickster characters within Indigenous storytelling provide us with many examples of lessons learned in the journey towards existing in good and respectful relationships.

Trickster remains as relevant today as he ever was—he is alive and well, teaching us stories about how to be in relationship to one another and to all of creation, as well as how to "walk in a sacred manner on the good red road" (Black Elk, cited in Neihardt 1961, 28). Black Elk tells us that the sacredness of the good red road is grounded in a life lived in balance, harmony, purity, and wellness—these are life lessons not just for Indigenous people, but for everyone, particularly for those who want to bring Indigenous knowledges into their pedagogies and practices. This is one of the ways that we can all move forward in respectful and meaningful relationships with one another that honour and respect Indigenous knowledges in ITE and ISTD, and indeed in all areas of the academy. I will leave you with the words of esteemed spiritual teacher

Kesheyanakwan, Arthur Solomon, from "There Is No Middle Ground" (1990):

There are many people who have seen the way things are,
And have asked almost in despair,
But what can I do?
And the only answer has been,
You have to do something about You. (67)

Notes

1. Dominant Western/Eurocentric—I think it is appropriate to put forward a cautionary note here that it is important to challenge the notion of Western thought as a hegemonic European construct. There have been many European people groups who have experienced colonization by other dominating European nations and who are now living out their own historical and contemporary colonial experiences. Therefore, for the purposes of this chapter the term "dominant Western" refers to a particular worldview that rises out of Eurocentricism—that is to say, the privileging of dominant Euro-centred cultural values and beliefs in education, scholarship, knowledge production, and the legitimization of intellectual capital, as well as networks and systems of power. Terms such as Western, European, or Eurocentric in this book are not intended to be a racial or hegemonic construct but rather are a way to articulate a particular worldview—dominant Western ideology.

2. Based on a comment by Ice-T made during an interview when he quoted KRS-One's lyric from "Sound of Da Police": "You'll never have justice on stolen land." KRS-One's lyrics are a protest against institutionalized racism, oppression, and violence (see http://articles.latimes.com/2012/jul/25/entertainment/la-et-ms-ice-t-speaks-out-against-gun-control-20120725).

3. The Peacemaker, we are told, was born among the Huron people and arrived first in the land of the Kanien'kehá:ka, the People of the Flint, known to the English as the Mohawks. The story is that "he crossed Lake Ontario in a stone Canoe" in order to establish "a union of peace under the principles the Hodenosaunee understand to be the natural laws of the universe" (Lyons 1992, 34). I have been told that his actual name is considered so sacred that it is not to be either spoken or written, and so I have not included it here.

References

Alfred, Taiaiake. 2005. *Wasáse: Indigenous Pathways of Action and Freedom*. Peterborough, ON: Broadview Press.

Assembly of First Nations. 2011. *2011 AFN School Survey Results*. Ottawa: Assembly of First Nations.

Bailey, S. 2008. "NDP Launches Campaign to Help 'Third World' Native Schools." *Tekawennake* (Ohsweken, ON), February 6, 2008.

Ball, David P. 2012. "'Educational Apartheid' Remains Despite New School at Attawapiskat." *Windspeaker* 30 (5). http://www.ammsa.com/publications/windspeaker/%E2%80%9Ceducational-apartheid%E2%80%9D-remains-despite-new-school-attawapiskat#sthash.JJ9oky6h.dpuf

Battiste, Marie. 2013. *Decolonizing Education: Nourishing the Learning Spirit*. Saskatoon, SK: Purich Publishing.

Chiefs Assembly on Education. 2012. "A Portrait of First Nations and Education." http://www.afn.ca/uploads/files/events/fact_sheet-ccoe-3.pdf

Criminal Code of Canada (RSC 1985, c. C-46). "Part IX: Offenses Against Rights of Property." http://www.canlii.org/en/ca/laws/stat/rsc-1985-c-c-46/latest/rsc-1985-c-c-46.html#sec321

Demosim Team. 2011. "Population Projections by Aboriginal Identity in Canada: 2006 to 2031." Ottawa: Statistics Canada. https://www150.statcan.gc.ca/n1/pub/91-552-x/91-552-x2011001-eng.htm

Graveline, Jean. 2002. "Teaching Tradition Teaches Us." *Canadian Journal of Native Education* 26 (1): 11–29.

Haig-Brown, Celia. 2010. "Indigenous Thought, Appropriation, and Non-Aboriginal People." *Canadian Journal of Education* 33 (4): 925–50.

Kanu, Yatta. 2011. *Integrating Aboriginal Perspectives into the School Curriculum: Purposes, Possibilities and Challenges*. Toronto: University of Toronto Press.

King, Thomas. 2003. *The Truth About Stories: A Native Narrative*. Toronto: House of Anansi Press.

Kuhn, Thomas S. 1962. *The Structure of Scientific Revolutions*. 3rd ed. Chicago: University of Chicago Press.

Loomba, Ania. 2005. *Colonialism/Postcolonialism*. 2nd ed. New York: Routledge.

Lyons, Oren. 1992. "The American Indian in the Past." In *Exiled in the Land of the Free: Democracy, Indian Nations, and the U.S. Constitution*, edited by Oren Lyons, 13–42. Santa Fe, NM: Clear Light Publishers.

Mendelson, Michael. 2008, December 10. *Improving Education on Reserves: A First Nations Education Authority Act*. Ottawa: Caledon Institute of Social Policy.

Mental Health Commission of Canada. 2012. *Changing Directions, Changing Lives: The Mental Health Strategy for Canada*. Calgary, AB: Mental Health Commission of Canada.

Milke, Mark. 2013. "Ever Higher: Government Spending on Canada's Aboriginals Since 1947." Report prepared for the Fraser Institute's Centre for Aboriginal Policy Studies. https://www.fraserinstitute.org/studies/ever-higher-government-spending-canadas-aboriginals-1947

Morin, Brandi. 2017. "First Nations Students Face Continued Funding Shortfalls, Advocate Says." *CBC News*, August 31, 2017. https://www.cbc.ca/news/indigenous/first-nations-students-face-continued-funding-shortfalls-1.4267540

Neihardt, John G. 1961. *Black Elk Speaks*. Lincoln: University of Nebraska Press.

Royal Commission on Aboriginal Peoples. 1996. *Highlights from the Royal Commission on Aboriginal Peoples*. Ottawa: Minister of Supply and Services Canada. https://www.aadnc-aandc.gc.ca/eng/1100100014597/1100100014637

Smith, Graham. 2012. Introductory Remarks for the session "Kumu 'Ula'ula: Who Are We and Where Are We Heading? Of the SIG Indigenous Peoples of the Pacific" at the 2012 Annual Meeting of the American Educational Research Association, Vancouver, BC, April 2012.

Smith, Linda Tuhiwai. 2012. *Decolonizing Methodologies: Research and Indigenous Peoples*. 2nd ed. New York: Zed Books.

Solomon, Arthur. 1990. "There Is No Middle Ground." In *Songs for the People: Teachings on the Natural Way*, edited by Michael Posluns, 67–8. Toronto: NC Press.

Statistics Canada. 2011. 2011 Census. https://www150.statcan.gc.ca/n1/pub/89-645-x/2015001/education-eng.htm

Styres, Sandra. 2017. *Pathways for Remembering and Recognizing Indigenous Thought in Education: Philosophies of Iethi'nihsténha Ohwentsia'kékha (Land)*. Toronto: University of Toronto Press.

Styres, Sandra and Dawn Zinga. 2013. "The Community-first Land-centred Research Method: Bringing 'Good Mind' to Indigenous Education Research." *Canadian Journal of Education* 36 (2): 284–313.

Tuck, Eve, and K. Wayne Yang. 2012. "Decolonization Is not a Metaphor." *Decolonization: Indigeneity, Education & Society*, 1 (1): 1–40.

United Nations. 2007. *United Nations Declaration on the Rights of Indigenous Peoples*. New York: United Nations.

Wilson, Shawn. 2008. *Research Is Ceremony: Indigenous Research Methods*. Halifax, NS: Fernwood Publishing.

3 | Kaupapa Māori within the Academy
Negotiating Sites of Struggle

LEONIE PIHAMA

Introduction

As a Māori woman academic, for the past 25 years I have been an advocate for *kaupapa Māori* and have worked to ensure not only that kaupapa Māori has informed my theoretical and methodological approaches, but that it is integral to all parts of my life and living. In a context of colonization, this is not an easy way to choose to live, as it brings virtually every site into a place of contestation. Linda Tuhiwai Smith (Mead 1996) has highlighted that as Indigenous Peoples we live in a context of deliberate colonially imposed fragmentation.

As Māori, we have a history of investigation. It is an ancient history of exploration and of navigation, not solely in the physical domain, but in ways that reach throughout the many dimensions of *te ao Māori* (the Māori world). These are all forms of research; they are all ways within which our people have developed knowledge and have located ourselves in the wider world. The searching for the source of the first sliver of light that emanated from between the armpits of Ranginui and Papatūānuku,[1] and the journey of our ancestor, Tanenuiārangi, to gather *ngā kete o te wānanga, te kete tuauri, te kete tuatea, te kete aronui*[2] are but two examples of how ancient Māori research is. The point is that research is not new for Māori people. Neither is the idea that as Māori we can take control of our own theories and research processes (Pihama 1993; G. Smith 1997; L.T. Smith 1999). What is new is the context within which many of us currently locate our research and ourselves. For many Indigenous researchers and scholars, that context is a Western university, an institution that has its foundations deep within colonial philosophical traditions and that has benefited from the oppression of Indigenous Peoples.

However, it is important that we understand that intellectual and scholarly thinking is not something that came with our colonizers. As a people, we have a rich tradition of research and knowledge. Education systems are a part of Te Ao Māori and processes of *ako* (learning and teaching) existed in all aspects of our daily living. More formalized processes ensured the maintenance of all forms of knowledge, with *whare wānanga* (higher schools of learning) being one example of highly formalized and ritualized forms of pedagogy.[3] The denial of this has been, and continues to be, a fundamental flaw in the existing education system. The active suppression of Māori knowledge in colonial legislation and through ideological warfare meant that much Māori knowledge has been actively attacked or forced "underground" (Pihama 2001). This suppression was instrumental in the development of the colonial education system that sought to take the place of Māori systems of knowledge transmission.[4]

The marginalization of Māori knowledge and Māori pedagogy has meant that our learning and teaching processes have been denied to generations of Māori people. This has without a doubt been the situation in the university system, both in academic teaching and research. Researching within institutional frameworks often means having to deal in a daily way with critical issues related to Māori research, being a Māori researcher, being a Māori academic, and being a Māori woman academic. These positions within the academy are not uncomplicated. Often, they bring us not only into direct conflict with our institutions, but also with colleagues and allies who work within the same disciplines or faculties. During my time as faculty and a doctoral student at the University of Auckland, Māori colleagues often discussed the struggles of working and studying in a Pākehā institution (Smith and Hohepa 1992). This is the experience of many Māori who enter tertiary education and other colonial institutions (Irwin 1992; Walker 1996).

Universities as Sites of Struggle

For Indigenous Peoples, the university is a site of struggle. Within that site, many Indigenous and minority-group scholars have also created spaces where radical thinking is engaged and developed (Deloria 1998; Mihesuah and Cavender Wilson 2004). This too has been the experience of Māori. There are many examples of both the struggle and the radical possibilities, from the development of Ngā Mōteatea by Apirana Ngata (1959) to provide "evidence" of Māori literature to the involvement of Māori students in organizations such as Ngā Tamatoa in the 1970s.[5] Cherryl Waerea-i-te-rangi Smith (1994) notes that upon entering the university, Māori students become aware that the university is not exempt from racism and colonial imperialism. Smith also reminds us that we cannot downplay the ways in which Māori have subverted the role of universities to create transformative spaces:

> I do not want to play down the fact that the universities have produced some of our most strident activists and a number of dissenting voices. In fact the universities are often the place where Māori students can first begin to learn Māori language and history. Also, there do exist within the universities (too few) radical educators who are concerned with creating strategies of resistance, liberation struggles and strategies for "decolonising minds." (14)

These contradictions and conflicts have become increasingly apparent to me as a Māori woman academic. We often work within institutions that have been antagonistic to our concerns. Struggle within the university occurs on multiple levels: culture, language, structures, staffing, access, retention of staff and students, and resources. These struggles are not new, but derive from a history of colonial imperialism. Universities, like other Pākehā-dominated institutions, are founded upon a history of colonial oppression. We are often denied real knowledge about such a history. For example, Andrea Morrison (1999) informs us that the "official" history of the University of Auckland written by Keith Sinclair for the 1983 centenary gives scant discussion of Māori involvement with the university. From the outset, the university was a place for Pākehā settlers and not for Māori.

The University of Auckland Calendar (University of Auckland 2000) tells us nothing about the involvement of colonial imperialism in the establishment of the university; rather, the history given in the Calendar bemoans the university's financial situation, noting that the "educational reserves were such poor land that they brought in very little" (3). It does not inform us of the Auckland University College Reserves Act of 1885, where confiscated land from the Waikato area and in Whakatane[6] was utilized to fund the development of the University of Auckland (Mead 1996). Linda Tuhiwai Smith notes that in concrete ways the University of Auckland has benefited directly from the losses suffered by one of her *iwi*, Ngāti Awa. The apparent insignificance of these events to Pākehā historians is evident in their documentation:

> The first paragraph of the history of Auckland University written by a prominent New Zealand historian Sir Keith Sinclair, for example, immediately connects the history of Auckland's university to the establishment of other universities in the "English-speaking countries." The official history acknowledges that land was indeed vested in the university but focuses more on the inability of the rent to provide a decent income for the new university because the land was "poor and heavily forested." There was scant official knowledge, even in hindsight that these lands belonged to Māori people. (Mead 1996, 98)

The University of Auckland was not the only university founded from colonial imperialism. Both Otago and Canterbury universities were developed as part of attempts to increase settlements in those areas (Morrison 1999). Legislation was also passed by the colonial settler government for the confiscation of lands for the benefit of other universities. The Opaku Reserve and Waitotara lands in South Taranaki were confiscated from "rebel Natives" through section 6 of the University Endowment Act 1868, which set aside a reserve for the endowment of a colonial university (Beaglehole 1949). The Opaku Reserve was essentially 10,000 acres of confiscated lands located near the town of Pātea. At that time, however, there was no university established in Aotearoa, and the funds were placed into a colonial university fund. The first university was established in 1870 in Otago, and it was deemed in section 30 of the New Zealand University Act 1874 that lands in the Province of Otago reserved under the University Endowment Act 1868 would be granted to the University of Otago.

It was not until 1878 that the recommendation was made for the establishment of colleges in Auckland and Wellington. It was suggested that those lands held in the North Island be put towards endowments for those colleges. By this time, the 4,000-acre Waitotara Reserve had been included in the schedule of lands via the New Zealand University Reserves Act 1875 (Beaglehole 1949). The Auckland University College Act 1882 established the University of Auckland, and the Auckland University College Reserves Act 1885 saw lands stolen from three iwi in the upper North Island, Ngāti Awa, Tainui, and Ngā Puhi, and vested in the Council of the Auckland University College (New Zealand Statutes 1885). The Victoria College Act 1897 brought the establishment of what is now known as Victoria University in Wellington, which Ostler notes was to provide higher education for Wellington, Taranaki, Hawke's Bay, Nelson, and Marlborough. Section 38 of that act set the Waitotara Reserve aside as an endowment. The Opaku Reserve was not included, however; instead, in 1905 the Opaku Reserve was diverted to the Taranaki Scholarships Trust to provide scholarships for Taranaki scholars to any of the universities in the country (Beaglehole 1949; Taranaki Scholarships Trust 1958).

Contested Spaces

Given the colonial beginnings of the university system and the dominance of monocultural ways of operating, it is not surprising that being a Māori academic can bring us into conflict within our institutions as a direct consequence of differing cultural values and expectations. In terms of cultural space, Morrison (1999) notes that Māori "space" is a notion that has multiple applications. It refers to physical, cultural, spiritual, spatial, and temporal concepts. In the university context, it also relates to constructions of theory and disciplinarity. Creating "space," then, for Māori within the university must happen on all these levels. As Morrison (1999) has argued, the unequal power relations that exist in the university context for Māori mean that this is not an easy task.

Linda Tuhiwai Smith (1992) argues that the struggle for Māori academics is that of creating both the space and the conditions for Māori knowledge to be engaged. The notion of space is a very broad one in Māori terms; when engaging an idea of creating space we are not solely talking of spatial and temporal notions, but are encompassing physical, intellectual, social, cultural, and spiritual ways of being. That presents a considerable challenge to Māori academics within university structures. Linda Tuhiwai Smith (1992) argues that the structural struggles are critical to creating space:

> Although at a social level it is important to make students feel comfortable by claiming a culturally appropriate space to work in and by developing support mechanisms for Māori students this does not begin to address the underlying structural issues which are concerned with what students are required to learn, how they learn and how this learning will serve them in their own practice. It is in their control over what counts as knowledge that the power of traditional intellectuals is paramount. (10)

Control over knowledge, what constitutes valid knowledge, and how knowledge is selected has been outlined in some depth by Michael

Young (1971). Graham Hingangaroa Smith (1997) asserts that questioning the basis of what counts as knowledge, how knowledge is produced, and whose interests are served by this exposes the myth that knowledge is neutral and therefore reveals that power underpins the ways in which education is constructed.

The imposition of Pākehā knowledge and ways of being has been our experience since colonization. It is evident that this is manifested in many ways within university settings. As an academic, there is an expectation that teaching and research will be couched within the various theoretical frameworks of one's discipline. This becomes problematic when those same theoretical frameworks have historically served to provide a platform for the oppression of Indigenous Peoples. The history of state education systems within colonized countries highlights that schooling was utilized as a mechanism for the denial of Indigenous languages and culture. The struggle over affirmation of Māori knowledge and Māori contributions to the university is ongoing. Leah Whiu (1999) documents developments in the Law School at Waikato University, highlighting that a lack of vision from the Foundation Dean, Margaret Wilson, led to the "bicultural objective" being viewed as a process of merely adding some Māori content to existing programs. Such processes do not bring about change for Māori in the university. Interviews with participants in the Waikato University Law School program raised issues of racism, marginalization of te reo Māori, and limited Māori presence in the curriculum content, particularly in the final year. Whiu (1999) summarizes her research findings as follows:

> In summary, the Law School is failing to provide an educational environment and experience in which: Māori students feel safe; Māori students and staff are free from racism generated by Pākehā (or tauiwi)[7] students and staff; the use of te reo Māori is promoted and actively supported by staff; Māori issues, values, aspirations, traditions and whakaaro can be freely discussed without opposition from

Pākehā (or tauiwi) students and staff; Māori content and a Māori presence pervades all courses and all levels of the Law School. (35)

Native Hawaiian academic Haunani-Kay Trask (1993) asserts that formal education in Hawai'i has been constructed in a context of colonialism. In a powerful critique, Trask highlights the role of universities in maintaining colonial objectives and racist structures through the legitimization of the colonizing cultures. She states:

> The University of Hawai'i stands atop the educational pyramid of public schools as the flagship campus for the State. With over 40,000 full and part-time students, it is a living symbol of colonization. In many ways, the University is an educational equivalent to the American military command center in Hawai'i. Both serve as guardians of white dominance, both support the State economy, and both provide a training ground for future technocrats. (202)

Contested Relations

The difficulties experienced by Māori and Indigenous academics are not solely related to structural issues. They are also located in a range of professional relationships. The relationship between Māori and Pākehā in the university can be fraught with danger for Māori staff and students. Māori are often considered available for any Pākehā staff or students who want to know about anything Māori. bell hooks (1994) refers to this as being placed in the role of "native informant," where a sole student of colour is placed in the position of the "native informant" to be objectified by white students (see also Parker 1997).

Māori staff and students experience similar objectification in the academy by Pākehā staff and students (Jenkins and Pihama 2001; Mikaere 2011). One example from my experience included the separation of a feminist perspectives course into two streams by ethnicity. The decision to separate into ethnic groups was made as a means of instigating separate space to more readily enable the Māori and Pacific women to express themselves without having to be concerned with the "feelings" of Pākehā women in the group.[8] Restructuring the course in such a way also enabled a process of interrupting the assumed validity of the dominant group's cultural capital as providing the basis for a whole range of structures and systems (Bourdieu and Passeron 1977). Journal entries from Pākehā students highlighted that a large number reflected negatively on the separation, and maintained a sense of having "missed out" on something (Jones 1999). This was in stark contrast to the Māori and Pacific Islands women, who saw the separate groupings as a means of having space to operate within their own cultural frameworks and felt validated and affirmed in their own identity as a consequence. The separation was perceived by the Pākehā students as a lost opportunity, as noted in their journals (Jones 1999):

> I would have thought it would be interesting for all the students to be able to share their unique cultural perspectives with each other. I know I would have found that valuable. I am sometimes quite ignorant and intolerant of other viewpoints, so a wider input would have been educational.

> It does not seem right. Could we not learn from each other? Wouldn't it be valuable to share our differences in experience?... It is different reading about it in books, or having it taught by teachers. It is better to hear it straight from the women who are having the experience. It is easier to relate to.

> When will I ever get to learn how Māori and Pacific Islanders perceive the world (since we are supposed to be so different) when we are continually separated? (301–02)

Journal entries discussing the physical separation of the Pākehā students from the Māori and Pacific Islands students highlight significant differences in response. For many of the Māori and Pacific Islands women, this was the first time in their academic careers that an entire course was taught in a way that validated who they are. For the Pākehā students, the feedback indicates that there is a sense of loss for the oppressors if oppressed groups seek their own space. However, journal entries for the Māori and Pacific Islands women highlight that having space is celebrated as an opportunity for further growth and self-affirmation (Jones 1999):

> This is the first time I have had a [course] which has been streamed, with Māori and Pacific Islanders in one and non-Māori in the other. I can not begin to describe just how much more I enjoyed coming to classes...
>
> I felt validated or even vindicated. Being in a class of Māori and Pacific Island students, I stopped feeling like I was the other. Instead I felt as though I had moved towards the centre and stepped into the centre where white people normally reside. It felt good.
>
> In the lecture room I witnessed an interesting sense of power-shift once it was suggested that Māori and Pacific Islanders would form their own group. Once the dominant Pākehā group had lost their "marker," things Pākehā seemed to suddenly lose their advantage. As Māori knowledge was being affirmed as being important, a comment from one of the students next to me was "It's alright for the Māori students. They have all the information." Suddenly there was a reversal as to what counts as knowledge and who was having it. (302)

The journal entries provide a number of insights. Māori and Pacific Nations peoples in Aotearoa rarely experience having their own space within the classrooms of the University of Auckland, and when they do in a context where they are recognized in themselves and in terms of the knowledge they bring, there is a sense of affirmation. That sense of affirmation is one that centres their experiences and understandings. For many of the Pākehā students, however, there is a sense of loss in that their "native informant" has been removed. Another point raised is the notion that Māori and Pacific students are there to "educate" Pākehā students, or to provide knowledge to the dominant other. Both Māori staff and Māori students are positioned as the "native informant" and are expected to deliver to Pākehā staff and Pākehā students.

The creation of Māori and Indigenous space within educational institutions has been hard fought for by Māori students, staff, and the wider Māori community for many years. The establishment of the educational initiative Te Kōhanga Reo in 1981 provided a pathway for the establishment of the kura kaupapa Māori and whare wānanga. These initiatives have been driven, and championed, by *whānau*, *hapū*, and *iwi*. They are grounded upon *tikanga*, te reo, and *mātauranga Māori* and have been critical in the assertion of kaupapa Māori approaches. As organic Māori education initiatives, Te Kōhanga Reo, kura kaupapa Māori, and whare wānanga have challenged the fundamental underpinnings of a colonial-based mainstream Pākehā education system. Since the establishment of these initiatives, there has been consistent challenging of the essence of kaupapa Māori education from many sources, including from within the academy.

At the forefront of kaupapa Māori theory and research methodologies in the 1990s was the Māori Education team at the University of Auckland (Pihama 1993; G. Smith 1997; Pihama 2001). This development is a clear example of the ways in which Māori staff and students in the academy have actively disrupted dominant institutional thought. For many Māori who have actively sought theoretical explanations for our experiences, kaupapa Māori theory provides a culturally defined theoretical space (Pihama, 2001). Kaupapa Māori is transformative. To think and act in terms of kaupapa Māori while experiencing colonization is to resist dominance. This is not something that Māori alone are engaging in, as it is the experience of vast numbers of Indigenous Peoples across the world. In the process of this ongoing struggle, the historical dominance of Western theorizing is being challenged at a very fundamental level, at the level of relevance to the Indigenous people of this land. For many Pākehā academics, this challenge is viewed as a threat. The possibility of Māori taking control of our own theoretical frameworks is a threat to the survival of many who have spent the best part of their academic lives theorizing "about" and "on" Māori.

As in other areas of our existence in the academy, as both teachers and students, theory and how we use theory are sites of contestation. As Māori academics, not only do we have to struggle against colonial systems of domination; we also increasingly have to struggle against Pākehā academics who assume a right to define and control kaupapa Māori discourses. There are a number of recent writings by Pākehā academics that maintain the marginalization of Māori assertions for the development of kaupapa Māori theory and methodologies by Māori. For example, Pākeha writer Elizabeth Rata (2005, 267) has argued that kaupapa Māori initiatives are based upon "separatist ethnic politics" because they are grounded upon Māori cultural identification through *whakapapa* (cultural ancestry and genealogy). According to her argument, ethnicity is grounded in biological and genetic determinations, and as a result she locates whakapapa as being equivalent to Western notions of biology and genetics. Perhaps the most relevant example to Māori and Indigenous education is the claim by Alison Jones (2012, 101) that kaupapa Māori assertions of "by Māori for Māori" are about "Māori inclusion rather than Pākehā exclusion." Jones (1999) provided discussion and critique of the Pākehā student journals above as being examples of Pākehā anxiety, while titling her 2012 article about kaupapa Māori "Dangerous Liaisons" refers to her interactions with two Māori women academics, myself and Jenny Bol Jun Lee; we both disagreed with Jones taking a role as editor for a journal about kaupapa Māori. In reading through Jones's 1999 article, it is clear that she is unable to "see" or understand her own white privilege and the assumption that she has a right as a Pākehā academic to take such a role in the journal process. What is clear is that Jones locates herself as the victimized white woman academic, much like the Pākehā students who became anxious about their "exclusion." Drawing on terminology from the journal article abstract, the article is fundamentally about "Pākehā exclusion anxieties." This is most clearly evident in the attempt by Jones to redefine one of the fundamental underpinnings of kaupapa Māori theory, that of *tino rangatiratanga*. Tino rangatiratanga (or the self-determination principle; G. Smith 1997) states that kaupapa Māori theory is defined by Māori, with control over Māori definitions of what constitutes kaupapa Māori being determined and controlled by Māori. However, regardless of the fact that Māori academics have stated the centrality of tino rangatiratanga as a defining way of understanding the need to have Māori be self-determining within the theoretical and research fields, Jones (2012) provides her views that

> the statement "Kaupapa Māori is for Māori, by Māori" can be read not as a form of objective logic, but as a statement about participation. It can be interpreted as asserting a fixed rule about who can and who cannot legitimately be involved in Kaupapa Māori work: Māori can, others cannot. It is relatively easy for Pākehā to take this reading, and interpret it as actively excluding them from engaging with Kaupapa Māori ideas. (102)

What becomes clear is that Jones is in fact referring to her own anxiety of exclusion, so that kaupapa Māori is no longer about Māori aspirations, but is about Pākehā academics feeling excluded. What is also highlighted is a personalized, privileged view of Māori critique of Pākehā research paradigms:

> Some will rightly point out that exclusion by Māori is not only and always a Pākehā anxiety: it can have practical effects—the refusal of two Kaupapa Māori scholars to contribute to this collection is an example. And we cannot ignore the fact that Māori scholars are sometimes negative about Pākehā researchers. As Linda Smith (1999) famously reminds us, "[Pākehā] 'research' is probably one of the

dirtiest words in the Indigenous world's vocabulary" (p. 1). This suspicion towards Pākehā researchers remains strong. Even for Kaupapa Māori researchers open to working with Pākehā, engagement requires justification and care. (103)

Firstly, the refusal to contribute to the collection was a political kaupapa Māori decision. The assumption that not contributing has some implications for us as Māori academics indicates the limited knowledge that editors have of our engagement within Māori communities. Nor does it recognize that kaupapa Māori is not dependent upon academic journals or publishing, but rather is dependent on our work with our people, our commitment to the *kaupapa*, our praxis. Secondly, the political decontextualization of such a statement reduces the critique of colonial research imposed upon Indigenous Peoples. The suspicion towards Pākehā researchers within Māori communities remains strong for a reason, and "being sometimes negative about Pākehā researchers" is grounded in lived realities for our people. Many Māori communities continue to deal with Pākehā researchers who operate within the same dominant Western-imposed research models and theoretical frameworks that our ancestors experienced. This also describes the work of Elizabeth Rata, who operates from a basis of feeling excluded and draws upon Western dominant theories of essentialism to assert that cultural identity has no place in educational initiatives (Openshaw and Rata 2008). Openshaw and Rata (2008) have actively attacked kaupapa Māori and mātauranga Māori, locating them as "cultural essentialism" (1) and claiming that those who critique cultural frameworks or develop a critique of "culturalism" are operating within a "repressive ideological climate" (16). Openshaw and Rata rely on colonial assumptions of Pākehā cultural superiority and Western notions of essentialism as a basis by which to deny Māori aspirations. They also create an argument to serve their dominant interests, similar to Jones (2012), whereby Pākehā are located as being oppressed by the assertion of Māori aspirations for Māori educational initiatives. Such an argument serves dominant

Pākehā interests and maintains the marginalization of Māori and Māori initiatives. Each of these Pākehā academics denies their white privilege within the academy and in doing so merely maintains the institutional racism that underpins that ongoing marginalization of Māori knowledge (Irwin 1988; Pihama 2001).

The issue of Jenny Lee and I not participating in the journal co-edited by Alison Jones and Te Kawehau Hoskins was not, as argued, about Pākehā engaging with kaupapa Māori ideas. We are very clear that kaupapa Māori theory and research methodologies are shared in order to create change and to challenge both thought and practice. Rather, the fundamental reason for declining participation in the journal was about a Pākehā academic assuming a role in editing a journal about kaupapa Māori and, therefore, assuming a power position in relation to kaupapa Māori and, in doing so, denying that role to Māori who have struggled to create spaces in which our theoretical developments are grounded upon our knowledge and kaupapa Māori praxis (G. Smith 1997). This is not a position that denies Pākehā researchers support and involvement with Māori researchers. It is about a decolonizing approach to theory and research that challenges dominant group control and power within education and beyond. It is Māori who have been at the forefront of the struggle for decolonization within Aotearoa, and there have always been Pākehā and Pacific nations support for that struggle; however, defining what constitutes tino rangatiratanga for Māori must remain with Māori. Such a place may be best described in terms of Pākehā researchers being *hoa haere*, those friends or allies who support Māori aspirations. Such a position, however, maintains the ability for Māori to define and control kaupapa Māori.

Conclusion

Māori students and academics have struggled within universities since their inception. Māori land provided the economic foundation for the establishment of universities in Aotearoa. The confiscation of hapū and iwi lands was a part of the wider colonization process, which was, again, a part of the colonial project in the oppression of our people. Generations of colonial descendants have benefited from the acts of colonization, as too have generations of Pākehā staff and students benefited from colonial ideologies and the dominance of Western knowledge and processes in the academy.

Few academics are aware of the colonial history of their own institutions. Few are aware of the significant oppression of whānau, hapū, and iwi across the country, upon whose backs the current university system has been built. Understanding the historical development of the university system provides a context through which to understand the cultural marginalization and subjugation experienced by Māori who enter into that system.

The creating of cultural space for Māori in education has been a key point of struggle for the past 50 years (C. Smith 2002). Māori movements such as the Young Māori Leaders, Ngā Tamatoa, Te Reo Māori Society, and Māori student associations, among others, have made significant challenges to the place of Māori language and culture within educational institutions, including universities (Walker 1990). The development of kaupapa Māori theory and methodologies in the 1990s built upon such movements and challenged the dominance of Western theories and research methodologies in the academy. Creating such space, structurally, theoretically, and methodologically, has been a part of the much broader aspirations of Māori to bring change within education and other social service sectors.

Te Kōhanga Reo and kura kaupapa Māori provided the political context within which kaupapa Māori theory and research gained momentum. Māori scholars and researchers have struggled for over 25 years for our theories and methodologies to be recognized within the academy as legitimate approaches to understanding and engaging with issues and research needs for Māori. The assertion of tino rangatiratanga is central to the ability of Māori to determine our future, not only within the academy but across all sectors within Aotearoa. Kaupapa

Māori theory and research is one way through which we assert those fundamental rights as Indigenous academics. At the centre of that assertion is Māori control and Māori self-determination as defined by and for our people. That is a site we have contested and struggled for since its expression within Te Tiriti o Waitangi. It may be difficult for Pākehā academics and researchers to understand, but Māori assertions of Māori control really have nothing to do with them. It is about us. It is about Māori space and Māori reclamation of te reo, tikanga, and mātauranga Māori. That is the essence of kaupapa Māori.

Notes

1. Ranginui is referred to by many as the sky parent and Papatūānuku as the earth parent.
2. *Ngā kete o te wānanga* refers to three baskets of knowledge that Tāne brought to earth from Iomatuakore, Io the parentless one, the Creator, to provide knowledge for people.
3. For discussion of Māori pedagogies refer to *Ako: Concepts and Learning in the Māori Tradition* (Pere 1994).
4. In the Native Schooling system there was a clear intention that te reo Māori be removed as a medium of instruction, and that in order to receive support for a Native School there be a commitment made to English as the medium of instruction, with te reo Māori being used purely as a means of facilitating the learning of English.
5. Ngā Tamatoa was a Māori activist group of the 1970s and 1980s that brought about major changes, in particular in terms of advocating for te reo Māori and fundamental Treaty rights.
6. Whakatane is an area in the mid-eastern part of the North Island.
7. *Tauiwi* refers to those non-Māori who have come and settled in these lands.
8. For discussion of an attempt at forming alliances where similar issues are raised, refer to *Bridges of Power: Women's Multicultural Alliances* (Albrecht and Brewer 1990).

References

Albrecht, Lisa, and Rose M. Brewer, eds. 1990. *Bridges of Power: Women's Multicultural Alliances*. Philadelphia: New Society Publishers.

Beaglehole, John C. 1949. *Victoria University College: An Essay Towards a History*. Wellington: New Zealand University Press.

Bourdieu, Pierre, and Jean-Claude Passeron. 1977. *Reproduction in Education, Society and Culture*. Thousand Oaks, CA: Sage.

Deloria, Vine Jr. 1998. "Comfortable Fictions and the Struggle for Turf: An Essay Review of 'The Invented Indian': Cultural Fictions and Government Policies." In *Native and Academics: Researching and Writing About American Indians*, edited by Devon Abbott Mihesuah, 65–83. Lincoln: University of Nebraska Press.

hooks, bell. 1994. *Teaching to Transgress*. London: Routledge.

Irwin, Kathie. 1988. "Māori, Feminist, Academic." *Sites* 17: 30–8.

———. 1992. "Becoming an Academic: Contradictions and Dilemmas of a Māori Feminist." In *Women and Education in Aotearoa:2*, edited by Sue Middleton and Alison Jones, 52–67. Wellington, NZ: Bridget Williams Books.

Jenkins, Kuni, and Leonie Pihama. 2001. "Matauranga Wahine: Teaching Māori Women's Knowledge Alongside Feminism." *Feminism & Psychology* 11 (3): 293–303. https://doi.org/10.1177/0959353501011003003

Jones, Alison. 1999. "The Limits of Cross-Cultural Dialogue: Pedagogy, Desire, and Absolution in the Classroom." *Educational Theory* 49 (3): 299–316. https://doi.org/10.1111/j.1741-5446.1999.00299.x

———. 2012. "Dangerous Liaisons: Pākehā, Kaupapa Māori, and Educational Research." *New Zealand Journal of Educational Studies* 47 (2): 100–12.

Mead, Linda Tuhiwai. 1996. "Nga Aho o Te Kakahu Matauranga: The Multiple Layers of Struggle by Maori in Education." PHD diss., Auckland University.

Mihesuah, Devon Abbott, and Angela Cavender Wilson. 2004. *Indigenizing the Academy: Transforming Scholarship and Empowering Communities*. Lincoln: University of Nebraska Press.

Mikaere, Ani. 2011. *Colonising Myths, Māori Realities: He Rukuruku Whakaaro*. Wellington, NZ: Huia Publishers.

Morrison, Andrea. 1999. "Space for Māori in Tertiary Institutions: Exploring Two Sites at the University of Auckland." Master's thesis, University of Auckland.

New Zealand Statutes. 1885. *Auckland University College Reserves [1885:1]*. Wellington, NZ: Government Printer.

Ngata, Apirana. 1959. *Nga Moteatea, Part I*. Wellington, NZ: The Polynesian Society and A.H. & A.W. Reed.

Openshaw, Roger, and Elizabeth Rata. 2008. "Flax Rope or Iron Fetter? How Cultural Essentialism Threatens Intellectual Freedom in the New Zealand Tertiary Education Sector." *The New Zealand Journal of Tertiary Education Policy* 3 (1): 1–27.

Parker, Gwendolyn M. 1997. *Trespassing: My Sojourn in the Halls of Privilege.* Boston: Houghton Mifflin.

Pere, Rangimarie Rose. 1994. *Ako: Concepts and Learning in the Māori Tradition.* Wellington, NZ: Te Kōhanga Reo Trust.

Pihama, Leonie. 1993. "Tungia te Ururua, Kia Tupu Whakaritorito Te Tupu o te Harakeke: A Critical Analysis of Parents as First Teachers." Master's thesis, University of Auckland.

———. 2001. "Tīhei Mauri Ora: Honouring Our Voices: Mana Wahine as Kaupapa Māori Theoretical Framework." PHD diss., University of Auckland.

Rata, Elizabeth. 2005. "Rethinking Biculturalism." *Anthropological Theory* 5 (3): 267–84. https://doi.org/10.1177/1463499605055960

Smith, Cherryl W. 1994. "Kimihia Te Maramatanga: Colonisation and Iwi Development." Master's thesis, University of Auckland.

———. 2002. "He Pou Herenga Ki Te Nui: Māori Knowledge and the University." PHD diss., University of Auckland.

Smith, Graham H. 1992. "Tane-nui-a-Rangi's Legacy: Propping Up the Sky. Kaupapa Māori as Resistance and Intervention." Paper presented at NZARE/AARE Joint Conference, Deakin University, Australia. http://www.aare.edu.au/92pap/smitg92384.txt

———. 1997. "The Development of Kaupapa Māori Theory and Praxis." PHD diss., University of Auckland.

Smith, Graham H., and Margie K. Hohepa. 1992. *Creating Space in Institutional Settings for Māori.* Auckland, NZ: RUME Auckland University.

Smith, Linda Tuhiwai. 1992. "Ko Tāku Ko Tā Te Māori: The Dilemma of a Māori Academic." In *Creating Space in Institutional Settings for Māori,* edited by Graham H. Smith and Margie Hohepa. Auckland, NZ: RUME Auckland University.

———. 1999. *Decolonising Methodologies: Research and Indigenous Peoples.* London: Zed Books.

Taranaki Scholarships Trust. 1958. New Plymouth, NZ: Avery Press.

Trask, Haunani-Kay. 1993. *From a Native Daughter: Colonialism and Sovereignty in Hawai'i.* Monroe, ME: Common Courage Press.

University of Auckland. 2000. *The University of Auckland Calendar.* Auckland, NZ: University of Auckland.

Walker, Ranginui. 1990. *Ka Whawhai Tonu Matou: Struggle Without End.* Auckland, NZ: Penguin Books.

———. 1996. *Ngā Pepa a Ranginui: The Walker Papers.* Auckland, NZ: Penguin Books.

Whiu, Leah. 1999. "Bicultural Legal Education: A Tool of Liberation or Merely Educating the Oppressor." Unpublished research paper, Waikato University, Hamilton, NZ.

Young, Michael F.D., ed. 1971. *Knowledge and Control: New Directions for the Sociology of Education*. London: Collier Macmillan.

4 | Contested Spaces

Indigeneity and Epistemologies of Ignorance

HUIA TOMLINS-JAHNKE

Ignorance is not something simple: it is not a simple lack, absence or emptiness, and it is not a passive state. Ignorance of this sort—the determined ignorance most white Americans have of American Indian tribes and clans, the ostrich-like ignorance most white Americans have of the histories of Asian peoples in the country, the impoverished ignorance most white Americans have of Black language—ignorance of these sorts is a complex result of many acts and many negligences.
—MARILYN FRYE, *The Politics of Reality*

Introduction

The academy remains a highly contested space for Indigenous scholars, where complex layers of ignorance are acted out on a daily basis, buttressed by a vast array of pervasive and oppressive institutional systems and structures that generate and reinforce ignorance. From the moment an Indigenous scholar enters the academy as a new entrant and throughout their student experiences, and perhaps as junior low-paid faculty or entering tenure track and promotion, the Indigenous scholar faces the sustained impact of normative and privileged ignorance. Attempts by Indigenous scholars to Indigenize the academy are fraught because it requires us to navigate a complex terrain that is hostile to Indigenous perspectives on the production of knowledge. In this chapter, I draw on Charles Mills's (1997, 2007) concept of epistemologies of ignorance and the works of other critical philosophers who have expanded on Mills's analysis, in order to understand the various forms and patterns of ignorance as they apply to the Indigenous experience within the confines of the academy, as well as to examine how they are actively produced and sustained. This sustained consideration reveals the politics of what is not known and what role this plays in supporting dominant group privilege.

In Aotearoa New Zealand the idea that mainstream tertiary institutions as collective entities are somehow external to the realities of Indigenous life and, therefore, irrelevant, is embedded in common place descriptors that categorize the academy as either "Western," "Pākehā," "European," "white," or "mainstream." The terms are used interchangeably in Indigenous discourse, underpinned by assumptions that the Indigenous scholar will be required to leave their Māori/tribal identities "at the gate" to achieve the cognitive switch necessary to comply with and adapt to officially sanctioned programs, structures, and processes. Each category serves to preclude certain possibilities inscribed in the Indigenous mind that either the hallowed sanctity of the ivory tower is beyond the reach of ordinary brown folk, or that by entering the academy they "learn to see the world wrongly" (Mills 1997, 18), based on evasion (such as the conceptual erasure of tribal language, histories, knowledge, and culture) and self-deception (such as the superiority of the English language and Eurocentric worldviews).

Mills's concept of an epistemology of ignorance emerges from his notion of the racial contract, an alternative frame to recognize and understand racism as a political system, using the vocabulary and apparatus developed for contractarianism. Based on the social contract tradition, the racial contract offers a powerful lens to show how the polity structures the norms, privileges, benefits, opportunities, and distributions of wealth in society. While a contract may be seen as an agreement between people, according to Mills (1997), the racial contract "is not a contract between everybody ('we the people') but between just the people who count, the people who really are people ('we the white people')" (3). And as a condition of membership of such a polity, an epistemology of ignorance is advocated whereby "one has to see the world wrongly, but with the assurance that his set of mistaken perceptions will be validated by white epistemic authority, whether religious or secular" (18).

Mills's mapping of "white ignorance" is useful because it offers a structural analysis of how oppressive systems generate ignorance, and the pervasive forms and features of ignorance as a basis for "reformulating an epistemology that will give us genuine knowledge" (Mills 2007, 16). Ignorance in this context is more than not knowing simple facts or displays of prejudicial behaviour; rather, it can be understood as nonknowing where race has played a determining role. The erasure of Indigenous knowledge, achievements, and history from the social canon; the reduction of populations through introduced diseases, wars, and policies; the usurpation of customary forms of government and social structures; and building Western societies on appropriated territories and vacated spaces through the displacement of decreasing Indigenous populations and increasing immigrant population (Tully 2000) are examples of the determining role of race in the grand narrative of a civilizing colonial history. In this narrative, the primitive native is juxtaposed with the developed, civilized European.

According to Mills, white ignorance is patterned on false belief and the idea that incorrect reasoning leads to misconceptions, and the absence of true belief (i.e., the acceptance of a proposition that has been examined and found to be logically sound, and which corresponds to facts of reality). Because white ignorance varies across populations, and is not necessarily confined to white people, since "blacks can manifest white ignorance also" (Mills 2007, 20), white ignorance as an organizing concept should be thought of as a cognitive tendency.

The link Mills makes between ignorance and interactive cognitive processes, such as perception, conception, memory, and so on, is instructive. The point is made that such processes are constantly interacting and shaping cognition, which in turn is influenced by an individual's socialization.[1] Common among Indigenous Peoples is a perpetual incredulity at the inability of white folk to comprehend ("to see us" and "to hear our voices") and to be cognizant of the Indigenous world, even when the facts of Indigenous realities past (historical) and present (contemporaneous) are set before them. In other words, ignorance by white folk operates with a particular kind of social cognition that distorts reality (Mills 2007) for brown and black folk. Epistemologies of ignorance become a constitutive norm and cognitive tendency that underpin categories of Eurocentrism. Cognitive processes lead white folk to reinscribe the Indigenous reality to a false belief and misconception that they would have us believe is the truth.

In the South Pacific nation of Aotearoa New Zealand, mainstream universities are essentially Eurocentric organizations structured on dominant group values, ethics, standards, culture, and aspirations. They are patterned on an unassailable conviction that emulating elite institutions of Europe and North America, seen as exemplary and superior based on epistemologies of ignorance, justifies embedding Eurocentric curricula, systems, and modus operandi at every level of the institution. When this is overlaid with home-grown values associated with biculturalism (Māori and non-Māori) and an acknowledgement of the Treaty of Waitangi, the founding document of Aotearoa, then the biases and non-knowing of the dominant group become even more apparent. Attempts to Indigenize the academy are filtered through skewed institutional lenses, and in the process such attempts are derailed, undermined, or marginalized.

Take, for example, the institution of *pōwhiri*, a formal Māori welcome, which has been adopted and become fairly commonplace in New Zealand institutions, most often taking place on institutional *marae*. Such marae are a fairly recent addition to institutional facilities, usually presided over by the obligatory Elder, where the customs and processes of pōwhiri are approximated if operationalized outside of tribal contexts. Marae and pōwhiri are deep symbols of Māori identity, cultural values, intergenerational socialization patterns, and ethical practice, and processes that have been irreparably impacted by the effects of colonization. Most non-Māori know little about marae protocol and feel uncomfortable with the pōwhiri process, often culminating in the ludicrous situation where non-Māori faculty act as strangers in a process that they themselves have agreed to, and in an institutional context where they hold majority power. Few non-Māori are socialized into Māori culture, despite 200 years of European/white settlement, and there exists a fear of Māori cultural practices based on epistemologies of ignorance. A narrative of one event that bears witness to categorical barriers for non-Māori in the welcome ceremony provides a relevant case study for analysis.

In one university in Aotearoa New Zealand a new Māori-centred program was launched, and the first intake of 27 first-year students and several hundred of their family members and friends gathered for the welcoming ceremony on the university marae. It was a momentous day for many reasons. It had taken four years to reach the point when the first students finally arrived. Significantly, the entire ceremony was conducted in the Māori language, in accordance with tradition not often witnessed within university environs. For the families, who represented the many tribes of Aotearoa, it was a proud occasion and the culmination of intergenerational aspirations embodied in the family member they were now supporting on their first day at university. For the students, all of whom are fluent speakers of Māori language, the day was overwhelming. Although the context of pōwhiri within a marae setting is familiar to them and helped ease frayed nerves, nevertheless, the combined weight of *whānau* (family) expectations evident in the stirring speeches of the Elders and the rousing *waiata* (songs) and *haka* (dance) performed by the students and their families as embellishment for each speech made it all the more palpable.

Earlier in the day, in a separate ceremony, about 100 first-year students in the mainstream general initial teacher education programs were also welcomed onto the university marae. Most of these students were non-Māori New Zealanders unfamiliar with the process of a pōwhiri and unable to understand the Māori language. To accommodate this lack of knowledge and experience, the ceremony was conducted in both English and Māori languages. A few students brought family members along in support, but otherwise this was a predominantly student/university-only affair. Unlike the later ceremony for the kaupapa Māori immersion students, there was a significant presence of university faculty in attendance. Class timetables restricted the length of time allowed for the welcome ceremony, so there was a limit to the number of speakers on behalf of the host and of the guests. As a result, the event was all done and dusted in less than 20 minutes, followed by a cup of tea and a cookie.

By contrast, it took an hour to welcome the 27 kaupapa Māori immersion students and their families, another hour to launch the program, and several hours for the *hākari*, the celebratory dinner, that followed. And later that evening, when their families returned home, the students were ushered into the *wharenui* (meeting house) to begin their first class of a week-long *wānanga* (lecture series), lasting late into the night.

These two separate ceremonies of welcome for students held in the same institution on the same day, for the same purposes and in the same cultural context of the university marae with some of the same actors (Māori and non-Māori faculty) in attendance, are underpinned by binaries of knowledge systems drawn from an epistemological understanding of the Indigenous world on the one hand, and a general ignorance of it on the other.

Cultural Spaces as Contested

Whether in urban settings or in tribal homelands, the marae remains a special place on which to hang an identity as the Indigenous people who once owned the whole country of New Zealand (Walker 1990). Institutional marae were established by Māori educators in the late 20th century as the primary means by which they could legitimately infuse Māori epistemology and pedagogy in the delivery of teacher education within a culturally relevant space (Penetito 2010). A major goal of these marae was to counter the Eurocentricity of mainstream institutions by conscientizing "Pākehā students to the Māori world view as a means of transforming their attitudes to being open to cultural difference and diversity; from embracing Te Tiriti o Waitangi to adapting to the needs of our Māori children in their classrooms" (Ka'ai 2008, 193-4). In the context of Eurocentric institutions, the marae represents a contested space where the needs of the majority non-Māori are often taken into account and the cultural ground moved to accommodate them. Marae are important symbols of Māori culture, identity, and values, and as such provide a relevant context and site for cultural continuity.

In the events leading up to the welcome ceremonies, there was resistance to a separate welcome ceremony for students in the kaupapa Māori program. The majority group of non-Māori senior faculty reasoned that, rather than separate events, a combined pōwhiri for all students was an opportunity for the non-Māori students to learn from the Māori students, to share in Māori culture and to come "together as one." These are legitimate ideals and goals to aspire to where there is intercultural exchange and learning in an "informalized" education between cultures. This standpoint becomes problematic, however, when the burden of up-skilling around values and cultural perspectives is placed on the Indigenous group as if it were their sole responsibility, and no expectation is held of the dominant group in terms of a two-way cultural exchange (Tomlins-Jahnke 2005). In such intercultural situations, the onus is almost always on Indigenous people to do the work of informing the ignorant. Furthermore, coming "together as one" is not so much about accounting for Indigeneity as it is about dominant group interests. This is what Mills (2007) considers the complacent luxury of ignorance that upholds "blind spots," where limitations of thought and action leads to only the interests of the dominant group being considered. In other words, who gets to be ignorant and uphold the privilege of not knowing are those who not only have the luxury of ignorance but hold the power to be ignorant.

Linda Alcoff (2007) suggests explaining ignorance as a feature of substantive epistemic practice, and that such practices as "willful ignorance" and "socially acceptable but faulty justificatory practices are structural" (40). This requires a structural analysis of the ways in which oppressive systems produce ignorance. Alcoff argues that substantive differences between knowers involve complex judgements, and that some epistemic advantages and disadvantages are not the same for all, but accrue to social and group identities, depending on the situatedness of the knower. Epistemic situatedness is based on four premises, related to the knower's position in time and space; the ways judgement calls are enacted; the fact that knowers are not mutually interchangeable; and the fact that "knowers are at once limited and enabled by the specificities of their locations" (42).

For example, returning to the welcome ceremony as a basis for analysis from an Indigenous standpoint is instructive. There were several underlying reasons why Māori faculty considered separate ceremonies were necessary. It was deemed inappropriate that at the launch of a flagship program predicated on contributing to the survival of the Māori language the institution would welcome new students and their Elders (fluent speakers of Māori) in a cultural ceremony where the English language predominated. Apart from the moral ignorance of such a proposition, Māori faculty reasoned that operating a cultural ceremony in English would send a message to Māori communities generally and the Māori language sector in particular about the institution's commitment, or lack thereof, to the revival and long-term survival of the Māori language the institution claims to support.

Institutional memory loss, evasion, and self-deception bely the politics of unknowing that shaped 19th-century colonial policy, which banned the speaking of Māori language from school precincts until the middle of the 20th century, and subjected Māori children to corporal punishment if they contravened, even if they were unable to speak English. As a result, Māori language remains seriously endangered. In 1999, Māori language was declared an official language, but only after a Treaty of Waitangi claim was brought against the New Zealand government, representing the Crown. In its deliberations, the Waitangi Tribunal found that in respect of the Māori language, the Crown had been operating in breach of the Treaty.

A significant consideration for Māori faculty was concerned with upholding the *mana* (integrity) of the marae, the subtribe within whose tribal area the university resides, and the university staff and students past and present; and it was important to uphold the mana of the university. Protocol necessitated allowing time for any number of Elders to stand and speak on behalf of their families. Therefore, controlling the number of speakers, as was the case with the mainstream ceremony, was simply not an option without causing offence to the tribes in attendance. There was also the cultural practice of catering for the guests with a celebratory feast in honour of the occasion. Compare this with the "tea and cookie" scenario provided to complete the mainstream ceremony, which did not go unnoticed by Māori faculty. The concept of *manaaki tangata*, hosting and providing food and nourishment for guests, is a core value in Māori culture, and the mana of the home people (in this case, the university, but by implication the local subtribe as well) depends on their ability to adequately host. Often at important occasions it is not the event itself that is long remembered but the food and the generosity of the hosts. The adage upheld by ancestors that it is better to offer too much food than too little is one that remains true and is still adhered to today.

Taking these factors together within the context of an institutional marae setting and the formalities of pōwhiri, there was agreement among Māori faculty that the occasion should be carried out according to *tikanga Māori*, or what is right customarily. Their judgement call brought to bear knowledge, experience, and understanding of the cultural values, traditions, and protocols associated with marae-based ceremonies. Furthermore, they were aware of what was relevant to mitigating any risk the institutional lack of knowledge might expose, such as causing offence to tribal communities, even if unintentional.

The unquestioned entitlement assumed by the dominant group serves to excuse them from any need to understand. It was only when it was clear that dominant group interests would be compromised in a combined event by sitting through a long ceremony they did not understand, listening to a language they did not know, and with no guarantee that the imposed tight time schedule would prevail that an agreement was reached to proceed with separate ceremonies. Māori faculty agreed that students should be given an opportunity to learn at a pōwhiri. They explained that according to customary practice, once the students at the earlier ceremony have been welcomed onto the marae, they then assumed a relational status as one with the "home" people of the university. The mainstream students would then be eligible to exercise this newly acquired relationship and assist the university faculty in welcoming the kaupapa Māori immersion students later in the day. However, efforts by Māori faculty to provide an authentic learning opportunity were largely ignored by the dominant group and, as a result, they remained in a state of unknowing and missed the chance to experience the full expression of the pōwhiri beyond that of symbolic effort (Asante 1995).

By contrast, the kaupapa Māori immersion students possess a level of knowing about the significance and process of the pōwhiri that comes from a deeply lived experience of the Māori world and knowledge of the Māori language. Most are graduates of an alternative kaupapa Māori system of education and schooling that was developed in Aotearoa by Māori for Māori outside of the "mainstream" system. Their schooling has promoted what counts as credible knowledge in *te ao Māori* (Māori world) and *te ao hurihuri* (the global world). They are grounded in an identity and genealogical connection with the flora and fauna, the land, mountains, and waterways of Aotearoa. Global perspectives of the earth and its environment, the people of the world and their societies, are thus understood from their position and situatedness as *tangata whenua*, first people of the land. Within the alternative kaupapa Māori system of education, it is not only a preoccupation with content and subject matter that counts, but also interpersonal relationships that give knowledge its full meaning (Malewski and Jaramillo 2011; Penetito 2010).

Eurocentric patterns and practices that naturalize and permeate an entire hegemonic social fabric within higher education serve to buttress and sustain the power and multiple modalities of ignorance, such as class, race, and gender, to promote and or sustain unjust social orders (Code 2007). Unwittingly, teachers have become complicit in the active production of "not knowing" that operates in multiple and varying ways, such as at the level of curriculum, teaching, philosophy, and teacher-student relationships (Jaramillo 2011). African philosopher Molefi Kete Asante (1995, 338) makes reference to "the tragedy of ignorance" as a condition of Eurocentric education. In the United States "the African American child has suffered disproportionately, but European children are the victims of mono-culturally diseased curricula" (338).

The Eurocentricity of the New Zealand history curriculum recently led one Māori Member of Parliament to express her concern that "schools are supposed to be teaching New Zealand history, and as part of that New Zealand history we would expect those schools to be talking about Māori history, but in fact we find that so many schools do not" (Tomlins-Jahnke and Warren 2011, 21). To give one glaring example, an analysis of the New Zealand secondary school social studies curriculum shows that units of study relating to the history of the Treaty of Waitangi, the nation's founding document, constitute 1.5% of the total curriculum (Tawhai 2007). As McClaren (2011, xv) so succinctly put it, "what we have in schools today are epistemologies of empire, that remain trapped in the 'what is'!"

Omissions and exclusions that lead to significant gaps in knowledge within our schooling system raise important questions about the role of education in ensuring citizens are informed and knowledgeable about the history of the nation and its people. What is the role of teacher educators in preparing graduate teachers for engaging with Indigenous learners and their families? How do Indigenous educators influence the racialized political hierarchy of knowledge that undervalues Indigenous epistemology at all levels of education and society?

Underpinning these questions, at least in Aotearoa New Zealand, is the knowledge that 90% of Māori children are located in mainstream schools and taught by a majority non-Māori teaching workforce. A high percentage of this workforce have little knowledge of how to engage effectively with Māori children and their families to lead to successful educational outcomes (Penetito 2010; Simon 1990). Māori children in mainstream schools are invariably positioned in the so-called "tail of underachievement" within statistical fields based on deficit theories. Māori learners are categorized by the state as "priority learners," and as such are grouped alongside learners who are Pasifika, low socio-economic status (SES), special educational needs (SEN), and English as an additional language (EAL). The power of ignorance by inciting such categories obfuscates the fundamental fact that Māori, as tangata whenua, the first peoples of the land, hold a Treaty of Waitangi relationship with the Crown (state/government), as well as the citizenship rights that extend to all New Zealanders, including Pasifika peoples, new migrants, and others with special needs.

By and large, tribal leaders consider Māori children at risk in the mainstream schooling system, which has led to some tribes collaborating with the Ministry of Education in efforts to ameliorate such risks through developing tribal cultural standards and emphasizing place-based education as a way of influencing curriculum and engaging with Māori learners and their whānau (Ngāti Kahungunu Iwi 2009; Tomlins-Jahnke 2011; Penetito 2010; Tomlins-Jahnke and Graham 2014).

Malewski and Jaramillo (2011, 1) argue that educators need to "challenge the ambivalence and…ignorance we witness in the construction of curriculum, teaching practices, research guidelines and policy mandates in schools." Epistemologies of ignorance refer to the active production of "not knowing" through actively obstructing or limiting the range of possibilities for the full participation of all people in society. What it offers are alternative perspectives to the assumptions underpinning disciplinary knowledge, including the selection of what counts as knowledge that goes into "building up a canon of central texts and ideas that make up a field" (2).

A focus on epistemologies of ignorance can be a positive endeavour, because it allows us to name and direct our attention to the gaps, omissions, and exclusions that our students and communities encounter within dominant institutional settings, and to focus attention on the global and systemic forms in which the selective process of what counts as worth knowing is institutionalized (Malewski and Jaramillo 2011). Within the academy, the conditioning influences of race are not accounted for in the intellectual agendas and practices, the epistemological standards, the canons and curricula subscribed to, and the sociological and demographical compositions of the various communities of the academy (Outlaw 2007). The damaging consequences of epistemologies of ignorance as they affect Indigenous people in the academy is what this chapter is concerned with.

A Case Study

The way ignorance of Indigenous people is systematically cultivated and current interests serve to block Indigenous knowledge within the academy can be seen in the experiences of developing and implementing an Indigenous-centred initial teacher education (ITE) program. If we understand ignorance as being "socially produced and distributed systematically across generations and legitimated by making it rationally pervasive" (Outlaw 2007, 198), then education is a principal way to effect systemic production, mediation, and legitimation of ignorance to achieve specific kinds of ordering of structures, processes, and practices. The results are a differentiated provisioning clearly apparent, for example, in accreditation processes that legitimate pedagogy, curriculum, and systems universal across universities. What happens when the complacent luxury of ignorance is disrupted? How does the privilege of not knowing work against marginalized Indigenous communities within the academy? If structures reinforce ignorance, then in what ways are relationships forfeited when ignorance rules or takes precedence? What space is contested and at what cost?

Take, for example, the case of an Indigenous faculty in Aotearoa who introduced a new Indigenous-centred ITE qualification into the academy that replaced an outdated Indigenous program. It took four long, hard years of struggle to navigate the myriad institutional barriers and contesting systems that underpin the approval processes of the university, as well as those of the external state accreditation process.

An academic review of the outdated program some years earlier by a panel of national and international Indigenous educators provided the recommendations upon which the new ITE program was to be based. The majority of the panel were Māori, thereby suggesting the institution recognized who is appropriate to carry out a critical examination of a Māori-centred program and why (given that the locus of such knowledge resides among Māori and Indigenous educators in the field). By and large, the panel recognized the worth of the program, but in an updated form.

Prior to the program review, government policies (Tertiary Education Commission 2005; Ministry of Education 2007) provided a potentially strong, positive, and supportive political environment within which to justify such a program. There was, and still remains, a serious problem of Māori teacher supply. As a distinctive university-based ITE program (marae-based, kaupapa Māori-centred, provider partnership with the Māori education sector), the potential for further development was high. This included taking account of tribal aspirations such as Māori language planning and identifying kura kaupapa Māori systems as their preferred settings for the education of Māori children. The new program thus aligned with tribal education plans, as well as government policy and university priorities.

The plan for the new program, however, was at risk, as the university moved to close small "uneconomic" programs in a move brought on by, among other things, government cutbacks, burgeoning debt, and a significant downturn in student numbers. Low enrollments in the old program were the result of a combination of factors, both internal and external. Internally, these were reduced resource allocation, such as low staffing levels and funding provisions; the unilateral application by university administrators of selection processes and entry criteria conceived for mainstream programs; and the lack of consultation about key administration decisions (e.g., the sudden cancellation of enrollments, excluding the program as an option on application forms, or lost application forms of known applicants) that, when taken collectively, served to negatively impact the old program over time. It was simply a case of the academy operating systems and processes that privileged mainstream agendas, while disadvantaging Indigenous programs, thereby naturalizing patterns of inequality and oppression.

The development of the new qualification included a series of consultation meetings with key experts and the Māori education sector. There was much optimism and excitement from these communities about what was envisaged and how ideas from the sector could be incorporated. Concomitant engagement with the university approval system was not so straightforward. An early notice form was submitted to the national Committee on University Academic Programmes (CUAP), responsible for approving programs within the New Zealand university system. Over the following two years, the CUAP proposal for the new Māori-centred degree was submitted back and forth, stalemated between four university committees, each charged with oversight of the academic merits and structure of new programs.

There was little criticism of the proposal regarding the content and conceptual framework; all the same, bureaucratic barriers were erected where agreement could not be reached, mostly around technical and administrative matters, or the formatting of the CUAP proposal document. For example, the full name of the degree was changed to fit the number of characters assigned by the university's computer software. Although not a requirement of a CUAP proposal, partway through the process a new policy requiring a business case for all new programs was added to the administrative tasks. There was also a national moratorium on new teacher education programs imposed by the Minister of Education, which required the Minister's permission to be lifted.

While other mainstream CUAP proposals were assisted by university administrators knowledgeable and experienced in the art of technical bureaucracy required by a CUAP proposal, such resources were not so forthcoming for the Indigenous proposal. Furthermore, the focus for approval shifted from administrative issues to a more substantive problem regarding whether or not the new program would be fiscally viable. Measuring viability was based on the enrollment history of the old program, which was delivered face-to-face, rather than on projections based on the online/internal mixed delivery mode proposed for the new program. There was no such history upon which projections could be made, but the Māori education sector had given insights about the appeal of an accessible ITE program to Māori communities. With this in mind, Māori faculty argued that the online delivery mode would make the program more accessible to prospective students across the country.

As oppositional barriers grew and continued to obstruct passage of the CUAP document, important deadlines were missed and sponsorship of the proposal at critical steps of the approval process proved unreliable. At the root of the problem is the fact that Indigenous-centred programs promulgate knowledge that is rarely sanctioned, confirmed, validated, or verified as authoritative. This is due in large part to the academy's mistaken perception regarding the relative superiority of Eurocentric tools as standards to measure Indigenous programs assumed and preconceived as inferior. Thus systemic beliefs that underpin the institution's complex systems and review processes, and senior faculty and administrators devoted to preserving the status quo, make it nearly impossible for Indigenous initiatives to succeed.

A decision by Māori faculty was to go outside the university and seek assistance from the community. The politics of Indigenous community partnerships and proactivity in advancing Indigenous education under the rubric of self-determination has been a critical factor, for example, in increasing access and participation of Native Hawaiian people in teacher education programs through Hoʻokulāiwi: Centre for Hawaiian and Indigenous Education at the University of Hawaiʻi (Maaka 2013). The Hoʻokulāiwi experience demonstrates powerful ways in which institutional barriers that conspire to control access to resources are circumnavigated through an appeal to community and political leaders. But action by community leaders is only guaranteed where there is evidence of reciprocal and authentic long-term commitment to the community by Indigenous academics situated within the academy (Maaka and Lenchanko 2008; Maaka 2013, 2009).

The strategy by Māori faculty of appealing to the Māori community was aimed at involving a key organization within the Māori education sector (MES). The approach was to identify a shared problem (Māori teacher supply), to assist with finding solutions, and, in partnership, to develop structures that enable the solutions to evolve in ways that embody the long-term vision of a strong Māori society. An important factor for the community in supporting the Māori ITE program was the strong relationships with Māori faculty that had been built up over many years. Many of the MES members and their whānau are alumni and well-known experts who have "walked the talk" in the politics of Māori education in Aotearoa. From the outset, Māori faculty sought from MES their combined knowledge, experience, and expertise about what counts in the preparation of Māori graduate teachers by having members assist with reconceptualizing and writing the new program. The assumption was that the credibility of the program within the Māori education sector depended in large part on the university's association with MES. At the same time, MES members recognized the advantage of utilizing the institution's vast distance learning facilities. Access would support their vested interest in ensuring a well-qualified workforce and an increased and sustainable teacher supply.

Conclusion

The combined weight of community and academy partnerships for Indigenous participation in the academy has served to disrupt the complacent luxury of ignorance, at least on the surface. The space remains contested and ongoing systemic critique is required to highlight the structural factors in the production and reproduction of injustice. The privilege of not knowing works against marginalized Indigenous communities within the academy. Structures that reinforce ignorance result in Indigenous people forced to take positions, where some support the status quo. Relationships are forfeited when ignorance rules and takes precedence over Indigenous priorities. The alarming spectacles of appointments that serve to weaken Indigenous leadership in the academy or the selection of Indigenous privatized intellectuals for professorial positions within corporatized academies[2] are emerging additions to the inventory of ignorance. The tacit reliance on ignorance of, and disregard for, the particularity of Indigeneity will ensure the academy remains a contested space.

Notes

1. For an in-depth discussion, see Mills (2007, 23-36).
2. I acknowledge Distinguished Professor Graeme H. Smith's concept of the privatized intellectual.

References

Alcoff, Linda Martin. 2007. "Epistemologies of Ignorance: Three Types." In *Race and Epistemologies of Ignorance*, edited by Shannon Sullivan and Nancy Tuana, 39-57. Albany, NY: SUNY Press.

Asante, Molefi Kete. 1995. "The Afrocentric Idea in Education." In *I Am Because We Are: Readings in Black Philosophy*, edited by Frederick Hord, 338-49. Amherst: University of Massachusetts Press.

Code, Lorraine. 2007. "The Power of Ignorance." In *Race and Epistemologies of Ignorance*, edited by Shannon Sullivan and Nancy Tuana, 213-29. Albany, NY: SUNY Press.

Frye, Marilyn. 1983. *The Politics of Reality: Essays in Feminist Theory*. Trumansburg, NY: Crossing Press.

Jaramillo, Nathalia. 2011. "Epistemologies of Ignorance." In *Epistemologies of Ignorance in Education*, edited by Erik Malewski and Nathalia Jaramillo, 1-30. Charlotte, NC: IAP.

Ka'ai, Tania. 2008. "The Role of Marae in Tertiary Education Institutions." *Te Kaharoa* 1: 193-202. https://doi.org/10.24135/tekaharoa.v1i1.142

Maaka, Margaret J. 2009. "Partnerships, Politics, Proactivity: Ho'okulaiwi and the Vitalization of Native Hawaiian and Indigenous Education." Paper presented at the Nankai Symposium and Workshop on the Higher Education of Indigenous Peoples and Minorities, Nankai University, Tianjin, China.

———. 2013. *Community Partnerships as Lived Experiences: Building Strong and Healthy Indigenous Peoples and Nations*. Kyoto, Japan: International Seminar of the Research Institute of Bukkyo University.

Maaka, Margaret J., and Mischa K. Lenchanko. 2008. "Hoʻokulaiwi: Self-Determination, Kuleana, and the Preparation of Native Hawaiian Leaders in Education." Paper presented at the Conference on the Influence of School, Place, and Culture on Indigenous Children's Learning, Providence University, Taichung, Taiwan.

Malewski, Erik, and Nathalia Jaramillo. 2011. "Introduction: Epistemologies of Ignorance." In *Epistemologies of Ignorance in Education*, edited by Erik Malewski and Nathalia Jaramillo, 1-30. Charlotte, NC: IAP.

McLaren, Peter. 2011. "Towards a Decolonizing Epistemology." In *Epistemologies of Ignorance in Education*, edited by Erik Malewski and Nathalia Jaramillo, viii-xvii. Charlotte, NC: IAP.

Mills, Charles W. 1997. *The Racial Contract*. New York: Cornell University Press.

———. 2007. "White Ignorance." In *Race and Epistemologies of Ignorance*, edited by Shannon Sullivan and Nancy Tuana, 13-38. Albany, NY: SUNY Press.

Ministry of Education. 2007. *Ka Hikitia—Managing for Success: The Draft Māori Education Strategy 2008-2012*. Wellington, NZ: Ministry of Education.

Ngāti Kahungunu Iwi. 2009. *Te Topuni Tauwhainga Framework*. Hastings, Hawkes Bay, NZ: Ngāti Kahungunu Iwi.

Outlaw, Lucius T., Jr. 2007. "Social Ordering and the Systematic Production of Ignorance." In *Race and Epistemologies of Ignorance*, edited by Shannon Sullivan and Nancy Tuana, 197-211. Albany, NY: SUNY Press.

Penetito, Wally. 2010. *What's Māori About Māori Education?* Wellington, NZ: Victoria University Press.

Simon, Judith. 1990. "The Place of Schooling in Māori-Pakeha Relations." PHD diss., University of Auckland.

Tawhai, Veronica. 2007. "He Moana Pukepuke e Ekengia e Te Waka: Persevering with Citizenship Education in Aotearoa." Master's thesis, Massey University.

Tertiary Education Commission. 2005. *Investment Guidance 2008-2010*. Wellington, NZ: Tertiary Education Commission.

Tomlins-Jahnke, Huia. 2005. "He Huarahi Motuhake: The Politics of Tribal Agency in Provider Services." PHD diss., School of Māori Studies, Massey University.

———. 2011. "Beyond Legitimation: A Tribal Response to Māori Education in Aotearoa, New Zealand." *The Australian Journal of Indigenous Education* 41 (2): 146-55. http://dx.doi.org/10.1017/jie.2012.28

Tomlins-Jahnke, Huia, and James Graham. 2014. "Te Pae Huarewa: Tribal Perspectives on Māori Education." In *Facing the Big Questions in Teaching: Purpose, Power and Learning,* edited by Alison St. George, Seth Brown, and John O'Neill, 146-55. Auckland, NZ: Cengage.

Tomlins-Jahnke, Huia, and Krystal Te Rina Warren. 2011. "Full, Exclusive and Undisturbed Possession: Māori Education and the Treaty." In *"Always Speaking": The Treaty of Waitangi and Public Policy,* edited by Veronica Tawhai and Katarina Gray-Sharp, 21-33. Wellington, NZ: Huia.

Tully, James. 2000. "The Struggles of Indigenous Peoples for and of Freedom." In *Political Theory and the Rights of Indigenous Peoples,* edited by Duncan Ivison, Paul Patton, and Will Sanders, 36-59. Cambridge: Cambridge University Press.

Walker, Ranginui. 1990. *Ka Whawhai Tonu Matou. Struggle Without End.* Auckland, NZ: Penguin Books.

5 | ***Homo Economicus*** and Forgetful Curriculum
Remembering Other Ways to Be a Human Being

DWAYNE DONALD

Introduction

How can human beings best live well in the world today? This question evokes a contested space wherein age-old contentions arise regarding the purpose and meaning of life and living. For the purposes of this chapter, the contested space under consideration resides within the human being, and the specific contestation has to do with the assumptions made by educators and curricularists regarding the forms of knowledge and knowing considered most valuable in creating the kinds of citizens they have in mind. Thus, in the process of making such decisions, the development of a particular kind of human being is being promoted. A significant space of contestation in the field of curriculum studies, then, is located within the human being, and this space is characterized by epistemological, ontological, cosmological, and axiological assertions regarding the meaning and purpose of life and living. Such contestations can be divisive because pondering the purpose of creation and existence is a fundamental part of human experience and thus heavily influenced by the various philosophies, ideologies, and faiths that people hold as true. This is what makes considerations of human being-ness a contested space.

In the context of this book chapter, I contest curricular conceptions of human being-ness derived from "Market Logic" (see Smith 2014, 58-61) and the divisive competitiveness that metastasizes from it. I share a deep-seated concern for the ways a North American settler dream imaginary[1] has slowly morphed into a curriculum mythology and ideology that promotes the market as a concept through which all forms of human living can and should be understood. Through story, I suggest a large-scale "letting go" of myopically anthropocentric understandings of life and living, and instead promote an educational project committed to acknowledging and honouring the complex connectivities that human beings have to the abundant more-than-human entities that live among us (Sheridan and Longboat 2006). In this spirit and with these intentions, I address this work to real human beings[2] and the extensive more-than-human relational networks that we are all enmeshed in and dependent upon for our survival. As real human beings, then, we proceed with acknowledgement of the sacred ecology that lives inside us. First and foremost, we acknowledge that the sun is literally the giver of life. We acknowledge that our bodies are comprised of sunlight-inspired energy that inhabits the air, water, minerals, plants, and animals that we consume. We acknowledge, too, that despite any current and future technological advances in how we live our lives, we will remain fully dependent on this sacred ecology to keep us alive. Whoever we are and wherever we may live, there is no way around this simple truth.

As I see it, the origin of current human struggles to balance the desire for economic development with ecological sustainability derives from a deep forgetting of those simple truths. What has taken its place in public consciousness and curriculum priorities is the embracing of a dream predicated on unfettered economic growth and material prosperity. This dream-way[3] manifests itself as a naturalized, universalized, and common-sense[4] logic that has come to have tremendous influence over public education curriculum initiatives in mostly subtle ways. The particular example of focus for this chapter is the Inspiring Education initiative undertaken by the Government of Alberta, which representatives of Alberta Education began promoting in 2009.[5] Inspiring Education is the consultative document that provides guidance on the unique demands of 21st-century learning to those working on the related project of curriculum redesign under the auspices of Alberta Education. This project involved a detailed revision of provincial programs of study, assessments, and teaching and learning resources, as well as processes for developing curricula to ensure they continue to be relevant and engaging to students. The revision brought greater focus on students developing competencies, which would enable the province to realize the vision of an educated Albertan as an engaged thinker and ethical citizen with an entrepreneurial spirit.

In 2015, the ruling Progressive Conservative Party lost the provincial election in Alberta and their Inspiring Education initiative was subsequently abandoned by the newly elected government. However, despite this political change, the market logics expressed in the Inspiring Education literature continue to have significant influence over educational policy development in the Province of Alberta. What I intend to do in this chapter is undertake a brief meditation on the significance of the mythological and ideological language used to support the Inspiring Education initiative, to show how it is implicated in some of the deepest difficulties we as human beings face today. For me, the difficulty of this contested space lies in understanding that these curriculum initiatives are predicated on the promotion of a particular kind of human being—*homo economicus*—who is primarily motivated by economic self-interest and the material gains that come with it. As an educator, I consider these initiatives as rooted in particular neo-liberal ideologies and mythologies that are often hidden in curriculum policy documents as incontrovertible statements of common sense. As such, I see such policy statements as active in the contested space of human being-ness as purveyors of violence, in that they serve to close down possibilities that children may have to imagine other ways to live their lives. Since, as human societies, we are now regularly experiencing the consequences of climate change and lifestyles dedicated to consumerism, it seems urgent to begin to guide students towards deeper and more ethically relational understandings of life and living guided by wisdom and understandings of sacred ecology. As one example of such sacred ecology insights and their connections to living like real human beings, I share a Blackfoot story on the origins of the Beaver Bundle.

Understanding Curriculum as Fundamentally Ideological and Mythological

The assertion that curriculum is ideological is not a new insight. For several decades now, prominent curriculum scholars have shown that formal education is a normative exercise geared towards the achievement of specific societal goals that align with the culture of those groups that hold social, political, and economic power in a society (for examples, refer to Freire 1970; Pratte 1977; Barton, Meighan, and Walker 1980; Giroux 1989; Eisner 1992; Bowers 1993; Apple 2004). Curriculum documents, and the educational priorities they emphasize, are thoroughly imbued with the cultural assumptions and prejudices that the majority of the members of a society have come to consider normal and necessary for young people to know and understand. In teleological terms, then, curricula can be understood as preparing children for a future that has been imagined on their behalf by adults. Thus, curriculum is basically an exercise in citizenship, and the success of this exercise is generally assessed according to how well the children have taken on the characteristics that the adults hoped they would. In curricular terms, the kinds of citizens that adults have in mind derive from orthodox, epistemic assumptions that are often characterized as common sense.

Thus, a key point when working to understand curriculum as ideological is to attend to the truth that curriculum ideologies derive from normative worldviews (Eisner 1992, 302). As such, they can manifest as powerful "religiouslike" orthodoxies that proclaim strong positions on important educational matters, but commonly operate with subtlety through conveyance of common-sense logics contained in conventionalized language forms and structures (303). These connections between culture, ideology, and curriculum are not necessarily surprising or problematic. They become so when the official curriculum ideologies become so pervasive and unquestioned that their followers are left unable to recognize them as cultural and ideological, and thus also left unable to imagine alternative possibilities (303). In such scenarios, the particular cultures and ideologies at work in curriculum priorities become dehistoricized, naturalized, and normalized expressions of epistemic orthodoxy. This dynamic makes it difficult for people to discern the ways in which curriculum priorities are expressions of cultural and ideological assumptions because they are typically framed in commonsensical terms. As epistemic orthodoxies, then, I contend that such curriculum ideologies eventually morph into mythologies.

By referring to mythologies, I am not arguing that curriculum ideologies are falsehoods. On the contrary, myths are actually insightful truths about peoples and cultures. The truths are the idealized versions of worldview that are simplified and made coherent when particular events, characters, and ideas are selected that seem to embody important cultural values that all good citizens should know. Following the ideas of Barthes (1972) in his provocative book *Mythologies*, we can say that "myth takes a purely cultural and historical object...and transforms it into a sign of universal value...it turns culture into nature. It is this duplicity of myth, a construct which represents itself as universal and natural, which characterizes its ideological function" (36-7). The point here is that official versions of worldview and ideology, which begin as cultural and contextual interpretations of events and ideas, morph into mythologies—that is, expressions of the existing epistemic orthodoxy of the dominant groups in a society. In this schema, then, mythologies are understood as invisibilized expressions of ideology that, despite their seeming obscurity, actually form the foundational roots of worldviews that guide the thoughts and actions of the people of a particular culture. The key point here is that people do not think about their mythologies; they think with them. They form the guiding common-sense normative frameworks with which the world is encountered, interpreted, and understood.

Since espousing a society's myths is a primary function of its institutions—and since schools are a primary conduit for this—curriculum documents can thus be considered mythological. So, then, what are the mythologies most strongly at play in curricula today? As is well understood, formal education, as we know and experience it today, has its roots in 19th-century industrialism and was conceptualized amidst the tremendous changes to everyday life that were instigated by the economic shift to factories and assembly lines under the general purview of market capitalism. Public education was created in response to an economic need for more qualified workers to be properly prepared for work in the emerging marketplace and to take full advantage of growing commercial opportunities.[6] Schools became places to prepare young people for this world of work, and the success of these preparations has been considered directly tied to the overall economic interests of the nation.

In light of these roots in economic functionalism, it should not be surprising that formal education today is still largely guided by curriculum mythologies predicated on the assumption that liberal market ideology is the key to human freedom and happiness. The following are some of the key mythologies and guiding cultural assumptions of education and curriculum today.[7]

Individualism

The promotion of the autonomous individual, separated from community, as the most advanced form of human being was the major impetus of the Age of Enlightenment in Europe and remains a fundamental tenet of modern liberal thought. In the classic liberal ideal, an individual citizen unbound by the shackles of tradition and free to act in self-interest will bring progressive benefits to the society as a whole. This worldview privileges the autonomous individual as the source of rational thought, innovation, and economic prosperity. Thus, the promotion of the free, autonomous, and possessive individual is viewed as a necessary precondition for societal success and so is intimately intertwined with curriculum thought.

Progress

Linked to the mythological dream-way of unfettered economic growth and material prosperity stemming from worship of market capitalism, this notion of progress has grown out of the colonial experience and the pursuit of ever-expanding opportunities to realize that dream. Progress, in this case, operates simultaneously as a rejection of tradition and as a celebration of the West as an autonomous entity that has grown progressively from this well-known chronological genealogy: Ancient Greece to Rome to Christian Europe to the Renaissance to the Enlightenment to the Industrial Revolution to the growth of political democracy (Wolf 1982, 5). The West, as the entity that has grown from this imaginary, is characterized by fervent faith in secular, rational, technical, and scientific approaches to life and living and is understood as embodying values that are considered acultural, and so universally good. As such, the West exemplifies a "moral success story" that tells of an always growing and expanding civilization built by people who have discovered the way to live well and have been trained to believe that their way should be emulated by all progressive right-thinking and freedom-loving peoples. Curricular worship of this linear notion of progress is ongoing, and the desire to maintain it as a guiding principle often manifests in curriculum documents as a call for innovation and forward thinking.

Anthropocentrism

Anthropocentrism—the commanding conviction that human beings are the most important life forms in the world—stems from the Enlightenment era and the preoccupation with separating people from the varied organisms, entities, and ecosystems that comprise the world.

Following the teachings of this myth, humans are trained to see themselves as rational beings who are pitted against the rest of nature and must do what is necessary to control and shape the so-called "natural world" to best suit their own needs and interests. Over many years, this deeply held cultural assumption of human superiority and lordship over all things in the world has been informed by a complex confluence of religious dogma, market capitalist principles, and Darwinian-inspired theories of evolution. In light of such cultural prominence, then, it is not surprising that anthropocentrism has become entrenched in curriculum documents. Over many generations, children in schools have been trained in largely unnoticed ways to believe that their interests and desires always supersede those of the entities that give them life.[8]

The Promotion of *Homo Economicus* as a Curricular Goal

The things we give ourselves to we become part of and
they can own us.
—WALTER LIGHTNING, "Compassionate Mind"

The mythologies above describe what we have given ourselves to in the field of education, and in a certain sense they have come to own us and any attempts to imagine other possibilities for curriculum. The key point here is that root mythologies act like mythical creation stories and become organizing principles that guide, but also simultaneously circumscribe and constrain, well-intended attempts to redesign curricula. Such mythologies act on us in deeply psychic ways that often go unnoticed.

An example of the deep influence that these mythologies have on curriculum thought is manifested in the character of homo economicus[9]— a unique form of the human species that is understood to possess a natural propensity to be "rational, individualistic, utilitarian, calculative and instrumental" in economic matters (Houston 2010, 842). In exercising these skills, homo economicus is understood as primarily motivated by a self-interested desire for wealth and the accumulation of material goods as a primary measure of success. It is understood that the success pursued by homo economicus can really only be achieved via an adherence to the tenets and principles of market capitalism (Williams 1999). For proponents of these tenets and principles, market capitalism guides human beings to conduct themselves in ways that bring benefits and economic prosperity to the society as a whole. In this context, the ontological question of what it means to be a human being is directly connected to the market and the benefits that accrue from it. Faith in and worship of the market is considered the primary purpose of humankind, and homo economicus constitutes the most natural and most developed form of human being in evolutionary terms. Questions regarding the meaning and purpose of human being-ness are answered with direct reference to this market rationality.

So, to what extent do schools today continue to follow a mythological, societal superstructure guided by an individualized and anthropocentric notion of progress that finds expression in the promotion of homo economicus as the human model for young people to aspire to be? An interesting example to aid in the exploration of the contested space in which these market-based insights are considered most useful in producing particular kinds of human beings is the curriculum redesign and Inspiring Education projects undertaken by Alberta Education and thus endorsed by the Government of Alberta beginning in 2009. For the most part, the curriculum redesign initiative was guided by a self-proclaimed state-of-the-art educational approach founded on the concept of "Competencies for 21st-Century Learning." In this approach, the conceptual framework undergirding the idea of "21st-century learning" seems to be largely framed in economic terms and in relation to a clear faith in the power of technology and innovation to spur economic growth:

> Our education system must both provide an inclusive environment where each student belongs, and equip them with the attitudes, skills,

knowledge, and competencies they need to be successful in tomorrow's economy...The continued development of a highly skilled, knowledgeable, innovative and productive workforce is critical to ensuring that Alberta sustains its competitive advantage in a global economy, allowing the province to attract investment, and high value-added industries. (Alberta Education 2010, 3)

This economics-first educational "Action Plan" is further guided by this vision: "All students are inspired to achieve success and fulfillment as engaged thinkers and ethical citizens with an entrepreneurial spirit" (Alberta Education 2010, 6). While this vision does seem to be student- and competency-focused, there is also a direct link given to an "entrepreneurial spirit," since this wording implies that to be an "engaged thinker" and "ethical citizen" of value requires a market-oriented spirit and outlook. According to this vision statement, an "entrepreneurial spirit" would be exemplified by a student

> who creates opportunities and achieves goals through hard work, perseverance and discipline; who strives for excellence and earns success; who explores ideas and challenges the status quo; who is competitive, adaptable and resilient; and who has the confidence to take risks and make bold decisions in the face of adversity. (Alberta Education 2011, 6)

This expressed vision of Alberta Education, which guided the work of both Inspiring Education and curriculum redesign, was controversial and divisive. Parents, concerned citizens, and political groups raised questions and gathered petitions stating opposition to discovery learning curriculum approaches in mathematics, as well as the involvement of oil and gas corporations in the curriculum redesign process (Salz 2014). In March 2014, Alberta Education Minister Jeff Johnson issued a "Curriculum Redesign Letter" in which he sought to clarify the overall goals of this initiative. It is worthwhile to quote from the letter at length:

I feel parents deserve to hear directly from me about my ministry's
efforts to ensure the provincial curriculum enables Alberta's students
to successfully compete in a dynamic, highly competitive world...
The modern economy demands creativity and problem solving, the
application of critical thinking and an ability to collaborate and
communicate. These skills lie at the heart of Alberta's curriculum redesign process. Top performing education jurisdictions, like Alberta,
have increased their focus on these 21st century skills. We can't
ignore that without strong abilities in these areas, our kids will be left
behind...At the end of the day we must ask ourselves, are we preparing
our children for their future or for our past?[10]

The subtle subtext of these policy declarations is that 21st-century
notions of how best to be a human being are largely derived from
neo-liberal understandings of innovation, progress entrepreneurship,
competition, success, and well-being in the interests of building an
economy. Youth are clearly positioned as future generators of economic
wealth, and their contributing value as citizens is directly dependent on
how well they replicate this prescribed value and build it into their
emerging identities. Such faith in muscular entrepreneurship is a prominent part of the socio-political mythology of Alberta (see, for example,
Harrison 2005; Lisac 2004). As earlier stated, I understand this ideological
thrust—concealed as common sense (Keil 2002)—to be a form of ontological violence that has direct impacts on the well-being of youth today.

While there is nothing inherently wrong with attentiveness to such
issues—economic issues are obviously a central concern of all human
societies—questions arise when youth are trained to believe that their
emerging identities as human beings are directly connected to neo-
liberal market logics and consumerism as a necessary lifestyle choice. In
the context of Alberta today, a frontier territory with substantial wealth
generated from oil and gas resource exploitation, this ideology teaches
that a person who is not participating in or benefiting from this prosperity is clearly doing something wrong and needs to be straightened out

(Masuda et al. 2008; Altamirano-Jimenez 2004; Pratt 2009; Donald and Krahn 2014).

Curriculum and "The Great Forgetting"

Such a mythological faith and worship of the market as the single concept most central to successful human living today is enmeshed within "The Great Forgetting" as described by Daniel Quinn (1996) in his book *The Story of B*. The Great Forgetting is the concept the teacher/lecturer (named B in the book) uses to describe the social and cultural dynamic we are currently living through, in which people have been carefully trained to disregard wisdom insights and stories from earlier eras. As I interpret this point in relation to my own concerns, what has been forgotten is that people lived well prior to the present era. By the time history began to be written down, and the Enlightenment process was well underway, it was assumed that human beings really only began to live as they were meant to during this time. The central message, then, is that before the current era nothing of significance happened (245). B argues that our knowledge and worldview today would be greatly altered had the foundational thinkers of our schooling cultures acknowledged that there was history beyond the beginning of their version of civilization.

In the book, B expresses the belief that circumstances have rendered the cultural mythology of progress untenable and unsustainable as a dream-way. B claims that the "Great Forgetting blinds us to the fact that we are a biological species in a community of biological species and are not exempt or exemptible from the forces that shape all life on this planet" (Quinn 1996, 307). B introduces the "Great Remembering" as the most urgent challenge facing human beings today. He declares that what was forgotten through the Great Forgetting must be remembered in order for us to recognize "that what cannot work for any species will not work for us either" (307). One of the consequences of fervent faith and worship of consumerism and market capitalism is a gradual forgetting of the entities that give us life and the stories that remind us of how we are all comprised of sunlight-inspired energy.

A series of interconnected questions emerge from consideration of these insights: To what extent are schools and curriculum documents today facilitating the perpetuation of this Great Forgetting? How responsible is it to insist on the ongoing production of young versions of homo economicus when there is every reason to believe that within a generation people will no longer be able to "be" that way? Which mythologies promote other forms of human being-ness beyond homo economicus? How can we begin to remember what the Great Forgetting has caused us to forget? As one way to respond to these questions, I offer the following Blackfoot story of the Beaver Bundle which, among many other insights, teaches ethical relationality, sacred ecology, and the interconnectivity of life. Importantly, the story describes the position of human beings within the relational kinship networks that generate life and living for all. In terms of the contested space that resides within the human being, and the curricular and educational significance of this space, this story provides brief insight into the Blackfoot imagination regarding how to live as a real human being. Consider this imagination in juxtaposition with the cultural mythologies of individualism, progress, and anthropocentrism seen in the imagined person of homo economicus as you read.[11]

Ksisskstaki Amopistaan: The Beaver Bundle

A long time ago, a man named White Grass brought his wife and infant son to live beside four large lakes at the base of the mountains. He worked so hard to support his family that his wife would see him only at night. Eventually, though, she grew lonely, and there was a young male beaver living at the lake who noticed this. One day, the bachelor beaver transformed himself into a man and charmed her into following him into his family's lodge.

When White Grass returned home that evening, his wife was nowhere to be found and their infant child was alone, crying and hungry. At first, White Grass was angry about his wife's negligence, and called out for her. When she didn't answer, he set off following her footprints, which led him down to the edge of the water, where they seemed to disappear. But the only thing he saw were the recent paw prints of a large grizzly bear. Then he knew, logically, that his wife must have been eaten.

That night, White Grass sat up late in his fire-lit lodge, the infant boy crying by his side, and he himself convulsing with tears, imagining the horrible fate that had befallen his beautiful young wife. White Grass may have cried himself to sleep. In the darkest period of night, just before dawn, an old man came into his lodge, sat down and told him not to mourn his wife. "She's not dead," the man told him. "She's been charmed underwater by a young beaver who appeared to her as a man. They are staying together in his parents' lodge. Do not mourn for her, and I will return again with instructions on how you can get her back."

When White Grass awoke the next morning, he wasn't sure if what he'd experienced was a dream, or if the old man really did come to visit. If it was a dream, it had been powerful. White Grass decided to do as he'd been told, to cease his mourning. He turned his attention instead toward consoling his infant son, who was now beginning to starve for the nourishment of his mother. But there was little White Grass could do in this regard.

That night he was again visited by the old man. "If you want to save the life of your son," the man told him, "you will need to steal a small beaver pup with white fur. This is the favourite child of the beavers, the ones whose older son took your wife. They guard this pup closely. Do not attempt to capture it until I return to give you instructions."

White Grass waited another stressful day. That third night, he was given precise instructions on how to successfully capture the beaver pup. The old man warned White Grass that once he caught hold of the pup, he was not to let go. Rather, he should take the animal into his lodge and await further directions.

When White Grass awoke on the fourth day, he was relieved to finally take action. Following the advice of the old man, he covered himself in duck droppings and concealed himself in a hole along the lakeshore. He waited all day in that hole for the white pup to appear. Just as he was ready to give up, the albino pup appeared and he quickly seized it.

As he sat in his lodge, holding both his own starving infant son and the young white beaver pup on his lap, the old man came to visit again. He told White Grass to hang onto the beaver pup at all costs. There would be an emissary sent to negotiate an exchange. This ambassador would ask White Grass to release the young beaver in exchange for his wife. But he was instructed to refuse this, remain in his lodge, and wait for the most elder beaver to come bearing gifts. The old man told White Grass what gifts he should demand before agreeing to the exchange for his wife's return.

Later that same night, an otter transformed into human shape entered his lodge. This otter man told White Grass that the beavers had sent him with a message: that if their favourite child was released, so too would the woman be returned. White Grass sat in place with his infant son on his lap while gently stroking the albino beaver's fur. "No," he said, "I think we'll keep him until my boy's mother has returned."

Hearing this, the otter man left, and all was quiet again. Sometime later, White Grass heard voices of many people singing as they approached the shore. These were the all the other animals and birds who lived in the lake. They were soon joined by some of the land animals—the buffalo, coyote, fox, badger, and others. It was a very large group, all walking single file in the night, singing as they went along. This procession made its way around the lodge four times before entering. They were led by the elder beaver and White Grass's wife, who carried a pipe bundle on her back.

When they came inside, White Grass was sitting on his bed, still holding his boy and the young albino pup on his lap. With hand signals, he motioned for his wife to sit next to him on his south side, and for the elder beaver to sit on his north. When all had found their seats, the elderly beaver turned toward White Grass and reasoned, "Your wife has been returned safe, now you should release my son." But White Grass, following the instructions of the old man who had visited him, sat still, gently stroking the young white pup. "No," he said, "It's good that you've returned my wife, but if you want to take this pup away, you will have to give me something more as well."

The elder beaver began to sing. As he sang, he brought items out of the pipe bundle that the woman had carried in, and set them in front of White Grass. The beaver man sang seven songs in total, placing in turn the eagle's tailfeathers, the pelt of a black coyote, red kit-fox, and fisher, the hide of a white buffalo calf, the pelt of a marten, and the hide of a cow elk. "This is the sacred Beaver Bundle," the old one said. "I'm transferring it to you in exchange for my son."

White Grass sat quiet, petting the young albino beaver. All the animals waited for his reply, but he just kept stroking that beaver until, finally, he looked up at the elderly one and said, "This is not enough."

Hearing those words, the beaver made an announcement. He called on all his relatives, the animals and birds who had come from the land, skies and underwater, to step forth and offer something to the bundle. After this was done, they all sat back and waited for White Grass to respond.

The trapper remained unimpressed, betraying little emotion as he sat petting the white pup on his lap. "It is not enough."

After all the animals had given him their most valuable belongings, White Grass saw that he had received everything the old man had told him about. At this, he consented to the exchange, and returned the beaver pup to its relatives.

With the exchange, the first transfer of Ksisskstaki Amopistaan was concluded. Since then, all of the birds and animals of both the upper Saskatchewan and upper Missouri watersheds were allied with the Blackfoot as relatives. And still today, twice a year, Beaver Bundles are opened in Blackfoot territory for performances that renew this earliest of transfers. It is to these openings—enactments of that waterside exchange—that many people go, in the first days of spring and just before winter, to dance as those animal spirits, restore harmonious relations, resolve sickness, and escape danger.

Imagining Curricula that Honour Other Ways to Be a Human Being

There are many wisdom teachings that can be derived from the story of Ksisskstaki Amopistaan. Important insights into Blackfoot imagination and worldview can be discerned by those who are committed enough to engage in careful study and interpretation of its various interconnected teachings. This can take a lifetime. However, it is important to remember that it is not just a story. Ksisskstaki Amopistaan conveys Blackfoot memory, experience, ceremonial ways, and worldview, which, more generally, provide guidance on how to live a good life. So, the spirit and intent of the story itself must inspire people to do something to honour the bundle exchange and the kinship alliance made that day with the birds and animals, or the wisdom it offers becomes static and inorganic. Nothing good grows from it unless people enact its teachings in their daily lives.

Of course, this is not a dynamic that is unique to the Blackfoot context. Most worldviews and mythologies are re-enacted daily by people who hold them as true. As human beings, we live in the logic of the stories we tell about the world and our place in it. It is for this reason that the story of Ksisskstaki Amopistaan was provocatively and purposefully juxtaposed with the opening sections of this chapter that focused on curriculum ideologies and mythologies derived from market logics. As a cultural experience, most readers would be quite capable of comprehending the main messages of the opening sections, because they bring focus on a cultural context that is familiar and presumably well understood. On the other hand, though, most readers would not have a cultural context for comprehending the story of Ksisskstaki Amopistaan. Juxtaposed with what is considered normal, universal, acultural, and commonsensical, as described in the opening sections, the story presents itself as an intensely cultural expression of a traditional way of life that is no longer viable. In this juxtaposition of ideologies and mythologies, the example from Blackfoot culture provided in the story of Ksisskstaki Amopistaan is interesting as an artifact of a former way of being, but is typically dismissed as unrealistic as a way of being today.

This juxtaposition is shared with the hope that it will spark creative responses to the question of how we might reimagine curriculum, meaningfully follow other ideologies and mythologies, and thus work towards honouring other ways to be a human being that are not fully circumscribed by market logics. It is one way to draw attention to the curricular contestations that arise whenever we deliberate on the meaning and purpose of life and living. A key point in this consideration is that the composition of curriculum is basically an exercise dedicated to the creation of a particular kind of human being. This is what makes considerations of curriculum simultaneously also about the contested space within the human being and suppositions held regarding how that person should live.

The complexity of these considerations cannot be addressed by simply replacing one story with another under the purview of inclusion.[12] If a story like Ksisskstaki Amopistaan is "infused" or "incorporated" into curricula as just a story, and without the necessary care and attention given the ideologies, mythologies, and ways of becoming real human beings it describes, nothing good will grow from it. In his scenario, the fundamental curriculum mythologies of individualism, progress, and anthropocentrism maintain their hegemonic influence as universalized common sense, and the story is marginalized based on those cultural assumptions.

So, what to do? It has become clear to me that the real work of reimagining curriculum and honouring other ways to be a human being involves the articulation of a new story that guides us to live on more ethically relational terms with humans as well as our more-than-human relations (Donald 2012). Of course, we cannot just make up stories that suit our interests and desires and expect people to follow them enthusiastically. Stories that give life emerge from people sitting together in the spirit of good relations and thinking carefully on their shared future as human beings. For me, such work is guided by the Cree concept of *wahkohtowin* (LaBoucane-Benson et al. 2012), which teaches that, as human beings, we are enmeshed in a series of relationships (human and more-than-human) that give us life. The model of a real human being that wahkohtowin provides is one who acknowledges those relationships daily and strives to live in ways that sustains them. To do otherwise is to act against life and the survival of those relational networks. I believe that the organic tension that is generated from enacting such ethical forms of relationality provides potential sources of creativity that can be simultaneously life-giving and life-sustaining for us all.

Notes

1. Here I am referring to the socio-cultural mythology of newcomers to North America that is guided by the "dream" of easily accessible resources and unfettered economic growth that will make them rich, successful, and thus happy. This "dream" originated during the high colonial era and has largely been maintained to the present (albeit in altered forms) as a guiding vision of the good life.
2. In many of the different Indigenous languages of North America, including the Cree and Blackfoot languages, which I am most familiar with, the people consistently refer to themselves as the "real people" or the "true human beings." While this could easily be interpreted as a sign that such people have a high opinion of themselves, I have been taught to understand this naming as declarative of the people's intentions to live humbly and in accordance with the laws of creation. In the languages and the cultural sensibilities connected to them, this is how *real* human beings are meant to live. For more on this, see Gatschet (1899) and Praet (2013).
3. This reference to the "way" is a purposeful nod to the concept of the path, route, or road as it is expressed within the teaching tenets of many different

wisdom traditions. Probably the most famous of these is the *Tao* as expressed in Chinese culture and East Asian philosophy and religion. I use the phrase here to emphasize the point that market capitalism has morphed into a way in its own right.

4. In the context of this chapter, the terms *common sense* and *commonsensical* refer to normative and hegemonically dominant attitudes and opinions on political, economic, cultural, and social issues espoused by majority members of a society. Following Kumashiro (2004), I consider such attitudes and opinions common sense because they are usually framed by proponents as acultural and apolitical positions that any normal, reasonable, and right-minded person would also consider true. Kumashiro asserts that common sense manifests in the field of education as a blockage to imagining alternative possibilities. In a context governed by common-sense logics, alternative approaches are dismissed on the grounds that they are inappropriate, inconsequential, or irrelevant, and thus incommensurable with the purposes of schooling (xxiii).

5. Alberta Education is the government ministry responsible for the supervision and administration of K-12 education in the Province of Alberta, Canada. For more details on the Inspiring Education initiative, see the report "Inspiring Education: A Dialogue with Albertans," at https://open.alberta.ca/dataset/45370ce9-3a90-4ff2-8735-cdb760c720f0/resource/2ee2452c-81d3-414f-892f-060caf40e78e/download/4492270-2010-inspiring-education-dialogue-albertans-2010-04.pdf

6. For an interesting example of this dynamic in the American context, see Kincheloe's (2000) explanation of Fordist production procedures with special emphasis on standardization, compartmentalization of tasks, and static assembly lines. These Fordist innovations were conceptualized so as to modernize and optimize industrial production, and have had tremendous influence on industry around the world. In astonishing parallel, these industrial innovations have also had deep influence over the assumptions guiding teaching, teacher education, and curriculum.

7. I rely heavily on Bowers (1993, 2007) in making these points.

8. It is important to add here that human superiority over nature has been extended to include a similar assumption of superiority over Peoples who follow more holistic ecological teachings. Peoples who consider themselves more civilized in their approaches to life and living have used their supposed superiority as justification for the exploitation and marginalization of Peoples they consider closer to nature and thus uncivilized (Bell and Russell 2000, 193).

9. See Persky (1995) for more on the origins of this concept. Following insights from Caruso (2012), I intend for this concept to be understood in anthropological and sociological terms rather than in purely economic terms.
10. This letter was retrieved on January 20, 2019 from http://www.greentreeschool.com/view.php?action=object&id=10725&stream=Homepage%20News
11. The story shared here is condensed from a written version shared with me by Ryan Heavy Head.
12. For more on this point, see Donald (2013).

References

Alberta Education. 2010. *Alberta Education Action Agenda 2011-2014*. Edmonton: Alberta Education. https://open.alberta.ca/dataset/ee9b9818-e603-409a-b615-7b5433196483/resource/60afeaa3-182d-4d19-993d-468fda3b3843/download/4912995-2011-actionagenda.pdf

———. 2011. *Framework for Student Learning: Competencies for Engaged Thinkers and Ethical Citizens with an Entrepreneurial Spirit*. Edmonton: Alberta Education. https://open.alberta.ca/dataset/4c47d713-d1fc-4c94-bc97-08998d93d3ad/resource/58e18175-5681-4543-b617-c8efe5b7b0e9/download/5365951-2011-framework-student-learning.pdf

Altamirano-Jiménez, Isabel. 2004. "North American First Peoples: Slipping Up Into Market Citizenship?" *Citizenship Studies* 8 (4): 349-65. https://doi.org/10.1080/1362102052000316963

Apple, Michael W. 2004. *Ideology and Curriculum*. New York: RoutledgeFalmer.

Barthes, Roland. 1972. *Mythologies*. Translated by Annette Lavers. New York: Hill & Wang.

Barton, Len, Roland Meighan, and Stephen A. Walker, eds. 1980. *Schooling, Ideology and the Curriculum*. Sussex, England: Falmer.

Bell, Anne C., and Constance L. Russell. 2000. "Beyond Human, Beyond Words: Anthropocentrism, Critical Pedagogy, and the Poststructuralist Turn." *Canadian Journal of Education* 25 (3): 188-203. https://doi.org/10.2307/1585953

Bowers, Chet A. 1993. *Education, Cultural Myths, and the Ecological Crisis: Toward Deep Changes*. Albany, NY: SUNY Press.

———. 2007. "Philosophy, Language, and the Titanic Mind-Set." *Language & Ecology* 2 (1): 1-16.

Caruso, Sergio. 2012. *Homo Oeconomicus: Paradigma, Critiche, Revisioni*. Florence, Italy: Firenze University Press.

Donald, Dwayne. 2012. "Forts, Curriculum, and Ethical Relationality." In *Reconsidering Canadian Curriculum Studies: Provoking Historical, Present, and Future Perspectives*, edited by Nicholas Ng-A-Fook and Jennifer Rottmann, 39–46. New York: Palgrave Macmillan.

———. 2013. "Teachers, Aboriginal Perspectives, and the Logic of the Fort." *ATA Magazine* 93(4): 27–30.

Donald, Dwayne, and Mandy Krahn. 2014. "Abandoning Pathologization: Conceptualizing Indigenous Youth Identity as Flowing from Communitarian Understandings." In *Critical Youth Studies Reader*, edited by Shirley Steinberg and Awad Ibrahim, 114–29. New York: Peter Lang.

Eisner, Elliot W. 1992. "Curriculum Ideologies." In *Handbook of Research on Curriculum*, edited by Philip W. Jackson, 302–26. New York: MacMillan.

Freire, Paulo. 1970. *Pedagogy of the Oppressed*. Translated by M.B. Ramos. New York: Continuum.

Gatschet, Albert S. 1899. "'Real,' 'True,' or 'Genuine,' in Indian Languages." *American Anthropologist* 1 (1): 155–61.

Giroux, Henry. 1989. *Critical Pedagogy, the State, and Cultural Struggle*. Albany, NY: SUNY Press.

Harrison, Trevor W., ed. 2005. *The Return of the Trojan Horse: Alberta and the New World (Dis)order*. Montreal: Black Rose Books.

Houston, Stan. 2010. "Beyond Homo Economicus: Recognition, Self-Realization and Social Work." *British Journal of Social Work* 40 (3): 841–57. https://doi.org/10.1093/bjsw/bcn132

Keil, Roger. 2002. "'Common-Sense' Neoliberalism: Progressive Conservative Urbanism in Toronto, Canada." *Antipode* 34 (3): 578–601. https://doi.org/10.1111/1467-8330.00255

Kincheloe, Joe L. 2000. "Cultural Studies and Democratically Aware Teacher Education: Post-Fordism, Civics and the Worker-Citizen." In *Democratic Social Education: Social Studies for Social Change*, edited by David W. Hursh and E. Wayne Ross, 97–120. New York: Falmer.

Kumashiro, Ken. 2004. *Against Common Sense: Teaching and Learning Toward Social Justice*. New York: RoutledgeFalmer.

LaBoucane-Benson, Patti, Ginger Gibson, Allen Benson, and Greg Miller. 2012. "Are We Seeking Pimatisiwin or Creating Pomewin? Implications for Water Policy." *The International Indigenous Policy Journal* 3 (3): 1–22. https://doi.org/10.18584/iipj.2012.3.3.10

Lightning, Walter. 1992. "Compassionate Mind: Implications of a Text Written by Elder Louis Sunchild." *Canadian Journal of Native Education* 19 (2): 215–53. https://doi.org/10.7939/R3J67946Z

Lisac, Mark, ed. 2004. *Alberta Politics Uncovered: Taking Back Our Province*. Edmonton: NeWest Press.

Masuda, Jeffrey R., Tara K. McGee, and Theresa D. Garvin. 2008. "Power, Knowledge, and Public Engagement: Constructing 'Citizenship' in Alberta's Industrial Heartland." *Journal of Environmental Policy & Planning* 10 (4): 359–80. https://doi.org/10.1080/15239080802332026

Persky, Joseph. 1995. "Retrospectives: The Ethology of Homo Economicus." *Journal of Economic Perspectives* 9 (2): 221–31.

Praet, Istvan. 2013. "Humanity and Life as the Perpetual Maintenance of Specific Efforts: A Reappraisal of Animism." In *Biosocial Becomings: Integrating Social and Biological Anthropology*, edited by Tim Ingold and Gisli Palsson, 191–210. Cambridge: Cambridge University Press.

Pratt, Sheila. 2009. "Martha and Henry Retire." *Alberta Views* 12 (5): 26–9.

Pratte, Richard. 1977. *Ideology and Education*. New York: McKay.

Quinn, Daniel. 1996. *The Story of B: An Adventure of the Mind and Spirit*. Toronto: Bantam Books.

Salz, Allison. 2014. "Alberta Education Critics from the NDP Says [sic] Corporations Have No Place in Shaping the Curriculum." *Edmonton Sun*. March 14, 2014. http://www.edmontonsun.com/2014/03/11/alberta-education-critics-from-the-ndp-says-corporations-have-no-place-in-shaping-the-curriculum

Sheridan, Joe, and R. Dan Longboat. 2006. "The Haudenosaunee Imagination and the Ecology of the Sacred." *Space and Culture* 9 (4): 365–81.

Smith, David. 2014. *Teaching as the Practice of Wisdom*. New York: Bloomsbury.

Williams, David. 1999. "Constructing the Economic Space: The World Bank and the Making of Homo Oeconomicus." *Millennium-Journal of International Studies* 28 (1): 79–99.

Wolf, Eric. 1982. *Europe and the People Without History*. Berkeley: University of California Press.

II Relationships
Negotiating Contested Spaces

6 | Contested Places in Education
The Radical Potential for "Being Māori"

WALLY PENETITO

Storyline

I was about 10 years old when I became involved in an argument swapping insults with Matiu—a classmate—about something I can no longer even remember. Yet, at one point in our difference of opinion, he suddenly bellowed at me, "You're not even a real Māori!" I distinctly remember my hackles rising and for a few moments I lost my cool. With fists flying, we tore into each other. Spit, snot, and blood flew in all directions. "Not a real Māori, eh? I'll show you who's a real Māori."

To this day I still puzzle over Matiu's accusation and my equally irrational response. I knew Matiu was Māori and not because he came from the *pā* (village), and I knew I was Māori but not because I didn't come from the pā. What was he trying to tell me by saying I wasn't a "real" Māori?

In later years, I was to experience a further corollary: "Yeah, but you're different!" These were the sentiments of Pākehā (European) schoolmates when I cautioned them for unjustly criticizing Māori over some situation, condition, or state. I can't even remember what it was. I was never sure whether I should accept their statement as a compliment or whether it was another form of the same ritual insult as Matiu's. Whatever the reasons are behind these insinuations, I definitely had a feeling of discomfort about them both. What were they trying to tell me? The point is, I suppose, that "being Māori" is something one has in one's DNA. But, just as importantly, it must also be about a process of "becoming"—that is, something one has to learn. Otherwise, in today's educational context, why would Māori want *kohanga reo, kura kaupapa, wharekura*, and *wānanga*? Why would they want more Māori content in mainstream[1] schools if the circumstances did not warrant it?

Statement of the Problem

The questions raised in this brief storyline are the main questions I set out to answer in this chapter: What does it mean to be Māori? What role does schooling play in enhancing/disrupting the process of becoming Māori? Why is this a problem? As the New Zealand education system struggles to find ways to counter the underdevelopment of Māori students in schools, the above narrative serves as a reminder of the very personal, grounded, and material problem facing Māori learners and their teachers in the New Zealand education system. Māori learners are complex, multi-faceted, infinitely flexible, and imbued with everything that is both malleable and intransigent, as with most other learners. The policy shift of raising Māori achievement levels through research-informed classroom pedagogies (Ministry of Education 2007), aligned with the ideological decision to support the perceived need to focus on realizing Māori student potential (Ministry of Education 2008), has created a kind of "breeder effect." A clear generation of new energy has arisen across the teaching and learning of Māori students, especially in secondary schooling (Ministry of Education 2013). Both these effects, the policy decision and the ideological decision, are welcome and necessary. However, I will argue that they are flawed initiatives without a clear understanding of the broader context of social justice and the necessity for both Māori and mainstream New Zealand to accept one of the most difficult obstacles facing Māori and Pākehā development, namely "denialism."[2]

The problem is that authority and control over every facet of mainstream schooling remains firmly in the minds, hands, and hearts of those who believe the reproduction of the dominant culture is the paramount goal of the education system. They may be right, but what does that say about an education system where compulsory, universal, and secular are the cornerstone principles for all learners? It is not as though one can choose not to attend schools, home-schooling being an exception for a very small minority. What does that reflect about New Zealand's particular brand of biculturalism, egalitarianism, and a fair go for all its citizens? At the societal level, there is a consistent message that has persisted for about 200 years that the dominant society legitimately, morally, and ethically is entitled to a greater share of the benefits of the fruits of Aotearoa New Zealand. They are the majority, they signed a treaty of cession with Māori in 1840, and they hold the position of power vis-à-vis Māori society. In a most insightful article published in 1977, Renwick, then the director-general of education for New Zealand, argued, "Rights are entitlements. They are claims that individuals have, against all other members of the society of which they are a member" (Renwick 1977, 3). Māori claim they have entitlements as tangata whenua or as the Indigenous inhabitants of this land. Māori also claim that the Treaty of Waitangi affirmed their status of *tino rangatiratanga* or absolute authority over their lands, waters, and possessions. The chiefs' abdication of this authority, asserted by some, is inexplicable. Māori further claim that those things, objects, or symbols valued by them (*taonga*) were also protected by the same Treaty. Mainstream New Zealand, in moments of greater clarity of thought, has made concessions on most of these entitlements, but the question of cession has never been open for debate since 1840. Specter (2010, 6) argues that the "most blatant forms of denialism are rarely malevolent; they combine decency, a fear of change, and the misguided desire to do good—for our health, our families, and the world." This is the brand of denialism practised by most

Pākehā New Zealanders. At its base it is patronizing and in daily life one is compelled to feel grateful for small mercies—hardly the foundation for mutuality and social justice. Among a significant proportion of the Māori population there is a utopian view that argues that the past can be lived in the present and projected into the future. This is a damaging denial, but unlike that of the Pākehā it makes no real impact on the rest of the population.

In my statement of the problem, I have tried to create a background where "contested places" are defined by competing conceptions of a broad range of interconnected perspectives, some of which are political, some theoretical, and some empirical. The point of debating contested places is to provide "new ways of seeing old problems that can lead to new questions and new possibilities" (M. Young 2008, 118). These are the thoughts I have in mind in developing this essay. There are three contested places identified. The first is politically oriented. Most forms of contestation can be described as being politically oriented, because that is the nature of a contest. Contest suggests struggle, encounter, and debate, but also winners and losers.

Mainstreaming or Māori Control of Māori Education

The fundamental contestation in Māori education at the present time is not about underachievement, participation, or retention in schooling but rather the answer to the question: Mainstreaming or Māori control of Māori education? The greatest fear for those who advocate mainstreaming is the issue of Māori separate development, but the problem is rarely framed in such terms. Preference is given instead to options designed to combat underachievement of Māori students in mainstream schools. Up-to-date research evidence from mainstream sources shows a closing of the "achievement gap" between Māori and non-Māori (Alton-Lee 2015). Two questions come immediately to mind: Will current practices lead to a closing of the achievement gap so that there will be parity within a reasonable period—for example, within a generation? Secondly, will closing the achievement gap make a real difference in the ongoing education of Māori learners? Māori *whānau* (families) want their children to be school achievers and at the same time enhanced in their identities as Māori. Most Maōri want mainstream schools to deliver the best possible education for their children, while also enhancing their identities as Māori. This is asking for no more than what Pākehā parents expect for their children as a result of 20,000 hours of compulsory schooling. They, too, want and expect both achievement and enhanced identities as Pākehā New Zealanders. A critical fact is that most Māori whānau enroll their children in mainstream schools; however, kaupapa Māori schools (Māori immersion) are not as available as mainstream (Pākehā immersion) schools. There is no research I am aware of that tells us whether more Māori whānau would enroll their children in kaupapa Māori schools if they were as accessible as mainstream schools. On the other hand, there is some evidence showing that an increasing proportion of kaupapa Māori schools are producing both high-achieving students and students who are strongly identifying with their Māori identities (Takao et al. 2010). These schools have been in existence for the last 30 years and there is a strong push from them, their teachers, their governing bodies, and their parent communities (whānau, *marae, hapū*) for full resourcing and authority to control themselves. Māori jealously hold fast to the aphorism, *Ma tātou anō, tātou e korero* (We speak for ourselves). The affirmation is as forcefully upheld among Māori as it is between Māori and non-Māori. It is likely to have its roots in traditional tribalism, but it also strongly manifests itself in the modern world in demands for consultation, cooperation, collaboration, and democratic principles such as the right to be heard and the responsibility to be listened to.

I argued elsewhere that Māori have already demonstrated a "radical potential" to both transform their own cultural positioning (Penetito 2005) and contribute to a transformation of society-at-large in the interests of all citizens (Penetito 2009; Mulholland 2006). This is a path perceived by some (Rata 2004, 2005; Rata and Openshaw 2006) as being potentially damaging on a number of scores. These perceptions involve New Zealanders' fanciful ideal of the country's empathetic race relations record and of English language competence as a basic requirement for citizenship, and, perhaps most detrimental of all, the challenging of conditions underlying the essentials for democracy. These claims sit firmly within the Popperian falsification scientific ethic (Fuller 2006), while there is, according to Rata (2004), an absence of scholarly critical scrutiny in the kaupapa Māori approach. She claims the approach is treated as non-problematic. This position, however, could be a problem for the leading Māori education advocates, the majority of whom are lay members of communities (whānau, hapū, iwi, marae) rather than academics, researchers, and officials. These Māori communities are traditionally layered in discourse.[3] The realization of the potential of kaupapa Māori in education, through the resurrection of what the American philosopher Lear (2006, 141) refers to as an "ego ideal of radical hope" was about Māori being courageous and taking action in line with an ideal and in response to the most dramatic destruction of their very subjectivity: loss of who they are through the loss of their language. What the academics, researchers, politicians, or anyone else has to say about the sacrificing of scientific method, rationalism, and even democracy is seen as trivial in comparison. Traditional Māori scholars like Tikao (Tikao et al. 1990) and contemporary ones like Graham Smith (1991) and Macfarlane (1997), researchers like Linda Tuhiwai Smith (2005) and Royal (2003), critical activists like Walker (1987, 1990) and Ramsden and Spoonley (1993), visionary psychologists like Durie (1998), pragmatic schooling innovators like Milne (2008), and educational reformers like Bishop, O'Sullivan, and Berryman (2010) have tirelessly reproduced the arguments and the rationale that contextualize the kaupapa Māori agenda within contemporary mainstream discourses. They have done this by answering as best they can the questions Māori have wanted answered. These questions are personal first before they can be answered institutionally. To quote once again from Popper (Lam 2013, 850), "The democratic institutions cannot improve themselves. The problem of improving them is always a problem for persons rather than for institutions."

When teachers consider questions about what it means for Māori learners to be Māori and why this matters, the beginning point is an appreciation of the need for a nuanced approach rather than the common equalitarian affirmation of "I treat them all the same" or "they need to learn to fit in."

In the next section, the contested place is mainly a theoretical discussion about one tenet of a social justice theory related to the prioritizing of the individual to such a degree that down-playing due reference to "difference" leads to cultural group oppression.

Social Justice Where Differences Are Not Deficits

I turn now to the quest for social justice as a strategy for redirecting the emphasis in how to approach an education for Māori that prioritizes their interests, their motivations, and their aspirations. From my earliest reflections on what to write about in this chapter on contested places, I have to admit to a sense of drowning in an over-supply of issues, each of which was worth contesting. The seemingly entrenched problem of shifting the locus of debate in Māori education from explaining what we already know to predicting what has yet to be known rests comfortably on keeping consistent with paths already travelled. Māori education since Europeanization has expanded the horizons of every Māori without exception, but the problem has been, in the main, a one-sided struggle for recognition and opportunity. The European horizon has also been enhanced through association with Māori, but for the most part minimally. Pākehā New Zealanders have made the deliberate choice in most cases to be exceedingly selective about those elements of the Māori world they will be familiar with, or will adopt or adapt to suit their requirements. Two examples include taking advantage of the Māori predisposition towards spiritual behaviour and proselytizing the Christian belief system, and later capitalizing on the Māori formalized schools of tribal learning (wānanga) and establishing mission schools in 1816. From 1867 on, Native Schools were established across the country (Simon 1998). From a Māori perspective, this created a dilemma. A passage from Bateson and Bateson (1988) encapsulates this dilemma:

> The issue of consistency is the issue of how things *fit together*, not of whether they are the same. Our ideas about [education] and about the [student] have to fit together with the [student's] own experience. A certain consistency is necessary to integration, but uniformity is surely one of those things that become toxic beyond a certain level. (68, emphasis in original)

Māori experience a toxicity as an over-bearing force for conformity, and it was never more emphatic as in the historical period of assimilation and integration from the 1930s to the 1970s. When the social reformists were asking how much diversity this society could tolerate (Hunn 1961), Māori were far more concerned about the question, How much conformity ought this society tolerate? As the popular press reported at the time, Māori were likening the government sponsoring of integration to "what the shark said to the snapper." Difference was definitely aligned with deficit over this period and, without realizing it at the time, Māori were struggling for their very existence as Māori.

Following the work of the distinguished feminist philosopher Iris Marion Young (1990), who argues the need to distinguish between an approach to equality and fairness that gives primacy to "having" and one that gives primacy to "doing," we need to address the following question: Given the dominance of New Zealand's colonial history, what conception of social justice "requires not the melting away of differences, but institutions that promote reproduction of and respect for group differences without oppression" (47)?

From its very beginning as a British colony, New Zealand was seen as a destiny for the taking. There are a variety of representations of this view, but the general consensus among historians is that Aotearoa would inevitably become New Zealand (King 2007), with authority and control shifting from Māori to the Crown. Beginning with the adventurers, then the traders from various parts of the world, then the missionaries, entrepreneurs, and politicians, all of whom arrived in Aotearoa to convert the natives or, if necessary, to obliterate them, but above all else to acquire the land. Such patterns of colonialism and imperialism were already well proven in other parts of the world, such as the Americas and Australia. The imperialist concept of "having" prioritizes materialist notions and is at base an economic concern, while "doing" suggests a more symbolic approach and leans heavily on moral principles such as self-respect, opportunity, power, and honour. The materialist application of social justice is epitomized by the scholarship of Rawls (1971) and his libertarian distributive principle,[4] whereas the symbolic application of social justice argues for a difference principle (I. Young 1990) on the grounds of incommensurability. Incommensurability highlights the radically different fundamental values that separate Māori culture from Pākehā culture. It would be nonsense to suggest a blanket denial of each other's core values, but at the level of fundamentals such as the priority of the collective versus the individual, the strong belief in secular versus spiritual orientations, and the priority of orality over literacy, the issue is not about difference per se but about significant differences. It is in the argument about significant difference that I think Young's book, *Justice and the Politics of Difference* (1990), speaks volumes for the Aotearoa New Zealand context.

Despite the fact that Māori traditionally share a great deal in common among their tribes, it is the differences between them that are held fast across generations. Māori share such values as *manaakitanga* (hospitality), language (te reo; there is only one language with a variety of dialects), spirituality (*wairuatanga* or the belief that there is a power greater than man), the rightness of one's actions (*tikanga* [custom]), community (the marae as the traditional home), and the genealogical connection or *whakapapa*. The saying is, *E kore koe e ngaro, he kakano i ruia mai i Rangiātea* (You will never be lost because you are the seed sown from the ancient marae of Rangiātea). The differences are honoured in the way orators tell their stories, which are particular to their place, even when the stories are interpreted differently in other locations. In Māori thinking there is no one right way to interpret the stories; each one is right for where they are and who they are. In Western minds this thinking epitomizes relativist logic, whereas in Māori minds it is a reflection of reality.

Contestation of Curriculum as Knowledge and Pedagogy

Over the last 30 years (1980–2010), Māori education policies have responded dramatically to a particularly volatile transitionary period in New Zealand's history. The most telling change was a major shift in the economy and consequently in politics from social welfarism to conservative neo-liberalism (Hughes and Lauder 1991; G. Smith 1992). The shift provided sufficient ambiguity across the education system and within public sector decision-making processes that a major opportunity for Māori to take the initiative and promulgate developments in their own interests became apparent. From bitter experience, Māori recognize that there are few times of relative peace and harmony when opportunities for them to make major advances in their own cultural and social wellbeing can take place without the impositions and constraints of the dominating culture. This time was one of those periods.

After almost 150 years of state-funded formal schooling, there are simply not enough Māori teachers in mainstream schools, nor are there enough Pākehā teachers with the depth of knowledge about the Māori child and his or her world to engender confidence among Māori parents that their children will continue to grow and develop as Māori and as future citizens of Aotearoa New Zealand. In response to this Catch 22, a significant proportion of the Māori public chose to vote with their feet. Throughout the 1980s, a cohort of courageous Māori took the initiative and established an alternative system of formal education, Kaupapa Māori, where everything is structured to fulfill the ideal of *kia Māori*, to be Māori, and simultaneously, to be educated (Nepe 1991; G. Smith 1997). These activists and those who worked with them are truly what the critical geographer Harvey (2000, 233) refers to as "insurgent architects at work."

As in the social justice discussion, there is no suggestion here that Pākehā teachers have consciously rejected acquiring knowledge of *te ao Māori* (the Māori world), only that most have not actively pursued, either through experience or through an in-depth understanding, Māori language, history, custom, and so on. Yet, whether rejected or not, too many Māori children have fallen by the wayside, and after 10 years of compulsory schooling have departed with few fond recollections of schooling and without the basic ingredients to pursue higher learning. All the debates about whether Māori are doing enough to help themselves educationally, whether non-Māori teachers are culturally responsive or not, whether kaupapa Māori schooling is separatist, or whether the curriculum in schools is culturally inclusive are valid queries that contribute to a central existential dilemma: Can a mainstream education system truly deliver an education to fulfill the aspirations of a non-dominant cultural group (Māori) intent on maintaining and developing its own educational futures? Probably the most intensive effort ever has been invested in attempting to bring about a positive answer to this question. The government, through the two key education agencies of state—the Ministry of Education (2011a, 2011b) and the Education Review Office (2014)—has been charged with ensuring everything they can do is targeted to bring about the necessary transformations. In the fields of research there have been corresponding investments, and the leading contractor in this area is undoubtedly Russell Bishop and his colleagues at the University of Waikato. Since 2003 the group (Bishop et al. 2003; Bishop and Berryman 2006) has produced ground-breaking research into explorations of the causes of Māori educational underachievement and strategies for reversing the trend. Despite the fact that real gains have been made, problems persist, such as confusion about the culture of the Māori child, uneven implementation of teacher professional development, and the problem of measuring student progress (Bishop 2012). From another angle, mainstream institutions are exceedingly difficult places to exercise values like *manaaki* (hospitality), *aroha* (love), and mana (respect), because these are emotion-driven activities instead of reason-driven.

The third contested place relates to the saying, *He waka eke noa*, meaning "We are all in this together." In answering the question posed above, the system has little choice but to meet the challenge and to enhance Māori culture as an integral part of New Zealand culture. Anything less would be tokenistic. The renaissance that Māori have experienced over the last 30 years provides the radical potential for transforming both the consciousness and materiality of New Zealand identity in a manner never experienced previously. Before that can happen, a critique of mainstream efforts to draw Māori cultural activities into mainstream institutions, seemingly without having to make major structural adjustments to those institutions, must be rejected. These cultural activities are not the naïve policy simulacra of assimilation and integration of the 1950s and 1960s, in that they are far more penetrative; they play on the hearts and minds of those who want to be a part of the whole while remaining separate, but lack the means to hold fast to the whole. The strongest appeal is made to the idea that as a society we must learn to live together if the society is to be a just one. It is the learning that is at the heart of this proposition. In order to bring about an equitable allocation of the resources within society, it is necessary to establish and maintain a socially and culturally just society. How much an education system at the secondary level can contribute to the allocation of resources, let alone having an allocation being an equitable one, is a moot point (Bernstein 1974). Nevertheless, I argue that the major gains Māori have achieved over the last three decades, running parallel with the disproportionate number of Māori living below the poverty line (Rashbrooke 2013), has created an extremely volatile situation that is potentially devastating for race relations.

It is this final point of familiarizing secondary school teachers with the culturally responsive practices for "being Māori" that I think is most problematic. To ensure Māori cultural survival, teachers need to include in their *kete* (tool kit) an appreciation and knowledge of the "materiality" of the Māori world. This is about historical, contemporary, and future thinking that is aligned with Māori knowledge and ways of knowing. Teachers must be equipped to legitimate a Māori subjectivity, and by that I mean being predisposed to accommodate the emotional and inner experiences Māori learners bring with them to classrooms. And they need to be able to confirm emancipatory Māori ways of knowing, for example through exposure to storytelling, to the beauty of memorization, and to a system of values that has survived for millennia.

Because of the nature of the first two contestations, mainstreaming and social justice, it is important to engage critically with the current mainstream theory, policy, and practice of raising Māori educational underachievement. The stance I take borrows from critical theory in the sense of challenging the taken-for-granted world of researchers, policy writers, and practitioners, especially where their advocacy impacts negatively on Māori aspirations. The curriculum is a construct that includes a selection of knowledge from the cultures of a society (Lawton 1983). Part of its definition includes pedagogy or what counts as a valid approach to the imparting of knowledge as experienced through the eyes of the learners. People in positions of influence decide what will count as knowledge. That truism holds whether the curriculum is designed for Māori, Pākehā, or any other social group. Despite the rhetoric, the curriculum is never culture-free or value-free. It is important, therefore, that the key learning objectives, their meanings, and the exploration of the most influential social relations is part of this critique. It is not obvious, for example, that from a Māori perspective outcomes should determine what is taught, how it is taught, and the way it should be assessed in advance of enacting the curriculum. The popular saying is, "If you don't know where you are going, how do you know when you have arrived?" From a Eurocentric point of view this seems to make logical good sense. The Indigenous literature does not affirm this stance as being either necessary, inevitable, or even sensible. Metaphors such as "the tree of life" (Sanga et al. 2005), "the circle of life," and "the web of life" (O'Sullivan 1999) underline the significance of the connectedness of all things, "a deep identification with all that is," to quote O'Sullivan (1999, 229). The iwi of the Ngāti Hauā region have a saying about their mountain: *"Ka huri tonu atu ki te tikitiki o Te Ihingārangi, ka hoki anō taku tihi maunga, ki taku taumata tonu, ki Maungatautari, I nohoia ai taku tupuna a Koroki e tau ana"*—"And thus it is a homecoming to the stronghold of my ancestor Te Ihingārangi and I return to the summit of my mountain, Maungatautari, blessed by my esteemed ancestor, Koroki and my mind and my heart are at ease." The saying expresses the profound sense of the relational quality of the unfolding process of evolution.

Democratizing the Education System, Emancipating Learning

Each of these three grounds for competing conceptions of social justice—language and culture, schooling, and the curriculum—are manifest in the education system. They constitute the primary contested places where Māori and Pākehā stand in a dialectical relationship[5] with each other. This process aimed at democratizing education for all its citizens is what the British scientists Rose and Rose (1982, 54) refer to as "a world becoming, not a world static."

Increasing the volume of Māori language teaching and learning in schools so that we can all learn to better live with each other is an admirable aspiration. Bilingualism could make a major contribution to an emerging, higher-order thinking among the citizens in both worlds. Graham Smith refers to the process as "cultural citizenship,"[6] which is a blending of mātauranga Māori systems and Western scientific systems. In bicultural terms, the blending is only incommensurable where there is no incentive to learn to live together. The real problem—so this argument goes—is how to make ingenious accommodations in order to broker two cultural contexts, simultaneously straddling the two worlds.[7] Tahupārae (1995) argues that Māori students and their teachers need to face a very personal challenge if learning "to be Māori" is to be meaningful. The solutions, he argues, lie within us: *Ko au te taupā kīhai i puāwai aku moemoeā*—"I am the obstacle to the fruition of my dreams." I think Tahupārae was only partly right. Agency is undoubtedly crucial, but other conditions prevail, like whether learning experiences are aligned with the material world students belong to, or whether the purpose of the exercise makes sense, or simply whether "to be Māori" is a choice I can make.

Returning to the opening storyline, the experiences of Māori children in mainstream schools is in most cases one of conflict and compromise. Matiu knew that I was Māori like him and that we shared whakapapa and belonged to the same marae. I also think he knew instinctively that because my immediate family and I lived in town with Pākehā neighbours, and that would mean I mixed outside school life with Pākehā friends, that I must in some intimate ways be compromised by that familiarity. Like me, he knew from experience that being Māori was not achievable in a school that practised a differentiated context through things that only Māori were asked to do. Only Māori children were asked to stand up and leave the classroom so the visiting nurse could check their hair for *kutus* or head lice and their bodies for *hakihaki* or scabies. These actions no longer take place in today's enlightened schools, but they are simply replaced by whatever is the current prejudice against Māori, as in guilt by association with gangs and drugs, violence, poverty, and neglect. My annoyance is also easily explainable; I knew Matiu was right about my out-of-school associations, even though I had no say in where I lived and little say about who my mates were outside the classroom. According to him, I wasn't the same sort of Māori he was. I had an English name, and so for him I was probably half-caste, a dismissive term often heard among adults that connected the holder to Pākehā or Māori, whichever side was being denigrated. I never really thought of myself as being half of anything, no matter who was using the term. Learning what it means "to be Māori" is like learning to be anything or anyone else. It will only be achieved by the acquisition of mātauranga (knowledge), tikanga (cultural practices), and te reo

Māori (communicative competence) at the level of everyday life within a socially just contemporary society. That is the challenge the contested place of schools has to face up to.

Notes

1. See Milne (2008). There is a growing concern among some about the use of "mainstream" to describe the dominant form of schooling in New Zealand. It seems to me to be accurate in that relations between Māori and Pākehā are hegemonic, and when that is no longer the case then mainstream would no longer be an apt description. However, I am reminded of the maxim that an "ought" does not follow logically from an "is." The New Zealand education and schooling system can accurately be described as a racist system, quoting Milne, and therefore her justification for describing it as "white-stream." I still prefer to use "mainstream" because as well as being racist, the system could also be described as ethno-centric (European-oriented), socio-centric (middle-class), and cognito-centric (analytic/linear-oriented).

2. Denialism is a concept I have borrowed from a book by Michael Specter (2010). The denialism he refers to concerns the general public's antagonism to science and the irrational thinking that surrounds new scientific discoveries and evidence-based conversations. Those who deny these advances in science opt instead for myths, shoddy investigation, and misinformation. It is my experience that Māori generally accept that Pākehā, as the majority population and as the Crown signatories to the Treaty of Waitangi, have the right to govern New Zealand citizens. They also have the obligation to recognize the status of Māori as *tangata whenua*, and they are obliged to ensure that Māori have an education that recognizes them as Māori and equips them to live in the world on the same basis as all other New Zealanders.

3. In a traditional Māori sense, every Māori is perceived as being his or her own person, as being a *rangatira* or leader in his or her own right. The food that sustains a chief is *kōrero* (talk). This is the meaning of the saying, *Ko te kai a te rangatira, he kōrero*. Such a definition flies in the face of those who take the view that the ordinary person, not just those of rangatira genealogy, is imbued with a strong sense of the self. The collective is highly significant but the individual is also powerful, full of *mana*.

4. The literature on distributive justice is massive, and all I can do in this chapter is refer to a selection of the key components of those works as an attempt to keep faith with their arguments.
5. There is a wealth of literature that deals with the concept of dialectical relations (e.g., Harvey 1996; Kemmis 1986), but what Wren says (1986, 119) is closer to how I want to use the term. He argues that dialectic refers to a unity of opposites, a clash of ideas or forces which are separate and opposed but whose contradiction includes or can give birth to a deeper unity. The relation between the ideal of social justice and the realities of power and conflict is dialectical—a unity of opposites, where each needs the other.
6. Personal comunication, July 16, 2014 at Ako Pai, Faculty of Education, Victoria University of Wellington, Tertiary Sector Māori Education Leaders Forum.
7. Personal communication regarding Te Wānanga o Raukawa, (2013) Wai 2258 Whakatupu Mātauranga Claim to the Waitangi Tribunal, Otaki, NZ, August 26, 2013.

References

Alton-Lee, Adrienne. 2014. *Ka Hikitia: A Demonstration Report. Effectiveness of Te Kotahitanga, Phase 5, 2010-12*. Wellington, NZ: Ministry of Education.

Bateson, Gregory, and Mary Catherine Bateson. 1988. *Angels Fear: Towards an Epistemology of the Sacred*. Toronto: Bantam Books.

Bernstein, Basil. 1974. "Education Cannot Compensate for Society." In *School and Society—A Sociological Reader*, edited by Ben Cosin, Roger Dale, Geoff Esland, and D.F. Swift, 61-6. London: Routledge & Kegan Paul.

Bishop, Russell. 2012. "Pretty Difficult: Implementing Kaupapa Māori Theory in English-Medium Secondary Schools." *New Zealand Journal of Educational Studies* 47 (2): 38-50.

Bishop, Russell, and Mere Berryman. 2006. *Culture Speaks: Cultural Relationships and Classroom Learning*. Wellington, NZ: Huia Publishers.

Bishop, Russell, Mere Berryman, Sarah-Jane Tiakiwai, and Cath Richardson. 2003. "Te Kōtahitanga: The Experiences of Year 9 and 10 Māori Students in Mainstream Classrooms." (Report to the Ministry of Education). Māori Education Research Institute (MERI), School of education, University of Waikato, Hamilton and Poutama Pounamu Research and Development Centre (PPRDC), Tauranga.

Bishop, Russell, Dominic O'Sullivan, and Mere Berryman. 2010. *Scaling Up Education Reform: Addressing the Politics of Disparity*. Wellington, NZ: NZCER.

Durie, Mason. 1998. *Te Mana, Te Kāwanatanga: The Politics of Māori Self-Determination.* Auckland, NZ: Oxford University Press.

Education Review Office. 2014. *Towards Equitable Outcomes in Secondary Schools: Good Practice.* Wellington: New Zealand Government.

Fuller, Steve. 2006. *Kuhn vs Popper: The Struggle for the Soul of Science.* London: Icon Books.

Harvey, David. 2000. *Spaces of Hope.* Berkeley: University of California Press.

Hughes, David, and Hugh Lauder. 1991. "Human Capital Theory and the Wastage of Talent in New Zealand." *New Zealand Journal of Educational Studies* 26 (1): 5–35.

Hunn, J. K. 1961. *Report on the Department of Māori Affairs.* Wellington, NZ: Government Printer.

Kemmis, Stephen. 1986. *Curriculum Theorising: Beyond Reproduction Theory.* Melbourne, Australia: Deakin University.

King, Michael. 2007. *The Penguin History of New Zealand, Illustrated.* North Shore, NZ: Penguin.

Lam, Chi-Ming. 2013. "A Popperian Approach to Education for Open Society." *Educational Philosophy and Theory* 45 (8), 845–59. https://doi.org/10.1111/j.1469-5812.2011.00829.x

Lawton, Denis. 1983. *Curriculum Studies and Educational Planning.* London: Hodder & Stoughton.

Lear, Jonathon. 2006. *Radical Hope: Ethics in the Face of Cultural Devastation.* Cambridge, MA: Harvard University Press.

Macfarlane, Angus Hikairo. 1997. "The Hikairo Rationale: Teaching Students with Emotional and Behavioural Difficulties." *Waikato Journal of Education* 3: 153–68. http://dx.doi.org/10.15663/wje.v3i1.499

Milne, Ann. 2008. "The Short End of a Smaller and Smaller Identity Stick." Keynote address at the NZARE Annual Conference, Massey University, Palmerston North, NZ, November 25, 2008.

Ministry of Education. 2007. *Developing the Second Māori Education Strategy.* Wellington, NZ: Ministry of Education.

———. 2008. *Ka Hikitia: Managing for Success: Māori Education Strategy 2008–2011.* Wellington, NZ: Ministry of Education.

———. 2011a. *Whakapūmautia, Papakōwhaitia, Tau Ana: Grasp, Embrace and Realise.* Wellington, NZ: Ministry of Education. https://www.pmawards.education.govt.nz/assets/Uploads/PageResources/Whakapumautia-Papakowhaitia-Tau-ana.pdf

———. 2011b. *Tātaiako: Cultural Competencies for Teachers of Māori Learners.* Wellington, NZ: Ministry of Education. http://www.teacherscouncil.govt.nz/required/tataiako.stm

———. 2013. *Ka Hikitia: Accelerating Success 2013-2017*. Wellington, NZ: Ministry of Education. https://www.education.govt.nz/assets/Documents/Ministry/ Strategies-and-policies/Ka-Hikitia/KaHikitiaAcceleratingSuccessEnglish.pdf

Mulholland, Malcolm, ed. 2006. *State of the Māori Nation: Twenty-First Century Issues in Aotearoa*. Auckland, NZ: Reed Publishing.

Nepe, T.M. 1991. "E hae e tenei reanga Te Toi Huarewa Tipuna: Kaupapa Māori: An Educational Intervention System." Master's thesis, University of Auckland.

O'Sullivan, Edmund. 1999. *Transformative Learning: Educational Vision for the 21st Century*. London: Zed Books.

Penetito, Wally. 2005. "Scenario for a Māori Education Authority: Mainstreaming or Māori Control." In *Education for Policy Directions in Aotearoa New Zealand: Is There a Third Way?* edited by John Codd and Keith Sullivan, 141-60. Palmerston North, NZ: Dunmore Press.

———. 2009. "The Struggle to Educate the Māori in New Zealand." In *The Routledge International Companion to Multicultural Education*, edited by James A. Banks, 288-300. New York: Routledge, Taylor and Francis Group.

Ramsden, Irihapeti, and Paul Spoonley. 1993. "The Cultural Safety Debate in Nursing Education in Aotearoa." *New Zealand Annual Review of Education* 3: 161-74. https:// doi.org/10.26686/nzaroe.v0i3.1075

Rashbrooke, Max. 2013. *Inequality: A New Zealand Crisis*. Wellington, NZ: Bridget Williams Books.

Rata, Elizabeth. 2004. "Ethnic Ideologies in New Zealand Education: What's Wrong with Kaupapa Māori?" Paper presented at Teacher Education Forum of Aotearoa New Zealand Conference (TEFANZ), Auckland College of Education, Auckland, NZ, July 2004.

———. 2005. "The Role of Cultural Fundamentalism in Māori Educational Underachievement." Refereed paper for the NZARE Conference, University of Otago, Dunedin, NZ, December 6-9, 2005.

Rata, Elizabeth, and Roger Openshaw. 2006. *Public Policy and Ethnicity: The Politics of Ethnic Boundary Making*. Hampshire, England: Palgrave Macmillan.

Rawls, John. 1971. *A Theory of Justice*. Cambridge, MA: Harvard University Press.

Renwick, W.L. 1977. "Rights of Individuals to Education." *Delta* 20: 17-21.

Rose, Hilary, and Steven Rose. 1982. "On Oppositions to Reductionism." In *Against Biological Determinism—The Dialectics of Biology Group*, edited by Steven Rose, 50-9. London: Allison & Busby.

Royal, Te Ahukaramū Charles, ed. 2003. *The Woven Universe: Selected Writings of Rev. Māori Marsden*. Otaki, NZ: Estate of Rev. Māori Marsden.

Sanga, Kabini, C. Hall, C. Chu, and L. Crowl, eds. 2005. *Rethinking Aid Relationships in Pacific Education*. Wellington, NZ: He Pārekereke, Institute for Research and Development in Māori and Pacific Education.

Simon, Judith, ed. 1998. *Ngā Kura Māori: The Native Schools System 1867–1969*. Auckland, NZ: Auckland University Press.

Smith, Graham H. 1991. "Reform and Māori Educational Crisis: A Grand Illusion." In *Proceedings of the Post-Primary Teachers' Association Curriculum Conference*, edited by Phillip Capper, 32–40. Wellington, NZ: PPTA.

———. 1992. "Tāne-Nui-a-Rangi's Legacy...Propping Up the Sky: Kaupapa Māori as Resistance and Intervention." Paper presented at NZARE/AARE Joint Conference, Deakin University, Melbourne, Australia, November 20, 1992.

———. 1997. "The Development of Kaupapa Māori: Theory and Praxis." PHD diss., University of Auckland.

Smith, Linda Tuhiwai. 2005. "On Tricky Ground: Researching the Native in the Age of Uncertainty." In *The Sage Handbook of Qualitative Research*, 3rd ed., edited by Norman K. Denzin and Yvonne S. Lincoln, 85–108. Thousand Oaks, CA: Sage Publications.

Specter, Michael. 2010. *Denialism: How Irrational Thinking Harms the Planet and Threatens Our Lives*. New York: Penguin Books.

Tahupārae, John. 1995. "Te Tūtukitanga Māori Achievement Symposium." Presentation to New Zealand Institute for Education, Wellington High School, Wellington, NZ, August 31 to September 2, 1995.

Tākao, Nuki, Denis Grennell, Kate McKegg, and Nan Wehipeihana. 2010. *Te Piko o Te Māhuri: The Key Attributes of Successful Kura Kaupapa Māori*. Wellington: New Zealand Ministry of Education Research Division.

Tikao, Teone Taare, and Herries Beattie. 1990. *Tikao Talks: Ka Taoka Tapu o Te Ao Ko Hatu, Treasures from the Ancient World of the Māori*. Auckland, NZ: Penguin Books.

Walker, Ranginui. 1987. *Nga Tau Tohetohe: Years of Anger*. Auckland NZ: Penguin Books.

———. 1990. *Ka Whawhai Tonu Mātou: Struggle Without End*. Auckland, NZ: Penguin Books.

Young, Iris Marion. 1990. *Justice and the Politics of Difference*. Princeton, NJ: Princeton University Press.

Young, Michael F.D. 2008. *Bringing Knowledge Back In: From Social Constructivism to Social Realism in the Sociology of Education*. London: Routledge Taylor & Francis.

7 | He Pelapela anei ka 'Ōlelo a ka Hawai'i?
Contested Values in Language Revitalization

K. LAIANA WONG & SAM L. NO'EAU WARNER

Background and Prospects for Survival

The great shift from Hawaiian to English coincided with the arrival of Captain James Cook in 1778[1] and continued until Hawaiian became moribund during the first half of the 20th century. It was only more recently that the first cohesive efforts were launched to reverse that shift. The establishment of the Pūnana Leo Hawaiian language immersion preschools in 1984 marked the advent of a language revitalization campaign targeting young children.[2] The nexus of this campaign was clearly located in a wider community within which English had become the lingua franca, and the number of native speakers of Hawaiian was decreasing rapidly. Since that time, and despite numerous obstacles, there has been significant advancement among youth who are now arguably fluent in Hawaiian. Many are now raising families of their own in Hawaiian. For some critics, however, this new version of Hawaiian has departed drastically from its pre-decline state.[3] One reason for this critique has been the creation of a plethora of new words designed to accommodate the pre-existence of English concepts in learners' repertoires.⁴ This problem is highlighted by a pervasive tendency to calque English ways of speaking and to employ English phonology in the production of Hawaiian.⁵ This critique is not without merit and challenges us to find remedies.

The issue of whether or not the emergent language will be considered authentic after undergoing these innovations is likely to become increasingly moot with the inevitable passing of elderly native speakers. That is, prescriptive notions that fuel the resistance to innovation are likely to subside in tandem with the collective memory of the community.⁶ Those old-timers who remain will find themselves holding the minority position. This is perhaps the strongest argument against prescriptivism as a strategy for promoting language survival.⁷ Nevertheless, the failure to salvage all aspects of the language, particularly those words and phrases whose English translations are offensive, is likely to limit the linguistic distance between Hawaiian and English.⁸ Resistance to such a process, however, can also be viewed as a prescriptive position. This chapter advocates for the latter, as it values all Hawaiian words and phrases, including those referring to body parts and bodily function, and strives to maintain separation between their meanings and the meanings of their English translations.

There is evidence from Hawaiian literature that appropriate contexts of use exist for most of the lexical items and phrases that might be considered censorable in translation. This evidence is embodied in a wealth of examples found in epic stories published and circulated throughout Hawaiʻi during the 19th and 20th centuries. A vast body of literature was made available to the public, including children, who were sometimes called upon to read to their Elders.⁹ As a public forum, we can assume that the newspapers made public any and all language that was appropriate for its readers. The failure to maintain certain aspects of the language leaves a gap in the logic that drives revitalization efforts.

In Hawaiʻi, policy has been established whereby primary and secondary school students may elect to undertake a course of study that is conducted in the Hawaiian language.¹⁰ The content of that course of study, however, is not delivered exclusively in Hawaiian. Some English is used to explicate concepts and topics for which the Hawaiian lexicon has no adequate counterparts. The state, however, has rather vague parameters in this regard and is primarily concerned with the adequate coverage of a set of nationally mandated content standards. Nevertheless, this overt use of English to cover certain subjects is less problematic than the use of a Hawaiian that is covertly imbued with English. There is no de jure policy that designates the particular forms of Hawaiian language that are to be excluded. As a result, there is nothing to curb this covert infiltration of English into Hawaiian, and avoidance of any part of the language can be attributed to the de facto influence of English.

Underestimating the Power of Words

Second language speakers of Hawaiian are often unaware of the power of words in their second language. Misconceptions of that power stem from a tendency to comprehend novel concepts in terms of those previously established. We rely on what Grace (1981) calls the "postulate of intertranslatability" to guide our estimation of the potency of words we encounter in our second language. That is, we assume that words are equal to their translations in the language with which we are most familiar, the consequences of which involve either underestimation of their potency and capricious overproduction, or overestimation of their potency and unwarranted underproduction. We will look first at problems of overproduction.

Second language learners may well be aware of the basic referential meanings of the words in their target language, but they are often unaware of the appropriate contexts for their use. Lack of experience can easily lead to capricious overproduction within inappropriate contexts. Overproduction marks the speaker as either unaware of or unconcerned with locating appropriate contexts for language use. Whereas a native speaker is generally aware of the social consequences of words in the native language, a second language learner is likely to have only a partial understanding of their potency, having acquired them more recently and comprehending them based on first language counterparts. With the first language as a reference point for these meanings and values, the learner is prone to unleash them at inopportune moments. It shortchanges children, in particular, who need access to language that facilitates the expression of anger. They need to be equipped with all the available options and to recognize appropriate contexts for their use.[11]

Beside the referential meanings, there are other, more metaphorical meanings that imbue such additions with power that is obscured from the learner's level of awareness. The relationships among words via homonymy or synonymy, for example, can extend meanings beyond those initially available to the second language learner. Not having the same linguistic experience as someone who has acquired the language natively, it is difficult to fathom the amount of perlocutionary force (i.e., the force that is perceived by the receiver; Searle 1990) exerted by certain lexical items.[12] In attempts to produce the new language, the second language learner is generally unaware of the full effect his or her words have on the receiver.

Cross-Linguistic Interpretation and Overproduction

The consequences of language shift resemble the problems encountered in cross-linguistic interpretation where there are numerous opportunities to underestimate the illocutionary force (Searle 1990) of relatively new additions to the lexicon of a second language learner. Here we focus on synchronic, cross-cultural differences in meaning. For example, a word such as "pussy" is currently a euphemism for other, more strident alternatives available in English referring to female genitalia. This word can also be used metaphorically as a derogatory reference to a male who is not considered sufficiently masculine. Despite the misogynous relationship between the two, there is no real ambiguity here. The intended meaning is generally clear from the context. In either case, an invective force clearly exists and an affront is clearly intended. In interactions among close friends, however, particularly in informal contexts, there is an expectation that speech will be candid. Although the use of the word "pussy" here would ordinarily constitute an affront to masculinity, the intent is ambiguous. On one hand it could be to insult, while on the other it could be designed to build solidarity (Wong 1999b). The ambiguity, of course, precludes this solidarity-building strategy from being risk free. Familiarity between interlocutors, and with this way of speaking, decreases that risk. The second language learner is more likely to make a faux pas in these contexts. Note the following example: When a non-native speaker of English was asked if she would be able to travel to a conference on her own (i.e., without her husband), she exclaimed that her husband had better agree or there would be "no pussy" for him. This was quite shocking to the small group of people present, but it was clearly not intended to offend. The speaker was attempting to promote solidarity among colleagues by saying something amusing and was simply unaware of the full force of her words.

It is not surprising that the second language learner, having a relatively incomplete command of the target language, is apt to use it awkwardly at times. This is also true in cases of slight dialectal differences. I first learned about the word "wanker" from a friend who is a speaker of New Zealand English.[13] This word was not part of my repertoire at the time and, although I was aware of the referential meaning (i.e., *masturbator*), and that it can be insulting to males, I had not internalized a full understanding of its power. This became evident when, one day while walking on the beach at Waikīkī, my friend and I came across a man wearing a Speedo-style bathing suit. It is highly unusual for a local person to wear such a bathing suit, so I assumed that he was a tourist, a common target of criticism among locals. In an effort to reinforce solidarity with my New Zealand friend, and perhaps to socialize him into a general intolerance for tourism, I attempted to use this word at the expense of the tourist. I turned to my friend and said quite audibly, "Check out this wanker." My friend's face immediately flushed with red as he chided me, "Oh no. Don't say that." I had assumed that, because it was new to me, the tourist would certainly not be privy to its meaning. My friend clearly had a different assumption. I had underestimated the perlocutionary force of the word, at least as it affected my friend. I can only assume that it had no effect on the tourist because it generated zero reaction. That experience taught me the power of that particular word, and gave me a new perspective on second language learning in general.

Another example occurred many years ago when a book entitled *Pidgin to da Max* was published (Simonson, Sakata, and Sasaki 1981). It was designed as a glossary of common Hawai'i Creole English terms, providing some explication of the language tourists might hear during their stay in Hawai'i while, at the same time, offering a humorous view of the language that would appeal to locals. When a critique of the book appeared in a local daily newspaper, highlighting some of the more interesting entries, two Samoan words, ufa *buttocks* and kefe *circumcise*, were highlighted as words to avoid when within earshot of Samoans. In much the same way as many of the other words listed, these were humorous examples chosen to pander to the reader and to sell copies. As it turns out, the book became a top seller in Hawai'i. Unfortunately, the use of these particular words was not humorous to everyone. A Samoan friend of mine wrote to the newspaper to complain about a failure on the part of the editors to censor these words. He pointed out that had similarly offensive words in English been used in the book, they would certainly have been edited out of the newspaper article. These particular words are widely recognized in Hawai'i as Samoan expletives, even though their English glosses might seem benign. This is a clear example of the failure to apprehend the full force of words cross-linguistically. Not unlike my use of "wanker" above, in the absence of native-like understanding, these words are susceptible to capricious overproduction.

Whether or not this final example qualifies as cross-linguistic depends on what we are prepared to recognize as a language (i.e., is the individual's language the same as that of the community?). I can recall the moment I first learned of the sexual connotations associated with the word cock. Somewhat inexplicably, it was not until the age of 11. My younger brothers and I had, perhaps due its guttural sound, found its production to be an amusing distraction. We produced it repeatedly and indiscriminately, laughing each time. Our stepfather, having heard us, called us together and asked if we knew what the word meant. I can remember saying that it was when you pull back the hammer of a gun. I also knew, from early Bible study, that it was another word for rooster. He explained that it also referred to the penis and that we should not use it carelessly. This, of course, served only to increase our fascination with the word.

At the community level, overt policies outlining the boundaries for appropriate language use are generally absent. Speakers are expected to censor themselves based on a communal sense of decorum. This constitutes a covert form of control that works fairly well when communication takes place within a particular group. Across groups, however, even when their languages are quite similar, the existence of mutual intelligibility cannot be assumed. This is illustrated in the examples above. Such assumptions can evoke a range of unintended outcomes, from rather benign temporary breakdowns in communication to outright hostility. Be that as it may, language censorship is hardly plausible when the possible language use scenarios are so complex[14] and when the majority of speakers have managed to communicate over long periods of time without the benefit of policy. As implausible as it is within a somewhat healthy homogeneous language community, it is perhaps impossible within the constantly evolving context that is inherent to revitalization.

'Ōlelo Pelapela and Unwarranted Underproduction

Interestingly, most speakers of Hawaiian today utilize the word pelapela when referring to what is glossed in English as "filthy, dirty, nasty, indecent, unclean, vulgar, lewd, obscene" (Pukui and Elbert 1986, 323).

Each of these glosses suggests a capacity to cause affront to the listener or reader, with or without intent. Whether or not the same responses existed in a traditional version of Hawaiian is questionable.

This word is obviously a reduplication of the base pela, which is defined as "fertilizer, any decomposed material, especially decayed flesh and intestines removed from a corpse" (Pukui and Elbert 1986, 323). The English glosses for the modifier pelapela, and perhaps extending to the glosses of its root pela, suggest that certain aspects of language are somehow unclean. This view is further intensified by the connection between words (as referential symbols) and actual decaying flesh. This raises the question of whether or not such a view of words as filthy is aligned with traditional Hawaiian ways of thinking. It is quite likely that it was imported from elsewhere. The connection between certain aspects of the language and filth cannot be assumed as universal, although it is certainly coincidental.

Despite the fact that the term ʻōlelo pelapela is commonly heard among speakers today, it does not appear as a citation in the Pukui and Elbert (1986) dictionary. There is a separate listing for each word, but the two are not collocated. In fact, the Hawaiian phrase for *obscene language* is ʻōlelo haumia, a term that is also not listed on the Hawaiian to English side of the dictionary. The failure to cross-list terms and phrases is perhaps a consequence of the effort to represent the collection of words in a bilingual format that only reinforces the connections between English and Hawaiian. A monolingual dictionary would certainly limit those connections. The most common connection that would remain would be found in transliterations of English swear words. According to Pukui and Elbert (1986, 539), "*No swear words existed other than exclamations and insults, and from English:* kanakapiki *(son of a bitch),* Kokami *(God damn),* and kokahele iā [iū] Paka *(go to hell, you bugger).*" The latter two examples reflect the heavy influence that Christianity has had on all aspects of Hawaiian culture. Despite anti-Christian sentiments in the early struggles for control in Hawaiʻi,[15] the shift to Christianity has since pervaded the Hawaiian worldview, particularly in the area of language.

This does not mean that there was a dearth of powerful, invective words in Hawaiian. In fact, there is a belief that words have the power to cause harm as well as to heal. A famous ʻōlelo noʻeau (*proverbial saying*) in Hawaiian commonly evoked by speakers today is "I ka ʻōlelo no [nō] ke ola, i ka ʻōlelo no [nō] ka make [*Life is in speech; death is in speech*]" (Pukui 1983, 129). It is possible that one might, with harmful intent, direct ʻōlelo pelapela towards an individual, but such language would more aptly fall under one of the following speech act rubrics, excerpted from Pukui and Elbert (1986):

kūamuamu: *to revile, blaspheme, curse, swear, damn, insult*
ʻanāʻanā: *place a curse*
ʻānai: *to curse*
hāʻiliʻili: *to revile, curse, blaspheme, speak evilly*
kā i ka ʻino: *to curse, do evil to*
hoʻohalahala: *to criticize, complain, find fault*
ʻōhumu: *to grumble, complain, find fault*
nema: *to criticize, find fault, censure*
hoʻowahāwahā: *to treat with contempt, scorn, despise, abhor*
wahaʻā: *to speak heatedly and rudely*
hoʻohiki ʻino: *violent oath*, e.g., "*Pau pele, pau manō*, consumed by volcanic fire, consumed by shark [may I die if I don't keep my pledge]" (Pukui and Elbert 1986, 239).
pāleoleoā: *loud reviling talk*
hoʻoulu: *to stir up, taunt*

This list is not exhaustive. It is merely intended to illustrate the fact that Hawaiians identified speech acts that are designed to cause harm or agitate, none of which really qualifies as pelapela. The relationship between words that indicate filth and words that are set loose in order to cause harm, if one exists, is more likely derived from the intent of their producer than the off-putting nature of their referents.

The Overestimation of Power and Subsequent Avoidance

Whereas underestimation can lead to overproduction, overestimation of the power of words can lead to underproduction and perhaps total avoidance. The kapu *taboo* factor attached to the translations of certain words can also stimulate overly effusive responses; that is, such words can have a pandering effect that would otherwise be absent in contexts of native speaker interaction. The justification for prurient connotations is derived from translation, thus belying the absence of impropriety in the original context. Pukui and Elbert (1986) define the word ʻōkole as follows:

> ʻōkole. n. 1. Anus, buttocks (less polite than *lemu*). ʻŌkole maluna, Hawaiian translation of the English toast "bottoms up" [this expression is condemned by older Hawaiians as vulgar and indecent because of the sacredness of the human body in old belief]. (PCP *kootole*.) 2. A sea creature, eaten cooked, perhaps a sea anemone. 3. A kind of birthmark; round, black, and raised higher than the surface of the skin; believed caused by the mother's eating an annelid when pregnant. (282)

None of these uses is patently pelapela except for ʻōkole maluna, which is a translation from the English phrase *bottoms up*. This phrase is clearly not traditional and the negative sentiments suggested in the definition above are not generated by some sense of vulgarity. They are derived, instead, from violating kapu *sacred* notions.

The word ʻōkoleoioi *moving buttocks* refers to the act of literally turning one's back on someone else. There is no invective force in the word itself or in any vulgarity assigned to its English translation. It is rather from the symbolic gesture of turning the back to show contempt.[16] There are several other, more benign compounds that utilize the word ʻōkole. ʻŌkoleʻoiʻoi *jutting buttocks*, for example, refers to the marigold flower. ʻŌkolehao *iron buttocks* is an alcoholic beverage distilled in an iron cauldron that was perhaps of similar shape to the buttocks.

'Ōkolepuʻu refers to a bustle-style dress that was once fashionable in Hawaiʻi. Finally, the popular Cantonese snack called siu mai, a dumpling commonly known as *pork hash* in Hawaiʻi, is called 'ōkole in Hawaiian, perhaps due to its shape.

One example, however, that is characterized as "vulgar" is 'ōkole kāmano (lit., *salmon backside*). This is an 'ōlelo noʻeau *poetical saying*: "#2470 'Ōkole kāmano. Salmon backside. A vulgar expression for a white person whose backside is pink. Also expressed *Kāmano ʻula* (Red salmon)" (Pukui 1983, 269).

It would seem that the offensive power of this saying relies more on the pale foreign phenotype than on the particular body part on which it is reflected.

Any notion that the word 'ōkole could qualify as pelapela is completely dependent on its translation into English. In the language revitalization context, the negative values associated with the anus in English are assigned to the use of its linguistic counterpart in Hawaiian. This results in an inaccurate assessment of the word's value to the speech community. In fact, the pelapela aspect of this word's translations in English can be humorous at times. For me, this became clear when I first encountered a small round black creature clinging to the side of a tide pool at Kaimū, Hawaiʻi, and was told that it was called 'ōkole. This revelation raised a chuckle, almost as if it had been called an anus or asshole in English. Moreover, when my colleague went to collect it, it shriveled up into a tight package that resembled the 'ōkole glossed above as *pork hash*. It is perhaps for this reason that this particular sea anemone is called 'ōkole emiemi *shrinking anus*. Then, when my colleague told me that it was edible, I was unable to contain my laughter. This incident, in hindsight, reinforces the concerns raised in this chapter. That is, my laughter was not derived from some humorous notion inherent to the Hawaiian word. It was instead reflective of my reliance on English to understand it.

Finally, the word kūkae *excrement* is not used invectively in Hawaiian. There is, however, a euphemism that might suggest otherwise (i.e., lepo *dirt*). English glosses of kūkae such as *shit* or *crap* are definitely used invectively (e.g., *shit head* and *full of crap*). Translations of these uses, however, would make little sense in Hawaiian. That is, poʻo kūkae *shit head* and piha i ke kūkae *full of crap* are not utilized in the same way. It should be noted that there is a metaphor in Hawaiian that does suggest the idea of "shit head." Since a shrimp defecates through its head, the phrase poʻo ʻōpae *shrimp head* is used invectively with a similar force to that of "shit head." Other collocations involving kūkae are actually benign. Here are just a few examples: kūkaepuaʻa *crab grass*, kūkaeuli *octopus ink*, and kūkaelio *mushroom*. The literal translations of these words are "pig shit," "dark shit," and "horse shit," respectively.

Shift and Reverse Shift: Retaining What We Have Yet to Know

As we know, languages change with time, and so do the meanings and values of their words and phrases. Appropriateness varies with context. That which is considered appropriate in one context might be completely inappropriate in another. This is particularly salient when such contexts are separated by time. Those of us who would endeavour to revitalize a language that has been left in the past are doing so from a different, arguably foreign, perspective. Even if the language has been extensively documented, we are not automatically privy to all the nuances of its former state. We have not experienced its use in the moment but, viewing it from a distance, we rely on our interpretations of its remnants.[17] Having not participated in its use during its period of viability, we must necessarily understand it within the parameters of what we know in the present.

In the language shift scenario, this change can be attributed to a shift in the value of words, and the force they carry with them when they are released into the world. Opponents of language revitalization argue that too much has changed, and, in the best interests of the current population, new ways of looking at the world must be reflected in the revitalized language. Fishman (1991, 386) warns that revitalization attempts can be misunderstood as "backward-looking" and anti-progressive. It is not the case, however, that what we do in the present is inherently superior to how we did it in the past. The censorship of any part of the original language ultimately diminishes the connection between that language and its successor, not to mention its linguistic resources. Loss of vocabulary, or the diminished range of associated meanings of a particular word, increases the distance between what we have and what we aspire to have.

The assumptions that underpin revitalization efforts do not call for the prohibition of certain segments of the target language based on our current sensibilities. Such a position can only be considered counterintuitive, given that the goal is ostensibly to revitalize the entire language and not just selected parts. The existence of words in the traditional language obviously presupposes appropriate contexts and purposes for their use. It makes little sense to censor them based on the values of their English counterparts, particularly those that are metaphorical in nature. An asshole in English literally refers to the anus, a part of the body, but is meant to metaphorically and derisively connect a person who engages in inappropriate behaviour to that part of the body. It is far less common to use the word anus in an attempt to produce the same result. "You anus!" does not generate the same force as "You asshole!"

Unfortunately, most current speakers of Hawaiian are native speakers of English. In the absence of prior experience in Hawaiian, we are prone to accommodate our communicative needs based on prior experiences in English. In other words, we construct our Hawaiian in a way that calques what we would normally say in English. Unless we have learned the appropriate Hawaiian for accomplishing certain communicative tasks, we are resigned to revert to our default system as a substitute. It was once said of the famous linguist Roman Jakobson, "He speaks Russian in six languages."[18] In this case, it might be said that we are inclined to speak English in Hawaiian. Calquing, although it supports communication, does not support efforts to revitalize Hawaiian, particularly if the goal is to speak Hawaiian in Hawaiian.

Before calquing the English, we should survey the traditional Hawaiian corpus for viable alternatives. Unfortunately, the disconnect we experience by way of language shift relegates us, as it seems to have done for Jakobson, to a strategy of connecting to Hawaiian by defaulting to English. We depend on what we know to understand what we hope to know, a kind of self-fulfilling prophecy, if you will. This default evaluation can lead to the mistaken assumption that certain words are inappropriate in educational contexts, and perhaps even to official censorship. On the other hand, the absence of policy leaves open the opportunity to teach a more complete representation of the traditional lexicon, along with a traditionally appropriate context for use.

When we cross over linguistic borders, it is necessary to try to understand the foreign as the foreigner does, and not from our own perspectives. In order to do so, we might choose to consider our understanding of a new language in terms of our native language as a bias built on self-deception. Whorf (1956) has pointed out that this bias, although it guides us to think in culturally patterned ways, is not insurmountable. It does not predetermine our understanding of new concepts. If, however, there is competition between the familiar and the strange, the advantage clearly lies with the familiar. Recognition of this deception opens the door for us to apprehend the meanings of new words and phrases within their native contexts.

Reference to Body Parts

We turn once again to the discussion of body parts and the view that their signifying words are pelapela. The word 'ōkole, as mentioned above, is not utilized in the same way as its English counterparts *ass* and *butt*. For the most part, its invective force is somewhat benign in Hawaiian. Other words indicating parts of the body, and whose English translations can be used invectively in English contexts, are often found in place names or in reference to common items. The word ule *penis*, for example, commonly indicates parts of plants as well as other non-volatile referents. The *aerial roots of the pandanus tree* are called ulehala. Ulehihi is a word for *yam*. Ule'ōhi'u is a type of *sugar cane*, and ule'ulu is the *male breadfruit flower*. There are also some more clinical referents, such as ule hilo *gonorrhea* and ule kahe, which signifies a *circumcised penis*. Ulepa'a is a *male who has not had sexual relations with a woman*, and uleule has two seemingly unconnected meanings. On the one hand, it is glossed as *pendulous* or *hanging*, while on the other it signifies a *sty*, as on the edge of the eyelid. These meanings are all very benign and none requires restricted use. There are, however, a couple of meanings suggesting the possibility of invective use. Perhaps related to the word ulehole *a channel marker in the ocean*, the phrase ule hole signifies a *pulled-back penis*. Pukui and Elbert (1986, 367) describe it as "an insulting epithet for men." Again, none of these items warrants censorship, and each was a part of the traditional linguistic repertoire of the community. The fact that these are homonyms opens up the possibility for innuendo, a feature that offers the speaker the benefit of deniability, if called to account.

Another word that might be considered inappropriate in translation is kohe, which is glossed as *vagina* in Pukui and Elbert (1986, 158) but carries numerous other common meanings (e.g., *mortise, crease, groove, barb on a fishhook*, etc.). It is not clear whether these meanings were derived from their more anatomical counterpart, or vice versa. The word kohe is also a part of the history of the Hawaiian Islands, particularly with regard to geographical names. Kohelepelepe *vagina labia minor*, for example, is the older name of what is commonly referred to as Koko Head today (Pukui, Elbert, and Mookini 1974, 190). It was called this because, in an attempt to escape attack from Kamapuaʻa, "Pele's sister Kapo sent her vagina to lure away the pig man. He followed it to Koko Crater, Oʻahu, where it left an imprint, and then flew off to Ka-lihi."[19] Notice that the English name, Koko Crater, has supplanted the Hawaiian name. This is not an uncommon phenomenon in Hawaiian geography. Another commonly referenced use of the word kohe is found in the name Kohemālamalama *shining vagina*, one of several ancient names for Kahoʻolawe,[20] the island that was desecrated by the US navy who, for many years, used it as target practice in order to improve bombing accuracy. Interestingly, some people today have parsed the name as Ko-Hema-Lamalama, *the southern light*.

There are many other examples of the open, unfettered use of terms that might warrant censoring if their meanings are only understood in translation. Two extremely common words, kanaka and kali, used by a wide range of speakers in a wide range of contexts, also have sexual connotations that might stigmatize their use. There are four sets of English glosses for kanaka in the *Hawaiian Dictionary* (Pukui and Elbert 1986). Most second language learners, however, acquire only the most commonly used of these, *human being*. The small phoneme inventory in Hawaiian, along with the open syllable structure (i.e., no syllable ends with a consonant and no consonant clusters), yields a relatively small inventory of lexical items. As we have seen, this feature of the language supports the possibility of homonymy. Moreover, each single item offers a rather large range of possible meanings. Kanaka is no exception. A survey of the list of glosses for kanaka reveals that it can also be glossed as *clitoris*. Needless to say, when students are apprised of this interesting tidbit, hilarity ensues. A similar result obtains when they find out that kali does not only mean *to wait* but can also be glossed as *vagina*. Some students, after being apprised of this meaning, began to use the word alia *wait*, in order to avoid kali. Since alia is only used as a command, the avoidance of kali generated the misuse of alia in statements. These reactions are clearly triggered by the taboo nature of the English counterparts. Silva (2004) describes the struggle, in the Hawaiian language newspapers, between the Hawaiian and haole positions on sexual references. She contrasts the puritanical sentiments of the missionaries with the more open treatment of sex by Hawaiians. Even children are privy to this topic. However unintended, the treatment of sexual topics as taboo merely contributes to the invective nature of the related Hawaiian lexical items.

ʻŌlelo Hoʻoulu *Taunting*: A Serious Business

Confrontational situations, particularly those involving impending physical hostility, lend themselves to the use of a certain amount of invective language (i.e., taunting, smack talk, fighting words, etc.). The actual power of the words is ultimately tested by a "moment of truth" in which one side vanquishes the other, or causes it to back down. In ancient accounts reflective of life prior to the arrival of Cook, and frequently represented by epic stories such as Kawelo (Hooulumahiehie 1909-1910), death or defeat determines the validity of those words. In effect, the words of the winner (survivor) are validated and the loser's words are revealed as inconsequential.

Early in the story of Kawelo, during his formative years, there are several incidents of violence that were initiated by 'ōlelo ho'oulu. In one case, Kawelo's cousin, Kauahoa, asks to come aboard Kawelo's canoe as he paddles up and down the Wailua River. Kawelo responds by saying, "Aia ma ka ikaika ka hoahanau e kau ai iluna o kuu waa" *Only if my cousin can do so by force will he be able to board my canoe.*[21] Kauahoa, who is described as being much larger than Kawelo and who, unlike Kawelo, has been trained in the art of warfare, decides not to engage physically at that point. He instead takes a parting shot, threatening Kawelo and calling him a po'o nui (literally translated here as *big head*). The author describes Kawelo's response as follows: "I ka puka ana o ka hua kuamuamu a Kauahoa ia Kawelo, i ke poo nui, aole i kana mai ka huhu o Kawelo" *When Kauahoa issued these insulting words to Kawelo, calling him a big head, Kawelo became incensed.* Kawelo tries to get off the canoe to take his rage out on Kauahoa, but trips over the side in the process. Meanwhile, Kauahoa makes off down the bank of the river, avoiding a physical confrontation.

There are a couple of issues in this excerpt that are worthy of note. One is the fact that Kauahoa clearly loses face by running away from the impending altercation with his smaller cousin. The second is the use of the word kūamuamu. Besides *insult*, it is also glossed as *revile, blaspheme, curse, swear,* and *damn* (Pukui and Elbert 1986, 171). These glosses appear slightly excessive from an English perspective. It is difficult to imagine how calling someone a big head could qualify for inclusion in any of these speech act categories. In Hawaiian, however, po'o nui clearly causes sufficient offense to elicit a violent response. Oddly enough, the literal gloss *big head* for this phrase is not actually listed in the dictionary. Moreover, its glosses *hangover, worried head,* and *worry* (342) do not seem to fit the context. A figurative meaning listed as *source of trouble* is perhaps the most appropriate gloss in this context. However, there are other instantiations of poʻo nui that support the literal gloss *big head*. Kawelo's head is, in fact, described as being larger than normal, and when attention is focused on this abnormality he becomes incensed.

Eventually, another cousin, Aikanaka, attempting to intervene on behalf of Kauahoa, calls Kawelo a "poo nui, maka aa" *big head with wide, staring eyes*, and further describes him as "kohu uu kani po" *resembling a surgeonfish that grunts at night*. Since no diacritical marks were used at the time, ʻūʻū *surgeonfish* could also be interpreted as ʻuʻu *masturbate*, producing an alternative gloss, *masturbator who grunts at night*. The under-specification of phonemes in the older Hawaiian orthography allows for such ambiguity, and authors at the time were apt to take advantage of the possibilities afforded. While either interpretation could work in this context, the author, whether intentionally or not, presents the reader with both possibilities.

Upon hearing this kūamuamu from Aikanaka, Kawelo warns him to measure his words lest they lead to irreconcilable differences. In this admonition, however, he takes the opportunity to call Aikanaka an "alii waha lepo" *filthy-mouthed chief*. These must have been fighting words because as soon as they are issued, Aikanaka attacks Kawelo—and gets knocked out for his effort. This is an example of the effect that words can have, even when they are not pelapela.

Speaking Hawaiian in Hawaiian

Insofar as it is feasible, the revitalization of Hawaiian should result in a Hawaiian that maximizes its independence from English. This cannot occur unless the dominance of English in determining the trajectory of that process is recognized as pervasive and actively mitigated. Many Hawaiian words and phrases associated with contexts of anger are not part of the repertoires of second language speakers of Hawaiian. They are, unfortunately, misguidedly avoided. In the absence of their ambient use, and without benefit of overt instruction, an important aspect of the language is repressed, leaving English words to fill the void. In order to speak Hawaiian in Hawaiian, it is necessary to revitalize the whole language, upgrading its capacity by making it relevant for modern contexts. No one wants to put in the effort necessary to learn a second language only to find out that, under the surface, it is really no different from the first.

Notes

1. This is the default date commonly used to delineate contact and pre-contact periods. It should be noted that, prior to that time, there were multiple migrations, suggesting multiple "contacts" and a heterogeneous population.
2. *Author's Note*: It is an important step in the process of decolonization that Indigenous writers work to Indigenize the precepts of compositional writing. As we strive to produce an Indigenous body of literature, including one that utilizes English as the matrix language, we should strive to elevate ways of writing that serve to honour our Indigenous worldviews. The authors have chosen to honour Hawaiian words by normalizing their use, i.e., by not marking them as different, but treating them instead as part of the normal text. As such, we have chosen to mark their English glosses (indicated by italics) as if they are foreign. Given that the chapter attempts to provide evidence for the inadequacy of translation, marking the English glosses with italics is an attempt to highlight that point. It is, in effect, a way to utilize compositional resource to effect a counter-hegemonic attack on an otherwise dominant mindset, one that is uncompromising for the very fact that its norms seem so normal. This chapter represents our attempt to contest a space that comes with preconceived notions of normalcy that subordinate native desires for recognition in our own right. In doing so, we recognize that Indigenous ways of knowing, and of presenting that knowledge, cannot be confined to a single style, as we all have unique ways of expressing ideas and various responses to their presentation. The idea that one size fits all stifles our individuality, levels the differences that identify our different peoples, and limits our creativity whether individually or collectively.
3. NeSmith (2003) has pointed out that a new version of Hawaiian has supplanted the old, and characterized it as "neo-Hawaiian."

4. See Kōmike Huaʻōlelo (2003). This volume is a collection, albeit not exhaustive, of new words coined before 2003. The majority of these represent a response to the pre-existence of some English concepts.
5. The term "calque" is commonly used in linguistics to indicate a literal translation that is sometimes inaccurate to speakers. See Odlin (1989).
6. This concept is borrowed from Ngugi wa Thiongʻo (1986, 15), who asserts, "Language as culture is the collective memory bank of a people's experience in history."
7. Wong (1999a) advocates for a "covert prescriptivism" as a strategy for language revitalization.
8. The term "language distance" is defined in Odlin (1989, 166) as "the relative degree of similarity between two languages."
9. Josephine Kaleilehua Lindsey, personal communication (May 11, 1993).
10. See Warner (2001), and also Wilson and Kamanā (2001), for further details on the establishment of the Hawaiian Language Immersion Program.
11. This idea is derived from numerous conversations with Professor Michael Forman, University of Hawaiʻi at Mānoa.
12. Searle distinguishes between the intended meaning (the illocutionary force) and the perceived meaning (the perlocutionary force) of an utterance. The word "receiver" is used here to signify both hearers and readers.
13. The stories in this section are written in the first person because they were experienced and retold by only one of the authors.
14. Greenawalt (1989) provides a more extensive look at the problems involved in determining the boundaries of acceptability in language use beyond which the state is likely to intervene.
15. See Kameʻeleihiwa (1992) for a more in-depth discussion of this struggle. See also Trask ([1993] 1999, 16), who aptly characterizes the cultural upheaval in which Christianity supplanted Hawaiian religion and English supplanted Hawaiian language as "cultural imperialism."
16. According to Pukui (Pukui, Haertig, and Lee 1972, 74), this gesture "huli kua" was inappropriate and carried with it severe consequences. "When someone came to you and asked for forgiveness, you could not *huli kua* [turn the back] on him. You had to forgive fully and completely. If you did not, the *aumakua* [ancestor gods] would *huli kua* on you."
17. This idea is analogous to Denning's (1995) concern about the relative accuracy of our interpretations of historical events.

18. An obituary article appeared in the *New York Times* (1982, 8) after the death of the well-known linguist Roman Jakobson, in which a fellow linguist stated, "Jakobson is a peculiar man...He speaks Russian fluently in six languages."
19. This story is listed under the place name "Puaʻa-kanu" (Pukui, Elbert, and Mookini 1974, 190).
20. Oliveira (2014) lists several other names for this island, including Kanaloa, Kahoʻolewa, Kohemālamalama, and Kohemālamalamaokanaloa *the shining vagina of Kanaloa*. This last name is worthy of note in that Kanaloa is a male deity.
21. English translations in this section are provided by the authors.

References

Denning, Greg. 1995. *The Death of William Gooch: A History's Anthropology*. Honolulu: University of Hawaiʻi Press.

Fishman, Joshua A. 1991. *Reversing Language Shift: Theoretical and Empirical Foundations of Assistance to Threatened Languages*. Clevedon, England: Multicultural Matters.

Grace, George W. 1981. *An Essay on Language*. Columbia, SC: Hornbeam Press.

Greenawalt, Kent. 1989. *Speech, Crime, and the Use of Language*. New York: Oxford University Press.

Hooulumahiehie-i-ka-oni-malie-a-pua-lilia-lana-i-ka-wai. 1909–1910. Ka moolelo hiwahiwa o Kawelo. *Kuokoa Home Rula*. Honolulu.

Kameʻeleihiwa, Lilikalā. 1992. *Native Lands and Foreign Desires: Pehea e Pono Ai?* Honolulu: Bishop Museum Press.

Kōmike Huaʻōlelo. 2003. *Māmaka Kaiao: A Modern Hawaiian Vocabulary*. Honolulu: University of Hawaiʻi Press.

NeSmith, Richard K. 2003. "Tūtū's Hawaiian and the Emergence of a Neo-Hawaiian Language." *ʻŌiwi: A Native Hawaiian Journal* 3: 68–76.

New York Times. 1982. "Roman Jakobson, a Scholar of Linguistics, Is Dead." July 23, 1982, 8.

Ngugi wa Thiongʻo. 1986. *Decolonising the Mind: The Politics of Language in African Literature*. London: James Currey.

Odlin, Terrence. 1989. *Language Transfer: Cross-Linguistic Influence in Language Learning*. Cambridge: Cambridge University Press.

Oliveira, Katrina-Ann R. Kapāʻanaokalāokeola Nākoa. 2014. *Ancestral Places: Understanding Kanaka Geographies*. Corvallis: Oregon State University Press.

Pukui, Mary Kawena. 1983. *ʻŌlelo Noʻeau: Hawaiian Proverbs and Poetical Sayings*. Honolulu: University of Hawaiʻi Press.

Pukui, Mary Kawena, and Samuel H. Elbert. 1986. *Hawaiian Dictionary*. Honolulu: University of Hawaiʻi Press.

Pukui, Mary Kawena, Samuel H. Elbert, and Esther T. Mookini. 1974. *Place Names of Hawaii*. Honolulu: University of Hawaiʻi Press.

Pukui, Mary Kawena, E.W. Haertig, and Catherine A. Lee. 1972. *Nānā i Ke Kumu: Look to the Source*. Vol. 1. Honolulu: Hui Hānai/The Queen Liliʻuokalani Children's Center.

Searle, John R. 1990. "A Classification of Illocutionary Acts." In *Cultural Communication and Intercultural Contact*, edited by Donald Carbaugh, 349–72. Hillsdale, NJ: Lawrence Erlbaum Associates.

Silva, Noenoe K. 2004. *Aloha Betrayed: Native Hawaiian Resistance to American Colonialism*. Durham, NC: Duke University Press.

Simonson, Douglas, Ken Sakata, and Pat Sasaki. 1981. *Pidgin to da Max*. Honolulu: Bess Press.

Trask, Haunani-Kay. (1993) 1999. *From a Native Daughter: Colonialism and Sovereignty in Hawaiʻi*. Honolulu: University of Hawaiʻi Press.

Warner, Sam L. Noʻeau. 2001. "The Movement to Revitalize Hawaiian Language and Culture." In *The Green Book of Language Revitalization in Practice*, edited by Leanne Hinton and Ken Hale, 133–44. San Diego: Academic Press.

Whorf, Bejamin Lee. 1956. "A Linguistic Consideration of Thinking in Primitive Communities." In *Language, Thought, and Reality: Selected Writings of Benjamin Lee Whorf*, edited by John B. Carroll, 65–86. Cambridge, MA: MIT Press.

Wilson, William H., and Kauanoe Kamanā. 2001. "Mai Loko Mai o ka ʻIʻini: Proceeding from a Dream." In *The Green Book of Language Revitalization in Practice*, edited by Leanne Hinton and Ken Hale, 147–78. San Diego: Academic Press.

Wong, K. Laiana. 1999a. "Authenticity and the Revitalization of Hawaiian." *Anthropology and Education Quarterly* 30 (1): 94–115. https://doi.org/10.1525/aeq.1999.30.1.94

———. 1999b. "Language Varieties and Language Policy: The Appreciation of Pidgin." In *Sociopolitical Perspectives on Language Policy and Planning in the USA*, edited by Thomas Huebner and Kathryn A. Davis, 205–22. Amsterdam: John Benjamins Publishing Company.

8 | Wisdom Maps

Metaphors as Maps

KATRINA-ANN R. KAPĀʻANAOKALĀOKEOLA NĀKOA OLIVEIRA

Introduction

In ancestral times, Kānaka did not have two-dimensional cartographic representations drawn on paper to locate ourselves on the landscape.[1] As an oral society, we utilized what cultural geographers refer to today as "performance cartographies" (Louis 2004). Mele, hula, ʻōlelo, and other modes of performance were used to "map" the topographies, weather patterns, geological formations, and historical accounts occurring at particular places over the course of time.

Since the process of "mapping" (on paper) was not an ancestral practice in ka pae ʻāina Hawaiʻi *the Hawaiian archipelago* during pre-contact times, there is an inherent tension when discussing Kanaka "mapping" practices. On one hand, there is an acknowledgement that our ancestors had the aptitude and skills to locate themselves on the landscape (and oceanscape) and to record the unique characteristics of their places. How else would they have been able to navigate purposefully and repeatedly throughout the Pacific without a system for locating where they were and where they were headed? Yet they did not have "maps" in the sense of cartographic representations on paper. How then does one begin a discussion about Kanaka "mapping" practices when the very notion of a "map" is contested? Even the ʻōlelo Hawaiʻi word for *map*, palapala ʻāina, carries Western-loaded connotations; palapala ʻāina is a "land document." By the very nature of the term palapala ʻāina there is an implication that maps are written documents. While palapala ʻāina adequately describes many Western maps, it does not take into account the performative nature of ancestral Kanaka cartographies. The term hōʻike honua *to show the earth; performances related to the earth* better approximates the notion of Kanaka performative cartographies; however, hōʻike honua is more commonly translated and understood to mean *geography* by most ʻōlelo Hawaiʻi speakers.

While "map" remains a highly contested notion for oral societies, the inclusion of concepts like "performance cartographies," "performance geographies," and "Indigenous epistemologies" in mainstream academic literature reaffirms that scholars are developing a deeper appreciation for the distinctive ways in which Indigenous Peoples connect with and relate to our places. Over the past decade, Indigenous scholars have made strides in informing and transforming the ways in which Western cartographers perceive Indigenous geographies. Many cartographers now agree that Indigenous Peoples have had their own unique "mapping systems" for thousands of years (Harley 1992; Johnson, Louis, and Pramono 2005). Although terms like "performance cartographies" have elevated the status of Indigenous cartographic practices in the field of geography, they still do not fully enunciate the importance of one's language and worldview in creating places and inscribing places with meaning.

As a geographer by training and a ʻōlelo Hawaiʻi academic by profession, it is my intention to (re)claim "mapping" as a Kanaka construct. In the past, I have purposefully refrained from the use of "mapping" with reference to Kanaka practices to the extent possible, preferring "performance cartographies" instead. The use of "performance cartographies" allowed me to evade many Western connotations while simultaneously employing a term that adequately approximates ancestral Kanaka practices. Recently, however, I have begun to rethink my position of tiptoeing around the use of the term with reference to Kanaka practices. While I generally prefer "performance cartographies" over "mapping," I also feel strongly that the time has come to reclaim Kanaka cartographic practices as "maps" so as not to marginalize our Indigenous practices as something less than Western practices.

The maps of my kūpuna *ancestors* are what I refer to as "wisdom maps." Encoded in their metaphoric oral maps are experiences, relationships, and histories that often cannot be reduced to paper; yet, like other maps, ancestral wisdom maps may be utilized to locate someone or something on the landscape. Another important reason that I refer to these practices as wisdom maps is because the degree to which these maps are understood is proportional to the level of wisdom, knowledge, and mastery the user possesses. Unlike Western maps that are fairly straightforward and widely understood, Kanaka wisdom maps require a depth of social, cultural, and linguistic knowledge that must be mastered over time. That is to say, while a tourist from almost any country in the world may use a Western map to find her or his way around a city, the same person new to Hawaiʻi may have difficulty understanding the layers of meaning encoded in Kanaka maps or performance cartographies.

Kanaka wisdom maps are a reflection of the metaphoric nature of ʻōlelo Hawaiʻi. Skilled ʻōlelo Hawaiʻi speakers effortlessly weave ʻōlelo hoʻopilipili *figurative language* into everyday speech, including wisdom maps. Through ʻōlelo noʻeau *proverbial sayings*, nane, welina, and mele, those fluent in ʻōlelo Hawaiʻi use the art of metaphor to both conceal and reveal multiple layers of meaning. The degree to which figurative language is understood is largely based on the listener's knowledge of a topic and her or his established relationship with the speaker, composer, or mapmaker (Herman 1999; Piianaia n.d.). As Herman (1999) suggests,

[The English language] does not have the sensitivity to the subtleties of light and color, wind and rain, and emotive landscape that these islands present. The countless names for individual winds and rains and for conditions of the sea, the cultural link with the earth, the spiritual link with unseen but clearly felt forces—in all, a great body of geographic knowledge and an entire way of understanding that is Indigenous and intertwined with this place—is lost with the peripheralization and near extinction of the Hawaiian language. (93)

Just as there is an absence in English to "the sensitivity to the subtleties" inherent in ʻōlelo Hawaiʻi, so too, are these subtleties absent in traditional Western maps.

ʻŌlelo hoʻopilipili and kaona *hidden meanings* are important components of both ʻōlelo Hawaiʻi and Kanaka mapping systems. ʻŌlelo noʻeau, nane, and welina that have been documented in newspaper articles, letters, and books as well as those preserved on audio recordings are both maps and windows into the past. These repositories inform our understanding of ancestral Kanaka worldviews and practices, as well as relationships to places. As Kanaka scholar Carlos Andrade (2008, 3) suggests, these repositories permit contemporary ʻōlelo Hawaiʻi scholars and speakers to "see the world through the eyes of the ancestors."

The layering of thoughts, ideas, and meanings is central to the mother tongue of ka pae ʻāina Hawaiʻi. ʻŌlelo hoʻopilipili are an integral part of the naming and mapping processes by which Kānaka inscribe place with meaning. The more knowledgeable a person is with a place, the more able a person is to refer to a place figuratively and the more likely a person is to understand the wisdom maps of others. What follows are examples of ʻōlelo hoʻopilipili that often serve as wisdom maps.

Welina

Aloha mai e ke hoa heluhelu mai ka lā hiki a ka lā kau *Greetings to you, the reader, from the rising of the sun to the setting of the sun.* The art of addressing a person or an audience can be a highly sophisticated Kanaka mapping practice. Besides extending one's aloha *greetings, love, appreciation,* perhaps the most important part of a welina is recognizing the different "places" of the people being addressed in a culturally acceptable order.

These "places" relate to both one's place on the landscape as well as one's place in society. A skillful orator is mindful and respectful of mapping both tangible and intangible places—those seen and unseen. An excellent contemporary example is the 2006 State of the Office of Hawaiian Affairs and the Hawaiian Community Address delivered by Office of Hawaiian Affairs Chairperson, Haunani Apoliona (2006), at the Kawaiahaʻo Church on the island of Oʻahu. She opened the address with the following greeting:

> Aloha mai kākou e nā ʻōiwi ʻōlino mai Hawaiʻi a Niʻihau a puni ke ao mālamalama. Aloha e nā kūpuna, nā mākua, nā ʻōpio, nā keiki a me nā kamaiki e ʻākoakoa mai nei, ma kēia hale pule laʻahia ʻo Kawaiahaʻo, a ma loko i ko kākou mau hale ʻohana a puni ke ao mālamalama. Aloha e nā kamaʻāina a me nā malihini kekahi. Aloha nō kākou a pau loa. Aloha.

> *Greetings to our esteemed fellow Kānaka from Hawaiʻi to Niʻihau and around this brilliant world. Aloha to the elders, adults, youth, children, and toddlers who have assembled here at this sacred church, Kawaiahaʻo, in your family homes, and around this brilliant world. Greetings to longtime residents and newcomers alike.*

Haunani Apoliona employed a traditional-style welina in a modern context, addressing everyone in the audience from eldest to youngest, resident and visitor alike. She also acknowledged the Kawaiahaʻo Church, the place her speech was being delivered, as well as the homes of those who might be viewing her speech on television. In her welina, she used metaphor to describe her fellow Kānaka from the islands of Hawaiʻi to Niʻihau as enlightened people.

A typical welina mirrors the one delivered by Haunani Apoliona. In general, welina seek to consciously include everyone as well as every place and everything between two expanses. In most cases, welina begin from the east and continue on to the west. One common welina style is to begin with the rising of the sun and to end with the setting of the sun; thus, everything from east to west is acknowledged. The locations where the sun rises and sets on the horizon are acknowledged as places. Similarly, an orator might recognize each of the four cardinal points. Should an orator elect to greet everyone on each of the four major islands in ka pae ʻāina Hawaiʻi, she or he would more than likely begin in the east with Hawaiʻi island, continue westerly to Maui and Oʻahu, and end in the west with Niʻihau. Sometimes, islands are referenced indirectly via the names of their famous chiefs; in such a case, greetings might be extended from Moku o Keawe *island of Chief Keawe* (a metaphoric reference to Hawaiʻi island), then to Nā Hono aʻo Piʻilani *the bays of Piʻilani* (a metaphoric reference to Maui), next to Oʻahu a Lua *Oʻahu of Lua* (a metaphoric reference to Oʻahu) or Oʻahu a Kākuhihewa *Oʻahu of Kākuhihewa* (a metaphoric reference to Oʻahu), and finally to Niʻihau o Kahelelani *Niʻihau of Kahelelani* (a metaphoric reference to Niʻihau).

Many welina also incorporate metaphoric references to places. Here is an example of a welina delivered for a lei *garland of flowers* making competition:

ʻAno ʻai kākou e nā pua mae ʻole o nēia pae ʻāina, mai ka lehua puāhilo o Kauakanilehua o Hawaiʻi, a i nā hono aʻo Piʻilani o Maui, e lei nō ʻoe i kou lei lokelani hiwahiwa i wili pū ʻia me ka lei hinahina ʻōlali o Kahoʻolawe, i hihia me ke kaunaʻoa o Lānaʻi, hanohano nō ʻoe i kou ʻalani, a mālamalama ʻo Molokaʻi i ke kukui i kui ʻia me ka pua ʻīlima lahilahi o Maunalahilahi o Oʻahu nei, a i ka lei mokihana o Hanalei ma Kauaʻi, a i ka lei pūpū o Niʻihau a hiki loa aku i ka lehu aloha o Lehua, me ʻoukou ka welina o ke aloha.

Greetings to all of us, the never fading flowers of this archipelago, from the delicate lehua flower of the Kauakanilehua rain of Hawaiʻi, to the bays of Piʻilani on Maui, you are adorned in your precious garland of roses interwoven with the delicate hinahina of Kahoʻolawe, intertwined with the kaunaʻoa of Lānaʻi, you are majestic in orange, and Molokaʻi is bright with the kukui that is strung together with the delicate ʻīlima flowers of

Maunalahilahi of Oʻahu, and the garland of mokihana berries of Hanalei of Kauaʻi, as well as the garland of shells of Niʻihau all the way to the great love of Lehua, with all of you are my greetings of love.

This welina was written for a specific event, a lei-making competition; thus, references to flowers, plants, and lei-making styles appear throughout the welina to both greet everyone in the audience and to acknowledge each of the major Hawaiian islands. People are compared to the famous flowers, plants, and shells of their own individual islands that are weaved into beautiful lei.

Welina of this nature illustrate the inextricable connection between people, their places, their ancestors, and their resources. The features of landscapes and the resources of the sea, land, and sky are celebrated and mapped. The previous welina figuratively suggests that like a lei of flowers, some Kānaka proudly "wear" their places with them. Whether it is a flower from their kulāiwi *ancestral homeland* or a memory of a past time there, people adorn themselves with their places.

Today, welina provide scholars clues about how traditional Kānaka "mapped" their places sequentially. The east preceded the west; the eldest preceded the youngest. There were socially accepted norms that dictated the order in which people and places were to be acknowledged.

ʻŌlelo Noʻeau

ʻŌlelo noʻeau are perhaps the most commonly known form of metaphor in ʻōlelo Hawaiʻi. ʻŌlelo noʻeau are interwoven into mele, oli *chants*, and welina. Mary Kawena Pukui, the foremost Kanaka scholar of the twentieth century, recorded and published a total of 2,942 ʻōlelo noʻeau in her book, *Olelo Noeau: Hawaiian Proverbs and Poetical Sayings* (Pukui 1983). Thirty per cent or nearly 900 of those ʻōlelo noʻeau include specific place names, thus reaffirming the importance of place to Kanaka poetry and metaphor. When one includes names of winds and rains associated with specific moku *large land district* and ahupuaʻa *land district generally extending from the mountains to the sea*, the percentage increases to 37%.

In addition to 'ōlelo no'eau that explicitly refer to place names, others implicitly refer to land without so much as mentioning the word 'āina *land*. The 'ōlelo no'eau "'Au i ke kai me he manu ala *swims out to sea like a bird*" metaphorically refers to a hill that is seen from a great distance at sea (Pukui 1983, 28). These two seemingly unrelated nouns, a bird and a hill, are compared, demonstrating that the use of metaphor can be quite complicated. Only people with an in-depth understanding of Kanaka poetry would be able to appreciate the various layers of meaning. Even those who speak 'ōlelo Hawai'i but have not been previously exposed to this particular 'ōlelo no'eau might not fully grasp the meaning of this poetic saying without visual clues, because the literal meaning, "swims out to sea like a bird," and its poetic reference, "a hill that is seen from a distance," are seemingly unrelated thoughts.

Kānaka, like other Pacific Island peoples, often view the ocean as a bridge that joins islands (Hau'ofa and Waddell 1993). This worldview is prominent in Kanaka poetry. Metaphoric references to land are accomplished by alluding to the ocean rather than the islands themselves. The 'ōlelo no'eau "nā kai 'ewalu *the eight seas*," for instance, refers to the eight major islands of ka pae 'āina Hawai'i. Emphasis is placed on the channels that connect the islands together, not the islands themselves. Similarly, a large land district on the island of Maui is collectively known as nā wai 'ehā *the four waters*. Within this district are four adjacent ahupua'a: Waikapū (*water of the conch*), Wailuku (*water of destruction*), Wai'ehu (*water spray*), and Waihe'e (*octopus water*). Each ahupua'a is named after the type of water prominent in that specific ahupua'a.

Perhaps the most common use of metaphor in relationship to place names is the use of pun in 'ōlelo no'eau. In many cases, place names are the foundation upon which an 'ōlelo no'eau is built. Without the place name, the 'ōlelo no'eau is meaningless. The place name literally and metaphorically grounds the 'ōlelo no'eau to a specific place. Kalalau is perhaps the most famous contemporary example of a place name that is known for its multiple meanings. People who lose their sense of direction as well as those who lose their train of thought are often jokingly said to be in Kalalau, Kaua'i. Lalau means to *go astray*; thus, several ʻōlelo noʻeau capitalize on the meaning of this place name. Two examples from *Olelo Noeau: Hawaiian Proverbs and Poetical Sayings* (Pukui 1993) are "Hala i Kauaʻi i Kalalau *gone to Kauaʻi, to Kalalau*" (52) and "Molale loa nō kumupali o Kalalau *clearly seen is the base of Kalalau*" (238).

Although Mary Kawena Pukui compiled and documented many ʻōlelo noʻeau, what is of particular interest here is the fact that the place name is the most important part of the ʻōlelo noʻeau. Thus, speakers of ʻōlelo Hawaiʻi often make up their own ʻōlelo noʻeau, ones that do not appear in Mary Kawena Pukui's book, by simply using the place name, Kalalau. In most cases, the name, Kalalau, is all that one needs to understand the intended pun. Today, people commonly say, "Aia paha ʻo ia i Kalalau *perhaps she or he is at Kalalau*" or "Hele akula paha ʻo ia i Kalalau *perhaps she or he is off to Kalalau*." Some even use the place name in English sentences, stating, "I think he just left for Kalalau."

A common ʻōlelo Hawaiʻi poetic device is to suggest where a person might have gone in order to draw similarities between a person and a place name. "Aia akula nō i Kiʻilau *she has gone to Kiʻilau*" is a play on the word kiʻilau *to fetch a lot*. Here, Kiʻilau, a place in ʻEwa, Oʻahu, is used as a poetic device to suggest that a person talks too much. "Aia akula paha i Kiolakaʻa *she has gone to Kiolakaa*" is a play on the word kiola *to throw away*. Here, poetic reference is made between the place, Kiolakaʻa, and a person who discards objects that are needed in the future (Pukui and Varez 1983). "Aia aku nei paha i Kaiholena *perhaps she has gone to Kaiholena*" suggests that a person has gone somewhere to lena *to loaf or to be lazy* (Pukui 1983).

In the saying "He lau hala lana," floating pandanus leaves are likened to people who drift from place to place (Pukui 1983). Many of the ʻōlelo noʻeau related to the notion of place acknowledge a close relationship between the Kānaka and our kulāiwi. "He lau hala lana" may be seen as a disparaging reference to those who lose touch with their kulāiwi and roam aimlessly from place to place. Aside from the loss of connection with a physical place, the abandonment of place symbolizes one's lack of commitment to land stewardship, as well as the many generations of her or his ancestors who resided there.

He ali'i ka 'āina, he kauwā ke kanaka *the land is a chief, a person is a servant* is an 'ōlelo no'eau in which the land is personified. Here, the land is revered as a chief, while people are servants to the land. This metaphor clearly depicts the level of respect that ancestral Kānaka had for the land. The land was not a possession to be bought and sold. Rather, it was believed to be both the older sibling and chief of the Kānaka.

Although it would be much easier to coin fictitious place names to illustrate a point, the beauty of this poetic form is that existing place names are used as puns to reveal implicit meanings. Perhaps part of the ingenuity of Kanaka metaphoric references is the fact that a speaker or writer may be very pointed with her or his words, yet not everyone in the audience has the skills with which to decipher the multiple layers of meaning inscribed and mapped in the words and phrases.

Interrelatedness of Kō ā uka and Kō ā kai

Ancestral Kānaka relied on the resources of the land and sea for sustenance. Thus, they developed a profound understanding of their ecosystems, including how conditions in the uplands directly affected the conditions in the lowlands. They were so in touch with nature that they were able to identify and map linkages between upland species with their counterparts at sea through appearance, function, name association, and other characteristics. The interrelatedness of kō ā uka *that belonging to the upland* and kō ā kai *that belonging to the ocean* is well documented in the Kumulipo, a Kanaka cosmogonic genealogy (Liliuokalani 1897). The Kumulipo suggests that balance is achieved through duality. The sun rises in the east and sets in the west. Daylight is balanced by nightfall. Ocean species are dependent on upland species.

These dualistic and symbiotic relationships serve as metaphoric mnemonic mapping devices. Often these associations are based on the appearance and/or names of plants and animals. One obvious example is the loli *sea cucumber* and the 'enuhe *worm*. While their ecosystems are quite different, loli and 'enuhe are similar in appearance and function relative to their own environments. The he'e *octopus* and alahe'e *a native shrub* are linked together by name association. Limu manauea *a small red seaweed* is closely associated with kalo manauea *a variety of taro*. Limu wāwae'iole *a type of seaweed* and wāwae'iole *a type of club moss* both resemble the feet of a rat; thus, they both carry the same name. The naupaka plant bears white flowers that appear to be half flowers. According to legend, two lovers were separated; one was sent to the ocean and the other to the mountains. Thus, the naupaka kahakai *naupaka found along the seashore* and naupaka kuahiwi *naupaka found in the mountains* are the manifestations of these lovers.

Wahi Pana

Wahi pana *storied places* are legendary places mapped by the names, resources, stories, historical accounts, and traditions associated with them. Sometimes Kanaka place names were given to commemorate events that occurred at a particular locale. Kepaniwai, for example, is the name of a stream and park in 'Īao, Maui where Kamehameha I's warriors conquered the island of Maui by defeating the warriors led by Kalanikūpule. The casualties of Kalanikūpule's forces were so great that the corpses in the stream partially dammed the water. Kanaka places were sometimes named for the resources that were commonly found in an area. Ke'anae, for instance, is a fishing and farming village on the eastern coast of Maui. Its name means "the mullet." Other places are named for their features. Wai'ehu, for example, means "water spray."

Kupa *natives of a place* are so closely connected to their places that metaphoric names are often attached to people based on their kulāiwi. In this way, the people are inscribed in Kanaka mapping systems as being a part of the landscape. People from the fishing and farming village of Kahakuloa, Maui, are sometimes figuratively called lehua. This single word has many layers of kaona. Since Kahakuloa is known for its fishing tradition, numerous expert fishers hail from this village; *expert fisher* is one meaning of lehua. Lehua is also a common variety of taro grown in the valley. According to Elders, the ʻōhiʻa lehua tree grows well in Kahakuloa, reflecting a third meaning of lehua. Additionally, flowers, in this case the lehua, are a common allusion for descendants; thus, kupa of Kahakuloa are often called lehua. Ancestral metaphoric references to kupa of Kahakuloa include e hoʻi ka lehua o Kaukini *return descendants of mount Kaukini* (Handy and Handy 1972), ʻohuʻohu ʻo Kahakuloa i ka pua lehua *Kahakuloa is adorned in lehua flowers*, Puʻu Koaʻe papā i ka makani *Puʻu Koaʻe, a place blown by the wind*, and Kuinālehua o Kaukini *the strung-together lehua flowers of Kaukini* (Kahananui 1875).

Through ʻōlelo noʻeau like these, contemporary scholars are better able to understand the ways in which their ancestors viewed and mapped their own kulāiwi. In the example of Kahakuloa, it is evident that the kupa likened themselves to the multiple meanings of lehua. Due to their connection with the mountains, the sea, the taro, the lehua tree, and their descendants, they were indeed ka lehua o Kaukini *the lehua of Kaukini*.

A few years ago, I was approached by a scholar who insisted that Kahakuloa did not and does not have ʻōhiʻa lehua trees; thus, songs that celebrate the "lehua" of Kahakuloa must be referring to the people and not the ʻōhiʻa lehua trees of Kahakuloa. I was astonished that a ʻōlelo Hawaiʻi teacher and mele composer had so easily forgotten that a single word could have so many meanings, and that kupa do not readily disclose the secrets of their kulāiwi to outsiders seeking the wisdom maps of their ancestors and their ancestral places.

Places of Politics

Figurative language is not limited to romantic references to place. ʻŌlelo hoʻopilipili are also used to advance political agendas by intentionally mapping the desirable features of some places and the undesirable features of others. A person from Oʻahu, for instance, may boast, "Oʻahu, ka ʻōnohi o nā kai *Oʻahu, gem of the seas*." An adversary from another island may respond, "He mamo ʻoe na Kākuhihewa *you must be a descendant of Kākuhihewa—the mistaken one—a famous chief of Oʻahu*." In a discussion about Kamehameha I, the chief who united ka pae ʻāina Hawaiʻi in the 19th century, a person from Hawaiʻi island might boast about the strength and intelligence of Kamehameha's warriors from Hawaiʻi. In response, a person from Oʻahu might insist that it was not the strength of Kamehameha's forces but the strength of the Western canon that secured his victory in battle. A person from Oʻahu might also challenge the intelligence of Kamehameha's forces with the remark, "Hilo palu lāʻī," insisting that no intelligent person would be seen licking a leaf for food as Kamehameha's forces had been seen doing when they lacked sufficient supplies of food. Further, a person with ties to Maui may assert that Kamehameha's biological father was Kahekili of Maui, not Keoua of Hawaiʻi island, so it is no wonder that the ruling chief of Maui allowed his son, Kamehameha I, to defeat his own forces while he was on the island of Oʻahu. Kupa of Kauaʻi might insist that theirs is the only island that Kamehameha failed to conquer. Kupa from any other island in ka pae ʻāina Hawaiʻi might taunt people from Kauaʻi, insisting that the people of Kauaʻi were so cowardly that they surrendered to Kamehameha I without even trying to defend their kulāiwi. Historical accounts that are told generation after generation gain mana *spiritual power* and serve as powerful wisdom maps, remembered and retold by those who know the history of a place.

Similarly, the ultimate compliment that could be paid to an aliʻi *chief* is to have her or his name and feats remembered for eternity. Today, the names of aliʻi appear on street signs, airplanes, hotels, state and federal buildings, shopping malls, and schools. Aliʻi whose names are synonymous with islands, such as Maui a Kama *Maui of Kamalālāwalu* and Kauaʻi o Mano *Kauaʻi of Mano*, continue to be remembered and mapped on the landscape in modern times, many generations after they have passed away.

The memories of other aliʻi are also celebrated and mapped via their profound statements. Today, the mottos kūlia i ka nuʻu *to strive for the summit*, ʻonipaʻa *to be steadfast*, and ua mau ke ea o ka ʻāina i ka pono *the sovereignty of the land is perpetuated in righteousness* are synonymous with their originators, Queen Kapiʻolani, Queen Liliʻuokalani, and King Kauikeaouli (also known as Kamehameha III), respectively, as well as the places where these statements were first proclaimed.

Mele

When one thinks of ʻōlelo hoʻopilipili, many think of mele. All of the poetic styles previously mentioned are commonly found in mele in ʻōlelo Hawaiʻi. Mele composed specifically for places are known as mele aloha ʻāina *songs for beloved lands*, mele inoa *name songs*, or mele wahi pana *songs for legendary places*. Mele of this nature are wisdom maps that enumerate the prominent features and outstanding qualities of places.

Within a single mele, there may be several layers of meaning—some of which are only known to the composer herself or himself. To the untrained ear, the mele may simply appear to be naming the peaks, waterfalls, and beaches of a place, but to the composer's lover, the song may be a road map of their escapades together. A family member of the composer might recognize various family names throughout the mele. The peaks and waterfalls mentioned in the mele might be metaphoric references to the maʻi *genitalia* of a beloved lover.

Due to the figurative nature of mele, it is not always possible for people to truly know what metaphors the composer intended in these wisdom maps. With regard to ancestral mele composed generations ago, these are the words and voices of our kūpuna. Through their wisdom maps in the form of ancestral songs, descendants today are able to learn the names of lesser-known places on the landscape, the names of the winds and rains of specific places, the resources of a place, and other historical facts about places.

Just as poetic references link people to their places, so too do mele. As a way of displaying their pride for their places, some Kānaka still practice the tradition of standing when a song is sung for their kulāiwi. An Elder once recalled how she was able to find her granddaughter in a large crowd during a concert by simply singing a song for their homeland and looking to see who was standing in the audience. In this way, the audience served as a visual map, and the mele as an audio map, of the people and places that were present.

Conclusion

According to Greg Dening (1980, 93), "Metaphor is an instrument of daily understanding within a closed system." By delving into the deeper meanings of place revealed by the mapping systems and language of those who inscribed places with meaning via names, stories, and ʻōlelo hoʻopilipili, we better understand the wisdom maps of our ancestors. As Dening suggests, only kupa can truly understand metaphors attached to their places. While this may be true, it is important for kupa and non-lineal descendants alike to recognize and appreciate the unique relationships that people enjoy with their ancestral lands, relationships that can only be enunciated through the language of one's ancestors. For Kānaka, metaphors provide us with a better understanding of the mapping systems and worldviews of our ancestors. Each time we say an ʻōlelo hoʻopilipili, we are quoting the poetry and wisdom of our ancestors and mapping our histories and places on the landscape.

Note

1. *Author's Note*: It is an important step in the process of decolonization that Indigenous writers work to Indigenize the precepts of compositional writing. As we strive to produce an Indigenous body of literature, including one that utilizes English as the matrix language, we should strive to elevate ways of writing that serve to honour our Indigenous worldviews. The author has chosen to honour Hawaiian words by normalizing their use, i.e., by not marking them as different, but treating them instead as part of the normal text. As such, I have chosen to mark their English glosses (indicated by italics) as if they are foreign. Given that the chapter attempts to provide evidence for the inadequacy of translation, marking the English glosses with italics is an attempt to highlight that point. It is, in effect, a way to utilize compositional resource to effect a counter-hegemonic attack on an otherwise dominant mindset, one that is uncompromising for the very fact that its norms seem so normal. This chapter represents my attempt

to contest a space that comes with preconceived notions of normalcy that subordinate native desires for recognition in our own right. In doing so, I recognize that Indigenous ways of knowing, and of presenting that knowledge, cannot be confined to a single style, as we all have unique ways of expressing ideas and various responses to their presentation. The idea that one size fits all stifles our individuality, levels the differences that identify our different peoples, and limits our creativity whether individually or collectively.

References

Andrade, Carlos. 2008. *Haena: Through the Eyes of the Ancestors*. Honolulu: University of Hawai'i Press.

Apoliona, Haunani. 2006. "State of OHA and the Hawaiian Community Address." Office of Hawaiian Affairs presentation given at Kawaiaha'o Church, Honolulu, December 6, 2006.

Dening, Greg. 1980. *Islands and Beaches*. Honolulu: University of Hawai'i Press.

Handy, Edward Smith, and Elizabeth Green Handy, eds. 1972. *Native Planters in Old Hawaii: Their Life, Lore, and Environment*. Honolulu: Bishop Museum Press.

Harley, John Brian. 1992. "Rereading the Maps of the Columbian Encounter." *Annals of the Association of American Geographers* 82 (3): 522-42. https://doi.org/10.1111/j.1467-8306.1992.tb01973.x

Hau'ofa, Epeli, and Eric Waddell, eds. 1993. *A New Oceania: Rediscovering Our Sea of Islands*. Suva, Fiji: School of Social and Economic Development, the University of the South Pacific in association with Beake House.

Herman, R. Douglas K. 1999. "The Aloha State: Place Names and the Anti-Conquest of Hawai'i." *Annals of the Association of American Geographers* 89 (1): 76-101. https://doi.org/10.1111/0004-5608.00131

Johnson, Jay T., Renee P. Louis, and Albertus Hadi Pramono. 2005. "Facing the Future: Encouraging Critical Cartographic Literacies in Indigenous Communities." *ACME: An International E-Journal for Critical Geographies* 4 (1): 80-98.

Kahananui, Abenera. 1875. "No ke Kalana o Kahakuloa a me kona mau Hiohiona." *Ka Nupepa Kuokoa* 14 (33): 1.

Liliuokalani. 1897. *An Account of the Creation of the World According to Hawaiian Tradition*. Boston: Lee and Shepard.

Louis, Renee Pualani. 2004. "Indigenous Hawaiian Cartographer: In Search of Common Ground." *Cartographic Perspectives* 48 (Spring): 7-23. http://dx.doi.org/10.14714/CP48.456

Piianaia, Ilima. n.d. *The Expression of Place in Hawaiian Folk Songs*. Unpublished manuscript, University of Hawai'i.

Pukui, Mary Kawena. 1983. *Olelo Noeau: Hawaiian Proverbs & Poetical Sayings*. Honolulu: Bishop Museum Press.

9 | What's in a **Name?**
Contested Eponyms

SPENCER LILLEY

TE REO MĀORI (Māori language) is the Indigenous language of New Zealand. By having this status, it has been the principal means of describing the relationship between humans and the *whenua* (land), and other natural features including rivers, lakes, streams, and mountains.

Te reo Māori has been embroiled in a war of linguistic politics since the 1840s, when schools that had been established by missionaries were given incentives by the colonial government to teach lessons predominantly in English. As a consequence, over the past 170 years, te reo Māori has undergone long periods of oppression through the introduction and implementation of policies and practices such as the Native Schools Code (1880), which was later reinforced by a policy of corporal punishment of children speaking Māori at school. Such actions led to the threat of the possible extinction of the language. Research undertaken in the 1970s by Benton (1979) revealed the language was in sharp decline and native speakers were predominantly in older age brackets. This decline has only been stopped through the innovative educational methods enacted by *kohanga reo* (language nests) and *kura kaupapa Māori* (Māori schools), where the primary language of instruction is te reo Māori.

Although popular public opinion within New Zealand favours the acquisition of a second language to complement English, the choice of te reo Māori as this second language is dismissed by many New Zealanders, particularly when there are suggestions that learning te reo Māori should become compulsory in the nation's schools. Most of this criticism is centred on views that the language has no relevance, and that it is spoken nowhere but New Zealand and therefore will not contribute to developing the country's export trade and international relationships. Despite a concerted effort over the past 35 years, the language revitalization movement continues to struggle due to inadequate resources and a diminishing number of native speakers in the older age brackets.

The focus of this chapter is not on language revitalization; instead, it contests the argument of those who view te reo Māori as irrelevant to our land by demonstrating that it has an important role. The nature of this position is that it provides the means for us to appreciate and understand the taxonomic context used by Māori to describe the relationship between humans and the environment. At the core of this discussion is the eponymic colonization of New Zealand by English explorers, settlers, and successive administrations in the form of central and local government authorities who have ignored and/or disregarded these original names and replaced them with others that have no descriptive value or have little contextual value to the land or features to which they are ascribed. The chapter commences with a description of the relationship between Māori, land, and te reo Māori, and relates the importance of the assignation of names to natural features and how Māori practices of naming differ from those of the Europeans who came to New Zealand from the 17th century onwards. Later in the chapter, the impact of these different naming practices is discussed, and there is an exploration of how the revival of these ancient names is enabling Māori to restore *mana* (prestige) back to these important places.

Māori Eponymic Origins

Prior to the first contact with the explorers, Tasman in 1642 and Cook in 1769, Māori had lived in New Zealand in relative isolation since first migrating in the first millennium. As the original inhabitants, Māori developed a relationship with the environment, defined by the descent of humans from Tāne, born from the union of Ranginui (Sky father) and Papatūānuku (Earth mother) and distinguished further by a common *whakapapa* with other living things. This relationship was built within an epistemological framework that gave land the utmost mana (status), as it was in effect honouring and protecting the integrity of our mother. The language of our whenua was and remains te reo Māori.

Te reo Māori is a member of the 1,200-strong Austronesian language group, which spans the Southeast Asian and Pacific regions. As a language, te reo Māori is closely related to Tahitian and Cook Islands Māori, consistent with known archaeological evidence that identifies Māori as having originated in East Polynesia. The origins of many Māori place names can be traced back to these places, including three names that are important to my tribal region, Taranaki: the name Taranaki itself, and the name of two towns, Hawera and Patea; all three names are found as a group in Tahiti (Davis, O'Regan, and Wilson 1990). Although at the time of this migration te reo Māori was quite possibly a unified language, over time dialectical differences emerged, with linguists identifying three major dialects: Eastern North Island, Western North Island, and South Island Māori (see http://www.Māorilanguage.info/mao_lang_faq.html). Differences in te reo Māori from other parts of the country are described as regional variations rather than dialects.

Until the early 19th century, te reo Māori was the dominant language of New Zealand, with the arrival of missionaries and settlers bringing English and other European languages.

Te reo Māori was not only a language for communication and conversation; it played an important role in the sense that it was also the language of the land. As such it was used as a means of naming places, landscape features, and natural resources, and these names became an indicator of the significance of these places and provided a rich tapestry of knowledge. Examples of this include a hill in Hawke's Bay called Taumatawhakatangihangakoauauotamateaturipukakapikimaungahoronukupokaiwhenuakitanatahu, which translates as the "hill where Tamatea the man with the big knees, the climber of mountains, the land-swallower who travelled about, played his nose flute to his loved one" (Whittleston 1979, 429). Similarly, the name Manawatū is derived from the reaction of Hau (a well-known Māori name giver), whose breath stood still when confronted with the depth, width, and coldness of the Manawatu River as he crossed it (McEwen 1986). Other common protocols with regard to naming places was to name them after people associated with that land or landscape features, with Walker (1969, 405) stating that personal and place names were of "functional significance in pre-literate Māori society as the fixed points of reference for orally transmitted traditions," being the "immutable, tangible markers of tradition." Examples of places named after people or features of the landscape include Otane (place of Tane), Otara (place of Tara; see Whittleston 1979, 325), Tararua (named to indicate the twin peaks of Pukemoana and Pukeahurangi; see Reed and Dowling 2010, 389), Paeroa (long mountain ridge; see Whittleston, 1979, 330), and Tauranga (a place for landing canoes; see Whittleston 1979, 422).

By their very existence, the names that Māori applied to the landscape around them mapped the relationship of one landmark to the next; as such, the names themselves provide the key, with the understanding of one name being dependent on the other markers they connect to. The names were often named after the exploits of an ancestor who journeyed through the land, or after important events such as sites of famous intertribal battles. This means that the place names were embedded in the history and traditions of a *hapū* or *iwi*, and could serve as another mnemonic to remind them of events and ancestors, thus safeguarding the memory.

Walker (1969) identifies that the manner in which proper names were used in the account of creation, and the myths and legends that followed, as a demonstration of the importance of the use of these names to Māori. Of particular significance was the use of proper names in Ngā Tama a

Rangi (the Sons of Heaven), the Maui cycle, and the Tawhaki (Tane) cycle myths, where Walker notes that in all of the "events depicted, heroes, villains and houses are all given proper names" (406). Walker continues by stating that the names of enemies and enemy tribes were always identified and never anonymous, due to the need for these enemies' actions to be avenged. Thus, the action of giving these significant names to children and descendants was one way of ensuring that the names of these individuals and places were remembered appropriately. Te reo Māori therefore provides another layer of knowledge; and without it being applied in these ways, this knowledge becomes lost and the names and places become inconsequential.

Historically, the names attached to these places were known, and like many other forms of knowledge they were passed on orally, either in the form of stories or in song. By assigning these names, a tribe enabled their traditions and tribal knowledge to be passed from one generation to the next, and the names gave them an enduring reminder of the importance of the people or events that occurred in these places. The tradition of naming places was evident from the first contact between Māori and the land that they discovered and occupied. The earliest Māori explorer was Kupe, who sailed from Hawaiki and systematically named landmarks on Te Ika-a-Māui (North Island), which his wife Kuramārotini named Aotearoa (long white cloud) (Davis, O'Regan, and Wilson 1990), the name that has characteristically been used as the popular Māori name for New Zealand. Walker (2004) identifies 11 place names in the North Island given by Kupe and a further 16 names in the region of Raukawa Moana (Cook Strait) to mark his voyage between the North and Te Waipounamu (South Island). Later explorers and name givers were identified as the *ariki* (paramount chief) of each of the *waka* (voyaging canoes) that made the journey from Hawaiki to New Zealand. Examples (Davis, O'Regan, and Wilson 1990) include Turi (allegedly the brother in law of Kupe), the ariki of the Aotea waka who named many of the features on the North Island's west coast; and Rākaihautū, the ariki of the Uruao waka, and his son Rokohouia, who between them traversed the South Island by sea and land, creating and naming places as they travelled, including the southern interior lakes and the east coast lakes and lagoons, which are known by South Island Māori as *Kā Puna Karikari a Rākaihautū* (the springs of water dug by Rākaihautū).

European Explorers

In 1642, the first colonial intrusion by Westerners took place with Abel Janszoon Tasman's search for the unknown great southern continent (Terras Australis Incognita), which instead rediscovered the South Island of New Zealand. The name given to the country was Staten Land. The place of the only physical contact with Māori was in the bay known as Taitapu by the local iwi, Ngati Tumatakokiri. This encounter was short and violent, ending with casualties on both sides. Consequently, this place was renamed Murderers Bay by Tasman, and marked accordingly by the cartographers on board. Thus started the process of subjugation of Māori place names, and the mana that was associated with these places was either disregarded or ignored. Ironically, Tasman was not immune to this, as his assignation of Staten Land was later changed to Nieuw Zeeland (Zealandia Nova) by an unknown cartographer of the Dutch East India Company (King 2003).

Captain Cook

No further voyages by Western explorers were recorded until the arrival of Captain James Cook and the HMS *Endeavour* in 1769. Cook has been described as a born surveyor (Wharton 1968) and had been responsible for charting parts of Canada, including the channels of the river near Quebec and Newfoundland. When commissioned to sail to and explore the Pacific, Cook was ordered to go to Tahiti to allow an observation of the transit of Venus, and to thereafter explore the Pacific to the south of Tahiti and to proceed to and explore New Zealand.

As an explorer and an expert surveyor adventuring into new territories previously unexplored and charted by Western explorers, Cook availed himself of the luxury of assigning names to places he "discovered."

Wharton (1968, xi) states that Cook would assign native names if they were known, but otherwise he would find a descriptive and distinctive appellation for each feature or place he "discovered." However, it seems that he, too, was mindful of the contribution made to his travels by patrons back in England. The map of the country that was charted by Cook during his circumnavigation shows this mixture of Māori and "new" names.

The allocation of 'new' names during the journey was often incident-based; for example, the promontory point, known as Te Kuri a Paoa (the dog of Paoa), was named Young Nick's Head by Cook after Nicholas Young, the assistant to the ship's surgeon who was the first crew member to sight land. Paoa was one of the captains of the Horouta waka, and to him the shape of the headlands resembled that of his dog. Cook was not immune to naming places after shapes either, naming one place Cape Table because of its shape and figure. Other place names were assigned by Cook after what was experienced there. So Turanganui a Kiwa (the place where Kiwa stopped) became known as Poverty Bay, because Cook and his crewmen were involved in some skirmishes with local Māori, resulting in the deaths of several Māori and leading Cook to leave the location without any of the supplies he and his crew wanted. Even though Cook commented in his journal that Tupaia (a Tahitian who was accompanying the *Endeavour*) was able to communicate with Māori, there appeared to be no attempt to find out what their name for this place was. This was a common but not entrenched trend for the remainder of his voyage, with another example being the bay off the east coast where Māori attempted to "kidnap" Tupaia's assistant, Tiata; the bay was subsequently named Cape Kidnappers. This area had been named Matahaupo Maui (the hook of Maui), representing the belief that the Māori demigod had fished up the North Island (Te Ika-a-Māui). However, an example of a place where the local name was learned and noted was the bay at Tolaga. The practice of naming places after prominent Englishmen was first encountered through the renaming of Heretaunga (named by legendary explorer Whātonga, as it was where his waka came to rest) to Hawkes Bay, after Sir Edward Hawke, the first Lord of the Admiralty. There are too many examples of Cook's naming protocols to focus on them all. However, I will focus on the names he assigned in Taranaki, and this will lead on to a fuller discussion of the impact that settlers made on this region in the 19th century.

Taranaki

On January 12, 1770, while sailing down the North Island's west coast, Cook notes in his journal that he saw the evidence of a peaked mountain to the south, but it was not until the next day, when the cloud had lifted from the mountain, that he named it Mount Egmont after the Earl of Egmont, who had strongly supported the expedition (Cook, Beaglehole, and Skelton 1955). In another bizarre twist of irony, the Earl passed away before Cook's return to England and never knew of the mountain named after him in New Zealand. The Māori name of this mountain is Taranaki (peak that shines); however, the name Egmont has stuck due to Cook's charts. Due to its name being registered on official charts, and thereafter maps, of New Zealand, the name of the mountain remained Egmont until 1986, when the Minister of Lands announced that Mount Taranaki would be the official alternative name to Mount Egmont, although the surrounding national park land would remain known as Egmont National Park. This announcement was not received with universal acclaim, and is still raised as an issue of discontent by those who were opposed to it and who refuse to refer to the mountain as anything else other than Egmont.

Illustrating the fact that Cook was not the only explorer renaming places without deference to already established names, Taranaki was also renamed by French explorer Captain Marion du Fresne in 1772. Du Fresne was unaware that Cook had already named the mountain, and when the French explorer sighted Taranaki he named it Le Pic Mascarin (presumably after his ship).

Captain Cook also displayed his sense of imagination (or perhaps humour) when he spotted the islands just off the coast (in the place now known as New Plymouth). Before Cook's observation, these group of islands were known to my iwi, Te Atiawa, as Ngāmotu (the islands). On the January 13, 1770, these islands were sighted by Captain Cook and renamed the Sugarloaf Islands, as they were covered in guano and reminded him of the shape of the lumps of sugar he took in his tea.

The most prominent of these islands is named Paritutu, and there are six smaller islands. Each of these islands has a name given to it either in memory of a *tipuna* or an event that occurred there; they have also been given English names that bear no relationship to their Māori names. The islands are in three different groupings, with inner and outer islands, and there are some smaller rocks. These islands are known to Te Atiawa as Mataora (Round Rock), Pararaki (Seagull Rock), and Motuotamatea (Snapper Rock). Mataora connects to the mainland at low tides, as does Motuotamatea on very low spring tides. The outer islands include Motumahanga (Saddleback Island) and Moturoa. The non-island rocks are Waikaranga and Tokatapu (Seal Rocks), which are several hundred metres offshore. Closer to the island of Moturoa lie Whareumu (Lion Rock), a vegetated stack and two barren rocks, and Tokomapuna (Barrett Reef). In ancient times these rocks provided shelter from invading tribes, a hunting ground, and a place where burials took place. In 1986 an aspect of their mana was restored through the creation of a marine reserve in the area surrounding the "Sugarloafs." This was further enhanced with the passing of the Sugar Loaf Marine Park Act in 1991. However, regardless of the protection, for Te Atiawa the fact that they are still known as the Sugarloaf Islands is a point of frustration.

Purchase of Ngāmotu

In 1838, Edward Gibbon Wakefield was accompanied by Dicky Barrett, a local whaler, who along with fellow whaler John Love had helped Te Atiawa defend their *pā* (fort) at Paritutu in 1833 from invading Waikato tribes. Love and Barrett had married Te Atiawa women. In recognition of his connection to Te Atiawa, Barrett was appointed as a land agent for the New Zealand Company and was an instrumental figure in the negotiations for the purchase of the land at Ngāmotu. The land was sold by

72 Māori on February 15, 1840. As most Te Atiawa had fled Taranaki after inter-tribal wars in the early 1830s, much of the land around New Plymouth was unoccupied, as only a small band of iwi members had remained behind, fulfilling an *ahi kā* (burning fires) presence, and the land they sold was surplus to their requirements.

The purchase of this land provided the settlement's leaders with a mandate to make it available to settlers and to start the development of the town. Before the colonization of the city in 1841, the location remained known as Ngāmotu. The renaming of Taranaki lands, however, intensified from 1841 onwards with the arrival of the first settlers from the Plymouth Company, a subsidiary of the much larger New Zealand Company. After purchase of the titles to the land, the new settlement was named New Plymouth after the place of origin of most of the Company's directors and settlers. Further assertion of their establishment rights came in the form of naming streets and landmarks of the area after prominent members of the Plymouth Company and places back in England.

Eponymic Colonization of New Plymouth and Waitara

The impact that the process of renaming by explorers and colonists of everything that they encountered without regard to the names already assigned by *tangata whenua* is immensely apparent to me in my hometown of New Plymouth. This is my *tūrangawaewae* (place where I belong), part of the province of Taranaki, situated on the west coast of the North Island. I affiliate with two prominent hapū: Ngati Te Whiti, which has the *mana whenua* (rights of occupation) over New Plymouth; and Pukerangiora, which is the paramount hapū of Waitara.

Examples of the imposition of new eponyms are apparent in both locations. In addition to the examples already discussed, the city of New Plymouth provides two other critical examples for Ngati Te Whiti of the impact that colonization and the subsequent renaming had on landmarks important to our hapū. This includes the renaming of the pā site of Puke Ariki. This was a stronghold that was commandeered and occupied, with a "bonded store, an imposing flagstaff, the signal store, the pilot and signalman's houses and the headquarters of the Armed Constabulary Force" (Tullett 1981, 27). It was subsequently renamed Mount Eliot after Lord Eliot (Edward Granville Eliot), a director of the Plymouth Company who, like the Earl of Egmont, never set foot in New Zealand. Adding insult to injury, they later bulldozed the site, using the excess soil as infill for the area surrounding it to create a flat-building platform, thus stripping the site of any remaining mana. In 2001, the mana was partially returned through the opening of the newly created integrated library and museum, named after the ancient pā site, but unfortunately still outside the control of the hapū. The other critical example relates to the formerly prominent pā site, Pukaka. This site had a panoramic view across the entire settlement. It was originally covered in bush and full of native birds, and the name Pukaka was representative of the fact that parrots were caught and hung there. The site was subsequently renamed Marsland Hill after a friend of the Plymouth Company's Resident Commissioner, who, like the Earl of Egmont, probably had no other link with New Plymouth or New Zealand. At the time of laying out the plan of the settlement, the hill had been identified as a suitable place for a cemetery; however, its prominent vista across the city made it a better location for a military base. The site was therefore chosen to house the military barracks, being levelled off to accommodate parade grounds and other necessary buildings. The troops dug trenches and barricades were erected, making the former pā site a safe refuge when there was a threat of Māori invasion. In later years the former pā became a public reserve, with a memorial statue being erected commemorating the names of officers, soldiers, and loyal Māori who lost their lives in the land wars of the 19th century.

Waitara

The township of Waitara was renamed Raleigh by the first European settlers, and then was changed back to Waitara in 1904. The origin of the name suggests that the correct name for it is Whaitara, which is abbreviated from Te Whai-tara-nui a Ngārue, derived from the magic *tara* (darts) given to Whare Matangi to help him find his estranged father. These darts, when thrown, hit the house belonging to Ngārue, which sat at the mouth of the Waitara River (Smith 1910). With it being known as Waitara, the common English translation of its name is "mountain stream," which is far removed from the original name given to it by Te Atiawa.

During the wars of the 1860s, several battles took place around the area surrounding Waitara, including the Te Atiawa stronghold Pukerangiora, where *pā* sites were taken over by the militia, including Te Morere, which was occupied by the troops and renamed Sentry Hill, and where a redoubt was built. To add further insult to its loss of mana, the hill was later levelled and used as quarry, thereby erasing it from the landscape. The name Te Morere, although effectively wiped from the landscape, has continued to survive within my *whānau*, having been handed down through several generations and so remaining as an ongoing memory of the links we have to this location and to our tipuna, who was the *rangatira* of the pā.

The street names of Waitara also reflect the colonial government's dominance of the former Māori stronghold, with several streets named after colonial politicians, military officers, and early settlers; there are very few streets with Māori names, despite the fact that 40% of the town's population identifies as Māori. The message sent by the assignation of these names is that the European founders and officials were important and worthy of commemoration, while the rangatira of Te Atiawa and its affiliated hapū were not.

Unfortunately, even when Māori place names have been retained, there is no guarantee that they will be respected; they are often shortened, as in the case of Whaitara, or their pronunciation is absolutely butchered through common usage and abuse. Two grating examples from Taranaki are Oakura, which has a common mispronunciation of Oh-auk-ra, and Kawaroa, which somehow gets mashed into Kar-rah.

Very many similar examples exist throughout the rest of New Zealand. It is difficult to know whether this mispronunciation is deliberate or just an example of lazy speech that has been perpetuated over successive generations of non-speakers of te reo Māori.

New Zealand Geographic Board

The entire length of New Zealand provides numerous examples of eponymic imposition by explorers, settlers, and public officials in the post-colonization period. The fact that these imported designations are privileged over their original Māori name continues to be contested by hapū and iwi who wish to recover the right to officially call these places by these names.

The New Zealand Geographic Board (Ngā Pou Taunaha o Aotearoa) is the official body that can assign or alter place names. As an agency of the Crown in New Zealand, the Board is required to ensure that it meets its Treaty of Waitangi obligations by ensuring that decisions are cognizant of Māori aspirations. First established in 1946, the Board has, among other functions, jurisdiction over assigning and altering official names (especially if names have been misspelled) and approving the discontinuation of official names. An increasingly important function of the Board is its ability to identify original Māori names and to encourage the use of these on maps and charts. For this purpose, it works closely with Te Taura Whiri i te Reo Māori (Māori Language Commission) to ensure that these names are orthographically correct. However, the process of renaming, correctly spelling Māori names, or assigning dual name status is not without controversy or opposition. Many of the proposals are sourced from the cultural redress process aligned with Waitangi Tribunal recommendations or the resolution of grievances negotiated with the Office of Treaty Settlements.

A prime example of the contestability of naming decisions is provided by the notification in 2013 that the Board was considering the names of the two main islands (North Island and South Island) and whether they should be assigned dual Māori and English names. The proposal put out for public consultation was that North Island and South Island, and the Māori names, Te Ika-a-Māui and Te Waipounamu, could become official alternative geographic names, and be used individually or together. In making this decision, the Board (New Zealand Geographic Board 2013) noted that the North Island and South Island had never been "official" names, and that Captain Cook's chart of New Zealand had only included the Māori names that had continued to appear on maps until about 1950. Submissions to the Board's plans were divided, with approximately 70% (n = 1842) supporting the changes in principle, and 30% (n = 766) objecting to the proposal. Although there were many submissions to the Board supporting the proposal, there were also a considerable number that contained comments that expressed disapproval of the changes proposed. Examples of these include:

> The proposal has racial undertones. No place in New Zealand for racial separation. Māori names too difficult and original settlers' claims questionable.

> New Zealand should be about equality and unity, not division based on Treaty of Waitangi 200 years ago.

> North Island & South Island names widely accepted and should be endorsed. New Ulster and New Munster more legitimate claim than Māori names. (New Zealand Geographic Board 2013)

This opposition was also reflected in wider circles, with discussions on talkback radio and through the use of social media tools, including blogs and discussion forums. Although some of this opposition was muted and relatively inoffensive, some was extremely vitriolic. Examples of the latter include:

> Stone age language. Should be left to die like the Inca, Mayan, Roman, Gaelic, Celtic, Ancient Greek and all the other dead and

useless languages that the world has passed by. More the [sic] half the language has been invented, why should I support it? (Comment by Hazards001, April 3, 2013, on Cameron Slater, "Shearer Enthusiastic about Maori Island Names," *WhaleOil* blog, https://www.whaleoil.co.nz/2013/04/shearer-enthusiastic-about-maori-island-names/)

Does Government have nothing else to do but pander to greedy lawyers and self-promoting racists in this way? Leave the names alone, get on with finding ways to stimulate and grow the economy. That is your real job, just do it!! (Comment by Hughwright, April 3, 2013, on David Farrar, "Naming the Islands," *Kiwiblog*, https://www.kiwiblog.co.nz/2013/04/naming_the_islands.html)

This is the most ridiculous suggestion we've ever heard!! For god's sake, enough is enough, there is nothing wrong with the North and South islands. Am sick and tired of all this Māori nonsense, and continually giving in to their wants!! It has to stop! (Comment posted March 15, 2013, on *New Zealand Centre for Political Research* blog, www.nzcpr.org.nz; the post has since been removed)

This level of opposition and commentary on the changes was not unexpected, given the highly politicized nature of Māori issues in New Zealand. However, it does provide a strong impression of the challenges that those advocating for the reinstatement of original Māori place names need to overcome. That there is resistance to the restoration of place names that were Indigenous to the landscape and other natural resources demonstrates that this will continue to be a contested space.

The last words of this chapter are left to a quote from a book published by the New Zealand Geographic Board in 1990 that reinforces the importance of Māori names to the places and natural features that they describe: "The most important role of place names in a society which traditions and history were transmitted orally was to serve as triggers for memory. They reminded those who spoke or heard them of events or episodes important in the history of tribe. They were the means by which the tribe's traditions and knowledge of its tūpuna were handed on" (Davis, O'Regan, and Wilson 1990, 7).

References

Benton, Richard. 1979. *Who Speaks Māori in New Zealand?* Wellington, NZ: New Zealand Council for Educational Research.

Cook, James, John Cawte Beaglehole, and Raleigh A. Skelton, eds. 1955. *The Journals of Captain James Cook on His Voyages of Discovery*. Cambridge: Cambridge University Press.

Davis, Te Aue, Tipene O'Regan, and John Wilson. 1990. *Ngā Tohu Pūmahara: The Survey Pegs of the Past, Understanding Māori Place Names*. Wellington, NZ: New Zealand Geographic Board.

King, Michael. 2003. *The Penguin History of New Zealand*. Auckland, NZ: Penguin Books.

McEwen, Jock M. 1986. *Rangitāne: A Tribal History*. Auckland, NZ: Reed Methuen.

New Zealand Geographic Board. 2013. "Alternative Geographic Name Proposals—Submissions Report." Wellington, NZ: New Zealand Geographic Board.

Reed, Alexander Wyclif, and Peter Dowling. 2010. *Place Names of New Zealand: Origins and Meanings for Over 10,000 Names*. Auckland, NZ: Penguin.

Smith, Stephenson Percy. 1910. *History and Traditions of the Taranaki Coast*. New Plymouth, NZ: Avery.

Tullett, James Stewart. 1981. *The Industrious Heart: A History of New Plymouth*. New Plymouth, NZ: New Plymouth City Council.

Walker, Ranginui. 1969. "Proper Names in Māori Myth and Tradition." *Journal of the Polynesian Society* 78 (3): 405-16.

———. 2004. *Ka Whawhai Tonu Mātou: Struggle Without End*. Auckland, NZ: Penguin.

Wharton, William James Lloyd, ed. 1968. *Captain Cook's Journal During His First Voyage Round the World Made in H.M. Bark Endeavour, 1768-71: A Literal Transcription of the Original Mss. Australiana Facsimile Editions*. Adelaide, Australia: Libraries Board of South Australia.

Whittleston, Edgar. 1979. *Wises New Zealand Guide: A Gazetteer of New Zealand*. Auckland, NZ: Wises.

10 | Contested Spaces of Indigenization
in Canadian Higher Education

Reciprocal Relationships and Institutional Responsibilities

MICHELLE PIDGEON

THE COMPLEXITIES OF "INDIGENIZING" the academy encounter multiple contested spaces. Marlene Brant Castellano (2014, par. 1) envisions Indigenized education to mean "that every subject at every level is examined to consider how and to what extent current content and pedagogy reflect the presence of Indigenous/Aboriginal Peoples and the valid contribution of Indigenous knowledge." For the purposes of this chapter, Indigenization is extended beyond curriculum and pedagogy to include the ongoing transformation and decolonization of post-secondary education, from institutional structures, policies, and practices through to intentionally including Indigenous ways of knowing and being, honouring the cultural integrity and diversities of Indigenous Peoples, and respecting the rights of Indigenous Peoples to articulate what of their knowledges, languages, cultures, and practices should be included in post-secondary spaces.

This view recognizes that universities and colleges are microcosms of the broader society and, for that reason, are places of contention and resistance for Indigenous Peoples (Alfred 2004). In "Being Indigenous:

Resurgences against Contemporary Colonialism," Alfred and Corntassel (2005, 600) question the broader issues of Indigeneity and colonization. This chapter explores how universities and colleges are "transforming" within the discourse of "Indigenization" and how institutions aiming to be better places for Indigenous Peoples "account for the dynamic nature of being Indigenous." Within higher education, this means asking what it means to authentically bridge an understanding of what it means to be Indigenous within institutional structures that are predominately based on colonial Euro-Western worldviews. Furthermore, how do institutions provide support services to diverse Aboriginal populations, address systemic and institutional racism, build relationships with and responsibilities to the broader institution and Aboriginal communities, and provide services within fiscal and political constraints and competing agendas both within and outside the institution?

This chapter first provides an overview of the Indigenous wholistic[1] framework that guides its organization. Next, readers are provided with a brief historical overview of the development of Aboriginal student services across Canadian colleges and universities and Aboriginal participation in higher education. The subsequent sections discuss, through the use of the Indigenous wholistic framework (including physical, emotional, cultural, and intellectual realms), the contested spaces and competing roles within higher education that are either helping or hindering (or both) Indigenous aspirations and the goals of higher education, specifically Aboriginal student services. The final section draws on the ideas of responsible relationships and Indigenization to articulate how universities and colleges authentically work towards transforming their policies, practices, and institutional cultures to honour the principles of Indigenous knowledges and education to be truly responsible for and accountable to Indigenous education. To begin this discussion, the guiding Indigenous wholistic framework is discussed.

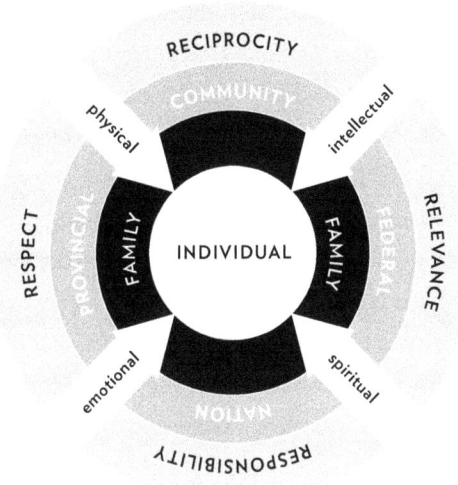

FIGURE 10.1 Indigenous wholistic framework.

Indigenous Wholistic Framework

The Indigenous wholistic framework (Figure 10.1) was developed in my graduate work as a theoretical framing for my research, informed by my cultural ways of knowing and understanding; subsequently, I have used this framework throughout my scholarship, as it provides guidance on how to address complex questions theoretically and methodologically while honouring Indigenous epistemology, ontology, and axiology (Pidgeon, Archibald, and Hawkey 2014; Pidgeon 2008, 2012; Pidgeon and Hardy Cox 2002). It is important to acknowledge that this is only one way of representing Indigenous knowledge(s) and there are other models and frameworks that also respect Indigenous knowledges in important and meaningful ways (Archibald 2008; Marsden 2006; Kovach 2009; Wilson 2008).

The Indigenous wholistic framework centres and privileges the Indigenous knowledges at the core of this chapter. As shown in Figure 10.1, Indigenous ways of knowing and being see the interconnections between the physical, emotional, cultural, and intellectual realms. These realms are overlapping and not viewed as separate; they all contribute to the whole. These realms also connect to the relationships we have as individuals to our families (nuclear and extended), communities (local, provincial, national, and international), and Nations, along with the relationships between federal, provincial, and Indigenous governments. The latter speaks to the unique (and not uncontested) relationship Indigenous Nations have with the federal and provincial governments as a result of the Indian Act (Royal Commission on Aboriginal Peoples [RCAP] 1996). Surrounding the framework are the Indigenous principles of the 4Rs: respect for Indigenous knowledges, responsible relationships, relevance, and reciprocity (Kirkness and Barnhardt 1991).

Kirkness and Barnhardt (1991) first proposed the 4Rs as a way to guide universities and colleges in supporting Aboriginal student success. Marker (2004) sees institutions still failing to truly honour the 4Rs; and, to some extent, even to this day institutional responsibility to Aboriginal education remains only pockets of presence across our campuses, primarily found within Indigenous academic stream programs and specializations or Indigenous student support services (Pidgeon 2008). I agree with Marker's assessment that higher education has been slow to adapt. In fact, even the interpretation of the 4Rs from an institutional perspective is at times contrary to how Indigenous Peoples think of the same concepts. For example, honouring the principle of reciprocity is not just about offering a one-time program and checking the "done" box; for many Aboriginal communities, it is an ongoing commitment to provide relevant programs and services that evolve with the needs of the community.

A Brief History of Indigeneity and Higher Education

Growth in Aboriginal student, faculty, and staff populations pushes back on notions of place and space within the academy and the landscape of higher education. Institutional shifts began in the 1970s and became more predominant in the 1990s, with Aboriginal academic programs and support services included for several reasons. Aboriginal students were arriving on campus needing wholistic support to overcome systemic challenges and barriers. More Aboriginal communities were encouraging their youth and young adults to attend post-secondary education to move towards goals of self-determination, community economic development, and empowerment (RCAP 1996). Another shift in the higher education landscape at this time was the introduction of federal and provincial funding that provided not only access to First Nations students (Malatest and Associates 2004, 2010) but also institutional grants and transfer payments that provided incentive for institutions to develop Aboriginal-specific academic programs and services (e.g., Provincial Advisory Committee 1990). These shifts resulted in more Aboriginal people being on our campuses as well as the inclusion of Indigenous content, programs, and services, which also required shifts in policy and practices. In many cases, non-Aboriginal people have had to recognize and come to understand the impact that residential schools and inadequate K-12 schooling had on Aboriginal Peoples, and that the supports required are not limited to academic preparation.

Since the late 1990s, notably after the Royal Commission on Aboriginal Peoples (RCAP) published its report in 1996, there has seemed to be renewed focus on Aboriginal student recruitment and retention in college and universities. Within the RCAP's (1996) discussion of education, the role that post-secondary education had to play within Aboriginal communities, urban and rural, on and off reserve, was clearly evident. If the current educational disparity between Aboriginal and non-Aboriginal people remains vast in both the K-12 (notably on-reserve; Richards 2014) and post-secondary sectors (Statistics Canada 2011), then the inequities (e.g., health, economic, and social determinants) we see today will continue.

Recognizing the systemic and societal barriers and the lack of relevant programs and services in higher education for Aboriginal students, one institutional response to supporting Aboriginal students was the creation of Aboriginal student services.[2]

Aboriginal Student Services

Aboriginal student services began in the 1970s in Canadian universities in response to increased Aboriginal participation in the newly established programs of the time: Native Teacher Education and First Nations Studies.[3] Aboriginal student services play a key role in supporting Aboriginal student success and bridging understanding in non-Aboriginal communities of the wholistic needs of students (Pidgeon 2005). Through wholistic service provision, physical (housing, health, food, finances), intellectual (tutoring, peer mentoring), emotional (peer counselling, Elders), and spiritual (cultural ceremony, Elders) needs of students are met to empower their success in university and college (Pidgeon 2008). Aboriginal student services continue to be sites of culturally relevant support to Indigenous students but also sites of resistance, decolonization, and Indigenization across the academy.

Across Canadian universities and colleges, there was a diversification of the ways in which specific support service provision was delivered to Aboriginal students through centralized and decentralized models, or a mix of both. For example, centralized services meant that there was one office in the institution that addressed all the needs of incoming and current Aboriginal students. While students had their academic departments to address their academic program needs, their personal, social, and cultural needs, and even their needs for extra academic help, were provided through this centralized office. A decentralized model took Aboriginal staff members and placed them within an existing unit in the institution; for example, Aboriginal recruiters were added to the recruitment office. A mixed model provided a "home away from home" for students, which was often the Aboriginal student services offices or building, but also had Aboriginal staff across academic and student affairs units to provide front-line support throughout the institution. All of these models, however, had the characteristic of providing specialized services for a "small" proportion of the student body, which will be revisited later in this chapter.

First and foremost, Aboriginal student services exist to support and empower Indigenous student success. Equally important is assistance with the reciprocal relationships that those within student services must navigate within the academy, including advocating for Indigenous issues, educating non-Aboriginal peoples' understanding and intercultural competency, and building relationships with Aboriginal communities (Pidgeon 2008). The presence of these services in over 90% of our colleges and universities sends a clear message to Indigenous students and their families that they do belong here.

In the beginning, Aboriginal student services comprised one individual hired on a contractual basis to provide culturally relevant support for Aboriginal students. These early pioneers, and even student affairs practitioners today, were and are cultural brokers in bridging two worlds for many: the Euro-Western academy and Indigenous communities (Pidgeon 2005). Today, over 40 years later, we see Aboriginal student services having critical roles to play in Aboriginal student success and in institutions' commitment to Aboriginal education. Not only have they evolved in many institutions to be a staff complement with diverse training and portfolios (e.g., Aboriginal recruiters, academic advisors, Elders-in-residence, financial aid advisors, housing support services) but there has also been the creation of Indigenous spaces on campuses through the creation of Aboriginal gathering spaces or specific buildings architecturally reflecting Indigenous cultures and designed specifically for Indigenous student services and academic programming.

Aboriginal Students Today

Nationally, Indigenous students make up approximately 3% of post-secondary students in Canada; however, this varies provincially and territorially. For example, in some universities in British Columbia, approximately 10% of the student population is Aboriginal. While the figures are influenced by population density across provinces, the reality is that Aboriginal Peoples are the fastest-growing population in the country (Statistics Canada 2008, 2013). Yet it is also true that the gap in post-secondary completion rates between Aboriginal (7%) and non-Aboriginal (20%) remains vast (Statistics Canada 2013). Consequently, universities and colleges have a renewed interest in attracting and retaining Indigenous peoples on their campuses, which are facing declining enrollments and increased competition over resources (both human and financial), continuing decreases in federal and provincial transfer payments, and diversifying teaching and research agendas, along with broader social and political shifts such as the Idle No More movement. This again becomes an important moment to pause and articulate that there are differences between institutions and Aboriginal perspectives on the role, purpose, and reasons for pursuing higher education.

Contested Spaces and Competing Roles Within Higher Education

Our universities and colleges are complex, negotiated spaces of power and privilege. The role of higher education within Indigenous communities is about empowerment and decolonization, not about "bums in seats" and target enrollments; it is about achieving success based on Indigenous values and maintaining one's cultural integrity while in these spaces (Pidgeon 2008).

Within the wholistic framework (presented in Figure 10.2) one can see that there are physical, emotional, cultural, and intellectual spaces in the academy that need to be considered in truly embodying the 4 R s as Kirkness and Barnhardt (1991) had envisioned them. The following sections describe each of these spaces in more detail.

Physical

Canadian higher education began in the 17th century with the establishment of church-funded post-secondary institutions (e.g., Université Laval in Quebec in 1660; King's College in Nova Scotia in 1789). Our university campuses are located on the traditional and often unceded

Physical
- Indigenous territory & protocol
- Indigenous space on campus (art; buildings)
- Indigenous "seen face" e.g., Aboriginal student services

Intellectual
- Indigenous academic programs and curriculum
- IK in the classroom (Instructor/Students)
- Culturally relevant support

Emotional
- Intergenerational trauma of residential schools
- Wholistic support: Aboriginal student services
- Elders

Spiritual
- Cultural protocol in practice and policy
- Public/private IK
- Elders
- Aboriginal student services

FIGURE 10.2 *Indigeneity in higher education.*

territories of Indigenous Peoples; acknowledging the place of Indigenous Peoples on this land shows respect for the fact that we are all in some ways visitors to their homeland. Borrowing on the ideas shared in Lilley's chapter in this volume on what is lost when Indigenous places are renamed in the act of colonization, we can ask, What happens when we begin decolonizing our campuses through the reclaiming and renaming of spaces and places through Aboriginal languages? This intentional act of naming is occurring in some institutions that have put their campus signage in the local First Nations language or that have Indigenous art and signage at sites of importance. In sharing the knowledge that these lands and territories and the spaces in between are Indigenous, we are saying that we belong; this is our space and our place.

As someone living and working within the Coast Salish territories in British Columbia, I am a visitor and respect the protocols I've been taught here on the west coast; I acknowledge that I am a visitor to the traditional territories of the Peoples whenever I am speaking in public in other spaces. This recognition of homeland is beginning to be part of the cultural protocol and responsibilities that institutions are taking up in their formal public business (e.g., convocation), yet it remains the case that many do not understand why such protocol is being followed. Corntassel (2011, 2) responds to these queries by stating, "It is to honour the ongoing relationships that Indigenous peoples have to their homelands." He also states that there is a clear political motivation in this acknowledgement, in what he sees as "a call for justice and returning stolen lands to the Indigenous peoples who maintain a special relationship with that place. But this kind of talk makes those who have benefitted—and continue to benefit—from living on Indigenous homelands a little uncomfortable" (3).

In my research and in my day-to-day experiences, I see this discomfort play out in several ways. One is the inconsistent honouring and acknowledgement of territory within the institution. For example, in Indigenous-focused events, protocol is typically followed; however, in other public events of the university it becomes less practised. Consistent and respectful acknowledgement is important, as it educates others as to why such protocol is central to the relationships institutions have with Indigenous Peoples and their homelands. Another is the visible discomfort with cultural protocols being practised in academic spaces (e.g., acknowledging of territory, Aboriginal languages being spoken, Elder's welcoming or blessings).

Indeed, some of this discomfort comes from a place of not knowing and not having the cultural understanding to know how to behave, but subverting this is a subtext that is deeper and, in many cases, racist. Some witness this subtext in vocalizations by non-Aboriginal people questioning why even to bother to include Aboriginal culture: Why should we do this for them? What about "other" minority groups? While those opposed to inclusion of Indigenous knowledge(s) may position their argument within the multicultural debate, what is clear is that some individuals do not want to give up any of their privilege and power in the academy (Pidgeon 2008). Others have witnessed the passive-aggressive actions of walking out of a room when an event is being opened with an Indigenous welcome (Pidgeon 2008).

Within our campuses, as noted earlier, Aboriginal student services became for many the first "physical" space on campus where Indigenous culture and knowledge was present and respected. However, we can also see that physical space on our campuses is political, and it is important to be aware of this position within the academy. For example, in the creation of space from the 1970s to 1990s, many Aboriginal student services units, which were often created with one contractual employee, were located in makeshift spaces, designated "Indigenous" without conscious thinking about what messages were being sent to Aboriginal students when they had to go to a small room with no windows, to the basement of a student union building, or within a building that was portable, temporary, or located in the far ends of campus. I recognize that sometimes reclaiming space takes time, and during this period using what space was available was a necessary first step to begin conversations about what space would be appropriate, and then actually raising the funds required to build a new space or building. Yet we should stay mindful of the challenges that taking space from others creates on a campus, even if the space wasn't being used. Space is probably one of the most political and contentious topics that administrators have to address: who gets space, who has resources to build space, and so on. So in claiming space as Indigenous, in order to create physical structures and spaces that allow for the cultural ceremonies and gathering of Indigenous Peoples, one must become and remain cognizant of the navigation and relationship-building that must go on, internal and external to the institution, to have a visible presence on campus.

The physical operations of holding cultural ceremony in buildings with central air and ventilation requires the Indigenous community and institutional administrators to work together to transform the buildings to allow such ceremonies to be held in an environment where no-scent policies are prevalent; the needs of others sharing that space also need to be considered. These may seem like simple things, but the complexity of balancing power within institutional spaces has been, and continues to be, contested and met with resistance—both subtle and overt.

Another tension within higher education has been the representation and inclusion of Indigenous culture on campuses through the visual display of Aboriginal art or cultural artifacts. While on one hand this is an important recognition of Indigenous knowledge(s) through contemporary and traditional media, the simple hanging of art does not create understanding or Indigenize the campus. Art holds an important role in many Indigenous Nations' cultures. Art is not just visual presentation; it involves story and teachings, about the piece itself or the artist who created it. Art is another representation of Indigenous ways of knowing and being, and should be respected as such. A cultural token presence without teaching or protocol challenges one to think about the messages that are communicated within the physical realm about Aboriginal Peoples and cultures. Another consideration is the cultural misappropriation of Indigenous culture and knowledges that we must continue to be mindful of in higher education (e.g., athletic team mascots and names; see Castagno and Lee 2007; King 2008; Reamey 2009) and how the colonial gaze on our cultures and protocols impacts the broader society's understanding of who we are as Indigenous Peoples.

In the creation of Aboriginal-specific spaces (or unique buildings), another dilemma occurs when such spaces become co-opted because of the architectural and cultural cache they have to outside groups who visit (predominately non-Indigenous people) and, consequently, the space is used to hold important university events (e.g., conferences, academic meetings, alumni gatherings, tour groups). It is not that these buildings, as university spaces, shouldn't be inclusive of such gatherings, but Indigenous meetings and gatherings must take precedence, and each visiting group (whether internal or external) to the building or space must have some cultural awareness education from those working at the building so that they understand the teachings behind the design and artwork of the space. Such spaces, then, become an opportunity for decolonization or overt centring of Indigenous knowledges in the day-to-day activities of institutions.

The physical realm is not limited to geography and building structures; people are also an important component of the physical realm. Linda Tuhiwai Smith (2012) introduced the Māori concept of "seen face" when speaking about researchers working in their communities. The seen face reflects the cultural responsibility of being present and engaged in community (Smith 2012). When we look to Canadian higher education, statistics demonstrate that, proportionately, Aboriginal students are consistently underrepresented in universities (particularly females) and overrepresented in trades (particularly males) in terms of student population; yet proportionately fewer Aboriginal Peoples attain a post-secondary credential than non-Aboriginal Canadians (Statistics Canada 2011). The seen face also is important for Aboriginal faculty, staff, and administration; recent reports show that Aboriginal faculty make up less than 3% of faculty across Canada (Canadian Association of University Teachers 2012). If we are to make substantive changes in transforming these spaces for Indigenous Peoples we also need to ensure that Indigenous Peoples are in these spaces. The seen face is also important for universities and colleges in terms of their presence and relationships in Aboriginal communities (Pidgeon 2008).

Spiritual

This realm is the one that has perhaps seen the most conversation and debate, as spirituality for many Indigenous Peoples is inherently connected to their culture. There is a difference, as well, between Indigenous spirituality and faith-based spirituality. While the two are not disconnected, many Indigenous Peoples blend their cultural teachings with their faith-based practices, while for others faith and spirituality/culture are two separate things. It is important, though, for us to understand that spirituality is a core realm and as thus one needs to ask the questions, What does it mean to authentically include cultural protocols and ceremony within university and college campuses? What kinds of cultural knowledge should be shared in these public spaces? For many of the Indigenous

Elders, academic, staff, and students with whom I have worked over the years, there was a clear separation between public and private knowledge, and some Indigenous practices, knowledges, and protocols are not meant for public sharing (Pidgeon 2008).

In my discussions with people who worked in Aboriginal student services from the 1970s to 1990s, many recounted experiences of having to justify the place of Indigenous ceremony within the provision of services; many in the academy questioned what cultural ceremonies such as smudging and sweat lodges had to do with academics and studying. What does it mean to have cultural protocol on campuses? Aboriginal student services providers are seen as cultural guides on campuses. In the provision of cultural ceremony such as smudging or sweat lodges there have been Aboriginal community protocols to honour, but also institutional protocols (e.g., fire and safety; physical plant operations). Those leading the ceremonies need to have the cultural knowledge and permissions to do so. In many cases, Aboriginal student services providers have had to navigate complex relationships with Aboriginal community cultural knowledge holders and a variety of institutional offices to gain permissions, and develop institutional policies, that allow cultural ceremony to be respected and honoured in spaces on campus. Elders play an important role in cultural and spiritual ceremonies; they are often the holders of the related knowledge and have the teachings on what is appropriate for these spaces.

Emotional

It is important for all of us to recognize and reconcile the intergenerational traumatic effects of residential schools, sometimes even reflected in the physical structures of contemporary institutions (e.g., red brick buildings on campus) or the historical relationship an institution may have had to residential schools in the province (Pidgeon 2008). The emotional reaction to these spaces provides insight into why some Aboriginal communities will not come to the campus; their trauma of being at a residential school that is now a functional university or college building is too hard. It also explains the emotional spaces that some of our students bring with them into the institution and experience quite viscerally when reading or hearing about their lived experiences in the classroom from instructors and classmates, whether these are appropriate representations, or worse, when they are misrepresented with biases and stereotypes.

Often emotional needs are seen to be "served" through counselling offices, yet in processing this intergenerational trauma or the emotional journey of discovering what being Indigenous means to them our students and staff are unable to "box" their emotions into such spaces and services. While some seek professional counselling, others may not want (or need) such formal relationships. Such individuals gain emotional support by sharing their experiences with those within the Indigenous Student Centres, such as Elders. Elders, in addition to being cultural knowledge holders, can be guides and listeners in a way that is different from a counselling setting; it is more relational, involving a shared understanding, and the intergenerational knowledge and grounding within these spaces is key to supporting Indigenous students along their post-secondary journeys (Pidgeon 2008).

Emotion within academic spaces is something that is not often discussed, yet we frequently feel emotions within our work—happiness, joy, anger, frustration, confusion, elation, or sadness. There is a continuum of emotions felt in the day-to-day activities of being in college or university. Within the Indigenous framework, having the ability to respectfully honour the continuum of emotions allows us to know that this is a space for us to feel safe. In this regard, Aboriginal student services centres and other Indigenous settings on campus are often described as a "home away from home" (Kirkness and Archibald 2001), or a place where one can be oneself and feel safe (Pidgeon 2008).

Intellectual

The inclusion of Indigenous knowledges within academic disciplines outside of First Nations studies and Aboriginal education has been met with some success and some tension. At the vice-president academic and dean levels, there seems to be a willingness to expand program delivery and curriculum content; however, tension seems to exist at the levels of department heads and faculty. On one hand, there is a push back in the name of academic freedom and not wanting to "make" someone include content in their courses, and on the other hand there is a keen eagerness by some faculty to be supportive and inclusive, even while, as non-Indigenous people, they feel totally unprepared or unskilled in undertaking such inclusive approaches in their teaching. Some institutions have responded by having Aboriginal student services staff act as liaisons for faculty and instructors, for instance as guest speakers, or as providers of resources and even professional development training. Others have hired, within their Teaching and Learning Centers, Aboriginal curriculum experts to work with the broader faculty. While some academic units have intentionally hired Indigenous faculty within their units to help "Indigenize" the content, in many cases these persons are called on to do so much of the work that they are distracted from (and then penalized for not doing) the work needed to earn tenure and promotion.

The disconnect between Indigenous and non-Indigenous Canadian worldviews was evident in stories, such as the lone Aboriginal staff member who had to speak up and represent all of those who couldn't speak, or Aboriginal students being challenged in classroom settings to explain "why Aboriginal peoples…" The responsibility of speaking for all when you are just one student, faculty, or staff person is a persistent and problematic issue across our campuses. Aboriginal students have long recounted stories of being singled out in class to speak for all Indigenous Peoples, or having to speak out against stereotypes or racist comments made by their peers or even instructors (Archibald et al. 1995; TeHennepe 1993). These stories continue to be repeated years later (Pidgeon, Archibald, and Hawkey 2014; Huffman 2008), in the ways students experience the construction of who the academy thinks they should be (e.g., they are status Indians with free education; or they are not "real" because they don't "look" Native) and how they understand and identify themselves as

Indigenous people. Such othering is problematic on so many levels, and demonstrates the ongoing effects of colonization. The continuum of what it means to be an Indigenous student on campus is tied to the colonial policies and practices (e.g., the Indian Act, residential schools, Bill-C37, Sixties Scoop) that have made it at times illegal to be Indigenous, that have disenfranchised families for inter-racial marriages, or that have taken children away from their families and raised them in non-Aboriginal homes with a denial of or shame at being Indigenous (RCAP 1996).

Understanding that each of our Aboriginal students is somewhere on a continuum allows us to see their cultural masks (Huffman 2001, 2008, 2010) and understand where they are coming from, and to learn what it means to be Indigenous from their perspective and all that this entails for them. This is where the wholistic framework becomes critically important in deepening our understanding of the successes, complexities, and tensions of being Indigenous within the academy. At this point, my discussion will turn to how Aboriginal student services have been integral in creating spaces on campus for Indigenous people to feel wholistically supported, while also increasing institutional awareness through relationships to Indigenous issues.

Relationships and Indigenization: Transforming Through the 4Rs

Within this shifting paradigm, to ensure Indigenous Peoples and knowledge(s) are part of the institutional fabric we need conceptualize success in higher education differently. In the United States, Native Americans have similar experiences in higher education, and until we reconceptualize success from an Indigenous, wholistic perspective, we will continue to struggle. Within an academy that continues to define success "as completing a degree within four to six years of consistent, full-time enrollment Indigenous students will continue to be framed as failures in higher education" (Huffman 2001, 2008, 2010). It is my hope that, within this chapter and the book as a whole, we can shift our gaze away from the deficit thinking that continually places Indigenous students as ones having shortcomings or failings and instead come to recognize how our educational system, specifically higher education, remains a contested space requiring transformation to truly honour Indigenous understandings of success. The next few sections of the chapter, framed within the work of the 4 Rs as defined by Kirkness and Barnhardt (1991), suggest ideas of how universities and colleges can work towards becoming places that empower Indigenous success.

Respect for Indigenous Knowledges

One means of creating a sense of belonging and space on a campus is through support services. There have been debates, some of which continue to this day, on what culturally relevant support services in a public institution look like: Are they truly about valuing and respecting Aboriginal knowledges and perspectives within the academy, or simply tokenistic representation that doesn't challenge the status quo? What does it mean to truly Indigenize the academy? As mentioned in the introduction to this chapter, the discourse of Indigenization creates a tension and fundamental question around who is setting the agenda. Is it the Euro-Western interpretation of Indigeneity (e.g., the institution determines and influences what is permissible within institutional spaces) or is it the Indigenous communities within and outside the institution?

I often wonder whether simply having more representation of Indigeinity through people, culture, curriculum and programs, and art on campus is enough to make fundamental shifts in higher education. Given the Euro-Western traditions of our higher education system, there is clearly a strong need for fundamental shifts in power and consideration of what constitutes legitimate knowledge within the academy (Kuokkanen 2007). What fundamental transformations are required for Indigenous scholars to be themselves, to be warriors in the act of decolonizing education through insurgent education (Alfred and Corntassel 2005; Corntassel 2011, 2012)? Corntassel (2012, 7) suggests that insurgent education "compels accountability and action to counter contemporary colonialism and to make amends to Indigenous peoples." This anti-colonial work and making amends within the Indigenous wholistic framework occurs through responsible and reciprocal relationships.

Responsible Relationships
Responsible relationships mean that both Aboriginal and non-Aboriginal peoples engaged in institutional changes have responsibilities and, in many cases, a call to a higher accountability that is embedded in cultural teachings and protocols but also legal responsibilities and policies (e.g., public missions, anti-racist and anti-bullying policies, and human rights). In this book, Wilson's chapter on community engagement and Zinga's chapter on non-Indigenous faculty working with Aboriginal communities are both good examples of responsible and reciprocal relationships. As Indigenous academics enter into their positions, it is important to be mindful of the political contexts surrounding them. In many ways, the forces (formal and informal) of the institutional structure will attempt to push them into the role of becoming a "private" academic (G. Smith 2000), in which they are expected to follow established practices of attaining tenure and promotion through teaching, research, and service. While the recommended 40-40-20 balance of these fields of work doesn't really work for most academics, Indigenous academics in particular are often placed in positions as "public" intellectuals—the purpose of their being in the academy goes beyond their own individual career goals and encompasses responsibility to the broader Indigenous community (as Debassige [2013] speaks of in his reflections of being Oshkabaywis and an academic). As public intellectuals, Indigenous scholars' work resides not just in the day-to-day work of teaching, research, and service; each component is more complicated, focused on being "directly relevant and centered on the needs of local Indigenous communities" (Corntassel 2011, 12). Corntassel (2011, 12) further suggests that "this is a challenge to Indigenous intellectuals and others who want to act in solidarity to become 'warriors of the truth,' both inside and outside the classroom. When we renew our responsibilities to defending and regenerating Indigenous land-based and

water-based cultural practices, we can move from insurgent to resurgent Indigenous peoples."

Kuokkanen (2007) reminds us that the tensions within the academy can be attributed to differences between Indigeneity and Euro-Western values, beliefs, and worldviews. Does this mean that understanding will never occur? No. In fact, we can see positive changes that have occurred within the academy as signs that relationship-building between Indigenous and non-Indigenous people is moving forward, creating spaces of inclusion, respect, diversity, and learning, even though we may not yet be fully at the point where "the values, principles, and modes of organization and behavior of our people are respected in, and hopefully even integrated into, the larger system of structures and processes that make up the [institution] itself" (Alfred 2004, 88). The work of those who have been the pioneers, the first to start this journey, has not been in vain; there has been much progress and continuing work to ensure that Indigenization of the academy continues to honour the integrity of Indigenous Peoples.

Relevance and Reciprocity

The last two of the 4Rs, relevance and reciprocity, are connected not only to relevant programs and services for Aboriginal Peoples within our universities and colleges but also to the successes that we have achieved within the academy: our scholarship, our voices, and our students. The work of Indigenous scholars as warriors of truth (Alfred 2004) is an act of reciprocity; institutional engagement in relationships with local Aboriginal communities to provide support and programs to the community is also another clear act of reciprocity—the gift of giving back. Universities and colleges have a responsibility to be relevant to Indigenous communities (Pidgeon 2008). The responsiveness of colleges and universities will determine whether or not their Aboriginal student population grows. As a participant said to me once, "Why would they come if it is not meeting their needs?" This speaks to the need for relevant programs, policies, and services to be part of institutional consciousness and practice (Pidgeon 2008). The challenge within these neo-liberal times is the funding and financial risks associated with such programs and services, which are often the first to suffer from cutbacks and unrenewed contracts. Institutions can do better at protecting programs and staff positions related to Indigenous initiatives.

Authentic Knowing and Being

Indigenizing the academy, insurgent education, decolonizing education—or whatever other concepts we use to speak to the authentic ways of Indigenous being and knowing—to support Indigenous student success to meet the broader goals of Indigenous self-determination and empowerment means transforming our educational system. Transforming the academy is not a one-step process, nor do I think that it has a measurable end; in fact, I think that Indigenizing the academy will always mean shifting and shaping forces and constantly being at work. Some in the academy will resist, and some will be the catalysts and tireless agents of change aiming at making our institutions better spaces for Indigenous Peoples. The ebbs and flows towards transformation will be influenced by those making the changes, as Indigenous and non-Indigenous people come to work together, each of whom are shaped by their own cultural teachings, knowledges, geographies, and broader understandings of political, social, and cultural movements within society. We need to raise our hands in thanks to all those who have struggled before us, to help us at the place we are at today; we need to acknowledge that for the next seven generations our work continues and this work is inherently part of who we are as Indigenous Peoples.

Notes

1. "Wholistic" is intentionally spelled with a "w" to reflect Indigenous understandings of being part of a whole, following the tradition honoured by Archibald et al. (1995).

2. These units, designed specifically to support Indigenous student success, have had several different titles; in the early 1970s they were known as "Native Student Services," which then evolved in the late 1990s into "First Nations Services" or "Indigenous Services." I use the term "Aboriginal student services" to reflect all of these names and note where appropriate the correct naming of a unit during a particular time period (Pidgeon 2001, 2005).
3. This section on Aboriginal student services in Canada stems from larger bodies of work (Pidgeon 2001, 2005).

References

Alfred, Taiaiake. 2004. "Warrior Scholarship: Seeing the University as a Ground of Contention." In *Indigenizing the Academy*, edited by Devon A. Mihesuah and Angela Cavender Wilson, 88–99. Lincoln: University of Nebraska Press.

Alfred, Taiaiake, and Jeff J. Corntassel. 2005. "Being Indigenous: Resurgences Against Contemporary Colonialism." *Government and Opposition* 40 (4): 597–614. https://doi.org/10.1111/j.1477-7053.2005.00166.x

Archibald, Joann. 2008. *Indigenous Storywork: Educating the Heart, Mind, Body, and Spirit*. Vancouver: UBC Press.

Archibald, Joann, Sheena Selkirk Bowman, Floy Pepper, Carl Urion, Grace Mirenhouse, and Ron Shortt. 1995. "Honoring What They Say: Post-Secondary Experiences of First Nations Graduates." *Canadian Journal of Native Education* 21 (1): 1–247.

Canadian Association of University Teachers. 2012. *The Changing Academy? A Portrait of Canada's University Teachers*. Ottawa: Canadian Association of University Teachers.

Castagno, Angelina E., and Stacey J. Lee. 2007. "Native Mascots and Ethnic Fraud in Higher Education: Using Tribal Critical Race Theory and the Interest Convergence Principle as an Analytic Tool." *Equity & Excellence in Education* 40 (1): 3–13. https://doi.org/10.1080/10665680601057288

Castellano, Marlene D. 2014. "Indigenizing Education." *EdCan Network Magazine*, June 10, 2014. https://www.edcan.ca/articles/indigenizing-education/

Corntassel, Jeff J. 2011. "Indigenizing the Academy: Insurgent Education and the Roles of Indigenous Intellectuals" (blog post). *Federation for the Humanities and Social Sciences*, January 12, 2011. http://www.idees-ideas.ca/blog/indigenizing-academy-insurgent-education-and-roles-indigenous-intellectuals

———. 2012. "Re-envisioning Resurgence Indigenous Pathways to Decolonization and Sustainable Self-determination." *Deocoloinization: Indigenity, Education & Society* 1 (1): 86-101.

Debassagie, Brent. 2013. "Building on Conceptual Interpretations of Aboriginal Literacy in Anishinaabe Research: A Turtle Shaker Model." *Canadian Journal of Education*, 36 (2): 4-33.

Huffman, Terry E. 2001. "Resistance Theory and the Transculturation Hypothesis as Explanations of College Attrition and Persistence Among Culturally Traditional American Indian Students." *Journal of American Indian Education* 40 (3): 1-23.

———. 2008. *American Indian Higher Educational Experiences: Cultural Visions and Personal Journeys*. New York: Peter Lang.

———. 2010. *Theoretical Perspectives on American Indian Education: Taking a New Look at Academic Success and the Achievement Gap*. Lanham, MD: AltaMira Press.

King, C. Richard. 2008. "Teaching Intolerance: Anti-Indian Imagery, Racial Politics, and (Anti)Racist Pedagogy." *Review of Education, Pedagogy & Cultural Studies* 30 (5): 420-36. https://doi.org/10.1080/10714410802426574

Kirkness, Verna J., and Joann Archibald. 2001. *The First Nations Longhouse: Our Home Away from Home*. Vancouver: First Nations House of Learning, University of British Columbia.

Kirkness, Verna J., and Ray Barnhardt. 1991. "First Nations and Higher Education: The Four R's—Respect, Relevance, Reciprocity, Responsibility." *Journal of American Indian Education* 30 (3): 1-15.

Kovach, Margaret. 2009. *Indigenous Methodologies: Characteristics, Conversations, and Contexts*. Toronto: University of Toronto Press.

Kuokkanen, Rauna. 2007. *Reshaping the University: Responsibility, Indigenous Epistemes and the Logic of the Gift*. Vancouver: UBC Press.

Malatest, R.A., and Associates. 2004. *Aboriginal Peoples and Post-Secondary Education: What Educators Have Learned*. January, 2004. Montreal: Canadian Millennium Scholarship Foundation.

———. 2010. *Promising Practices: Increasing and Supporting Participation for Aboriginal Students in Ontario*. Toronto: Higher Education Quality Council of Ontario.

Marker, Michael. 2004. "The Four Rs Revisited: Some Reflections on First Nations and Higher Education." In *Student Affairs: Experiences in and Through Canadian Post-secondary Education*, edited by Lesley Andres and Fiona Finlay, 171-88. Vancouver: UBC Press.

Marsden, Dawn. 2006. "Creating and Sustaining Positive Paths to Health by Restoring Traditional-based Indigenous Health Education Practices." *Canadian Journal of Native Education* 29 (1): 135–45.

McKinley Jones Brayboy, Brian, Amy J. Fann, Angelina E. Castagno, and Jessica A. Solyom. 2012. *Postsecondary Education for American Indian and Alaska Natives: Higher Education for National Building and Self-determination.* ASHE Higher Education Report, 37, no. 5. Hoboken, NJ: Wiley & Sons.

Pidgeon, Michelle. 2001. "Looking Forward…A National Perspective on Aboriginal Student Services in Canadian Universities." Master's thesis, Memorial University of Newfoundland.

———. 2005. "Weaving the Story of Aboriginal Student Services in Canadian Universities." *Communique* 5 (3): 27–9.

———. 2008. "It Takes More than Good Intentions: Institutional Accountability and Responsibility to Indigenous Higher Education." PHD diss., University of British Columbia.

———. 2012. "Transformation and Indigenous Interconnections: Indigeneity, Leadership, and Higher Education." In *Living Indigenous Leadership: Native Narratives on Building Strong Communities*, edited by Carolyn Kenny and Tina Ngaroimata Fraser, 136–49. Vancouver: UBC Press.

Pidgeon, Michelle, Jo-ann Archibald, and Colleen Hawkey. 2014. "Relationships Matter: Supporting Aboriginal Graduate Students in British Columbia, Canada." *Canadian Journal of Higher Education* 40 (1): 1–21.

Pidgeon, Michelle, and Donna Hardy Cox. 2002. "Researching with Aboriginal Peoples: Practices and Principles." *Canadian Journal of Native Education* 26 (2): 96–106.

Reamey, Becky. 2009. "Native American Mascots in Contemporary Higher Education: Part 1: Politically Acceptable or Ethnically Objectionable?" *Community College Journal of Research & Practice* 33 (12): 995–1008. https://doi.org/10.1080/10668920801980880

Richards, John. 2014. *Are We Making Progress? New Evidence on Aboriginal Education Outcomes in Provincial and Reserve Schools.* Toronto: CD Howe Institute.

Royal Commission on Aboriginal Peoples (RCAP). 1996. *Report of the Royal Commission on Aboriginal Peoples.* Ottawa: Minister of Supply and Services.

Smith, Linda Tuhiwai. 2012. *Decolonizing Methodologies: Research and Indigenous Peoples.* 2nd ed. New York: Zed Books.

Statistics Canada. 2008. "2006 Census: Aboriginal Peoples in Canada in 2006: Inuit, Métis, and First Nations, 2006 Census: Findings." Ottawa: Statistics Canada. http://www12.statcan.gc.ca/census-recensement/2006/as-sa/97-558/p3-eng.cfm

———. 2011. *The Educational Attainment of Aboriginal Peoples: National Household Survey (NHS) 2011*. Ottawa: Statistics Canada.

———. 2013. *The Education and Employment Experiences of First Nations People Living Off Reserve, Inuit, and Métis: Selected Findings from the 2012 Aboriginal Peoples Survey*. Ottawa: Statistics Canada.

TeHennepe, Shelia. 1993. "Issues of Respect: Reflections of First Nations Students' Experiences in Post-secondary Anthropology Classrooms." *Canadian Journal of Native Education* 20 (2): 193–260.

Wilson, Shawn. 2008. *Research Is Ceremony: Indigenous Research Methods*. Black Point, NS: Fernwood Publishing.

III Knowledge
Practice and Pedagogy

11 | Confronting Indigenous Identities
in Transcultural Contexts

FRANK DEER

MANY ASPECTS of personal and regional identities are, and have been, absent from mainstream education in Canada (Roland 2008), a development that has its roots in traditional, "one-size-fits-all" educational programming (Battiste and Semaganis 2002). Identities that do not correspond to that of the dominant culture have been frequently absent from such mainstream programming, as are those that do not emphasize international development or economic imperatives. Although Canadian multiculturalism policy has codified the importance of ethno-cultural diversity in Canada, such diversity is not sufficiently prevalent in Canada's schools (Schissel and Wotherspoon 2003). Ethnic marginalization in education is particularly prevalent for Canada's Indigenous Peoples (Johnson 2006). Numerous writers have asserted that educational programming in Canada's schools should reflect the cultural milieu of their students and community (Goulet and Goulet 2014; Long and Dickason 2011; Kanu 2012; Emberley and Newell 1994; L. Lee 2008). Unfortunately, many educational jurisdictions teach to broad behavioural standards because such programming is easy to employ and rationalize (Robertson 1998) and may represent efforts to indoctrinate students of minority ethnic groups into the dominant cultural perspective (Giroux 1997). Although social studies curricula provide for the study of such topics as community traditions and practices (Conderman and Bresnahan 2008), such programming frequently occurs in isolation from other school-based activities (Friesen and Friesen 2002).

Developing standardized curricula or uniform sets of educational resources for use in all schools may be problematized by imperatives associated with teaching and learning that correspond with and are sensitive to the diverse Indigenous identities that may be associated with a particular school (Battiste 2013; White, Maxim, and Spence 2004). Supporting the development of curricula, pedagogical practices, and appropriate school cultures and climates may necessitate the empowerment of principals and teachers to initiate such developments that are congruent with the values of the community (T. Lee 2007). The developing imperative of localized identity exploration in public schools is one that is not lost on Indigenous communities in Canada that have ventured to affirm and celebrate collective values for cultural revitalization.

The contested space that is the focus here is the contemporary Indigenous self. Although not a physical space and perhaps one that is subject to our personal and socially constructed perspectives and values, this contested space is important because of how contemporary transcultural society may affect the Indigenous identity of children and youth. The personal and collective identities of Indigenous Peoples may have a variety of ancestral, cultural, national, political, legislative, and language-based influences. The manner in which educators, among others, facilitate relevant learning experiences that will support identity development among Indigenous children and youth has become increasingly important given that our transcultural society offers other influences whose sources are essentially non-Indigenous. Drawing upon personal and professional experience, the following will explore the contested space in which the development of Indigenous identities may be problematized in ethno-culturally diverse, transcultural, educational contexts. Also, this chapter will explore how Indigenous identities can be operationalized in Canadian schools in an effort to facilitate identity awareness in educational programming. The discussion will be predicated on the notion that culture, which may be characterized as "systems of behavior, attitudes and values" (Ashcroft, Griffiths, and Tiffin 2000, 60) should be regarded as a subset of the broader concept of identity, which not only allows for the existence of culture as a potential personal characteristic but also can incorporate such characteristics into personal and collective continuity (Perry 2002).

Contextualizing an Indigenous Identity

I grew up on a First Nations reserve in Quebec called Kahnawake. Known more in Canadian consciousness for the infamous Oka crisis of 1990 when people from my community erected roadblocks on all roads and highways leading into the community (thus closing the Mercier Bridge and preventing direct access between Montreal and numerous communities in the South Shore area), Kahnawake represents a rich environment of Indigenous heritage and language that has facilitated cultural revitalization and affirmation. In a climate of fervent (sometimes militant) nationalism, Kahnawake's potential as a focal point for understanding the possibilities of Indigenous activism and cultural assertion is perhaps supported by its geographical location adjacent to a major urban centre on the southern shore of the St. Lawrence River. I only came to appreciate the importance of such location when I moved to Manitoba and began to understand how communities that are geographically remote relative to Canada's other, more populated regions can easily be forgotten in the grand scheme of things. With francophone nationalist sentiment just a heartbeat away, the cultural and linguistic dichotomies that exist between English/French Québécois and the Kahnienkehaka of Kahnawake have provided an opportunity for improved awareness of the Canadian Indigenous experience.

One day, sometime in the early 1980s when I was in elementary school, one of my parents asked me what I wanted to do when I grew up. I mentioned that I wanted to be an air force pilot (perhaps informed by the fact that one of my siblings was in the American military and another had a fascination with military conflict that was manifest in popular comic books). This career plan didn't last very long, perhaps due to my fear of flying that I discovered shortly afterward. My future ambitions changed quite frequently during my youth—at one time or another during elementary school I aspired to become an ice hockey player, chef, radio DJ, construction worker, fitness instructor, dancer, computer technician, toy designer, inventor of obscure household devices (I watched a lot of infomercials), paperback writer, marine biologist, professional golfer, gas station attendant (a position I did occupy for about three years up to the age of 19), quarry man, and avant-garde artist. The thought that went into these temporary career aspirations was inspired by the emergent pressure by family and, to a lesser extent, school to begin exploring potential avenues of prospective employment. This notion that personal success is defined by appropriate career choices in adulthood was not lost on those around me. That question that my parents asked me all those years ago reflected that notion well. What was I going to be? What was that "thing" that would define the rest of my life? The direction that my parents attempted to offer was governed by the importance of gainful employment in the form of a respectable career.

Although focus on a prospective career waned during my early adolescence—not only had I discovered girls but also the importance of trying to be cool (among my small circle of friends, there was a tacit understanding that being "cool" meant not caring)—the periods of introspection and response to external pressure to acquire an education that would suit a prospective career were embedded in an ethno-cultural context that represented one of the few identifying imperatives that was at all consistent in my life: the consistent need to identify with something. In retrospect, this consistency was crucial—not because it helped me to become more proud to be an Indigenous person (that pride came a bit later in life), not because it strengthened my relationships with other community members (those relationships weren't very strong to start with), and not because it helped in my personal and cultural development (my development in this regard occurred through relationships that were not governed by shared ancestry). The consistency that characterized my ethno-cultural context was (and still is) crucial because it provided me with a story—an unfinished narrative of who I was and, with that governing context, who I may turn out to be (assuming I possess the agency to control such developments).

Imagine how life would be if this were not the case. For those who hold their career as the litmus for their life's success, perhaps this is why they would not wish to win millions of dollars in the lottery; their motivation for moulding and maintaining their identity may become inhibited by the quick acquisition of stacks of money. In a similar manner, many may wish to not venture too far from their home community; whether to maintain the kinship of an extended family or the familiarity that comes with a shared language, the ability for moulding and maintaining their identity may become inhibited by distance.

One might suggest that the quality of an ethno-cultural context may not be as important as the fact that it exists at all. I could be a Palestinian trying to make a life for myself in the tense region of Palestine, or a Yidinji attempting to overcome the legacies of colonialism in Queensland, Australia. Regardless of the context, the existence of a story seemed to provide me with that "thing" that could allow me to feel as though I am something of a complete person—that distinctive characteristic that simultaneously connects that person to the outside world and distinguishes himself or herself from others. Essential to personal identity stories is the notion that they are almost always a work in progress; whether constructed by the self or imposed by an outside agent or entity, one's identity is subject to a constituent framework as it/they are manifest at a particular point in time. The focus here is the ethno-cultural framework and its constituent parts.

I frequently ponder the phenomenon of childhood, as it offers some of the most cogent paradigms that may allow one to appreciate how identity is developed. To employ some of the arguments developed by Steven

Pinker (2007), whether we see children as tabula rasa—blank slates on which experience provides knowledge—"noble savages" that are contaminated by societal influence, or as individuals with the capacity to make decisions independent of the body, the vast expanse of new experiences coupled with the biological changes that are characteristic of early childhood are commensurate with classical views of the self and how the child turns into an adult. Questions such as "To what degree is one's past an indication of how one will behave?" may lead to a more ominous question, with respect to identity theory: Is an adult truly the same person as his or her younger self? In exploring individuality and personality theory, Particke Johns Heine (1971) wrote:

> The question then becomes: How relevant is the life history and how lasting is its relevance to the way we enact our roles? Are there typical sequences or stages on the way to becoming a person? Are they generalizable over time and from place to place?...[T]he cumulative effect of socialization studies has not brought personality to the foreground but made it relative to time and place and circumstance. The idea of uniqueness, of the development of person in response to environmental conditions has almost disappeared; the idea that the "child is father to the man" endures as a metaphor because it tells us something about patterns of childhood, not the certain distinctiveness of *this* child or *this* man. (71, emphasis mine)

Personality is *relative to time and place and circumstance*. So what is the implication for one's personal identity? If personality is indeed relative to time, place, and circumstance, then personal identity might be regarded not as a static reflection of the self that can escape the existential debates about the self, but rather as a dynamic set of characteristics that allow the individual to simultaneously distinguish themselves from others and affirm a measure of allegiance with that "thing" that facilitates association with others. The story of the self cannot exist without a context—and time, place, and circumstance provide the contextual inspiration that informs the continuity of such stories.

There have been periods of my youth when the contested space of focus here, Indigenous identity development in a transcultural society, was a more acute influence. In mid to late adolescence, that "thing" that facilitated both association and distinctness for me had less to do with ethnic identity and more to do with fitting in with non-Indigenous peoples. The final four years of my secondary education occurred in private and public schools outside of my home community where most of my friendships were formed with non-Indigenous people of various backgrounds. The preoccupation with fitting in continued into college and university—a period of time that has led me to regard post-secondary education as the double-edged sword: the necessity of acquiring a university education frequently requires Indigenous youth to leave their communities to pursue such post-secondary studies. This pursuit placed me in a community of fellow students where career aspirations were of principal focus and ethno-cultural differences did not lead to any obvious tensions. The acquisition of an education and the development of relationships that can lead to life partnerships can lead to a change in personal priorities over time. I never returned to life in Kahnawake—my career, spousal partnership, and other personal circumstances have taken me elsewhere. At least no one can accuse me of not following parental direction all those years ago.

My career and personal trajectories that emerged from my experiences in my home community have led to a professional focus on issues of Indigenous identity that may be developed through adolescence and adulthood. Presenting ethno-cultural identity as a fluid notion as opposed to something that is more static may be regarded as problematic in some quarters—problematic because cultural and linguistic revitalization movements among Indigenous peoples in Canada are, in part, predicated on the notion that traditional manifestations of Indigenous culture and language are exactly that: traditional and should be maintained. The contested space of Indigenous identity in a transcultural society may be particularly affected by these traditional influences. For nearly half a century, Indigenous Peoples in Canada have attempted to organize themselves socially and politically in an effort to facilitate revitalization of Indigenous Peoples' interests, including their cultures and languages. Indigenous Elders have been and continue to be relied upon for their knowledge of culture and language. Indigenous communities have ventured to rediscover their Indigenous roots—a process that has involved such initiatives as the renaming of communities/territories with ancestral languages. Primary and secondary schools, particularly those that are managed by First Nations, have employed culturally relevant programming that is intended to expose students to cultural and linguistic perspectives. Initiatives such as these reflect a desire on the part of Indigenous Peoples to reclaim their cultural identities, a desire that may be readily understandable when one considers the history of colonization and marginalization that they have endured. These hardships were particularly prevalent in primary and secondary schools where the most vulnerable demographic of any population, young children, were separated from family and made the recipients of assimilative teachings. As Julia Emberley (2007) once wrote:

> These schools were the site of an extraordinary "policing" operation inasmuch as they set out to regulate aboriginal children's bodies to the assimilatory objectives of colonial dispossession, transforming those bodies into agricultural and domestic labourers. Such an operation eventuated in the loss of Native languages, the destruction of spiritual and cultural practices, and, with the dissolution of kinship relations, the collapse of a network of emotional, intellectual, spiritual, and physical support. (5)

Heightened awareness of histories such as this have, in part, led to the contemporary Indigenous Peoples movements. There are a number of notable historical events that have led to the contemporary sociopolitical movements among Indigenous Peoples. Leftist sentiment among Canadians following the Second World War led to increased awareness of previously marginalized peoples such as immigrants and women. Though not at the forefront of this developing sentiment, some issues associated with Indigenous Peoples, particularly status Indians, did garner some governmental attention. Broadly, the Hawthorn report of 1966 may be regarded as a seminal moment as it identified some of the problems in First Nations communities related to such issues as health, education, and participation in the labour market. Although Hawthorn's recommendations were largely ignored in government at the time, the crises highlighted in the report informed the development of the now-infamous discussion paper, the 1969 *Statement of the Government of Canada on Indian Policy*, popularly referred to as the White Paper. Rightfully regarded as a means of assimilating Canada's status Indians into Canadian society through the repeal of the Indian Act and participation in mainstream Canadian society, the White Paper represented what may have been regarded at the time as the "last straw" for First Nations Peoples in Canada. The responses to this proposed legislation, which frequently asserted the importance of traditional perspectives on First Nations life (particularly language and culture), has led such institutional changes as band-managed schools on First Nations, post-secondary and university educational programs that focus on Indigenous issues, and agencies devoted to Aboriginal child welfare services. These developments, and many others like them, are predicated on the notion that Indigenous knowledge, heritage, consciousness, and tradition are essential to the contemporary Indigenous experience in Canada. However, perhaps it is incumbent upon educators to consider that traditional knowledge, heritage, and consciousness can and should be considered as that which informs, not governs, one's ethnic identity. *Wahbung: Our Tomorrows* (Manitoba Indian Brotherhood 1971, vii), Manitoba First Nations chiefs' 1971 response to the White Paper, asserted that "we are a 20th-century people, not a colourful folkloric remnant. We are capable and competent and perfectly able to assess today's conditions and develop ways of adjusting positively and successfully to them."

One of my favourite quotes from the literature on education might represent a truth about this struggle for understanding Indigenous identity and its association with Canadian education: "Education stands or falls by the principle that virtue can be taught" (Emberley and Newell 1994, 3). This perspective informs my career as a faculty member at a university in a rather significant way: if one accepts that virtue is not a constant among ethnic groups in Canada, what characterizes virtue for Indigenous Peoples? The diversity represented by that word, "Indigenous," makes this question rather difficult to answer, but the notion that ethno-cultural identity should be regarded as heterogeneous due to the constant socio-cultural evolution associated with Canadian life may require an outlook on Indigenous identity that is truly contemporary and responsive to social change. Therefore, is it not incumbent on us to discover what virtue is for a particular Indigenous group or community? Should such virtue be regarded as an essential part of a collective's self-concept, then my role as a public intellectual appears clear, and my responsibility in the acquisition of an appropriate understanding of a people's virtue is what continues to inform my work. In regards to the contested space reflected here, it is perhaps essential for education professionals to consider the unique manifestations of virtue that may be prevalent among Indigenous communities and families. Such virtues may be related to divergent ontologies, epistemologies, and worldviews and may be rather important to consider in the development of learning opportunities that facilitate Indigenous identity development for children and youth.

The acquisition of an appropriate understanding of virtue, within the context of the Indigenous Peoples in Canada, may be an important task for those who operate in the contested space of Indigenous identity development in a transcultural society. The implications for education and awareness of Indigenous issues may be too significant to overlook. Currently, in the midst of a movement towards inclusion of, and respect for, the Canadian Indigenous experience, authorities in public education have attempted to develop programming that is responsive to this movement in a rather short period of time. A number of regional ministries have required any graduate of a teacher education program to take at least one course in Indigenous education. Many school districts have attempted to increase the number of Indigenous teachers and support staff in their jurisdictions and have created learning support centres for Indigenous students. Some major Canadian universities have attempted to attract prospective Indigenous students and have created faculty positions specific to Indigenous education. Some Canadian campuses have even erected buildings devoted to Indigenous students where ceremonies and gatherings can take place.

But all of these initiatives, and others like them, require an essential recognition: that with every aspect of culture that is cited, with every building that is erected, with every traditional activity that is performed, and with every artifact that is displayed and analyzed, there is a perspective—that commentary that explores the people and experience associated with a given initiative. At times, such exploration is not as rich as it could otherwise be: physical education teachers sometimes introduce lacrosse in an acultural manner; history teachers sometimes discuss the life of Louis Riel from a colonist's perspective; and education professionals of numerous fields frequently discuss spirituality in opposition to mainstream perspectives in a manner that ridicules ancestral beliefs. That is why the term "perspective" is so important: it emphasizes the focus on the unique manifestations of specific Indigenous Peoples' experiences. To overlook the importance of perspective is to run the risk of tokenism—the employment of Indigenous education as an exercise in activity-based learning without insight into the Peoples with which they are associated. This may be an essential task for those educators who operate within the contested space of Indigenous identity development in a transcultural society: a perennial problem that has become appreciated more in recent years, of how easy it may be to trivialize Indigenous content in schools. One might enter, for instance, a physical education class, hand out the lacrosse sticks, and be rather proud that something Indigenous had taken place. What of the Indigenous people associated with this activity? Why was it played? How did it lend to communal and international relations? Otherwise posed, what is the perspective associated with this activity? The perspective, the exploration of the people, histories, narratives, and values, is as essential to Indigenous identity development as any activity, artifact, or other referent reflected in a student outcome.

Responding to the emergent significance of Indigenous identity as a part of educational programming across Canada has yielded an important question: is the employment of Indigenous perspectives an exercise in exploring just the past? Manitoba Education and Youth (2003, 2) presented these goals for Indigenous students: "To develop positive self-identity" and "To participate in a learning environment that will equip students with the ability to fully participate in the unique civic and cultural realities of Aboriginal communities."

These objectives may be important because they have the potential to reflect the changing social climate among all Canadians. Also, these goals may be regarded, in part, as a way of reflecting the transcultural nature of a Canadian society that has begun to accept and celebrate the contributions of Indigenous Peoples. The affirmation of these societal changes may be important because of the evolution of Indigenous perspectives that have been conditioned by colonial and post-colonial impacts. Here emerges another imperative associated with the contested space of Indigenous identity development in a transcultural society: exploring the Canadian Indigenous experience through appropriate school programming may also support non-Indigenous peoples' appreciation of Indigenous contributions to society. Harmonious coexistence among a country's citizenry requires understanding and empathy. Essential to this cross-cultural dimension of the contested space of Indigenous identity development may be the affirmation that this space is occupied by both Indigenous and non-Indigenous peoples. To achieve recognition and affirmation of these shared contested spaces requires efforts towards mutual understanding.

Identity Issues and Indigenous Education

In Canadian schools that struggle to negotiate the provision of quality programming with the socio-linguistic imperatives of Indigenous communities, aspects of localized Indigenous identity may be overlooked as broader theories and terminology are incorporated. Advocates of culturally appropriate education for Indigenous students have asserted that aspects of Indigenous identity such as language, socio-cultural perspectives, and cultural mores should be incorporated into education in an effort to retain traditionally prevalent aspects of identity. Aspects of school changes that are associated with citizenship education suggest that such aspects of identity require broad incorporation across all school activities and programming in order to ensure success. Considering that the contested space explored here is that of Indigenous identity development in transcultural education contexts, a brief exploration of identity as a concept may be called for.

Identity: A Fundamentally Contested Space

Identity may be characterized as the set of personal or group characteristics that allow an individual or collective to assert a form of distinctiveness (Rohmann 1999). Identity is frequently defined along ethnic or racial lines (Johnson 2006), a definition that may also be influenced by respective cultural mores (Holder 2006). Personal identity and collective identity can share a symbiotic relationship (James 2003), one where personal affirmations and distinctiveness regarding beliefs, ideals, and ways of life strengthen a collective of similar individuals and vice versa (Heine 1971). Whether considering its personal or collective manifestation, the central tenet essential to the concept of identity is the continuity of those characteristics that are prevalent to the individual or group in question (Williams 1989). The importance of identity for a person's self-concept was articulated by Perry (2002, x) who stated, "We seem to ourselves to be of basic and important things, and the identity of basic and important things should not be matters for the conventions of language and the vagaries of commerce or even the Supreme Court to decide. Who I am, whether I am the same as a person who did something in the past, ought to be clear, given the facts." Perry's quote reflects the notion that identity is a particularly important matter for ethnic minorities in Canada (Tully 2006), including Indigenous Peoples (Leslie 2004). As Perry's (2002) quote suggests, identity may be characterized by one's connection with a past self. Extended to encompass racial and ethnic dimensions, identity can represent an essential link to the past, to ancestors, to languages, and to cultural traditions.

Identity in the Canadian Mosaic

The broad regional context in which this current discussion is situated is that of Canada. Adhering to this regional context in a discussion on the contested space of Indigenous identity development in transcultural educational environments requires an exploration of the quality of the Canadian mosaic in which these contested spaces are situated. Canada is replete with divergent racial and ethnic groups, each of whom may be distinct in regards to their respective racial/ethnic backgrounds, experiences, languages, and cultural mores (Stewin and McCann 1993). In spite of the fact that multiculturalism, the "ideal of the harmonious coexistence of differing cultural or ethnic groups in a pluralist society at its core" (Cashmore 1996, 244), is codified in Canadian law, its existence as an ideal in Canadian society is problematic for social equality across ethnic groups. Eisenberg (2006, 6) wrote that the rationale for multiculturalism was "to ensure that each individual has equal access to a secure cultural context and that possessing a minority cultural identity is viewed as conventional and fully accepted within mainstream society." Such access is frequently not prevalent for ethnic minorities in Canada (Ignatieff 2000). Such a state of affairs has resulted in a national cultural mosaic that is characterized by social tension and can be fragmented along ethnic lines (Cohen 2007).

In criticizing social policies of countries other than Canada, Magsino (2002, 70) asserted that "the continuing debate about multiculturalism in the United States indicates a refusal to face the changed reality in that country. Whether or not minority groups in (the United States) will persevere in claiming their rights remains to be seen." Magsino's work, which interestingly asserted that Canada has made a "commitment of respect for the plural character of the body politic and thus to provide for the rights and well-being of minority communities" (70), demonstrates how marginalized peoples in a democratic country can exist on the periphery of society. In spite of Magsino's affirmation of Canada's commitment to social equality, it may be important to note that the current state of many Indigenous Peoples in Canada does not corroborate this sentiment (Alfred 1999). Critics of multiculturalism have posited that it equates to a version of ethnic pluralism that does not adequately address social positioning or equality (Cohen 2007; James 2003). Spending time in Indigenous communities and discussing these matters with socially, politically, and economically marginalized peoples suggests that Indigenous Peoples do not feel that they are a part of any Canadian identity but rather feel very much on the periphery. Thus, at the current time, the notion that all ethnicities and cultures can flourish under a national banner may be regarded as a difficult goal to achieve (Strong-Boag 1996). Canada's Indigenous Peoples, to a very large extent, are not flourishing in Canadian society and there are many institutional barriers that are preventing them from flourishing while living a lifestyle that is congruent with their traditional backgrounds (Frideres and Gadacz 2008). The potential influence that divergent national affiliations may have on the discourses on individual and communal identity in educational contexts can be considerable. The contested spaces where Indigenous identities may be personally and collectively negotiated may be affected by such fragmented national affiliations. In my experience, Canadian, Québécois, and American affiliations were, at the least, additional layers to such development and, at most, aggravating factors in the establishment's goal of an Indigenous community where Indigenous children and youth exercised and celebrated grassroots Indigenous knowledge and customs.

Indigenous Identity in Canadian Education

Identity can have a problematic relationship with contemporary education (Cogan 2000), a relationship that reflects tension between relevant national, regional, and community values and ideals (Macleod 2006). Schools in Canada have developed a systemic tendency to emphasize broad academic standards; such emphasis is frequently exercised at the expense of educational programming that offers students insight and development of localized heritage, languages, and cultural mores (Volante 2008). Although some educational improvements regarding the inclusivity of culturally relevant programming have taken place in Canada, contemporary schooling does not sufficiently reflect what minority groups desire, nor does it do an effective job of addressing the contested space explored here: culturally relevant education that reflects the ethnic identity of the local community (Abele, Dittburner, and Graham 2000). It may be important to note that the development and implementation of educational programming that is congruent with the identity of the local community goes beyond mere curriculum implementation and amended course subject matter; pedagogical practices, school climate, community involvement, and language should also be amended to reflect the character of the local community in an effort to address the contested spaces in which Indigenous identity development are situated (Deslandes, Fournier, and Morin 2008; Watt-Cloutier 2000).

The discourse on Indigenous identity in Canadian educational contexts has been explored in a variety of ways through numerous theoretical lenses, some of which may merit mention here. For instance, it has been suggested that school programming may be affected by the imposition of an anti-racist framework that could influence school activities (St. Denis 2007). Such an anti-racist framework that affirms the importance of racial background as an important part of one's identity could positively impact harmony among staff and students in a school. Secondly, in investigating the significance of the roles of women among Indigenous Peoples, Hammersmith (2002) affirmed that women's roles are different from community to community and are an important aspect of traditional ways of life. In regards to citizenship, Deer (2008) asserted that one of the important aspects of Indigenous Peoples' self-concept in Canada is the right to such entitlements as land and self-government. Alfred (1999) suggested that modern-day Indigenous self-concepts in Canada are predicated on the negative effects of post-colonial life that have obfuscated cultural knowledge. A survey of academic discourses such as these support the notion explored in this chapter: that the localized exploration of Indigenous identities in educational contexts are important to the maintenance of Indigenous culture and language.

Some have asserted that numerous dimensions of Indigenous identity should be reflected in what Canadian schools provide to Indigenous students (Barman, Hébert, and McCaskill 1987; Castellano 2000). The integration of aspects of Indigenous identity such as culture, history, and other relevant dimensions of the Canadian Indigenous experience in school activities may be enhanced by school-based interventions that include language exploration (Fettes and Norton 2000), content, and academic themes and topics that are reflective of Indigenous knowledge and traditional pedagogies. The integration of features such as these that may enable the introduction of Indigenous identity into general school activities can aid in the achievement of Indigenous cultural revitalization. There is one rather fundamental imperative that these actions serve that is directly relevant to the contested space of Indigenous identity development in transcultural educational contexts, and that is related to one of the purposes of contemporary primary and secondary schooling. Primary and secondary schooling may be perceived as a means of preparation for the labour market; citizenship development that is responsive to vague or unarticulated social imperatives; and preparation for post-secondary educational experiences.

However, the fundamental purpose of primary and secondary schooling may be rightfully seen as one of the numerous ways in which individuals who are developing along personal and communal journeys that are informed by ancestral, cultural, national, and language-based social trajectories may be better situated to discover moral truth in our world. These journeys may be best appreciated when we consider how our own children may be situated in them. Few would argue that it is important for families to inform their children's development through the transmission of values, worldviews, languages, and even frameworks for moral perspectives. The cultural continuity that this supports can be powerful for Indigenous Peoples and should be considered an essential part of the contested space of Indigenous identity development in educational settings.

References

Abele, Francis, Carolyn Dittburner, and Katherine A. Graham. 2000. "Towards a Shared Understanding in the Policy Discussion about Aboriginal Education." In *Aboriginal Education: Fulfilling the Promise*, edited by Marlene B. Castellano, Lynne Davis, and Louise Lahache, 3-24. Vancouver: UBC Press.

Alfred, Taiaiake. 1999. *Peace, Power, Righteousness: An Indigenous Manifesto*. Don Mills, ON: Oxford University Press.

Ashcroft, Bill, Gareth Griffiths, and Helen Tiffin. 2000. *Post-Colonial Studies: The Key Concepts*. New York: Routledge.

Barman, Jean, Yvonne M. Hébert, and Don N. McCaskill. 1987. "The Challenge of Indian Education: An Overview." In *Indian Education in Canada Volume 2: The Challenge*, edited by Jean Barman, Yvonne Hebert, and Don McCaskill, 1-21. Vancouver: UBC Press.

Battiste, Marie. 2013. *Decolonizing Education: Nourishing the Learning Spirit*. Saskatoon, SK: Purich Publishing.

Battiste, Marie, and Helen Semaganis. 2002. "First Thoughts on First Nations Citizenship: Issues in Education." In *Citizenship in Transformation in Canada*, edited by Yvonne M. Hebert, 93-111. Toronto: University of Toronto Press.

Cashmore, Ellis. 1996. *Dictionary of Race and Ethnic Relations*. 4th ed. New York: Routledge.

Castellano, Marlene B. 2000. "Education and Renewal in Aboriginal Nations: Highlights of the Report of the Royal Commission on Aboriginal Peoples." In *Voice of the Drum: Indigenous Education and Culture*, edited by Roger Neil, 261-76. Brandon, MB: Kingfisher Publications.

Cogan, John J. 2000. "Citizenship Education for the 21st Century: Setting the Context." In *Citizenship for the 21st Century: An International Perspective on Education*, edited by John J. Cogan and Ray Derricott, 1-21. London: Kogan Page.

Cohen, Andrew. 2007. *The Unfinished Canadian: The People That We Are*. Toronto: McClelland & Stewart.

Conderman, Greg, and Val Bresnahan. 2008. "Teaching Big Ideas in Diverse Middle School Classrooms." *Kappa Delta Pi Record* 44 (4): 176-80.

Deer, Frank. 2008. "Aboriginal Students and Canadian Citizenship Education." *Journal of Educational Thought* 42 (1): 69-82.

Deslandes, Rollande, Hélène Fournier, and Lucille Morin. 2008. "Evaluation of a School, Family, and Community Partnerships Program for Preservice Teachers in Quebec, Canada." *Journal of Educational Thought* 42 (1): 27-51.

Eisenberg, Avigail. 2006. "Introduction: New Approaches to Freedom in Canada." In *Diversity and Equality: The Changing Framework of Freedom in Canada*, edited by Avigail Eisenberg, 1-14. Vancouver: UBC Press.

Emberley, Julia V. 2007. *Defamiliarizing the Aboriginal: Cultural Practices and Decolonization in Canada*. Toronto: University of Toronto Press.

Emberley, Peter C., and Waller R. Newell. 1994. *Bankrupt Education: The Decline of Liberal Education in Canada*. Toronto: University of Toronto Press.

Fettes, Mark, and Ruth Norton. 2000. "Voices of Winter: Aboriginal Languages and Public Policy in Canada." In *Aboriginal Education: Fulfilling the Promise*, edited by Marlene B. Castellano, Lynne Davis, and Louise Lahache, 29-54. Vancouver: UBC Press.

Frideres, James S., and René R. Gadacz. 2008. *Aboriginal People in Canada*. Toronto: Pearson Education.

Friesen, John W., and Virginia Lyons Friesen. 2002. *Aboriginal Education in Canada: A Plea for Integration*. Calgary: Detselig.

Giroux, Henry A. 1997. *Pedagogy and the Politics of Hope: Theory, Culture, and Schooling*. Boulder, CO: Westview.

Goulet, Linda M., and Keith N. Goulet. 2014. *Teaching Each Other: Nehinuw Concepts and Indigenous Pedagogies*. Vancouver: UBC Press.

Hammersmith, B. 2002. "Restoring Women's Value." In *Nation to Nation: Aboriginal Sovereignty and the Future of Canada*, edited by John Bird, Lorraine Land, and Murray Macadam, 120-30. Toronto: Irwin.

Hawthorn, Harry, ed. 1966. *A Survey of Contemporary Indians of Canada: Economic, Political, Educational Needs and Policies*. 2 Vols. Ottawa: Queen's Printer Press.

Heine, Patricke Johns. 1971. *Personality in Social Theory*. Chicago: Aldine Publishing Co.

Holder, Cindy. 2006. "Culture as a Basic Human Right." In *Diversity and Equality: The Changing Framework of Freedom in Canada*, edited by Avigail Eisenberg, 78–96. Vancouver: UBC Press.

Ignatieff, Michael. 2000. *The Rights Revolution*. Toronto: House of Anansi Press.

James, Carl E. 2003. *Seeing Ourselves: Exploring Race, Ethnicity and Culture*. 3rd ed. Toronto: Thompson Educational Publishing.

Johnson, Walter. 2006. *The Challenge of Diversity*. Montreal: Black Rose Books.

Kanu, Yatta. 2012. "In Their Own Voices: First Nations Students Identify Some Cultural Mediators of Their Learning in the Formal School System." In *Canadian Curriculum Studies: Trends, Issues, and Influences*, edited by Susan E. Gibson, 236–64. Vancouver: Pacific Educational Press.

Lee, Lloyd L. 2008. "Reclaiming Indigenous Intellectual, Political, and Geographic Space: A Path for Navajo Nationhood." *American Indian Quarterly* 32 (1): 96–110.

Lee, Tiffany S. 2007. "Connecting Academics, Indigenous Knowledge, and Commitment to Community: High School Students' Perceptions of a Community-Based Education." *Canadian Journal of Native Education* 30 (2): 196–216.

Leslie, J.F. 2004. "The Policy Agenda of Native Peoples from World War II to the 1969 White Paper." In *Aboriginal Policy Research: Setting the Agenda for Change*, Vol. 1, edited by Jerry P. White, Paul Maxim, and Dan Beavon, 15–28. Toronto: Thompson Educational Publishing.

Long, David, and Olive P. Dickason. 2011. *Visions of the Heart: Canadian Aboriginal Studies*. Don Mills, ON: Oxford University Press.

Macleod, Colin. 2006. "Interpreting the Identity Claims of Young Children." In *Diversity and Equality: The Changing Framework of Freedom in Canada*, edited by Avigail Eisenberg, 134–52. Vancouver: UBC Press.

Magsino, Romulo F. 2002. "From Eclectic Theory to Coherence: Citizenship Virtues for Our Time." In *Citizenship in Transformation in Canada*, edited by Yvonne M. Hebert, 57–80. Toronto: University of Toronto Press.

Manitoba Education and Youth. 2003. *Integrating Aboriginal Perspectives into Curricula: A Resource for Curriculum Developers, Teachers, and Administrators*. Winnipeg: Manitoba Education and Youth.

Manitoba Indian Brotherhood. 1971. *Wahbung: Our Tomorrows*. Winnipeg: Manitoba Indian Brotherhood.

Niezen, Ronald. 2003. *The Origins of Indigenism: Human Rights and the Politics of Identity*. Berkeley: University of California Press.

Perry, John. 2002. *Identity, Personal Identity, and the Self*. Indianapolis, IN: Hackett.

Pinker, Steven. 2007. *The Stuff of Thought: Language as a Window into Human Nature.* New York: Viking.

Robertson, Heather-Jane. 1998. *No More Teachers, No More Books: The Commercialization of Canada's Schools.* Toronto: McClelland & Stewart.

Rohmann, Chris. 1999. *A World of Ideas: A Dictionary of Important Theories, Concepts, Beliefs, and Thinkers.* New York: Ballantine Books.

Roland, Karen A. 2008. "Educating for Inclusion: Community Building Through Mentorship and Citizenship." *Journal of Educational Thought* 42 (1): 53-67.

Schissel, Bernard, and Terry Wotherspoon. 2003. *The Legacy of School for Aboriginal People: Education, Oppression, and Emancipation.* Don Mills, ON: Oxford University Press.

St. Denis, Verna. 2007. "Aboriginal Education and Anti-Racist Education: Building Alliances Across Cultural and Racial Identity." *Canadian Journal of Education* 30 (4): 1068-92.

Stewin, Leonard L., and Stewart J.H. McCann. 1993. "Implications of Ethnic Diversity." In *Contemporary Educational Issues: The Canadian Mosaic*, 2nd ed., edited by L.L. Stewin and S.J.H. McCann, 81-2. Mississauga, ON: Copp Clark Pittman.

Strong-Boag, Veronica. 1996. "Claiming a Place in the Nation: Citizenship Education and the Challenge of Feminists, Natives, and Workers in Post-Confederation Canada." *Canadian and International Education* 25 (2): 128-45.

Tully, James. 2006. "Reconciling Struggles over the Recognition of Minorities: Towards a Dialogical Approach." In *Diversity and Equality: The Changing Framework of Freedom in Canada*, edited by Avigail Eisenberg, 15-33. Vancouver: UBC Press.

Volante, Louis. 2008. "Equity in Multicultural Student Assessment." *Journal of Educational Thought* 42 (1): 11-26.

Watt-Cloutier, Sheila. 2000. "Honouring Our Past: Creating Our Future: Education in Northern and Remote Communities." In *Aboriginal Education: Fulfilling the Promise*, edited by Marlene Brant Castellano, Lynne Davis, and Louise Lahache, 114-28. Vancouver: UBC Press.

White, Jerry, Paul Maxim, and Nicholas Spence. 2004. "An Examination of Educational Success." In *Aboriginal Policy Research: Setting the Agenda for Change*, Vol. 1, edited by Jerry P. White, Paul Maxim, and Dan Beavon, 129-48. Toronto: Thompson Educational Publishing.

Williams, Christopher J.F. 1989. *What Is Identity?* Oxford: Oxford University Press.

12 | Preparing Teachers for Indigenous Language Immersion Classrooms

MARGIE HOHEPA & NGAREWA HAWERA

Introduction

This chapter argues that a commitment to producing teachers who can successfully teach in Māori medium classrooms is an essential component to ensuring educational success of Indigenous Māori learners in Aotearoa New Zealand schools. Māori medium schooling has been playing a critical role in the regeneration and development of te reo Māori (Māori language), *mātauranga Māori* (Māori knowledge), and *tikanga Māori* (Māori cultural practices). Māori medium teacher preparation programs are an important support element in the language, knowledge, and culture regeneration agenda. This chapter explores initial teacher education aimed at preparing teachers for Māori medium education.

"Māori medium education" itself is a contested term. The term has been used as an umbrella to cover a range of Māori language immersion levels in educational settings. Until recently, the term was used to describe educational settings that used Māori language as a medium of instruction at least 31% of the time (Education Information and Analysis Group 2010). Māori medium education is now officially used to describe education settings in which teaching and learning occurs through Māori language 51% to 100% of the time.

Although the study of the Māori language has been formally included in initial teacher education programs in Aotearoa New Zealand since 1939, Māori medium initial teacher education has a recent history. The first programs that prepared students to teach through the medium of Māori did not emerge until the late 1980s. This was the case even though the provision of bilingual Māori-English schools began in the early 1970s (Benton 1981), quickly followed by the development of other bilingual programs, *kura kaupapa Māori* (independent full immersion schools based on Māori philosophy and practice), and other full immersion schools and programs.

This chapter provides an historical overview of the place of te reo Māori in the preparation of teachers in Aotearoa New Zealand and examines the emergence of Māori medium initial teacher education programs—along with the challenges they have faced, and continue to face—as "contested places."

Background

The Māori language has played a role in teacher preparation since Western-style schooling was first introduced to Aotearoa New Zealand in 1816. Set up by missionaries to introduce Māori to literacy and Christianity, the first school soon folded. But by the 1830s, Māori interest in literacy and schooling had risen dramatically, with a corresponding increase in the number of schools located in Māori settlements and attached to church mission stations (Jackson 1975).

Most of the early missionary schools opted to teach in the Māori language, and teaching resources and texts were also produced in the language. It can be assumed that teachers for the missionary schools needed to develop a level of fluency in the language in order to teach in Māori and to use Māori language teaching resources. This could be understood as the first instance where Māori language was included in teacher preparation. In 1847, however, the introduction of state funding for mission schools was accompanied by the requirement that those schools teach English. A series of legislative ordinances and acts brought about the transition from schooling through the medium of Māori language to schooling through the medium of English (Simon et al. 2001). Mission schools were subsidized by the state if they met certain conditions, which included instruction in the English language. This was followed by the establishment of the Native Schools system for Māori children in 1867, which existed up until 1969. The 1867 Native Schools Act required instruction in schools to be in English.

Although the medium of instruction was English, bilingual Māori-English texts were supplied to the first Native Schools during the early 1870s. However, the expectation was that they would be used to facilitate the learning of English only, and it is unclear whether teachers were expected to develop a level of Māori language fluency in order to use the bilingual texts. Until the establishment of Aotearoa New Zealand's first teachers' training college in 1876 in the South Island at Dunedin, teacher preparation took a range of forms and methods across the country, including importation of trained teachers, prescriptions of standards, on-the-job examination and certification, and pupil-teacher, probationer, and teacher assistant systems (Openshaw and Ball 2006).

The next development of note with regards to Māori language and the preparation of teachers is the 1880 Native Schools Code.[1] The Code included the statement that teachers did not need to "be acquainted with the Māori tongue." However, in something of a contradiction, the Māori language was included in what might be regarded as the teacher training syllabus in the Code. Teachers were divided into five classes, ranging from uncertificated teachers to first-class certificated teachers, and needed to undergo examination should they wish to receive a higher classification. Knowledge of Māori language was included in teacher examinations and certification from 1880.

Although included in teacher examinations and certification, it was not until 1939 that the study of the Māori language was formally included in the curricula of teacher training colleges. The then Wellington Training College developed a third-year specialist training course in Native Education, and the course also included lessons in Māori language. While only four students were enrolled in the specialist course, other students were attracted to the Māori language lessons. Māori language classes also began at the Auckland Training College, taught by a part-time teacher (Simon et al. 2001).

In 1960 the government received the Hunn Report (Hunn 1961), which called for a greater emphasis on policies and resources that supported significant improvement for Māori achievement in education. Previous policies had resulted in Māori becoming greatly disadvantaged in a number of areas, including education. The report recognized Māori voice in determining which features of their language and culture they wished to keep.

At this time Māori language continued to be an option in initial teacher education to support programs in schools that introduced basic Māori language with key aspects of Māori culture. It was envisioned that such programs would suffice for the future of society in Aotearoa New Zealand.

The 1970s saw the beginning of a renaissance of Māori language and culture that was part of a movement for self-determination by Māori to regain control of their lives. Initiatives such as the beginning of Māori-language broadcasting and the opening of the first bilingual (Māori-English) school in 1978 added to the revival and recognition of the validity of being Māori.

In the early 1980s Māori leaders and families initiated *kōhanga reo* (Māori immersion "language nests") to provide a different system of education for their preschoolers and families. The main focus of kōhanga reo was the maintenance and strengthening of the Indigenous language, knowledge, and philosophies through the immersion of young children with their families in Māori language and culture. Development of kōhanga reo added further impetus to the movement of self-determination by Māori. The subsequent growth of these language nests then created a demand for their graduates to attend alternative schools that also operated through the Māori language.

An alternative education system, kura kaupapa Māori (independent full immersion schools based on Māori philosophy and practice), designed by Māori for Māori, challenged the hegemony of the present system. Māori were disenchanted with the results of the English medium system and sought to design one they considered more relevant, which would help address the inequities of the current situation. They called for greater autonomy and a shift in power from a centralized government system that was reluctant to acknowledge and share control (Nepe 1991).

Māori leaders and communities recognized that schools based on a kaupapa Māori framework that privileged Indigenous values, attitudes, and practices could be a powerful vehicle for facilitating long-term change for Māori. They believed that the results of such education would have a significant impact on the cultural, academic, and socio-economic position of Māori in Aotearoa New Zealand.

In the late 1980s Māori medium initial teacher education emerged as a response to demand by Māori communities for appropriately qualified teachers to support children's learning in Māori medium settings or schools. Māori communities viewed the capacity to speak their own language as an integral part of being Māori, and the regeneration and maintenance of the language and culture became a priority. The ability to teach a curriculum based on kaupapa Māori ideas through the medium of the Māori language became an imperative.

The responses by initial teacher education providers at the time were varied. The first Māori medium initial teacher education program in 1990 was specifically constructed and designed by Māori to provide specially trained teachers "aimed at reproducing Kaupapa Māori knowledge for successive Māori generations" (Nepe 1991, 124). Student teachers were fluent speakers of Māori (although many were second language learners), preparing to be knowledgeable in kaupapa Māori and have the appropriate skills, attitudes, and values necessary for teaching in kura kaupapa Māori. While this initiative began under the umbrella of a large, established initial teacher education institution, the desire for autonomy and control of the program by Māori leaders was not supported by that organization. Māori initiators deemed the situation irreconcilable and located alternative premises to continue the program. For these leaders autonomy and control of the program were synonymous with *tino rangatiratanga* or the drive for self-determination. If more successful educational outcomes for Māori children were to be achieved, Māori needed to take more responsibility to ensure that occurred.

In order to meet the demands of Māori medium settings, an alternative pathway was taken by another large initial teacher education institution to provide an appropriate Māori medium initial teacher education program. Instead of designing and initiating a completely new program, an already established program was "adjusted" by Māori staff. Where the established program focused on the provision of teachers for bilingual settings that incorporated some Māori language and culture, the modified program focused on providing teachers for Māori immersion settings (Kana 1999). The established degree structure would continue except for the option papers. Those papers were revised to focus on Māori education and improving student teacher proficiency in the Māori language (especially for teaching curriculum areas). Māori medium initial teacher education students were also expected to gain requisite teacher knowledge and pedagogy for Māori medium as well as English medium settings. Although this program recognized elements of the local *iwi* (tribe), such as their location, history, and dialect, it differed from the previous program in that not all aspects were taught in the Māori language. Where speakers of the Māori language were not available (about half of the program) from within the incumbent staff, those papers would continue to be taught by largely non-Māori with a focus on English medium classrooms. Even though this program did not emerge specifically from within the movement for self-determination for Māori, it did evolve to add support for those ideals.

In 1990 the Education Amendment Act was introduced and another avenue for Māori medium initial teacher education was created. Māori *wānanga* or universities located within Māori communities in townships were officially recognized. These wānanga had developed as a result of Māori striving to advance and legitimate the dissemination of Māori knowledge through teaching and research. While the wānanga were located in small towns, they were not restricted to local iwi and have since developed a pan-Māori clientele to whom they endeavour to cater through e-learning programs or the facilitation of workshops where students are located. A later development in Māori medium initial teacher education saw the establishment of smaller independent wānanga located within particular iwi. Such wānanga have a strong focus on promoting local language dialect, tribal history, and values. Because of the origin of wānanga, close relationships with local iwi are a general feature.

In 2005 further impetus was added to Māori medium initial teacher education by TeachNZ, a unit within the Ministry of Education charged with the national monitoring of teacher recruitment and supply. TeachNZ launched the provision of Māori medium scholarships, with the aim of increasing the number of classroom teachers. The scholarships were designed to offer support to candidates with some proficiency in the Māori language who might be considering entering the teaching profession. In 2013, TeachNZ chose to focus scholarships on areas of high demand, such as teaching in the Māori language, or teaching other subjects through the medium of that language at the secondary school level. As a further retention measure, the scholarships are "bonded," requiring the recipients to remain in teaching for a stipulated time after graduation (usually two years for each year of scholarship funding received; Ministry of Education 2014).

Features of Māori Medium Initial Teacher Education Today

A defining feature of Māori medium initial teacher education in Aotearoa New Zealand today is its diversity. This in part results from the challenge to prepare teachers for diverse Māori medium education settings. Māori medium education spans different philosophies, levels of language immersion, and levels of schooling, including secondary.

Most Māori medium education settings adhere to a particular philosophical position. A large number of kura kaupapa Māori schools identify with *Te Aho Matua* (New Zealand 1989), a document that espouses educational principles underpinned by widely held Māori values, beliefs, and practices. Another significant group of schools known as Kura ā Iwi focuses on tribal identity, knowledge, language, and values as central to teaching and learning.

Māori medium initial teacher education responds to philosophical diversity in a number of ways. Some programs have developed out of philosophical positions and aim, first and foremost, at preparing their students for schools that adhere to a particular philosophical position. Other programs aim to familiarize their students with different philosophical positions so they will be able to teach appropriately across different school settings.

As well as preparing teachers for Māori medium settings, 8 of the 10 current Māori medium initial teacher education programs state that they also prepare teachers for English medium settings. The programs include content from the New Zealand Curriculum document, and at least one course or paper delivered mainly through English. This approach aligns with the obligations placed on the Ministry of Education and education sector agencies via the Māori Language Strategy (*Tau Mai Te Reo*) 2013-17, to ensure that a connected and cohesive approach is pursued to support and strengthen the Māori language in the Māori medium sector and English medium settings. The inclusion of an English medium focus also relates to ensuring viable student cohorts and/or increasing a sense of students' employability. The dual focus for students in Māori medium programs, however, does raise the question, What counts as Māori medium initial teacher education?

Essential Elements of Māori Medium Initial Teacher Education

We propose that there are five essential elements that form the bases of Māori medium initial teacher education today. These elements recognize that Māori medium education evolved out of Māori whānau, community, *hapū* (subtribes) and iwi aspirations, leadership, and activism to establish education pathways that will make a difference for learners in Māori medium settings. The elements also recognize the fact that Māori medium initial teacher education is a relatively recent development striving to recognize and meet the needs of different philosophies and approaches that have emerged from a variety of perspectives.

1. He Taonga Tuku Iho (Treasures Handed Down)

Māori medium initial teacher education programs are underpinned by the principle of *taonga tuku iho* (cultural aspirations), which relates to the regeneration and perpetuation of the Māori language, Māori customs and values, and mātauranga Māori (Māori knowledge). The promotion of these components in Māori medium initial teacher education programs is "taken for granted" (Smith 1992, 20). Understanding that the Māori language is central to Māori cultural aspirations is an important idea for Māori medium initial teacher education students, many of whom require support to become proficient in the language. Programs therefore need to also support student development of Māori language, traditional Māori knowledge, and understanding the role of culture in education (Cram et al. 2012).

2. Rangatiratanga (Self-Determination)

Māori medium education is about transformation for Māori by Māori (Smith 1997). Self-determination or rangatiratanga includes Māori autonomy over education for their children, and supporting the retention of the Māori language and culture. Māori parents, *whānau* (families), and communities have been instrumental in the establishment of Māori medium schooling. Their demonstration of political leadership led to the recognition of kura kaupapa Māori as a category of school (Robinson,

Hohepa, and Lloyd 2009). Māori medium initial teacher education focuses on making a direct contribution to the strengthening of teaching and increased student achievement in Māori medium classrooms, while supporting the aims of parents, families, and iwi. This requires programs to ensure that Māori medium student teachers develop knowledge of and commitment to Māori self-determination, and that they understand the roles demanded of them with regards to realizing cultural and educational aspirations of children, families, and tribal groups.

3. Ako (A Focus on Learning and Teaching)

Ako, as a Māori pedagogical principle, emphasizes the unified cooperation of learner and teacher and the reciprocal nature of the teaching and learning process. It challenges established models of what it means to be a student and a teacher (Hemara 2000). Māori medium initial teacher education programs need to prepare student teachers to understand and practise ako in the classroom and contribute to the ongoing development of effective teaching and learning practices that are valued by Māori. Such a contribution requires knowledge of and critical engagement with Māori pedagogy, research evidence, and other forms of pedagogical knowledge. As well as encouraging the critique and use of Māori pedagogy, Māori medium initial teacher education programs should also support students in engaging with Western theories of learning and knowledge construction.

Māori medium initial teacher education programs are expected to ensure that student teachers consider their own processes for learning and how learning might occur for others. Learning to teach is complex, and programs need to provide student teachers with opportunities to examine their beliefs about learning and consider new ways of thinking about teaching that may help them to understand the cultural and social nature of teaching. Being supported as they reflect on their own learning and learning processes will enhance student teachers' reflexive capacities and help them to understand the extent of their role as teachers in a Māori medium setting.

Māori medium initial teacher education programs are expected to encourage active use of assessment information in order to understand and enhance effective teaching practice. Program design needs to support student teachers in understanding the learning needs of individuals and exploring how schools are endeavouring to meet them. Learning about effective curricular, instructional, and assessment approaches that enhance Māori medium student learning and contribute to greater achievement is integral to Māori medium initial teacher education programs. Using evidence to identify learner strengths and weaknesses to improve teaching and children's learning and closing engagement and achievement gaps for learners in the Māori medium are emphasized in programs.

School and university contexts are different. Practicum time within Māori medium initial teacher education programs offers important opportunities for student teachers to consider, refine, and practise implementing ideas that they have been exposed to in the university context. Such ideas relate to bilingual and second language acquisition, second language teaching competency, curriculum knowledge, information and communication technology (ICT) skills, and practise skills deemed important to establish and manage a classroom of learners (Cram et al. 2012). A practicum offers valuable opportunities for observing experienced teachers and incorporating aspects of those observations into practice. The expertise of associate teachers supporting student teachers to broaden their content and pedagogical skills while working with children in a range of curriculum areas is not to be underestimated (Hohepa et al. 2014).

4. Whanaungatanga (A Focus on Building Relationships)

Recent research reflects the importance of programs that support the practice of *whanaungatanga* (relationships; White et al. 2009) with Māori adult learners and highlights the significance of space for cultural imperatives such as *karakia* (prayers), *tikanga* (customs), *manaaki tangata* (caring for others; McMurchy-Pilkington 2009), *kanohi ki te kanohi* (face to face), and *whakawhitiwhiti kōrero* (discussions), when they are required. A strong feature of Māori medium initial teacher education programs is recognition of the importance to student teachers at university of belonging to a distinct group or whanau. Programs that acknowledge this cultural perspective and situate student teachers within a particular cohort or group where being Māori is the norm, and where key cultural understandings and practices underpin pedagogy in their program (Hohepa et al. 2014), are appreciated by Māori medium student teachers.

Actively promoting traditional Māori values of *āwhina* (seeking help) and *mahitahi* (collaboration; Mlcek et al. 2009) to student teachers in their studies, and considering issues regarding their practice, is another feature of Māori medium initial teacher education. This orientation to seeking help supports an inquiry-based approach promoted in curriculum documents for Māori medium settings.

Providers of Māori medium initial teacher education programs seek to ensure that the close relationships they develop in the local community with Māori are strengthened and maintained. When considering developing and maintaining important relationships outside the physical confines of an institution, *kanohi kitea* (a face seen) is a significant aspect for Māori and an important component of Māori medium initial teacher education. To this end, Māori medium initial teacher education programs provide opportunities for students to spend time in Māori medium schools and their communities to develop relationships while broadening their language, knowledge, and pedagogical skills.

Māori medium initial teacher education programs understand the value of relationship networks that exist within and across kura, and often extend into hapū and iwi, and appreciate the support these relationships can offer for the individual learning needs of children. Programs endeavour to support student teachers in developing as agents of change by encouraging an awareness and development of the theoretical tools and practical experiences required to critique and build on what they experience. In the context of Māori medium initial teacher education, hapū and iwi aspirations and strategic directions with regards to education also need to be acknowledged as other important knowledge sources. The critical role of partnership between Māori medium initial teacher education programs and Māori medium schools, which appropriately encompasses hapū and iwi in preparing student teachers to take responsibility for their own classes, cannot be overstated (Hohepa et al. 2014).

5. Te Ahureitanga Me Te Pito Mata (Understanding Uniqueness and Building from Difference)

Understanding and valuing diversity and difference as sources of uniqueness and potential that can generate inclusive educational space is another essential element in Māori medium initial teacher education. Programs seek to support student teachers in knowing and valuing the knowledge and skills that children bring with them to Māori medium settings (Te Tāhuhu o te Mātauranga 2010).

In Aotearoa New Zealand, as well as having cultural and pedagogical knowledge, understanding, and skills, teachers need to be committed to teaching students in ways that are responsive to diverse needs and backgrounds (Simpson and Grudnoff 2013). Teachers need to understand that their role includes building teaching programs starting from difference rather than accommodating for difference to improve achievement (Bishop and Glynn 1999).

Children in Māori medium settings come from various backgrounds and display a range of proficiencies in the Māori language. Some will be strongest in the Māori language while others will be stronger in English. Other learners will demonstrate dual proficiency in Māori and English, while a fourth group may also have some proficiency in additional languages (Rau 2008). It is essential that Māori medium initial teacher education programs support students in understanding their responsibility to build on these language differences. Programs therefore need to support student teacher learning to include knowledge of research and theory about bilingualism and second language development (May, Hill, and Tiakiwai 2004), to inform their teaching of learners with diverse levels of Māori language skills and knowledge.

Avenues for understanding and drawing upon Māori perspectives regarding giftedness in order to build on difference is also another important factor that Māori medium initial teacher education programs need to consider. As well as noting key features of Western theories that support further development of special needs children, Māori medium initial teacher education programs seek to ensure that student teachers are encouraged to explore pathways that incorporate cultural viewpoints from extended whānau and iwi that will build on the strengths that children bring with them. It is important that programs support student teachers in developing the necessary skills and knowledge to provide quality education that supports special needs learners as they engage with their learning (Bevan-Brown 2006). In doing so, programs must offer opportunities for student teachers to explore their own frame of reference and how that shapes their views and responses to uniqueness and potential. Catering to special needs learners while embracing diversity and difference in Māori medium educational settings requires, in reality, a commitment to social justice.

Teachers are agents of social change and play a crucial role in making a more just society. It might be expected that student teachers, on entry to Māori medium initial teacher education programs, will already have some understanding of cultural responsiveness (Education Information and Analysis Group 2010). This may include an understanding of their own identity, language, and culture (often but not always as Māori); an understanding of the relevance of culture in New Zealand education; and an understanding of and openness to Māori knowledge and expertise.

Difference is recognized across both individual and philosophical dimensions. Māori medium education settings reflect a range of philosophically and/or iwi-driven kaupapa. Māori medium initial teacher education programs are expected to develop and draw on understandings of philosophical differences and the importance of tribal groups that are foundational to Māori medium education. The exploration of these ideas is essential for understanding the diverse range of Māori medium contexts that currently exist in the compulsory school sector.

Challenges and Implications

That most programs include a stated focus on preparing teachers for English medium settings raises questions: What is a Māori medium initial teacher education program? Who are these programs providing teachers for? A definition will need to be one that not only ensures the integrity of Māori medium initial teacher education but also supports the diversity of philosophies and aspirations found across programs.

If the aim of Māori medium programs is to produce quality teachers for Māori medium settings, expecting those programs to also produce quality teachers for English medium classrooms is, in effect, doubling the workload of staff and students. This situation is clearly illustrated in the fact that while English medium programs will generally require students to only focus on the New Zealand Curriculum document throughout their time at university, Māori medium initial teacher education programs expect students to become familiar with that document as well as the national document for Māori medium settings (Kane et al. 2005). This "overload" of material might also be extended to include a third document if or when students are considering developing their own curriculum document for their local Māori community. The challenge for Māori medium initial teacher education programs in meeting the demands of two curriculum documents (and sometimes three) can generate tension for Māori staff and schools attempting to create "space" for students to develop traditional Māori knowledge perspectives about children's learning. Such tension is a result of programs attempting to achieve dual aims and purposes. The situation requires careful management to align program goals with the stated aims of the institution (Murphy, McKinley, and Bright 2008).

Such tension can have a considerable impact on an institution that aims to provide Māori medium initial teacher education. Increased awareness of identity by Māori, continued growth in demand from Māori communities to be involved in their children's education, and recent government policies that actively pursue inclusion of Māori in their children's education (Ministry of Education 2013a, 2013b) has meant that Māori medium initial teacher education needs to be more aware of Māori tribal and school voice in education. The notion of institutions being the sole or key "provider" of teachers for schools is evolving towards a "partnership" model. For many involved in Māori medium education, the development of such a situation is to be applauded. Devolving power to Māori communities seeking to gain greater involvement and control over their children's education coincides with the drive by Māori for self-determination. Māori medium initial teacher education programs readily acknowledge, value, and support a more active role for Māori schools and tribal groups in ensuring quality teachers for their children's education. The challenge for Māori medium initial teacher education will be to construct and share meaningful responsibility with key stakeholders who come from a spectrum of diverse philosophically located positions, to support quality teacher education and how it might be facilitated.

Teachers who work in immersion language settings require a high level of language proficiency for programs to succeed (Skerrett 2014), because such classrooms involve the teaching of a minority language by mainly second language speakers of Māori. "While teacher fluency is a crucial condition for the success of bilingual/immersion education, it is not, in itself, a sufficient condition. Teaching a minority target language as an L2 also requires an understanding of issues concerning second language acquisition" (May, Hill, and Tiakiwai 2004, 121). Finding time in Māori medium initial teacher education programs for students to explore and develop the necessary knowledge of bilingual theory, second language acquisition, and pedagogy is a challenge for student teachers enrolled in a three-year qualification.

Māori medium initial teacher education programs include student teachers who display a range of competencies in the Māori language. Programs therefore seek to ensure that students develop the necessary proficiency to teach all curriculum areas competently in the Māori language. Graduates are expected to display quality language as well as appropriate pedagogical skills for total immersion settings. Draft language competencies of graduating teachers for Māori medium learners (Murphy 2012) have been developed by the New Zealand Teachers Council to guide entry and exit assessments prior to graduation from Māori-medium initial teacher education programs. Program providers will be seeking to use the draft framework to ensure their graduates are sufficiently proficient to successfully teach in Māori-medium and immersion kura, school, and early childhood settings. As the majority of staff teaching in Māori-medium initial teacher education programs are second language learners of Māori, the need for professional support becomes an issue. Finding time for program leaders to develop language proficiency, as well as to support students in this area while they develop necessary teacher knowledge and skills, is a challenge.

In order to support cultural and educational aspirations that underpin Māori medium education, and to overcome teaching and learning challenges that teachers may meet as they work in kura, there is a need for programs to ensure that student teachers develop an appreciation of research and evidence-based decision-making and how these might influence their pedagogical practice and children's learning. The critical analysis of research-based evidence for its relevance and applicability in Māori medium settings is important (Hohepa 2010). Programs that support research and evidence-based decision-making are supported by Darling-Hammond (2000, 166) who suggests that we need to "expand professional [teacher] training to prepare teachers for more adaptive, knowledge-based practice." Teachers need to develop greater expertise in adapting their teaching more readily to meet the diverse needs of children in Māori medium settings. Such adaptation in instruction should be based on evidence indicating ideas that children are learning, and an understanding of how learning in that particular curriculum area can progress. The adaptive expertise model advocates a change from the practice model currently promoted in Māori medium initial teacher education programs, and requires an understanding of the concept of learning progressions as espoused by Duschl, Maeng, and Sezen (2011).

Māori medium initial teacher education programs need to offer opportunities for students to make further connections between practical knowledge and research-based knowledge. The inquiry-based approach, with ensuing opportunities for reflexive practice, positions student teachers to challenge and develop their thinking about teaching in Māori medium contexts. The emphasis on reflexive practice and on understanding kaupapa Māori approaches to teaching, learning, and research will also provide a basis for student teachers to become teachers who are able to inquire into and research their practice as they move into the Māori medium educational arena. Improved student achievement is dependent on teachers asking questions about their practice, gathering data, and being able to use the data to make sound judgements and decisions. Māori medium initial teacher education programs need to ensure that students understand and develop their commitment to this process.

Growth and development in technology provides greater opportunities for connectivity and influences how people engage with information and generate knowledge. As well as ensuring that student teachers develop the necessary Māori language proficiency and curriculum knowledge, Māori medium initial teacher education programs are expected to ensure that ICT is integrated into both the learning environment and pedagogical practice of graduates. Programs where student teachers critically examine the effectiveness of ICT used to support learning through the Māori language are required. Research has indicated that the use of ICT to enhance children's learning in Māori medium classrooms has been a challenge for graduates from Māori medium initial teacher education in the past and requires attention (Ham et al. 2006). The integration of ICT is aimed at more successfully meeting the needs of all learners in classrooms by reflecting the world outside formal Māori medium settings, by interrupting traditional teaching and learning practices, and by personalizing learning.

Conclusion

Māori medium initial teacher education is relatively new, and faces issues and challenges that specifically relate to the Māori medium context. Programs were originally initiated by Māori to support language and cultural regeneration and to help address inequities in education that were largely a result of early government policies in Aotearoa New Zealand.

The impetus and growth of identity and self-determination for Māori by Māori since the 1980s presents a key challenge for Māori medium initial teacher education programs. There is high demand from Māori tribes, communities, and families to ensure that they prepare teachers with the appropriate knowledge and skills to teach within a range of philosophically diverse settings that emphasize language and cultural regeneration, as well as for increased academic achievement by Māori learners.

Māori medium education is an intervention that is about the transformation of Māori through the promotion of traditional values and knowledge, which therefore need to be central to Māori medium initial teacher education programs. Such programs need to reflect and support the integration of these ideals and the ways they can serve the needs of Māori in the 21st century. The further development of Māori medium initial teacher education program structures and content, as well as innovative teaching through the medium of the Māori language, will require substantial research and development.

Note
1. The text of the Act can be accessed at http://atojs.natlib.govt.nz/cgi-bin/atojs?a=d&d=AJHR1880-I.2.2.3.7

References
Benton, Richard. 1981. *The Flight of the Amokura: Oceanic Languages and Formal Education in the South Pacific*. Wellington, NZ: New Zealand Council for Educational Research.

Bevan-Brown, Jill. 2006. "Teaching Māori Students with Special Education Needs: Getting Rid of the Too Hard Basket." *Kairaranga* 7 (special edition): 14-23.

Bishop, Russell, and Ted Glynn. 1999. *Culture Counts: Changing Power Relations in Education*. Auckland, NZ: Dunmore Press.

Cram, Fiona, Vivienne Kennedy, Miromiro Kelly-Hepi Te Huia, and Kirimatao Paipa. 2012. *Background Papers: Māori Medium ITE Outcomes. Graduate Profile and Effective Practicum and Induction Experiences*. Prepared for the Ministry of Education. Auckland, NZ: Katoa Ltd.

Darling-Hammond, Linda. 2000. "How Teacher Education Matters." *Journal of Teacher Education* 51: 166-73. https://doi.org/10.1177%2F0022487100051003002

Duschl, Richard, Seungho Maeng, and Asli Sezen. 2011. "Learning Progressions and Teaching Sequences: A Review and Analysis." *Studies in Science Education* 47: 119-77. https://doi.org/10.1080/03057267.2011.604476

Education Information and Analysis Group / Group Māori. 2010. *Ngā Haeata Mātauranga—The Annual Report on Māori Education, 2008/09*. Wellington, NZ: Ministry of Education. http://www.educationcounts.govt.nz/publications/series/5851/75954/mori-language-in-education

Ham, Vince, Peter Moeau, Sandra Williamson-Leadley, Toubat Toubat, and Michael Winter. 2006. *ICTPD Through Three Lenses: An Evaluation of the ICTPD School Clusters Programme 2001-2003, Report to the Ministry of Education*. Christchurch, NZ: Christchurch College of Education. https://www.educationcounts.govt.nz/publications/series/5819/5787

Hemara, Wharehuia. 2000. *Māori Pedagogies*. Wellington, NZ: NZCER Press.

Hohepa, Margie. 2010. "Whakapakari Kura: Learning and Inquiry in Māori-Medium Education." In *Weaving Evidence, Inquiry and Standards to Build Better Schools*, edited by Helen Timperley and Judy Parr, 93-111. Wellington, NZ: NZCER Press.

Hohepa, Margie, Ngarewa Hawera, Karaitiana Tamatea, and Sharyn Heaton. 2014. *Te Puni Rumaki: Strengthening the Preparation, Capability and Retention of Māori Medium Teacher Trainees*. Report commissioned by the Ministry of Education. Hillcrest, NZ: Wilf Malcolm Institute of Educational Research, University of Waikato.

Hunn, Jack Kent. 1961. *Report on Department of Māori Affairs*. Wellington, NZ: Government Printer.

Jackson, Michael. 1975. "Literacy, Communications and Social Change." In *Conflict and Compromise: Essays on the Māori since Colonisation*, edited by Hugh Kawharu, 27-54. Wellington, NZ: A.H Reed & A.W. Reed.

Kana, Fred. 1999. "The Effectiveness of a Māori-Focused Teacher Education Programme." *Waikato Journal of Education* 5: 133-7.

Kane, Ruth, Pam Burke, Joy Cullen, Ronnie Davey, Barbara Jordan, Colleen McMurchy-Pilkington, Ruth Mansell, et al. 2005. *Initial Teacher Education: Policy and Practice*. Wellington, NZ: New Zealand Ministry of Education and New Zealand Teachers Council.

May, Stephen, Richard Hill, and Sarah Tiakiwai. 2004. *Bilingual/Immersion Education: Indicators of Good Practice*. Wellington, NZ: Ministry of Education.

McMurchy-Pilkington, Colleen. 2009. *Te Pakeke Hei Ākonga: Māori Adult Learners*. Wellington, NZ: Ministry of Education.

Ministry of Education. 2013a. *Māori Medium Kaiako Survey*. Wellington, NZ: Ministry of Education.

———. 2013b. *Tau Mai te Reo: The Māori Language in Education 2013-2017*. Wellington, NZ: Ministry of Education.

———. 2014. *TeachNZ Career Changer Scholarships Guide*. Wellington, NZ: Ministry of Education. http://www.teachnz.govt.nz/scholarships/teachnz-career-changer-scholarships/

Mlcek, Susan, Ngareta Timutimu, Carl Mika, Monte Aranga, Nikora Taipeti, Te Rurehe Rangihau, Te Makarini Temara, Yvonne Shepherd, and Haturini McGarvey. 2009. *Te Piko o te Māhuri, Terā te Tupu o te Rākau: Language and Literacy in Marae-based Programmes*. Wellington, NZ: Ministry of Education.

Murphy, Hineihaea. 2012. "Language Competencies of Graduating Teachers for Māori-Medium Learners: Draft Framework." Prepared for the New Zealand Teachers Council.

Murphy, Hineihaea, Sheridan McKinley, and Nicola Bright. 2008. *Whakamanahia te reo Māori: He Tirohanga Hōtaka: An Exploration of Issues and Influences that Effect te reo Māori Competence of Graduates from Māori Medium ITE Programmes*. Wellington, NZ: New Zealand Teachers Council.

Nepe, Tuakana Mate. 1991. "E Hao Nei Tenei Reanga te toi Huarewa Tipuna: Kaupapa Māori: An Educational Intervention System." Master's thesis, University of Auckland.

Openshaw, Roger, and Teresa Ball. 2006. "New Zealand Teacher Education: Progression or Prescription?" *Education Research and Perspectives* 33 (2): 102-23.

Rau, Cath. 2008. "Literacy Acquisition, Assessment and Achievement of Year Two Students in Total Immersion in Māori Programmes." *International Journal of Bilingual Education and Bilingualism* 8 (5): 404-32. http://doi.org/10.1080/13670050508668622

Robinson, Vivienne, Margie Hohepa, and Claire Lloyd. 2009. *School Leadership and Student Outcomes: Identifying What Works and Why—Best Evidence Synthesis Iteration*. Wellington, NZ: Ministry of Education.

Ross, Catherine. 2008. *Culturally Relevant Peer Support for Māori and Pasifika Student Engagement, Retention and Success*. Lower Hutt, NZ: Open Polytechnic of New Zealand. https://ako.ac.nz/knowledge-centre/culturally-relevant-peer-support-for-maori-and-pasifika-student-engagement-retention-and-success/

Simon, Judith, Linda Tuhiwai Smith, Fiona Cram, Margie Hohepa, Stuart McNaughton, and Maxine Stephenson. 2001. *A Civilising Mission? Perceptions and Representations of the Native Schools System*. Auckland, NZ: Auckland University Press.

Simpson, Mary, and Lexie Grudnoff. 2013. "From Preparation to Practice: Tensions and Connections." *Waikato Journal of Education* 18 (1): 71–82. http://doi.org/10.15663%2Fwje.v18i1.140

Skerrett, Mere. 2014. "Policy and Inhibitors of Bicultural/Bilingual Advancement." In *Early Childhood Education in Aotearoa New Zealand: History, Pedagogy, and Liberation*, edited by Jenny Ritchie and Mere Skerrett, 56–69. New York: Palgrave Macmillan.

Smith, Graham Hingangaroa. 1992. "Tane-nui-a-rangi's Legacy, Propping up the Sky: Kaupapa Māori as Resistance and Intervention." Paper presented at NZARE/AARE Joint Conference, Deakin University, Victoria, Australia, November 1992.

———. 1997. "The Development of Kaupapa Māori: Theory and Praxis." PHD diss., University of Auckland.

Te Tāhuhu o te Mātauranga. 2010. *Tū rangatira: Te kaitātaki i te mātauranga kaupapa Māori* [Māori Medium Educational Leadership]. Te Whanganui-a-Tara: Te Tāhuhu o te Mātauranga, 2010.

White, Hera, Tania Oxenham, Marion Tahana, Kim Williams, and Kimi Matthews. 2009. *Mā te Huruhuru Ka Rere te Manu: How Can Language and Literacy Be Optimised for Māori Learner Success?* Wellington, NZ: Ministry of Education.

13 | Teaching as the Creation of Ethical Space
Indigenous Student Learning in the Academy/University

DAWN ZINGA

INDIGENOUS[1] STUDENTS ENTERING UNIVERSITY face the complex challenge of negotiating contested spaces and places within those institutions of higher education. This contestation involves students trying to maintain their cultural integrity and achieving success on their own terms in the face of colonial oppression and the devaluing of their cultures and ways of knowing that is embedded in these educational contexts. This oppression and devaluation occurs in many places and spaces on campus and frequently is expressed through the absence of spaces and places that respect and acknowledge Indigenous cultures and ways of knowing. Many Indigenous students find universities to be places where their identities are defined by others and subsequently challenged and/or discounted. Students have spoken of being asked to speak for all Indigenous Peoples in class discussions as well as encountering and navigating racist content in curriculum (Battiste 2013, 2018; Hare and Pidgeon 2011; Kuokkannen 2007; St. Denis 2011; St. Denis and Hampton 2002). Many navigate these challenges alone and feel alienated within the university while others find support through Indigenous-focused programs, Indigenous faculty, Indigenous community members, and occasionally non-Indigenous faculty who have extensive experience working within Indigenous contexts. Despite the challenges faced by Indigenous students, 8.7% of individuals who identified as First Nations, 5.1% of individuals who identified as Inuit, and 11.7% of individuals who identified as Métis report having a university degree (Statistics Canada 2013a).

As a non-Indigenous faculty member in a mainstream university, I often feel unequal to the task of supporting Indigenous students on campus. I am implicated in colonial networks and relations of power and privilege, which continue to oppress and devalue Indigenous cultures and worldviews both systematically and administratively through Canadian institutions, including universities, and through the paternalistic relationship that the Canadian federal government continues to impose on sovereign Indigenous communities. In this chapter, I will focus on the experiences of Indigenous students within the contested spaces of higher education, and, specifically, the ways Indigenous students navigate the space and negotiate how they choose to engage and disengage both within the learning environment as well as with their peers and their instructors, who are usually non-Indigenous. I will provide a consideration of the context that informs the contestation present in universities, as well as an examination of the ways individuals and institutions are implicated in the maintenance of universities as places that fail to reflect, affirm, and value Indigenous cultures and ways of knowing, even as those individuals and institutions are located on the ancestral lands (ceded and unceded) of Indigenous people who have existed and continue to exist in relationship to their lands and territories since time immemorial. By exploring Ermine's (2005) application of ethical space within learning contexts, I will discuss what it means, as a non-Indigenous instructor, to teach Indigenous students within these contested spaces. Furthermore, I will consider what it means as a non-Indigenous instructor to teach non-Indigenous students within these contested spaces, as well as the ways in which we, as non-Indigenous people, are implicated in them. I will also introduce the concept of teaching as the creation of ethical space and discuss the ways such spaces can be co-created and maintained.

Prior to reviewing the context that informs the contested spaces and places on university campuses, I would like to share a story that a colleague shared with me about her experiences as an Indigenous student entering undergraduate studies. My colleague, Lindsay Cosh,[2] had been accepted at a university that was seven hours away from her home community and located in the territory of other Indigenous Peoples. She was nervous and expected that the transition might be challenging but she was unprepared for the hostility of the university environment, how alien it felt, and how it challenged and devalued her core values and identity. She described most of her undergraduate years as being very dark and isolating—her "dark days." She has completed her university studies and gone on to be a contributing and very productive member of the local Indigenous community near the university, and she continues to remain connected and actively involved in the university she navigated to receive her degree. However, she attributes her successful completion to both her personal strength of will and to the drum, as she explains below.

> Born and raised in Northern Ontario I found myself very alone in a southern urban city. Making the decision to leave my family in order to pursue my academics in university was one of the most difficult decisions of my life. During my first two years attending school away from my home, I felt extremely alone and isolated. I began to feel depressed, as within this educational environment as I was not able to continue learning my history, language, cultural and spiritual practices as well as find a course nor a place to connect to my heritage and identity as a First Nations person. I slipped into a dark depression and no increased amount of pills nor counselling sessions helped in pulling me out. The beginning of my third year, what finally pulled me out from my darkest years was the big drum. I had found myself wondering in the little forest by the university and that big drum called to me. It drew me in like a mother's calling. I followed its call and found to my surprise a whole new world of connection with my people and opportunity to practice my culture through the Aboriginal Student Services

(ABSS) and the Aboriginal Student Association (ASO). The day I heard that drum was the same day the ABSS in partnership with ASO was providing a welcome back lunch to their students just on the edge of campus. I felt a piece of home come back to me that day and a heavy cloud lifted from my spirit. We shared and connected from that day forward. I give all my thanks and gratitude to the ABSS and ASO. The space, the services, and the support they provided enabled me to feel a connection once again and allowed me the strength to climb out of the dark into the light and helped me find my way through the contested spaces within the university. I not only found hope, but became the leader of ASO during my final years, and facilitated a full-day educational culture event, "Returning to our Roots," for all students to find space and a greater connection to our earth, its medicines, and our traditional healing practices. I graduated university and continued on my career path of helping Aboriginal people live healthy, find a place in a contested space, and strengthen their own connection to the culture of our Aboriginal people.

Within most Indigenous circles, the beat of a drum is considered to be Mother Earth's heartbeat and it is a comforting, familiar sound that calls to her. Her story is one of many and is informed by the important contextual factors that shape the ways Indigenous students experience Canadian education systems.

Setting the Context

Indigenous students enter institutions of higher education with diverse learning experiences and backgrounds. Like other college and university students they have unique family backgrounds and cultural experiences that may find resonance with other students from similar backgrounds. The key difference is that the identity of Indigenous students has been politicized and they carry with them consciously or unconsciously the history of colonization and the scars that colonial acts have inflicted on themselves, their families, and their Peoples. Indigenous students access Canadian education institutions that have an assimilationist history: the 1876 amendment to the Indian Act required the enfranchisement or unwilling relinquishing of Indian status to gain entry to higher education, and around 1911 the government amended the act again to make school attendance mandatory for Indigenous children. Some residential schools were in place as early as the 1840s, the 1900s saw a huge increase in forcible enrollment of Indigenous students in the residential school system, and the last residential school did not close until 1996 (Battiste 2013). Entering college or university is considered to be a transition requiring adjustment for all entering students, but while universities and colleges have made strides in learning to welcome new students to campus and ease that adjustment, the majority of the faculty, staff, and administrators in higher education fail to appreciate the impact of this assimilationist history or how alien and unwelcoming the campus spaces and places are to Indigenous students.

As Pidgeon discusses in her chapter in this volume (chapter 10), universities and colleges have become more interested in Indigenous student retention but have not gained the requisite skills in making campuses more welcoming places for these students. Battiste (2013, 159) refers to education and its associated institutions as being "neither culturally neutral nor fair" and further argues that Canadian education has been created out of a "patriarchal, Eurocentric society." Thus, education systems continue to oppress individuals on the basis of gender, group identification, and cultural background while also serving to reaffirm the privilege and status of mainstream individuals. These systems simultaneously devalue and subjugate those who do not fit the mainstream mould and seek to assimilate them into "proper" university material and "global citizens." It is a self-perpetuating cycle, and those who are seen to be mainstream are indoctrinated in the beliefs and ideologies that act to subjugate and devalue beliefs, ideologies, and peoples who do not fit the prescribed mould. Thus, the individual students, staff, administrators, and instructors within these institutions perpetuate the imposition of colonial power by becoming what Foucault (1977, 98) refers to as "willing vehicles of power." Institutions of higher education carry this colonial history within their structures, policies, procedures, and classrooms and yet struggle to understand why their specialized outreach programs for Indigenous students are not more effective without realizing that the root of the problem can be found in what Kuokkanen (2007, 66) refers to as "epistemic ignorance."

Kuokkannen's (2007) conceptualization of epistemic ignorance draws upon Spivak's (1990) idea of sanctioned ignorance, which refers to the tendency of the academy to justify and reward the failure within the academy to recognize or acknowledge others, such as Indigenous people, as producing knowledge or theories. Kuokkannen builds on this idea and expands it beyond a "failure to know" to theories, practices, and discourses that deny other epistemologies or ways of knowing, thus requiring Indigenous students to put their own ways of knowing aside for the dominant Western epistemology. To further compound the problem, Indigenous students are usually required to self-identify as Indigenous to access these services with little appreciation by the institutions and its members of the multiple political layers associated with Indigenous identity.

Alfred and Corntassle (2005, 597) state that Indigenous identity is "constructed, shaped and lived in the politicized context of contemporary colonialism." Palmater (2013) has written about the various ways that Indigenous identity can be defined and about the attempt to control and legislate who is or is not Indigenous through the Indian Act and the division of individuals into status or non-status. Indigenous students are the only students attending higher education who may have a legislatively defined identity. Like Palmeter, Lawrence (2004, 173) has written about the complexities and challenges associated with Indigenous identity for Indigenous Peoples within Canadian society: "Aboriginal peoples' racial identities are fraught with complexities hinging on legal definitions of Indianness, cultural knowledge, and connection to Indigenous land base. In everyday terms, however, Nativeness also depends on how you are defined by others—which, in white society, depends to a phenomenal extent on how you look." Deer (2011) discusses how the understanding of Canadian identity in schools serves as a dominant post-colonial influence that can interfere with Indigenous identity and Indigenous students' self-concept. He also points to recent initiatives in higher education to recruit Indigenous students and make campus spaces and places more welcoming by providing areas and opportunities for ceremonies, creating support centres, increasing the number of Indigenous faculty and staff, and establishing new buildings designed around Indigenous worldviews. However well-intentioned these initiatives may be, there are important considerations in the ways these initiatives are implemented and the impact they have on the institution and its members. Pidgeon (this volume) also discusses higher education initiatives related to space and the display of Indigenous art, as well as the attempt to recognize and honour cultural protocols. She points to the importance of doing this work mindfully and respectfully so that it both recognizes and values Indigenous Peoples while also working to educate mainstream individuals and combat racism. Any initiatives implemented within higher education must be designed with an understanding of the complex histories and the associated wounds that have been experienced by Indigenous students and communities through either their forcible or their voluntary involvement with Canadian education systems.

There are decades of research pointing to the fact that Indigenous students in Canada face significant challenges when negotiating the multiple levels within Canadian education systems (see Archibald et al. 1995; Battiste 2005, 2013, 2018; Indian and Northern Affairs Canada 2002; Canadian Teachers' Federation 2001; Coon Come, Gosnell, and Young 2002; Furniss 1995; Mattson and Caffrey 2001; Royal Commission on Aboriginal Peoples 1996; Statistics Canada 2008; St. Denis and Hampton 2002). Frequently, this research is positioned in a way that points to a "crisis" in Indigenous education. For example, the Hon. Jim Prentice (2007, n.p.), former minister of Indian and Northern Affairs Canada, is quoted as arguing that Canada's approach to Indigenous education is "achieving the lowest educational outcomes certainly anywhere in Canada" and that Indigenous children are "the only children in Canada who have lacked an education system." Similarly, the Standing Committee on Aboriginal Affairs and Northern Development (2007) identified Aboriginal education as a crisis that is unanimously agreed upon, a rarity within social policy circles. More recently, Atleo (2014) stated that the work in Indigenous education began over 40 years ago with the Indian Control of Indian Education document in 1972, and he highlighted the importance of education as one the primary reasons for his resignation. His resignation occurred amidst criticism concerning the Harper government's proposed First Nations Education Bill. It is interesting that in his last statement as the AFN National Chief, Atleo (2014, n.p.) never referred to Indigenous education as being in crisis but rather referred to the importance of the work and the need to "smash the status quo."

Generally speaking, mainstream Canadians are more comfortable with a crisis than facing that there is a significant problem with the status quo in education. The national and provincial trends indicate that Aboriginal youth ages 12–18 tend to leave school before completing high school, and drop-out rates among Indigenous youth aged 15 and over are a reported 40% in comparison to 13% rates for their non-Indigenous counterparts (Statistics Canada 2008). Much of the research has identified systemic problems within Canada's education systems and schools, such as alienation, devaluing of Indigenous culture, othering, and racism (see Antone 2003; Battiste, 2013, 2018; Fryberg et al. 2013; Furniss 1995; Hare 2004; Hare and Pidgeon 2011; Leroy 2001; Neegan 2005; Samson 2003; St. Denis and Hampton 2002; Whattam 2003; Zinga and Gordon 2014). While this research points to systemic problems, it is often interpreted by others through what Ermine, Sinclair, and Jeffrey (2004, 12) refer to as a "pathologizing lens" that is characteristic of other research that has been done on, but not with, Indigenous Peoples. Smith (1999, 92) acknowledges this history of research on Indigenous

Peoples as being responsible for the widespread understanding among Indigenous Peoples that "the word research is believed to mean, quite literally, the continued construction of Indigenous Peoples as the problem."

More research is not needed to identify systemic problems within Canadian education systems, nor is it needed to help individuals understand why Indigenous students have to navigate contested spaces in all levels of education, including higher education. What needs to be researched and deconstructed is why so little has been done to address these systemic problems or, as Atleo (2014, n.p.) contends, to "challenge the status quo."

Why are mainstream Canadians more comfortable with a crisis in education, or, as it is often stated, in Indigenous education? A crisis is a neat way of sidestepping systemic issues and placing the blame on Indigenous students and communities. It triggers the idea that there is an urgent issue that has emerged and needs to be addressed while minimizing the reality that what has been labeled as a crisis is really an entrenched standard operating procedure, or status quo, in education. A crisis sounds new and urgent. It can cloud the issue that there are long-standing concerns with historical roots that have been perpetuated by current and historical systems and structures. Furthermore, focusing on Indigenous education serves to separate it from mainstream education and promotes the use of the pathologizing lens through which Indigenous students and their communities become the problem. Any changes or initiatives within Canadian education systems can then be seen as "favours" or a show of good will to help Indigenous students without mainstream administrators, staff, and educators ever having to interrogate how the mainstream system continues to perpetuate the status quo and serves to undermine such initiatives. In contrast, the understanding that the status quo and the systems that perpetuate hegemonic views rooted in colonialism are the problems that need to be addressed is much more uncomfortable for mainstream individuals, as it necessitates discovering and coming to terms with how they are implicated in this perpetuation. Further, such knowledge then prompts a simple question with significant implications: Now that you know how you are implicated, what are you going to do about it?

What Is Ethical Space?

The creation of ethical space provides one avenue through which individuals can engage with their own implication in the perpetuation of colonialism. In discussing ethical space, I am drawing upon Ermine's (2005) conceptualization of ethical space as a space for ethical action and conversation that occurs when Indigenous and Western knowledge systems come into contact with each other. Ermine built upon Poole's (1972) idea of ethical space by reconceptualizing it and applying it to the space between Indigenous and Western knowledge systems. Poole conceptualized ethical space as the confrontation between two sets of intentions. In reading Poole, each set of intentions can be seen as creating their own space, and ethical space is automatically created when the two sets of intentions confront each other. For Poole, it is the space between the two sets of intentions that is important. Ermine agrees with Poole that the space between the intentions is not empty but full of possibility and of the unspoken thoughts, interests, and assumptions that will influence any engagement between the two. In applying the concept of ethical space to Indigenous and Western knowledge systems, the space between the two becomes full of their entrenched differences. These entrenched differences often act to disrupt communication and interfere with authentic dialogue, as hidden within them are the unquestioned social constructs, assumptions, and perceived understandings through which individuals belonging to either group view the world. At best, the clash of these worldviews results in misunderstandings, and at worse it leads to significant negative outcomes such as marginalization and oppression. In my conceptualization of this space between Indigenous and Western intentionalities, I see the space between the two groups in two specific ways. Like Poole and Ermine, I see the space as being ethical space that can allow for the ethical engagement of the entrenched differences to move forward in positive ways. In addition, if the space is unexamined or not engaged with in ethical ways by the intentionalities, then it can be thought of as the status quo that the dominant group is not interested in examining.

Ermine (2007, 196) stresses the importance of understanding how we have arrived at the status quo. In the North American context, he describes it as a "time-lagged issue" that is the result of a pattern of "divergence and mal-adaptation" that is characterized by interaction between Indigenous Peoples and the colonizers. These interactions reflect repetitive cycles of engagement and disengagement, connection and disconnection, and union and rupture that date back to first contact and continue to be replicated through current interactions that remain entangled in and influenced by previous historical patterns of interaction. Ermine argues that these patterns have resulted in intercultural confusion and undermined the ability of either the Indigenous Peoples or the colonizers to establish rules of engagement that could be used to bridge the chasm between the two groups.

In an interview about ethical space, Ermine discusses his conceptualization of ethical space as being a place between knowledge systems where he could engage with Indigenous and mainstream/Western worldviews (Coleman and Ermine 2010b). Thus, ethical space is a place of engagement. Ermine (2005) also refers to it as a neutral zone in which there exists the opportunity to engage in critical dialogues. In the interview, Ermine describes ethical space as creating ideas and dialogue where we take control back from the systems that perpetuate both unethical engagement through the privileging of one worldview and the oppression of Indigenous worldviews and cultures. For Ermine, we must do this by challenging the embedded assumptions and associated prescriptions from the institutions and systems that continue to shape our lived realities (Coleman and Ermine 2010ab). He goes on to discuss how it is convenient for non-Indigenous people to hide behind the systems and institutions that privilege them and to fail to question the status quo, but suggests that in reality, non-Indigenous individuals are as caught in the system as Indigenous individuals. Thus, if non-Indigenous individuals perceive themselves as being caught in the system and streamed through it such that they are in the position to replicate and reinforce mal-adaptive interactions and oppression, there is more motivation to examine the status quo and push back against the systems and institutions.

Ermine (Coleman and Ermine 2010b) poses two challenges. He challenges people to take control of their own humanity and visioning by pushing aside the prescribed knowledge delivered through institutions and systems that are rooted in intercultural confusion and unhealthy patterns of engagement dating back to first contact, so that we can shape our own lived realities and revision relationships. He acknowledges that this can be done very theoretically with no resulting change, and so his second challenge is for people to take the concept of ethical space and to do something with it.

Teaching as the Creation and Engagement of Ethical Space

Teaching as the engagement of ethical space is both a concept and an action. As a concept, I am building on Ermine's (2005, 4) conceptualization of ethical space as a "space between the Indigenous and Western spheres of culture and knowledge relative to research issues" by applying it to the context of teaching, and I am conceptualizing teaching as providing opportunities for the creation of and engagement in ethical space. As an action, teaching as engagement in ethical space addresses the challenge posed by Ermine to take up the concept and do something with it.

Ermine's (2005) ethical space is a concept that I have been working on with colleagues for some time in various research contexts. Poole (1972) conceptualizes ethical space as being automatically created when two intentionalities collide, whereas Ermine (2005) posits that ethical space is a place in which to engage with the two worldviews and that there is a level of engagement required in the ethical space in order to trigger meaningful dialogue (Ermine 2007). When working through this concept within research contexts (Styres et al. 2010; Styres and Zinga 2013), we conceptualized ethical space as being created as a possibility when intentions and assumptions collide, but said that mindful engagement of the space was necessary for the ethical space to be realized. Power relations are another important consideration within ethical space. In choosing to engage in ethical space, an individual chooses to engage with his or her positionality and associated baggage, including the power relations that are connected to the positionality. For example, as a non-Indigenous academic I am responsible for dealing with the colonial baggage that I have inherited and for being aware of the power relations that are enacted by membership in the dominant Eurocentric group. It is not something that I can take off at will, like a coat; it is part of my very being and my understanding of it will inform who I am and how I choose to act.

In the classroom context, intentions and assumptions frequently collide and power relations are enacted. There are no actions that can be taken to eliminate power relations when there is a teacher who will grade and a student who will deliver work to be graded. However, power relations can be acknowledged and engaged with in various ways. In higher education, classrooms focus on the dissemination and questioning of knowledge, assumptions, intentions, and related issues. Therefore, if we apply Poole's (1972) conception of ethical space, it follows that the creation of ethical space is a regular occurrence in classroom contexts. The creation of ethical space is not the critical element to focus on, as that creation is often triggered; what is essential is the engagement of that space.

This brings us back to my earlier question: Now that you know how you are implicated, what are you going to do about it? While non-Indigenous faculty and students may be unaware and frequently choose not to address how they are implicated in contested spaces, Indigenous faculty and students do not have the privilege of being unaware of contestation or of being able to set it aside as something they would rather not address. Indigenous students in higher education continually negotiate contested spaces and places within colleges and universities, and one of the most frequently contested spaces is the classroom. Worldviews frequently collide in the classroom and those collisions can be engaged with in various ways. Unfortunately, collisions between Indigenous and Western worldviews are usually engaged with in ways that perpetuate Western dominance and colonial relations, reaffirming the status quo and resulting in contested spaces for Indigenous students. When this occurs, ethical space is created by the collision and the possibility for the engagement of that ethical space is not realized due to the imposition of colonial power.

When colonial power is imposed, the instructor has become what Foucault (1977, 98) terms "a willing vehicle of power" and has consciously or unconsciously turned away from engaging ethical space. How might an instructor unconsciously turn away from ethical space? Is it possible to be that unaware of the tangled colonial relations that have brought us to this point in our shared histories? I allow that it is possible for students who have not been made aware of the implications of such histories to be unconscious of these relations, as students have been mired in Eurocentric curricula and therefore may be unaware of their turning away from the engagement of ethical space. In contrast, I find it difficult to see how an instructor in higher education can unconsciously turn away. At some level there has to be an awareness of the contestation, the clash of worldviews, and an active choice to assert mainstream privilege and not engage in ethical space. So I will focus on reasons why an instructor may consciously turn away from ethical space as I question the authenticity of an unconscious turning away as anything but a convenient excuse and an enactment of privilege that perpetuates contested spaces.

The instructor may consciously turn away from engagement for a number of reasons. It could be that the instructor feels constrained by context or circumstance and has decided that it is not an appropriate time to engage. The instructor may not value the engagement or may not be interested in engaging. It is also possible that the instructor may resist being aware of the ways in which he or she is implicated in colonial relations. Regardless of the reason the instructor fails to engage in ethical space, the end result is that power relations are imposed and the educational space in which the interaction occurs is reinforced as being contested for the Indigenous student(s). Non-Indigenous students have also been deprived of an opportunity to engage in ethical space in this scenario.

It is important to note that failure to engage in ethical space reinforces educational spaces as contested places. As discussed earlier, university and college settings are places of contestation for Indigenous students, as these places have been envisioned and created through the lens of Western thought and largely informed by Eurocentric approaches to pedagogy and curriculum that devalue and frequently misrepresent Indigenous ways of knowing. This is true even in spaces that have been designed to provide respite to Indigenous students within academia, such as Aboriginal Student Service departments or special gathering places such as the University of British Columbia's First Nations Longhouse. One would expect that these spaces would be uncontested, but unfortunately that is not always the case, as politics and the imposition of colonial relations can result in contestation even in places that have been set aside as spaces for Indigenous students and faculty.

Indigenous students work hard to achieve their educational goals in institutions of higher education and navigate the contested spaces that such institutions perpetuate. Engaging ethical space creates opportunities for these students to engage with learning in deeper, authentic ways, and the failure to engage reinforces the contestation, often making the space even more challenging to navigate. Instructors have an important role to play in being party to the opening up of those ethical spaces in several important ways.

Engaging Ethical Space in Higher Learning

Engaging ethical space is complicated and requires a willingness to confront, engage with, and question one's implications in colonial relations as well as the resulting baggage and influences on how one views the world. Poole (1972) drew on the imagery of two people sitting on a park bench and the resulting space between them being the ethical space as a helpful way for people to think about the concept. Ermine (2005, 2007; Coleman and Ermine 2010ab) has talked about ethical space as being a place where he could engage with Indigenous and Western worldviews. In the classroom there are many possible different configurations of ethical space engagement. There is one that does model the park bench scenario and this occurs when an interaction is between an instructor and an Indigenous student. For example, an Indigenous student may approach the instructor and question something that was discussed in lecture or a reading. Frequently, the configuration is quite different from the park bench imagery.

In higher learning, one-on-one interactions are not the only type of interactions that could engage in ethical space. There are many other configurations that are possible; I will review some of the most common, and it is important to understand that the possibility to engage in ethical space occurs in more configurations than those reviewed in this chapter. Being mindful of when such opportunities arise is essential to being able to engage in ethical space.

Opportunities to engage in ethical space can occur during lecture or class discussions, in group sessions with students, in the provision of feedback on readings, during conversation between instructors, in meetings, and in symposia, talks, and conferences. Each configuration impacts Indigenous students within higher education contexts, with some configurations impacting Indigenous students more directly than others. Regardless of whether the impact is direct or indirect, the engagement of ethical space impacts the contested space that Indigenous students occupy, as the following examples illustrate. Some of the examples will also illustrate one of the unique, but not often explicitly discussed, features of ethical space, namely that there do not need to be two individuals to create ethical space and that there can be as few as one individual involved, as well as more than two individuals involved. Ermine (2005, 2007; Coleman and Ermine 2010) talked about ethical space as a place where an individual could engage with the two worldviews and he also alluded to ethical spaces as being engaged in between groups of people or an individual and a group.

Engaging ethical space is complex, as illustrated by the following example. This example is a combination of individual engagement in ethical space, engaging in ethical space in lecture and class discussion, and in one-on-one engagement. When planning one of my lectures for a large first-year course (two sections of 350 students), I wanted to challenge the students to consider the dangers of only using a Western perspective to understand children and youth by introducing them to Indigenous ways of knowing. I was concerned about how deeply I could discuss Indigenous worldviews in that setting while keeping the students engaged in developing an appreciation for what Indigenous worldviews could offer, as well as communicating that while the Western worldview frequently devalues other ways of knowing, the Indigenous ways of knowing do not devalue other ways. Essentially, I was modelling the engagement of ethical space that can occur when an individual engages with two worldviews. The students in the lecture might choose to engage in ethical space themselves within their own minds, be largely unaware of what I was modelling, tune out, or consciously resist the modelling.

I decided that I would review the three Holistic Lifelong Learning Models (First Nations, Métis, and Inuit) that are freely available through the Canadian Council on Learning website. I felt that the choice would accomplish what I sought to do in the classroom and offered a good first introduction that students could examine in more detail through the website. The lecture went well and afterwards a number of students came up to discuss various concerns. One of the students came to me to share that there was more to the worldviews than what I had covered, and she discussed the origins of Turtle Island. I thanked her for coming up to me and let her know that I had purposefully chosen not to share deeper knowledge with the class due to the setting. I felt somewhat uncomfortable as there were many students around and did not engage with her as deeply as I would have liked to do before she left. I was left questioning whether my discomfort was about my concerns for her in that group setting or whether it had more to do with being questioned as an instructor. I did not reach a conclusion but remained unsatisfied by the exchange and concerned that I had not engaged with the student as I would have liked, but I could not find any resolution as I did not know the student's name.

Shortly after the lecture she contacted me by email to apologize for questioning what I had done in class, which confirmed my fears that we had not engaged in ethical space together. I emailed back that I had been wishing to apologize for not engaging with her more after class. I thanked her for coming up to me to discuss the lecture and stressed how much I appreciated her doing so and being willing to share her knowledge with me. I discussed the reasoning behind my choices and we had a much more authentic conversation.

In this example, I engaged in ethical space in several configurations. I engaged in the space as an individual by engaging Indigenous and Western worldviews to plan my lecture and by planning how to expose students to that ethical space. I also engaged in ethical space by designing the lecture and associated discussion such that I modelled the engagement of ethical space to the students and opened the opportunity for engaging in ethical space to the students in the lecture hall. I provided appropriate supports to assist the mainstream students in thinking through how their Eurocentric education and their Western lens influenced their thinking. In that same lecture and discussion, I was also honouring the Indigenous ways of knowing, which were represented through the learning models to invite Indigenous students into the space and discussion. The challenge of this group engagement was that each individual chooses to engage or not and may engage at varying levels. The introduction of ethical space in the classroom in this way pushes back against the contested space in the classroom by opening up opportunities for ethical dialogue that questions the entrenched differences referred to by Ermine. There was also the one-on-one configuration with the student following the lecture and the subsequent email dialogue. Following the lecture and associated experiences, I also went back into the ethical space individually through my questioning of how I had planned the lecture and, given the one-on-one experience with the student, how I might have done things differently.

In upper-year courses, I design opportunities to engage in ethical space in various areas of course work. As in the previous example, I model the engagement of ethical space in the classroom and then go further with these upper-year students to open more opportunities during large group discussions. The students are also provided with opportunities to engage through small group discussion and through individual reflections on readings. In my understanding of engagement in ethical space, it is, at its core, a choice. Students should be exposed to modelled examples of engagement and invited to engage, but it is the student who choses whether or not to engage. The mindful opening of opportunities to engage in ethical space can shift some of the dynamics of contested spaces by exposing the nature of the contestation and the dangers of the status quo for all students. Battiste (2013) has discussed the benefits of opening the curriculum to other ways of knowing for all students and argues that Canada needs to move towards decolonizing education and using ethical space in curricula.

Instructors also need to be aware of barriers that may make it difficult for students to take up opportunities to engage in ethical space. Some barriers can be addressed by the instructor, while other barriers must be navigated by the student. These barriers include, but are not limited to, the following: personal history and experience, lack of knowledge, lack of trust, guilt and feelings of implication, stereotypes, not feeling safe, Eurocentric thought, discomfort with engagement, protective strategies students have developed to navigate contestation, and the contested space itself. Both Indigenous and non-Indigenous students encounter barriers to engaging in ethical space. Instructors can address some of these barriers by creating safe classroom environments and establishing trust within the classroom, as well as by discussing stereotypes, guilt, and feelings of implication.

Instructional strategies can also be used to address barriers to engagement. The use of proximal distance can also be a helpful strategy, as it allows a certain level of distance that can assist students in engaging without feeling immediately threatened. By proximal distance, I am referring to choosing something that is not in the students' immediate environment but at some distance so that the issue to be examined is not intimately close but also not too distant. For example, in several upper-year classes I used the case of the Thorold Blackhawks as an example of cultural appropriation and stereotypes that created contested spaces for young people. The Thorold Blackhawks is a Junior B Hockey organization whose logo is a stereotypical cartoon depiction of an Indigenous man that many Indigenous and some non-Indigenous members of the Niagara community find to be racist and offensive. In class we collectively examined the logo and reviewed the media reports about the controversy that ensued when the Indigenous community pushed the hockey organization to change the logo. There are many examples that I could have chosen from national teams, but those would have been too distant. As this team is located in close proximity to Brock University, where I teach, it was proximally distant and allowed students to examine the contested space created in sport for Indigenous players as well as the role of the logo and those individuals who failed to see any issue with the logo (those who maintained the status quo) in continuing to perpetuate contested spaces. The situation mirrored some of the contested spaces experienced in the university such that students could draw parallels and begin thinking about those contested spaces without having to directly confront them. At the same time, the engagement with the issue of the Thorold Blackhawks logo within the classroom challenges the status quo that maintains the contested spaces in the university.

There are other opportunities presented to engage in ethical space that do not directly impact classroom spaces. These are opportunities that come up at meetings and in conversation with other instructors and members of the higher education community. There are times in such conversations when Indigenous and Western ways of knowing collide, and a choice must be made about whether or not the ethical space is engaged in. For example, in discussions about convocation procedures and protocols, ethical space can be opened up to discuss how such procedures and protocols could be changed to make the ceremony more welcoming to Indigenous students and their families while also honouring the ancestral lands upon which many institutions of higher education are located. The opportunity may arise when discussing the distribution and booking of space within the institution, or the allocation of space, or when trying to find a compromise between Indigenous protocols around honoraria and compensation for services and institutions' financial accounting policies. While these conversations do not have direct impacts on Indigenous students in classrooms, they do filter down and either positively or negatively impact the overall institutional climate and educational experience. Often these conversations are opportunities to examine and challenge the status quo that reinforces educational spaces as contested spaces for Indigenous students.

In addition to the opportunities presented in meetings and at different points in the structural and managerial levels of the university, there are other educational opportunities that exist outside the formal classroom or associated interactions between students and teachers. As places of learning, universities and colleges often host academic conferences and visiting scholars. During these events, professors and other speakers present talks that are designed according to the understandings and theoretical perspectives of the given speaker and through the speaker's exercise of academic freedom. There have been a number of incidents at various institutions of higher learning in which the content or visuals shared during a talk were offensive to Indigenous students and Indigenous community members, as well as other members of the audience. While it is clear that academic freedom exists, speakers also have an obligation to engage with the audience in relevant and respectful ways and to explain their use of content and visuals. All too often, academic freedom and academic conventions are used as a shield so that the speaker can abdicate their responsibilities to respectfully engage with or explain the content or visuals that are embedded in or connected to colonial relations. In choosing not to engage and abdicating that responsibility, the speaker transfers the responsibility to engage to members of the audience who are aware of the contestation, such that members are in a position of either condoning through a consenting silence or engaging through disruption. This transference of responsibility and the associated challenges it poses are clearly illustrated in the example provided below.

The following example will help uncover the multiple layers of contested spaces that can confront Indigenous students in their academic pursuits, as well as illustrate how these occurrences can negatively impact educational spaces for Indigenous students and reinforce contestation. An Indigenous graduate student, Laurie Sherry-Kirk,[3] shared her experience at a prestigious national conference with me. One of the key invited talks at the conference featured a Trudeau scholar who was speaking on a book that she had written using a social justice framework. A member of the organizing committee, who was also a key faculty member in Laurie's graduate program, asked Laurie to prepare a question to open the question and answer period following the talk. Laurie was honoured by the request. She eagerly prepared by reading the book and familiarizing herself with the scholar's other work in order to prepare a thoughtful and informed question. As Laurie describes in her own words, she was not prepared for what happened during the talk.

> The speaker began by discussing how she believed that the concept of settler society has been disappearing as such and that the time had come for meaningful change in immigration policies. As she discussed immigration policies, she displayed a slide that contained an image of two men with Hollywood-style Mohawk haircuts with a solitary feather sticking up from their heads. They were dressed in breech cloths holding a tomahawk in one hand while extending the

other to welcome a man, woman, and child who were stepping off a Mayflower-type ship.

Words cannot express the sense of pain and anguish that I experienced while I sat and listened to a representative from settler society discuss what should now be done with the traditional lands of my people. The speaker continued to argue for the elimination of borders to ensure that no one in this country could be labelled as illegal. According to her, the term "illegal" allows a country to gain the benefits of cheap labour while at the same time ensuring that the state does not have to share the benefits gained from their contribution. What is absent from the discussion is the input of the original peoples of Turtle Island. Nor was there a conversation surrounding the issue of unresolved land claims and dishonoured existing treaty rights that continue to be the motivating factor behind the Idle No More movement.

Words cannot give justice to the way that I felt as I gazed at that picture; with my heart pounding in my chest, it was the voice of my ancestors that prevented me from abandoning my responsibility to the address and bolting from my chair. To make matters worse, the speaker concluded the lecture with another slide featuring Indigenous imagery. This slide was extremely offensive as it contained the imagery of First Nations people in caricature. At no point during the lecture did the speaker acknowledge the existence of First Nations people, nor did she provide a rationale for the use of Indigenous imagery.

Laurie described to me how she became hyperaware of the multiple levels of contested space that occurred during the talk and the discussion that followed. She described her feelings of needing to speak up for her ancestors and yet being aware that she did not want to disappoint the faculty members from her graduate program. She was aware of the power differentials and of the larger contested spaces around land and treaty rights that had been revealed during the talk. She still opened the question and answer period but with a new question that she wrote as she listened to the talk and not the question that she had prepared. The question Laurie asked was:

> Does the end of settler society mean the end of Indigenous Canada? We are the forgotten people, the originally displaced refugees of what was once a land of plenty—a place where my ancestors welcomed new people—greeted them with openness and sharing. We had no laws of immigration indeed—no one was illegal. Have you considered the role the First Nations people will play in the proposed New Politics of Immigration?

The speaker seemed stunned by the question and indicated that she was not in a position to speak to that question and that she would have to let First Nations people speak to that question. Ironically, the individual handling the microphone promptly took it away from Laurie before she could respond or offer any other contributions. Laurie described the awkward silence that followed her question and how the issue that she raised was not taken up or validated until a white member of the audience posed a similar question. It was only after that happened that Laurie received any nods of approval or support from the audience. Even the silence has layers of contestation, as within mainstream conventions silence can be interpreted as tacit consent, whereas within many Indigenous worldviews silence does not confer consent and silence is used to convey specific and nuanced messages that communicate important information in multiple ways. In abdicating the responsibility to engage with the question, the speaker transferred the responsibility to Laurie, who faced very difficult choices about the ways she might engage and the ways she might be silenced, the most obvious silencing being the removal of the microphone. The speaker introduced a new layer of contestation through the abdication and transfer of responsibility. The speaker chose to include the visuals and also chose not to engage with that inclusion, actively using power and privilege to put the responsibility onto Indigenous Peoples to respond while simultaneously framing any possible response as the "problem." Thus, the Indigenous individual taking up the responsibility to deliver that response is seen as deviant or problematic and therefore one who, based on that stepping outside the norm in the response, could be discounted, silenced, and delegitimized.

Laurie was deeply disturbed by the trauma that she experienced and brought the incident to the attention of the Aboriginal Education Council (AEC) at the university where the conference was hosted. The AEC consists of Indigenous community members, Indigenous members of the university community, and non-Indigenous members of the university community who work together to advise the administration on matters related to Indigenous education and whose primary function is to support Indigenous students. While many members of the AEC were supportive of Laurie's concerns and felt that the situation must be addressed, Laurie encountered challenges in having the issue promptly addressed by the AEC due to protection of academic freedom and concerns around how to address the situation with the speaker. The weight of the transferred responsibility continued to impact Laurie as she sought to have the incident appropriately addressed through official channels. Despite the support that she received from many members of the AEC, there was an undercurrent tied to contestation that led in some ways to Laurie being revictimized and framed as the "problem." The contested spaces associated with that framing were not engaged with and deconstructed in meaningful and respectful ways that could have led to rich conversations within ethical space. Instead, there was a silencing and the use of power and privilege by some non-Indigenous members of the AEC to constrain Laurie and to attempt to give permission and approval to both the collective response by the AEC and the student's personal response to the speaker. Laurie resisted what she perceived as attempts to either control or approve her response and decided to send her personal response independently. It took almost a year from the date of the incident before the issue was addressed with the speaker and even then Laurie felt that it was not a satisfactory resolution. Instead she felt that multiple levels of contestation within academia had been reinforced throughout the AEC's handling of the situation.

In this example, there were many opportunities for the engagement in ethical space and for individuals or groups to challenge the contested spaces in the university. When the speaker dodged the question about the images, a faculty member could have supported Laurie and redirected the speaker back to the question. Simply put, if the speaker felt that she was in a position to include such images in a talk, then she had accepted the responsibility to speak to that decision. If the speaker was unprepared or unwilling to address the question, then the faculty member could have made arrangements for a private conversation between the faculty organizers, the student, and the speaker. Concerns could have been brought to the conference organizing committee immediately. Not taking action was a conscious reinforcement of the contested space, whereas taking action would have offered an opportunity to engage in ethical space; even if the speaker was not willing to engage, there were other opportunities for engagement available within the situation that would not have reinforced the status quo. Furthermore, the AEC missed an important opportunity to engage in ethical space when the contestation associated with an official response was not engaged with and addressed.

The Importance of Creating Ethical Space

Teaching as the creation of ethical space is complicated, challenging, and messy. It is demanding, hard work that offers many opportunities for missteps and mistakes. So, why is it so important? Why should instructors seek to teach by creating ethical space? As previously discussed, statistics around the success rates of Indigenous students and the implications of the current status quo provide compelling reasons, as does the tangled history. Returning to my earlier question—Now that you know how you are implicated, what are you going to do about it?—poses another compelling reason to engage in teaching as the creation of ethical space.

The opportunity for Indigenous students to engage in ethical space works towards making their educational spaces safer and more welcoming spaces for learning. It addresses the contestation in educational spaces that you as the reader are now aware of and implicated in either maintaining or challenging. It is important for non-Indigenous students and instructors to engage in ethical space as they are complicit in maintaining the contested nature of educational spaces by maintaining the status quo and by failing to see any contestation in the educational spaces that they occupy. Engaging in ethical space offers opportunities to see how spaces can be contested and to work towards ways of addressing and resolving the contestation. As mentioned previously, engaging or not engaging in ethical space is a choice that each individual makes in multiple ways. There is the ethical space that is created when two worldviews collide and an individual enters into ethical space to engage with their thoughts about the worldviews and work through those tensions, challenges, and contradictions (Ermine 2005, 2007; Coleman and Ermine 2010ab). There is also the engagement of two or more people in the ethical space as also discussed by Ermine (Coleman and Ermine 2010a, 2010b). What is important to consider in an educational setting is the co-creation of the space. In the examples of ethical space, I have stressed the modelling of ethical space and the opening of opportunities for engaging in ethical space. Once that space is engaged in by more than one individual, it is a co-created and co-maintained space, and it is out of that co-creation that deeper learning occurs, as students must bring themselves into the space. In class discussions, students may repeatedly engage in and disengage from the ethical space, resulting in a constantly shifting dynamic in the space. When that space is between two people, disengagement ruptures the space, whereas when the space is engaged in by more than two people, such as by a class of students, the movement in and out of the space by individuals shifts the dynamics within the space but does not rupture the ethical space.

Smith (2012) identified five conditions that exist in the struggle for decolonization. These conditions are critical consciousness, reimagining the world and one's role in the world, the intersection of disparate ideas, movement or disturbance, and conceptualization of structure and power relations. Smith has argued that these five conditions capture the contestations and struggles that Māori have experienced in their struggle for decolonization. Within ethical space these five conditions can be fostered and explored. While Smith introduced the conditions in relation to her own lived experience and the Māori context, they have a resonance that extends beyond the specific context to speak to the larger context of decolonization and the impact of colonial relations. They speak to the contested spaces within institutions of higher education that have been maintained through systemic and structural realities that reinforce colonial relations and fail to question the status quo. Battiste (2013) calls upon educators to question the current system of education, understand their own complicity within the system, and take action to remake and imagine education in different ways.

This begs the question of how to answer the call. This need within educational contexts to address contested spaces by opening up dialogue that will help us to better understand our implications in colonization has been present since the creation of Canadian education systems. Too often, non-Indigenous individuals do not see it as their place to act or question, or they do not want to deal with the discomfort that exploring such issues may create. Yet that choice relegates Indigenous students to an educational reality that is beyond discomfort. The status quo must be challenged. I am often asked by students and occasionally by other faculty about how we might challenge the status quo. One of the questions most frequently posed by students is, "What are we supposed to do? Give these ancestral lands back?" In posing the question, the students are missing the most salient points of the contestation, namely that we should not choose to opt out and to not engage with the complex issues associated with treaties and land claims. We need to find ways of honouring the ancestors who walked these lands before us. The layering of concrete does not erase the stories contained in the covered lands. Rather we must find a way of moving forward in the realities in which we find ourselves and choose to reconceptualize and reconfigure the ways in which we choose to move education forward. Within education, this means engaging with the tough questions, letting go of the belief that there is one solitary right answer, and being open to other ways of knowing. Teaching as the creating of ethical space addresses the questions that instructors and students often ask: What can I do about it? Have the courage to confront the status quo and to consciously engage in teaching as the creation of ethical space. As non-Indigenous people, we need to acknowledge the privilege afforded to us by the status quo, we need to engage in ethical space, and we need to act to collaborate on ways to reframe educational contexts as spaces that are inclusive, safe, and supportive for all students. The question that we need to consider is not What can I do about it? but rather Now that you know how you are implicated, what are you going to do about it?

Notes

1. Within the context of this document the term "Indigenous" refers to the original or first people of any country and is used interchangeably with the term "Aboriginal." In Canada it also includes First Nations, Métis, and Inuit unless otherwise specifically noted.
2. Lindsay Cosh, BA, has provided permission to share her story within this chapter. She chose to share most of it in her own words and wanted to have her name associated with her experience. She shared her story orally, and participated with me in establishing the written version.
3. Laurie Sherry-Kirk, MA, has provided permission to share her story within this chapter. She chose to share most of it in her own words and wanted to have her name associated with her experience. She shared her story orally, and participated with me in establishing the written version. She and I have never shared a direct student-teacher relationship.

References

Alfred, Taiaiake, and Jeff J. Corntassel. 2005. "Being Indigenous: Resurgences Against Contemporary Colonialism." *Government and Opposition* 40 (4): 597–614. https://doi.org/10.1111/j.1477-7053.2005.00166.x

Antone, Eileen M. 2003. "The Changing Face of Aboriginal Education in Rural and Northern Canada." *Education Canada* 43 (3), 24–8.

Archibald, Jo-ann, Sheena Selkirk Bowman, F. Pepper, Carl Urion, G. Mirenhouse, and R. Shortt. 1995. "Honoring What They Say: Post-Secondary Experiences of First Nations Graduates." *Canadian Journal of Native Education* 21 (1): 1–247.

Atleo, Shawn. 2014. "Shawn Atleo's Statement of Resignation." *CBC News*, May 2, 2014. http://www.cbc.ca/news/aboriginal/shawn-atleo-s-statement-of-resignation-1.2630279

Battiste, Marie. 2005. "Bringing Aboriginal Education into the Contemporary Education: Narratives of Cognitive Imperialism Reconciling with Decolonization." In *Leadership, Gender and Culture: Male and Female Perspectives*, edited by John Collard and Cecilia Reynolds, 142–8. Maidenhead, England: Open University.

———. 2013. *Decolonizing Education: Nourishing the Learning Spirit*. Saskatoon, SK: Purich Publishing.

———. 2018. "Reconciling Indigenous Knowledge in Education: Promises, Possibilities, and Imperatives." In *Dissident Knowledge in Higher Education*, edited by Marc Spooner and James McNinch, 123–48. Regina, SK: University of Regina Press.

Castellano, Marlene B., Lynne Davis, and Louise Lahache, eds. 2000. *Aboriginal Education: Fulfilling the Promise*. Vancouver: UBC Press.

Coleman, D. [Interviewer], and Willie Ermine [Interviewee]. 2010a. "Ethical Space in Action. The Different Knowings Speaker's Series: Prof. Willie Ermine." YouTube, September 2, 2011. https://www.youtube.com/watch?v=ZUfXu3gfVJ8

Coleman, D. [Interviewer], and Willie Ermine [Interviewee]. 2010b. "What Is Ethical Space? The Different Knowings Speaker's Series: Prof. Willie Ermine." YouTube, August 30, 2011. https://www.youtube.com/watch?v=85PPdUE8Mbo

Coon Come, Matthew, Ginger Gosnell, and Terry Young. 2002. "Presentation to the Senate Standing Committee on Aboriginal Peoples." Paper produced by Assembly of First Nations, June 11, 2002. http://files.eric.ed.gov/fulltext/ED474686.pdf

Deer, Frank. 2011. "Aboriginal Identity: A Perspective on Hegemony and the Implications for Canadian Citizenship." *Education* 17 (3): 2–16.

Ermine, Willie. 2005. "Ethical Space: Transforming Relations." Paper presented at the National Gatherings on Indigenous Knowledge, Rankin Inlet, Nunavut, May–June, 2005.

———. 2007. "The Ethical Space of Engagement." *Indigenous Law Journal* 6 (1): 193–203.

Ermine, Willie, Raven Sinclair, and Bonnie Jeffery. 2004. *The Ethics of Research Involving Indigenous Peoples*. Report of the Indigenous Peoples' Health Research Centre to the Interagency Advisory Panel on Research Ethics. Saskatoon, SK: Indigenous Peoples' Health Research Centre.

Foucault, Michel. 1977. "Two Lectures." In *Power/Knowledge: Selected Interviews and Other Writings 1972-1977*, edited by Colin Gordon, 78-108. New York: Pantheon Books.

Fryberg, Stephanie A., Wendy Troop-Gordon, Alexandra D'Arrisso, Heidi Flores, Vladimir Ponizovskiy, John D. Ranney, Tarek Mandour, Curtis Tootoosis, Sandy Robinson, Natalie Russo, and Jacob A Burack. 2013. "Cultural Mismatch and the Education of Aboriginal Youths: The Interplay of Cultural Identities and Teacher Ratings." *Developmental Psychology* 49 (1): 72-9.

Furniss, Elizabeth. 1995. *Victims of Benevolence. The Dark Legacy of the Williams Lake Residential School*. Vancouver: Arsenal Pulp Press.

Hare, Jan. 2004. "They Beat the Drum for Me." *Education Canada* 44 (4), 17-20.

Hare, Jan, and Michelle Pidgeon. 2011. "The Way of the Warrior: Indigenous Youth Navigating the Challenges of Schooling." *Canadian Journal of Education* 34 (2): 93-111.

Indian and Northern Affairs Canada. 2002. *Fall 2002 Survey of First Nations People Living On-Reserve: Final Report*. Ottawa: Indian and Northern Affairs Canada.

Kuokkanen, Rauna. 2007. *Reshaping the University: Responsibility, Indigenous Epistemes, and the Logic of the Gift*. Vancouver: UBC Press.

Lawrence, Bonita. 2004. *"Real" Indians and Others: Mixed-Blood Urban Native Peoples and Indigenous Nationhood*. Lincoln: University of Nebraska Press.

Leroy, Carol. (2001). "'No Friends, Barely': A Voice from the Edge of Indian Identity." In *Resting Lightly on Mother Earth: The Aboriginal Experience in Urban Educational Settings*, edited by Angela Ward and Rita Bouvier, 83-92. Calgary, AB: Detselig Enterprises.

Mattson, Linda, and Lee Caffrey. 2001. *Barriers to Equal Education for Aboriginal Learners: A Review of the Literature*. A BC Human Rights Commission Report. Vancouver: British Columbia Human Rights Commission.

Neegan, Erica. 2005. "Excuse Me: Who are the First Peoples of Canada? Aboriginal Education in Canada Then and Now." *International Journal of Inclusive Education* 9 (1), 3-15.

Palmater, Pamela. 2011. *Beyond Blood: Rethinking Indigenous Identity*. Saskatoon, SK: Purich.

Pidgeon, Michelle. 2008. "It Takes More than Good Intentions: Institutional Accountability and Responsibility to Indigenous Higher Education." PHD diss., University of British Columbia.

Pidgeon, Michelle, Jo-ann Archibald, and Colleen Hawkey. 2014. "Relationships Matter: Supporting Aboriginal Graduate Students in British Columbia, Canada." *Canadian Journal of Higher Education* 40 (1): 1–21.

Poole, Roger. 1972. *Towards Deep Subjectivity*. New York: Harper & Row.

Prentice, Jim. 2007. Comments before Parliament. Standing Committee on Aboriginal Affairs and Northern Development, no. 054, 1st Session, 39th Parliament, evidence, May 29.

Royal Commission on Aboriginal Peoples. 1996. *Gathering of Strength, Volume 3. Report of the Royal Commission on Aboriginal Peoples*. Ottawa: Minister of Supply and Services.

Samson, Colin. 2003. "Sexual Abuse and Assimilation: Oblates, Teachers and the Innu of Labrador." *Sexualities* 6 (1), 46–53.

Smith, Linda Tuhiwai. 1999. *Decolonizing Methodologies: Research and Indigenous Peoples*. London: Zed Books.

———. 2012. *Decolonizing Methodologies: Research and Indigenous Peoples*. 2nd ed. New York: Zed Books.

Spivak, Gayatri Chakravorty. 1990. *The Postcolonial Critic: Interviews, Strategies, Dialogues*. Edited by Sara Harasym. New York: Routledge.

Standing Committee on Aboriginal Affairs and Northern Development. 2007. *No Higher Priority: Aboriginal Post-Secondary Education in Canada*. Report to Parliament, 39th Parliament, 1st session. Ottawa: House of Commons.

Statistics Canada. 2008. "2006 Census: Aboriginal Peoples in Canada in 2006: Inuit, Métis, and First Nations, 2006 Census: Findings." http://www12.statcan.gc.ca/census-recensement/2006/as-sa/97-558/p3-eng.cfm

———. 2011. *The Educational Attainment of Aboriginal Peoples. The National Household Survey (NHS) 2011*. Ottawa: Statistics Canada.

———. 2013a. *The Educational Attainment of Aboriginal Peoples in Canada*. Statistics Canada Catalogue no. 99-012-X2011003. Ottawa: Statistics Canada.

———. 2013b. *The Education and Employment Experiences of First Nations People Living Off Reserve, Inuit, and Métis: Selected Findings from the 2012 Aboriginal Peoples Survey*. Ottawa: Statistics Canada.

St. Denis, Verna. 2011. "Silencing Aboriginal Curricular Content and Perspectives Through Multiculturalism: 'There Are Other Children Here.'" *Review of Education, Pedagogy, and Cultural Studies* 33 (4): 306–17.

St. Denis, Verna, and Eber Hampton. 2002. *Literature Review on Racism and the Effects on Aboriginal Education*. Prepared for Minister's Working Group on Education. Ottawa: Indian and Northern Affairs Canada.

Styres, Sandra, and Dawn Zinga. 2013. "The Community-First Land-Centred Theoretical Framework: Bringing a 'Good Mind' to Indigenous Education Research?" *Canadian Journal of Education* 36 (2): 284–313.

Styres, Sandra, Dawn Zinga, Sheila Bennett, and Michelle Bomberry. 2010. "Walking in Two Worlds: Engaging the Space Between Indigenous Community and Academia." *Canadian Journal of Education* 33 (3): 617–48.

Whattam, Tracey. 2003. "Reflections on Residential Schools and Our Future: 'Daylight in Our Minds.'" *Qualitative Studies in Education*, 16 (3): 435–48.

Zinga, Dawn, and Megan Gordon. 2014. "Racism Under the Radar: Student Perceptions of School Experiences in a Multicultural Setting." *Race, Ethnicity and Education*, 19 (5): 1088–116.

14 | Exploring Teacher Candidate Resistance
to Indigenous Content in a Teacher
Education Program

JEAN-PAUL RESTOULE & ANGELA NARDOZI

Introduction

Educating Canadian elementary and high school students about Aboriginal histories, cultures, and contemporary issues and the role of all Canadians in past and current Aboriginal-Settler[1] relations is crucial for catalyzing social and political change. While many provinces across the country have recognized the importance of updating the Aboriginal content in their curriculum documents, teachers are the primary decision-makers with regards to what is taught in their classrooms and how the information is presented.

In 2010, the Association of Canadian Deans of Education issued an accord affirming the need for teacher training programs across Canada to incorporate training with regards to Aboriginal content in their curriculum (Association of Canadian Deans of Education 2010). The Ontario Institute for Studies in Education of the University of Toronto (OISE/UT) is one of the many signatories who committed to enhancing the place of Aboriginal ways of knowing and improving the experience of Aboriginal students.

We, the authors of this chapter, are members of the Deepening Knowledge Project (DKP), an initiative based at OISE/UT, whose mandate is to infuse understandings about Indigenous-Settler relationships, both past and present, into all areas of the Initial Teacher Education program. This group consists of Indigenous and Settler professors, teacher instructors, and graduate students who come together because of a shared belief in the importance of better educating teachers in how to teach about Indigenous-Settler relations. In our efforts to advocate for and deliver information about these relations, as well as to impart knowledge of Aboriginal histories, current issues and events, or pedagogies, we have encountered spaces of contestation within the teacher training program.

OISE/UT is a Western academic space. The university system of which it is a part has historically been, and is presently, a site of colonization (Smith 1999) where knowledge is produced that limits and controls what Indigenous Peoples can know and are capable of thinking, doing, and being. It can also be a site of potential liberation where ideas about Indigenous self-determination can be expressed. In teacher training, the spaces can be highly charged and tense when narratives of state and Settler innocence come into conflict with Indigenous discourses of anti-colonialism. Indigenous people are underrepresented in the teacher education program at OISE/UT. Indigenous students who do study here are entering hostile spaces where their lived experiences and those of their families may be completely absent or, if introduced, examined dispassionately by Settlers engaging in what they consider to be a critical exercise, and where racist sentiments may be shared with the justification of "free speech." Indigenous populations are experiencing a boom that means more Indigenous youth will be in classrooms at all levels in future. Will these spaces represent them or continue to be experienced as hostile or dismissive of them?

The contestation we're focusing on is the introduction of Indigenous thought, experience, perspective, and knowledge into a previously white-normative environment where raced bodies are othered and where Indigeneity is seen as either exotic and romantic, primitive and irrelevant, or threatening to Settler security on this land. Re-establishing this material as a valuable way of knowing and of being on this land and within these spaces is the focus of our work and of this chapter. These contested spaces emerge while instructors negotiate the amount of space and time dedicated to teaching these topics in the well-established, mainstream teacher training program. They also arise within the presentations we deliver to teacher candidates, whose privileges and Settler identities result in taken-for-granted narratives of the Canadian state and in both spoken and covert resistances. The prospect of teaching Aboriginal content also gives rise to the anticipation of future contested spaces on the part of teacher candidates who foresee difficulties in bringing Indigenous issues into their classrooms. Without challenging these spaces, the mainstream elementary and secondary classroom will continue to be a place of contestation for Indigenous students who do not see themselves, their communities, their nations, or their histories reflected in what they are learning. In this chapter we will name and explore these contested spaces, and reveal what strategies we are using to help teacher candidates examine their reasoning and overcome resistance.

The various forms of resistance displayed by teacher candidates demonstrate the contested ground that Indigenous realities and experiences must tread upon when taken up in teacher education programs. Conventional Canadian education systems are mandated to tell narratives of Canadian nationhood and sovereignty as founded on peace, order, and good government. Tuck and Gaztambide-Fernández (2013, 73) argue that within mainstream educational space, "the settler colonial curricular project of replacement...aims to vanish Indigenous Peoples and replace them with settlers, who see themselves as the rightful claimants to land, and indeed, as Indigenous." To teach about Aboriginal histories contests these national narratives and confronts the Canadian Settler subject's privilege, and his or her sense of innocence and goodness. It is a small wonder, then, that when white supremacy is challenged, many students react strongly to protect their identities and Canada's foundational myths. To Indigenize curriculum is to contest ideological territory and to incite a battle that erupts in mainstream teacher education classrooms across the country. In this chapter we examine how that occurs in our own classrooms at OISE/UT.

Settler Teachers' Reluctance to Teaching Appropriate Indigenous Content

Blood (2010), Kanu (2011), Kaomea (2005), and Zurzolo (2010) have all studied why Settler teachers do not take up Indigenous content in their classrooms. Blood (2010) cited lack of confidence, lack of knowledge of Indigenous content, lack of ability to access members from the Indigenous community, lack of initiative to ask for school support, lack of school support when asked for, lack of professional development opportunities, lack of knowledge of what exactly they are supposed to teach, and a lack of comfort with teaching the subject because they are not Indigenous. Kanu (2011, 180) found teachers worried about whether they had "the right" to teach the material as non-Indigenous teachers. Teachers in both Kanu (2011) and Kaomea (2005) reported that a lack of time prevented them from including Indigenous content in their curriculum.

In Blood (2010) and Zurzolo (2010), teachers reported that their students resist Indigenous content, and that some react with racism. In Kanu (2011), teachers expressed concern that in teaching Indigenous content in their classrooms they make themselves professionally vulnerable, and fear negative reactions from not only students but also colleagues, school and board administration, and parents.

Zurzolo (2010) identified that teachers who do want to take up Indigenous content do not feel supported by school board policy or professional development opportunities, and were critical of the lack of diverse Indigenous voices represented. According to Kanu (2011), teachers who teach Indigenous content want school boards and administrators to provide better resources to support their work, and teachers who are not yet comfortable also want resources but desire assistance strengthening their professional efficacy.

Teacher Candidate/Teacher Identity and Indigenous Content

Teacher candidates at OISE/UT hold both white Settler and Settler diasporic identities (Cannon 2011), the latter defined as peoples who have left or been pushed out of their homeland due to political or socio-economic struggle, and who settled on Indigenous territories. However, much of the teacher candidate population is made up of white middle-class women (Solomona et al. 2005). Most teacher candidates enter the program with little-to-no awareness of their social privilege or the existence of white supremacy (Solomona et al. 2005; Schick and St. Denis 2005). Aveling (2006, 264) argues that "exploring 'race' and racism with White students goes to the very heart of our socially constructed identities."

Kaomea (2005), Dion (2009), and Kanu (2011) all argue that Settler teacher identity is the ultimate barrier to willingness to teach Indigenous content. Kaomea (2005), Dion (2009), Cannon (2012), and O'Dowd (2012) argue that an unexamined identity, especially with regards to Settler investments in the Settler nation state, ultimately prevents teachers from teaching the content desired by Indigenous Peoples. Zurzolo (2010) reports that Settler teachers who do teach Indigenous content retain some level of discomfort due to their identities.

The Deepening Knowledge Project

In 2008, the Deepening Knowledge Project (DKP) was created by a group of professors and instructors at OISE/UT, with the help of a grant from the Aboriginal Opportunities Fund from the Ontario Ministry of Training, Colleges and Universities. OISE/UT has one of the largest teacher preparation programs in Canada and, until 2014, graduated approximately 1,000 teacher candidates per year. Over the years, the DKP has grown from a group of interested practitioners exploring ways to integrate Aboriginal content within the Initial Teacher Education (ITE) program, and has developed a number of concrete strategies designed to reach every teacher candidate at least once during their program. Members of the DKP deliver a series of workshops across the program, with every class receiving, at minimum, a 90-minute introductory session on pre-contact histories, treaties, stereotypes, the Indian Act, residential schools, and the Sixties Scoop. Classes will often invite presenters back for additional sessions, resulting in up to six hours of instruction. Some of these presentations are given in subject-specific courses, in which DKP members will tie content and lesson planning techniques into particular areas, such as science, social science, and philosophy. The DKP team has developed a popular website for teacher resources, which is accessed by a wide audience across North America (www.oise.utoronto.ca/deepeningknowledge). The DKP also facilitates guest speakers and hosts workshops outside of class time for interested teacher candidates.

The DKP formed a special partnership with one professional learning community in the ITE program named Central Option.[2] This cohort consisted of approximately 70 teacher candidates each year, all of whom are studying to become primary or junior educators, and who are qualified to teach Grades K through 4. Central Option historically had a stated focus on both drama education and conflict resolution; however, in 2010, one instructor of the cohort, Nancy Steele, who is also a member of the DKP, added a specific focus on Aboriginal content and pedagogies to the curriculum offered in Central Option. Steele identifies as a white Settler on Turtle Island. She has a long history of teaching social justice to elementary students. As an instructor in the ITE program and a member of the DKP, she began to build relationships with Indigenous community members and professors at OISE/UT, and immersed herself in learning about Indigenous perspectives on history and current events. Together with a team of Settler and Indigenous educators, Steele has worked to bring in guest speakers and Elders to the ITE program, while incorporating documentary films, instruction on historical and contemporary issues, and targeted assignments into Central Option that encourage teacher candidates to bring Aboriginal content and perspectives into their classrooms. In 2013, the ITE program hired John Doran, a Mi'kmaw educator, to teach Central Option's School and Society course, a half course that all Options are required to offer that looks specifically at issues of equity.

Sources of Information

Since the DKP came into existence in 2008, its members have been collecting data from both instructors in the ITE program and teacher candidates about their willingness and readiness to incorporate Aboriginal content into their practice. At all stages of this collection, resistance has emerged, and this chapter brings together these resistances in an attempt to sort and categorize so that we can better understand the strategies we can implement to address and overcome resistance. The sources of data we call upon in this chapter include anonymous and optional instructor surveys completed in 2011; one-on-one interviews with professor and instructor members of the DKP completed in 2011; evaluations completed by teacher candidates after viewing the DKP introductory workshops from 2011–14; and surveys and one-on-one interviews conducted in 2012–13 and 2013–14 with teacher candidates in the Central Option professional learning community at OISE/UT.

The Workshops

Since the spring of 2011, instructors in the ITE program have had the option of having members of the DKP visit their classroom to deliver workshops on Indigenous-Settler relations. When initially conceptualizing these workshops, Kathy Broad, then-academic director of the ITE program and co-founder of the DKP, and Jean-Paul Restoule, co-author of this chapter, recognized that the identity of those who were selected to deliver these workshops was just as important as the content the workshops contained. They decided that such a workshop should be delivered by a team of two presenters, the first of whom would necessarily be Indigenous. This was of critical importance so that his or her voice, wisdom, knowledge, and firsthand perspective would form the foundation for the team and the resulting presentation the team would develop. It was decided that the second person should be someone who identified as a Settler, who had experience working in solidarity within various Indigenous communities, and who was recognized as having done so in a way that was respectful of protocol and through an anti-colonial lens. This workshop has thus far been delivered by two successive Indigenous/Settler teams, the first consisting of Angela Mashford-Pringle and Angela Nardozi (who wrote about their experiences in "Aboriginal Knowledge Infusion in Initial Teacher Education at the Ontario Institute for Studies in Education at the University of Toronto" in 2013), and the second team, starting in 2012, consisting of Doran and Nardozi. Together, these presenters enter classrooms across the program and navigate the contested space that emerges as teacher candidates face material that conflicts with their identities and prior beliefs about the nation of Canada.

Mashford-Pringle is an urban Algonquin scholar with an MA in Aboriginal and Adult Education from OISE/UT and a PHD in Aboriginal Health from the Dalla Lana School of Public Health at the University of Toronto. Her knowledge and experience shaped the presentations during the first two cycles of delivery in 2011. After she moved on from the role, John Doran, who is Mi'kmaw from Sipekne'katik First Nation, near Shubenacadie, Nova Scotia, was brought on and the presentations took a different tone based on his perspectives. Since he has joined the team, Doran has repeatedly shared his story of being taken by the Canadian government in the 1960s and placed in an international adoption, which many teacher candidates have expressed as having a strong impact on them. Co-author of this chapter Angela Nardozi, who is a Settler whose family immigrated to Turtle Island from Italy, was selected by Restoule and Broad to co-lead the workshops. As a recent graduate of the BEd program who had experience working and living in a remote First Nation, Nardozi was uniquely positioned to help teacher candidates evaluate their own role in Aboriginal-Settler relationships. Her background in teacher education meant that she had a strong understanding of the program, and of the state of mind of teacher candidates as they navigate their identities as teachers, teaching in practicum, and the workload at various points in the program. Her relationship with the community mentioned above and with Indigenous communities in Toronto meant that she was aware of some community protocols and that protocols existed with which she was not familiar, and she had a strong sense of spaces, both those into which she was invited and those in which she was not invited to participate. She had knowledge of the perspectives being communicated, and she was on a journey of examining her relationship with Indigenous communities and her privileges based on her Settler identity. Although the inclusion of a Settler presenter in the workshops has sometimes been met with critical questioning by teacher candidates, it is the DKP team's belief—a belief that has been confirmed by the workshop evaluations—that the positive and respectful relationship between the two presenters is instructive for teacher candidates. By sharing her own journey of recognizing and acknowledging her own complicity in colonialism, Nardozi makes the content highly approachable, inviting teacher candidates, the vast majority of whom are Settlers on this land, to examine their own roles. Nardozi takes direction from her Indigenous co-presenters, actively listens as they tell their stories, and explains and examines her privileges in a way that is unthreatening to the audience, inviting them to do the same. Through working together, Nardozi and Doran have developed a close working and personal friendship, checking in before the presentations, supporting one another when enmeshed in that contested space, and checking in again during the debrief as they process the candidates' reactions and reflect on the impact on their bodies, minds, emotions, and spiritual well-being.

One of the most effective teaching strategies that we have employed in the DKP is the centring of First Voice testimony. In the last two cycles of presentations, teacher candidates most frequently indicate on evaluations that the portion of the workshop they find "most interesting" is co-presenter Doran's story of being a survivor of the Sixties Scoop as well as the other stories he shares. However, on those same evaluations, teacher candidates tell us that their confidence to teach this content has not been significantly raised. When we return to classrooms to do follow-up presentations, and over the year in Central Option, many oppositions to teaching this material emerge. What we have realized is that in order to truly change deeply entrenched mindsets within teacher candidates, we need an extended period of time with them, over multiple meetings, in which we can employ a variety of strategies that not only educate teacher candidates with content, but also explore their identities and build their confidence in teaching these lessons. This extended, dedicated time exploring teacher candidate identities is not always available to the DKP team; the time they are allotted with each Option can vary from up to six hours in Central Option to as little as 45 minutes in some others, and this is determined by the lead instructor in each case.

Resistance to Aboriginal Content and Perspectives

Resistance to Aboriginal content and perspectives within the contested space of the presentations has been an ongoing theme since the DKP began. Mashford-Pringle and Nardozi (2013, 13) document their experience with resistance during their first year delivering presentations, revealing that during and after presentations (sometimes on evaluations), "[s]ome (teacher candidates) made comments about the political nature of the presentations, and how they were delivered with bias. Others could not yet see culture beyond the representations of 'artefacts' and 'spiritual routines.'" The experiences that Mashford-Pringle and Nardozi document represent, sadly, a fraction of the pushback and opposition the DKP team has experienced over the course of its work thus far. Most often these reactions do not express outright hatred for Indigenous Peoples, but instead betray an implicit dehumanization that places the oppression of Indigenous Peoples in a category separate from others. For instance, in February 2014, one student raised his hand after listening to a description of residential schools, saying that he was tired of hearing about the negative side of residential schools and wanted to hear about the positive impacts they had. When these sentiments are spoken out loud during the presentations, an immediate emotional response is felt by the facilitators, who may struggle to articulate a response that is measured but strong in its opposition. This comment had a strong emotional impact on Doran, whose family members suffered trauma at the expense of the schools. Nardozi responded to the student at Doran's request, explaining that based on the research they had done, the system sought to assimilate Indigenous Peoples into white Canadian society and rid the country of their cultures and languages, and that the meagre education some of the children may have received, if they survived the horrible conditions and abuse, could not be separated out of the larger context of the schools as a "benefit." After the break, Doran brought up the example of the system of slavery in the United States, and asked if candidates would ever ask the question, "But can you tell me about the good points of slavery?" He reasoned that "even if slaves were able to sing songs and find some enjoyment in their day, they did so within a system which viewed them as less than human and took away their freedom." After the presentation Doran and Nardozi both expressed their uncertainty regarding whether or not their responses had affected that candidate's mindset, or the others who may have agreed with him, and reflected on how multiple meetings with the group may have better served to challenge their attitudes. Below we group the resistances we have experienced into two categories: outright resistance and covert resistance, and we explain the strategies we have employed to address them.

Outright Resistance

As we work to bring Indigenous content into the ITE program (including in Central Option), there have been a handful of individuals who have persisted in strong and outright resistance, and even racism, against

Aboriginal Peoples and perspectives, as what we are teaching comes into direct conflict with white Settler and Settler diasporic identity. This identity is so entrenched that individuals will repeat timeworn stereotypes, despite being presented with facts to the contrary, and use statements such as "why should we glorify Aboriginal people?" While important to address, we have found that individuals who hold such extreme views often are not open to the information instructors provide, and persist in their views despite our arguments. Our team has found that the emotional and spiritual energy put into extended periods of arguing with such views seems to be lost on the individual, while leaving the instructor emotionally and spiritually drained. Individuals making these comments often feel comfortable making statements that contain sweeping generalizations, or appealing to logic that blames Indigenous individuals for their lot in life when there is clearly systemic, institutionalized injustice operating. For these individuals, the space of the classroom is one where anything can be said as long as it does not question their own senses of self. When Indigenous experiences are dismissed, or when Canada is defended as a meritocracy without a history of colonialism,[3] the classroom space is declared to be a space where "free speech" and "thought" should reign. When counter-arguments are made by the DKP visiting instructors to explain the lower socio-economic status of most Indigenous people in Canada, or about the effects of intergenerational trauma from residential schools on how many Indigenous youth learn today, these vocal teacher candidates see this as closing down free speech or as silencing them. They clearly see the classroom space as ideologically invaded by our perspectives, and we have to prove what we are saying. The onus is on us, despite the little or faulty evidence provided to substantiate their stereotypical thinking or defence of Canadian meritocracy. We, however, are not seeking to silence these speakers but rather to engage them in a more rounded picture of how things have come to be. Despite this approach, inevitably there are a handful of evaluations that accuse the speakers of demonstrating "bias" in the presentations or claim the lectures are not "factual."

Currently, we are experimenting with two pedagogical strategies to counter these views within these spaces. The first is an attempt to pre-empt them during initial teaching by disarming the audience through humour. In the DKP presentations, both presenters maintain a light-hearted approach during appropriate sections of the presentation, which ultimately creates balance within the space, providing a counterweight to the heavy emotional material discussed in other sections. One popular video, which has received positive feedback, is "Soapbox" by Wab Kinew (2012), which originally aired on the CBC TV show *George Stroumboulopoulos Tonight* in early 2012. This video is a great example of a contemporary Indigenous person speaking with truth by using disarming humour about the reality of five major stereotypes that Canadians have about Indigenous Peoples.

The second strategy is to project care onto these individuals, while asking them to self-reflect. This is similar to a strategy that Laara Fitznor (2014) of the University of Manitoba employs with Settler teacher candidates in her work. In these instances, Nardozi, from her position as a Settler, will echo the candidate's concern as one she used to hold, and then compassionately explain the flaws in the candidate's argument in a way which, rather than isolate and blame, invites him or her to move beyond the identity positions he or she was taught to embody. When views are expressed in these contested spaces that reflect racism and project negative energy onto the presentation leaders, it has an emotional impact, and during their debrief, both presenters often speak to their pain and frustration. However, special care is taken to support Indigenous colleagues at these times. Prior to each presentation, for instance, the two presenters will check in with one another and Doran will advise what material he feels comfortable covering that day. If a strong teacher candidate reaction emerges in the space, Doran and Nardozi may decide to take a break, and a debrief may occur at this time in which Doran will advise as to what material should be covered after the break. The support of Indigenous colleagues is especially crucial in our presentations, since Doran, like other presenters, has agreed to share personal stories that can take an emotional toll.

Covert Resistance

Not all resistance to including Aboriginal content into teaching practice that we have encountered within the contested space of teacher training is outright. Indeed, the example cited above regarding residential schools is an example of covert resistance that hides behind stereotypes of Indigenous Peoples as exotic and romantic or primitive and irrelevant, and which culminates in their dehumanization. More covert resistance to Indigenous perspectives that we have worked with is detailed below. These resistances are subtle, releasing tension into the space. Below we discuss the pedagogical strategies that we are currently employing in these contested spaces to encourage teacher candidates to move through their resistance.

Strategy: Instruction in Content

It is clear from the DKP research that the majority of teacher candidates enter into their professional program lacking understanding of Aboriginal histories, cultures, and contemporary issues and communities. On surveys and evaluations this lack of knowledge is often cited as a reason why teacher candidates do not feel they can take up this content in their classrooms. From our experience, common knowledge about Indigenous content among the teacher candidate population at the start of the program rises a bit year after year, although overall levels are still very low. This is reflected in the general population, as studies by the Coalition for the Advancement of Aboriginal Studies (CRRF 2002) and Restoule (2008) also found that Canadians know very little about their Aboriginal neighbours. Teacher candidates enter the program with misunderstandings about Aboriginal Peoples, which often bolster stereotypes in their minds that have been passed down through Canadian culture. For instance, during almost every presentation the DKP mounts at OISE/UT, teacher candidates ask about the myth that Aboriginal people in Canada pay no taxes. For most of our audience, simply giving the correct information dispels this myth.

Despite focused instruction in some areas of the program, such as Central Option, there remain challenges in teaching Settlers this material. Some candidates express the sentiment that they do not know enough to teach Aboriginal content, a sentiment that is out of place when considering all the other subjects candidates are asked to teach and with which they may be unfamiliar (Western New South Wales 2015). Rather, their discomfort reveals an awareness on their part that if they were to take up this teaching in their classrooms, their teaching and curriculum would become contested space—a challenge that they may not feel up to taking on. Other candidates continue to use the language of the past tense to refer to Indigenous issues, which is especially frustrating in Central Option. Whether or not candidates feel that they are equipped to teach Indigenous perspectives in their own classrooms after benefiting from the Option, they should at the very least be able to recognize the contemporary existence of Indigenous Peoples and communities in the city of Toronto and beyond. Central Option receives multiple Indigenous guest speakers, screens clips from numerous contemporary sources, and provides instruction on current events. Instruction in content must necessarily be coupled with work on privilege and an analysis of Settler colonialism with teacher candidates. This will be discussed in greater detail below.

Advocating for time for the teaching of Indigenous content with other instructors within the space of teacher education can be tricky. We often hear resistance from them, which can be paraphrased as, How do I fit in Aboriginal topics when there is so little time? In an interview with the authors in 2014, Rose Torres, an instructor affiliated with the DKP, recounted his experience introducing lessons centring Indigenous perspectives to his colleagues:

> Beyond integrating these materials and the pilot lesson into my own course, I spoke to my foundation instructors about the materials. And the first time I spoke to them, the group was not very receptive; they were concerned the curriculum was very crowded and they were not ready, and it seemed like something that they wanted to do but they were not prepared to do.

Instructors have also told us they are concerned about not knowing how to deal with potential reactions from teacher candidates, and if they have ventured to teach Indigenous content, how the experience has been challenging. From these reactions it becomes clear that the curriculum within teacher training is itself a site of contestation. Settler instructors may not have begun to examine their own privilege and complicity in Settler colonialism. Others may also recognize the discord and unsettledness that comes to a space when the content enters it, and they may be reluctant to meet that discord head on. Still others may not feel comfortable with their level of knowledge and feel unprepared to answer any content questions that may come up. We suspect that the root of their fear of appearing unready or unknowledgeable lies in wanting to avoid disrupting comfortable spaces with ideas that contest colonial normativity. Their refusal to engage in contesting hegemonic space thus reproduces an order that maintains colonialism. At the risk of feeling discomfort, some teacher candidates choose not to engage at all, allowing cycles of stereotyping, prejudice, discrimination, and racism (Sioux Lookout Anti-Racism Committee 1998) to continue unchallenged.

Strategy: Experiential Learning

Central Option's stated focus on Aboriginal content has allowed it to incorporate numerous instructional strategies and extensive content about current events, histories, and perspectives over the course of the entire program year. Candidates begin the year by venturing to Toronto Island where they hear from Indigenous community members and Elders about the history of the land and partake in activities on the land. In the following weeks they receive hours (nine in the latest year) of instruction on Aboriginal histories and current realities. As the year progresses, numerous guests visit the class to share political perspectives, dramatic enactments, and dance and its meanings with the candidates.

Unlike any other teacher candidates in the ITE program, Central Option teacher candidates are required to complete three assignments, two major and one minor, which challenge them to either prepare for or enact instruction in their practicum placements about topics related to Aboriginal Peoples (this will be discussed in more detail later). According to our research, when combined together, these strategies result in most teacher candidates growing in their self-perceived readiness and willingness to incorporate Aboriginal content into their work. Information about Aboriginal content is also shared with Central Option teacher candidates on two online knowledge sharing platforms: on Pepper, the ITE-wide knowledge forum platform, and on the DKP website.

Examining Identity and Privilege

Schick and St. Denis (2005) argue that resistance to Aboriginal Peoples and histories often reflects a misunderstanding of the colonial foundations of Canada and reveals a lack of awareness on the part of teacher candidates of their own social privilege. A lack of understanding of these two elements can lead to covert resistance to incorporating Aboriginal content and contribute to the upholding of contested spaces. One such resistance we hear within these spaces is a claim to universalism, in which candidates will argue that "We're all just people," "I try to be colour-blind," "We're all Canadians in this together," "If I teach difference, we end up polarizing each other." These arguments fail to recognize the specific place in history and current events that Indigenous Peoples occupy on this land, and it silences this history. This argument is related to the resistance statement, "Why should I focus on Aboriginal cultures when there are so many other cultures represented in my class?" Similarly, some wonder why the focus is on Aboriginal culture instead of "multicultural."

While we have had many teacher candidates bravely take up this work and challenge themselves, we have also had occasion to notice just how contested the classroom space is for real divining of Aboriginal perspectives. Teacher candidates have expressed annoyance at having their privileges pointed out to them or for having to reflect critically and personally upon these privileges. Some have reacted with anger, and some expect special gratitude for trying to be accommodating. For instance, upon entering classrooms our DKP presenters (as recounted to Angela Nardozi in personal communication, 2012) heard comments such as "I don't feel like feeling guilty today" and "I am all equitied out." A respondent indicated on the 2011-12 post-presentation evaluations, "It's hard to put effort in teaching Aboriginals when we don't know how much they value us. If they're resistant to Western school system, why should we accommodate if we are not appreciated?" On numerous occasions teacher candidates expressed anger that their own relatives had immigrated over and had eventually found financial success, and that Aboriginal Peoples were given too much by the government. One teacher candidate expressed the opinion that people all around the world are suffering and the fact that Aboriginal Peoples get any sort of financial recognition from the government is fortunate, and so they should stop complaining (anonymous teacher candidate, personal communication with Nardozi, 2011). In one case a teacher candidate asked, "When are we going to stop having to owe them, when will they be satisfied?" (evaluation comment 2011-12). One instructor noted the difficulty for instructors to engage their teacher candidates in this type of lesson, given the many political implications. The instructor wrote, "This was not an easy lesson to teach—especially the notion of decolonization that fundamentally confronts Canada as a white Settler colony with attendant benefits, privileges, and entitlements provided to white subjects" (Instructor Survey Respondent Five, November 2011).

Toronto, where our institution is located, is a highly diverse and multicultural place, and it is true that in recent years OISE/UT and local school boards have implemented numerous programs and initiatives to address the needs of students from a variety of backgrounds. As with multiculturalism policy, this then relegates Aboriginal Peoples to being another "special interest group," and an invisible one at that. This is set in the conditions created by Settler colonialism, which Tuck (2013, 326) argues "is the context of the dispossession and erasure of poor youth and youth of colour in urban public schools." Elementary and secondary education thus becomes a contested space where perspectives of Indigenous Nations on their own histories and current realities struggle for visibility. Tuck (326) further argues that "Indigenous responses to settler colonialism provide salient insights for urban school reform." Educating teacher candidates is a crucial step in making room for these responses in the mainstream school system. Most teacher candidates are shocked to hear, during our presentations, that Toronto is home to the largest population of Indigenous Peoples in Canada. To counter this lack of knowledge, teacher candidates need to be made aware of the colonial foundations of this nation and the rights to the land that Indigenous Peoples hold under the treaties and as a result of unceded territory. As future teachers, they also need to know and understand that colonizers have long recognized their sovereignty under the Royal Proclamation of 1763 and the Treaty of Niagara, as well as having a strong understanding of how colonialism operates today and how Indigenous rights continue to be denied. Armed with these important perspectives on the history of this land and the original agreements that governed it, candidates can be inspired to create space for these perspectives in their curriculum. Otherwise, the result of candidates' lack of knowledge would be creating by omission a contested space for Indigenous students within the education system. Finally, Settler teacher candidates, whether their families arrived on this land generations ago or whether they have recently made Canada their homes, need to understand their privilege in relation to Indigenous Peoples whose land they now occupy. One of the tensions in the space of teacher instruction is between state-sanctioned curriculum that omits or marginalizes Indigenous presence, and attempts like the DKP to centre that presence in opposition to state narratives that treat dispossession as a fait accompli. Discussion of these unresolved issues can lead to frustration, guilt, anger, shock, and a range of emotions in the Settler who has been discomforted (Regan 2010). Learned forgetting or purposeful omission of Indigenous education seems to be a state strategy for creating exalted subjects (Thobani 2007), essentially reproducing a system with favoured European racial identities ruling new(er) immigrants who themselves are more entitled to occupy the dispossessed land than the original inhabitants. However, when the DKP challenges these notions in the classroom, the space becomes charged because the legitimacy of nearly everyone in that room to occupy that land, previously an unquestioned assumption, becomes the very subject of debate.

Sometimes teacher candidates ask, "Why should I prioritize Aboriginal history, issues, and perspectives when there are many social justice issues that the students in my classes have?" Teacher candidates need to understand that the systems of oppression that are currently at work in this country are built upon that foundation.

The notion of increasing the amount of space and time dedicated to Indigenous issues, both in the teacher training program and in the mainstream curriculum, is a contested one for some of those whom we encounter in our work. Teacher candidates have argued that they don't feel the need to teach Aboriginal content because it does not belong in their grade level or their subject area. This has also been a struggle with instructors in the ITE program. The notion that Indigenous content belongs only in a specific grade level or a particular subject area is a privileged one, and one that takes for granted the dominance of Euro-Western perspectives on all subjects, not just history and social studies. While tools like the Dean's Accord on Indigenous Education (Association of Canadian Deans of Education 2010) and the Ontario College of Teachers guidelines, which now require teacher training programs to include instruction on Aboriginal content in order to acquire accreditation, help counter this, teaching about privilege and colonialism is a necessary component of understanding the deep roots of this work.

Teaching candidates about privilege and colonialism is an emotional project. Examining the foundations of Canadian identity—an identity that most schools in the nation take care to foster from the earliest years—can rock the core of teacher candidates and elicit anger, frustration, guilt, and sadness because it forms the foundation of who they believe they are, what they think their roles are as Canadian citizens, and all the various meanings that this citizenship brings with it. Pedagogical approaches that instruct and challenge teacher candidates on their connections to colonialism and their own social privilege are of vital importance so that the teacher candidates can become more receptive to Indigenous content and then bring that content into their classrooms, which then has the potential to transform their future classrooms from contested spaces for Indigenous students to spaces where their histories and present realities and identities are reflected.

Assignments Requiring Aboriginal Content

Although an optional course in Aboriginal education exists for all teacher candidates, Central Option teacher candidates are the only teacher candidates in the ITE program required to complete assignments about topics related to Aboriginal Peoples. Many Central Option teacher candidates told us that "being forced" to bring Indigenous content into their classrooms made them teach beyond their comfort zones in a way they would not have chosen to otherwise. There are many types of resistance that we understand this pedagogical strategy of incorporating Aboriginal histories and/or current perspectives into lessons to counter, and we detail them here.

First among these is a fear of appropriation. Some teacher candidates cite this fear as debilitating, preventing them from attempting to teach Indigenous content. For instructors and teacher candidates alike, we can counteract these fears by pointing out that they can teach social justice issues and history, and that it is not necessarily their place to teach culture. Closely related to this anxiety around appropriation is the fear of offending. Teacher candidates express this fear often. Some tell us that they have made a mistake or two in the past and were called out on it, and they feel discouraged as a result. Indeed, during the interviews, one instructor identified this as a potential reason why teacher candidates disengage during sessions. The instructor commented, "Some, I believe, shut down because they saw themselves as not being able to cope with controversy, given that they lacked knowledge" (Instructor Survey Respondent Nineteen, November 2011). Concerns about proper implementation exist among instructors, too. One instructor wrote,

> I have seen the pilot lesson and think it's excellent. My concern is that I wouldn't do it justice in using it, which is why I haven't tried it to this point. I don't want to do it wrong! And if it stands out from the rest of my course, it ends up looking like an add-on, rather than infused in the course, which I know is exactly what we don't want. (Instructor Survey Respondent One, November 2011)

Teacher candidates also reported finding it difficult to imagine what incorporating Indigenous material into their curriculum would look like, as many of their own teachers did not model this infusion while they were progressing through the school system. While this expressed reservation seems to have some merit, there were some teacher candidates who went to great lengths to explain away and dismiss our positive models and examples. For example, BEd students across multiple Options who viewed a video of Grade 4 students speaking about residential school had dismissive reactions. After each viewing by a group, at least one teacher candidate responded that while the students were impressive, they were clearly the top of their classes, and that this level of learning would not be possible with all students. The teacher candidates were then informed that, in both cases, these students were not the most academically capable students. Instead, depicted students were chosen to participate based on whether they had parental permission to be recorded rather than on their academic capability. In our experience, additional resistant reactions that teacher candidates have after viewing this video include arguing that they would not be able to teach the content to that depth in their schools, that such focus would not be allowed, that the curriculum would not provide enough time for it, or that children are too young to learn about or understand emotional subjects such as residential school.

Nevertheless, teacher candidates from Central Option told us that assignments that required them to teach the material were the second-most important for their learning (following First Voice strategies in the top spot). Assignments that require them to teach Aboriginal content in class rank high over the two years for teacher candidates when asked what strategies in the cohort contributed to their knowledge. On our closing survey with Central Option, candidates were asked if they had taught Aboriginal content in their own classrooms. Some said no, explaining that their mentor teachers did not support their teaching such content, or that the demands of their teachers were such that they could not fit such content in. Among those who did teach it, some of them told us how they would do it differently next time. Some were bolstered by the positive reactions of their students. Others told us that they did not get the reaction they had expected from their students, and reflected on what they would change to better engage them.

Teacher candidates from across the ITE program often tell us that they would like the opportunity to practise teaching Aboriginal content in front of their colleagues prior to teaching about these topics in front of schoolchildren. Having an opportunity to rehearse may ease teacher candidates' fears of offending students, especially Aboriginal students, other teachers, and staff. Viewing the teaching of others may also help to clarify strategies and content for teacher candidates. Restoule used this approach for two offerings of a teacher education course in 2010 and 2011 and found that it greatly increased confidence and helped teachers work collaboratively through weaknesses in a lesson plan. Teacher candidates from primary and junior grades, or from similar subject areas in higher grades, could share the plans that others in the class had developed.

Conclusion

Teacher training at OISE/UT is a Western space where mainly Settler teachers are trained to work in Western schools. These institutions are designed to, among other things, reinforce notions about Canadian citizenship. A central fact of Canadian settlement that has been mostly absent from these spaces is that it has been and is occurring on Indigenous lands, often on dubious moral and legal grounds. Through our work within the DKP and Central Option, we are contesting understandings of the doctrine of discovery, *terra nullius*, stereotypes, and other myths that support dispossession and colonialism and narratives of Canadian identity. The DKP has done this by carving out space within the ITE program for educators to explore and implement new strategies to build the understanding and skills of candidates with respect to content about colonialism on Turtle Island.

Contesting these understandings in these spaces puts Settler teacher candidates on the defensive and requires us to "prove ourselves." Especially when we challenge candidates to teach Aboriginal issues and examine their own complicity in colonialism, our work is frequently met with pushback, and we cannot expect that initial reaction to change. However, we must continue to find ways to challenge candidates to move beyond those first instincts. This work has great relevance to the future of Indigenous-Settler relations in this province, as teachers have a large role in setting the foundation of understanding for generations of Canadians. Without contestation, these ideologies, discourses, and myths would go unchallenged, meaning that the space of mainstream education would continue to be one of assimilation and pain for Indigenous students, while Settler students continue to hear the same half- and untruths about Indigenous Peoples in their curriculum.

We will continue to advocate for more time to be devoted to these issues and for these issues to be made accessible to more teacher candidates and instructors. We will continue to argue for the legitimacy of these ways of knowing and of this understanding the world to be central in the training of future teachers. Through relationship and dialogue, members of the Deepening Knowledge Project are finding new ways to help candidates move through their resistance to a place of hope and responsibility.

Notes

1. Here we use the term "Aboriginal" to echo the Canadian government's terminology in defining the original peoples of this land in the Constitution Act, 1982, which includes Indians (First Nations), Métis, and Inuit. We use this term interchangeably with the more global "Indigenous." The term "Settler" refers to all non-Aboriginal people living on Turtle Island, whether it was they or their ancestors who immigrated to this land from other parts of the world.
2. OISE's consecutive program used to organize its teacher candidates learning to become elementary teachers into professional learning communities called "Options." The Deepening Knowledge Project worked within all of them, but worked particularly closely with the Central Option.
3. Stephen Harper (in)famously boasted in 2009 at a G20 summit meeting in Pittsburgh, Pennsylvania, that Canada did not have a history of colonialism, a year after making a historic apology for Canada's role in running Indian Residential Schools.

References

Association of Canadian Deans of Education. 2010. "Accord on Indigenous Education." Delta, BC: ACDE. http://csse-scee.ca/acde/wp-content/uploads/sites/7/2017/08/Accord-on-Indigenous-Education.pdf

Aveling, Nado. 2006. "'Hacking at Our Very Roots': Rearticulating White Racial Identity Within the Context of Teacher Education." *Race Ethnicity and Education* 9 (3): 261–74.

Blood, Tracy Lynn. 2010. "Integrating an Aboriginal Perspective: Issues and Challenges Faced by Non-Aboriginal Biology Teachers." MED thesis, University of Alberta.

Canadian Race Relations Foundation (CRRF). 2002. "Learning about Walking in Beauty: Placing Aboriginal Perspectives in Canadian Classrooms. A Report from the Coalition for the Advancement of Aboriginal Studies." Toronto: Canadian Race Relations Foundation. http://www.crr.ca/en/policy-a-research/334-crrf-research-reports/23526-learning-about-walking-in-beauty-placing-aboriginal-perspectives-in-canadian-classrooms

Cannon, Martin J. 2011. "Changing the Subject in Teacher Education: Indigenous, Diasporic, and Settler Colonial Relations." *Ideas Can...Canadian Federation for the Humanities Social Sciences* (blog). May 17, 2011. http://www.ideas-idees.ca/blog/changing-subject-teacher-education-indigenous-diasporic-and-settler-colonial-relationsx

———. 2012. "Changing the Subject in Teacher Education: Centering Indigenous, Diasporic, and Settler Colonial Relations." *Cultural and Pedagogical Inquiry* 4 (2): 21-37.

Dion, Susan D. 2009. *Braiding Histories: Learning from Aboriginal Peoples' Experiences and Perspectives*. Vancouver: UBC Press.

Fitznor, Laara. 2014. *Anthropologists, Indigenous Scholars, and the Research Endeavor: Seeking Bridges Towards Mutual Respect*. London: Routledge.

Kanu, Yatta. 2011. *Integrating Aboriginal Perspectives into the School Curriculum: Purposes, Possibilities and Challenges*. Toronto: University of Toronto Press.

Kaomea, Julie. 2005. "Indigenous Studies in the Elementary Curriculum: A Cautionary Hawaiian Example." *Anthropology and Education Quarterly* 36 (1): 24-42.

Kinew, Wab. 2012. *Soapbox: Wab Kinew on First Nations Stereotypes*. Originally aired on CBC *George Stroumboulopoulos Tonight*, November 24, 2012. https://www.youtube.com/watch?v=llGo8ltW9Ho

Mashford-Pringle, Angela, and Angela Nardozi. 2013. "Aboriginal Knowledge Infusion in Initial Teacher Education at the Ontario Institute for Studies in Education at the University of Toronto." *The International Indigenous Policy Journal* 4 (4): Art 3. http://ir.lib.uwo.ca/iipj/vol4/iss4/3

O'Dowd, Mary. 2012. "Engaging Non-Indigenous Students in Indigenous History and 'Un-History.'" *History of Education Review* 41 (2): 104-18.

Regan, Paulette. 2010. *Unsettling the Settler Within: Indian Residential Schools, Truth-Telling, and Reconciliation in Canada*. Vancouver: UBC Press.

Restoule, Jean-Paul. 2008. "Fostering Aboriginal Awareness in Social Studies." In *Initial Teacher Education: School Improvement and Teacher Education: Collaboration for Change*, edited by Carol Rolheiser, 6-12. Toronto: Ontario Institute for Studies in Education. http://www.oise.utoronto.ca/oise/UserFiles/File/MG%20PUBLICATION_FINAL.pdf

Schick, Carol, and Verna St. Denis. 2005. "Troubling National Discourses in Anti-Racist Curricular Planning." *Canadian Journal of Education* 28 (3): 295-317.

Sioux Lookout Anti-Racism Committee. 1998. Workshop on Stereotypes. Originally delivered at CFTC, Toronto, Ontario, November 1998.

Smith, Linda Tuhiwai. 1999. *Decolonizing Methodologies: Research and Indigenous Peoples*. London: Zed Books.

Solomona, R. Patrick, John P. Portelli, Beverly-Jean Daniel, and Arlene Campbell. 2005. "The Discourse of Denial: How White Teacher Candidates Construct Race, Racism and 'White Privilege.'" *Race, Ethnicity and Education* 8 (2): 147-69.

Thobani, Sunera. 2007. *Exalted Subjects: Studies in the Making of Race and Nation in Canada*. Toronto: University of Toronto Press.

Tuck, Eve. 2013. "Neoliberalism as Nihilism: A Commentary on Educational Accountability, Teacher Education, and School Reform." *Journal for Critical Education Policy Studies* 11 (2): 324-47.

Tuck, Eve, and Rubén A. Gaztambide-Fernández. 2013. "Curriculum, Replacement, and Settler Futurity." *Journal of Curriculum Theorizing* 29 (1): 72-89.

Western New South Wales Regional Aboriginal Education Team. 2015. "I Don't Understand." http://8ways.wikispaces.com/I+don%27t+understand! (website no longer exists).

Zurzolo, Cara. 2010. "Where Does Policy Come from? Exploring the Experiences of Non-Aboriginal Teachers Integrating Aboriginal Perspectives into the Curriculum." *Our Schools/Our Selves* 19 (3): 275-89.

15 | Kia Mahi Hei Waewae Mo Te Atawhai

MARI ROPATA-TE HEI

He hokinga mahara ki a koutou mā kua haere ki tua o te ārai, e ōku rangatira
haere, haere, haere atu rā.
Kātou i para ai i te huarahi nei kia whai mana motuhake mātou te iwi Māori ka nui te
mihi ki a koutou katoa, ka kore rawa koutou i warewaretia e mātou.
Ko mātou kua mahue nei, kia hikina te tōtara taumaha hei kawe tonu atu, kia kaha, kia maia, kia manawanui mātou te kokiri tēnei kaupapa miharo,
ā tēnā tātou katoa.[1]

Introduction

Every person has a story to tell as to how they were raised. My reflections on growing up a Māori child, following some of the core aspirations instilled in me by my Elders that eventually led to my chosen career in teaching, offer a way of understanding the effects their teachings have had on me.

There is little doubt that my childhood and early experiences have been deeply influenced by the intergenerational socialization methods employed by my parents and grandparents. These methods included instilling the importance of Māori cultural beliefs and practices that have made me who I am as an individual and have contributed to the values and principles I practise as an educator in the kaupapa Māori education sector.

Historically the freedom to speak the Māori language openly, as a normal part of New Zealand everyday life, was problematic for Māori generally and for my grandparents in particular, which impacted on me and our *whānau* (family). The alienation of the Māori language from modern life was a significant goal of the colonization agenda.

However, it was not until the birth of my children and my involvement in the revitalization of the Māori language movement that my passion for te reo Māori activated a reconnection to my cultural identity and my roots that have resulted in a lifetime commitment. I was fortunate, because my value systems were nurtured and developed within a close-knit Māori whānau and combined with being raised by the teachings of my *tūpuna* (ancestor).

This chapter reflects on some of my experiences, which provide a unique perspective for considering their impact on my practice as an educator, including within a university context. In particular, I look at the tensions and challenges of teaching in a unique, university-based kaupapa Māori immersion initial teacher education program, Te Aho Tātairangi.

Contested Spaces in Kaupapa Māori Education

Te Aho Tātairangi requires that students meet the graduating standards set down by the New Zealand Teachers Council. However, as part of the leadership of the program what is more important to me in the provision of Te Aho Tātairangi is fulfilling the aspirations and expectations of Te Rūnanga Nui o Ngā Kura Kaupapa Māori o Aotearoa (The Executive Council of Māori Foundation Schools of Aotearoa), its community and members with which I am associated, as well as ensuring we uphold our own *tikanga Māori* (Māori protocols and procedures) and te reo Māori (the language of Māori). Operating within a Pākeha (European descent) institutional framework and delivering a Māori-centred program is regarded by many Māori as perhaps the biggest compromising situation to be in.

Contextualizing the contested spaces and connecting the perspectives, standards, aspirations, and expectations of all parties involved with Te Aho Tātairangi demands my avid attention. I am cognizant that my values and cultural principles will strongly influence my praxis.

The provision of a kaupapa Māori program within a Eurocentric university environment presents many conflicting situations that constantly compromise my ability and efforts to uphold tikanga Māori and to fulfill the needs of my community. The challenge before me is to reassure my community that, regardless of where we work as educators, we can advance our *kaupapa* (foundation/base) successfully, but it requires dedication and perseverance.

I have purposely named my chapter from part of a proverb left by my grandfather to our family, which I believe provides the inspiration that underpins my work as an educator:

...kia mahi hei waewae mo te atawhai...

...work diligently as a pillar for humanity...

Background

My decision to follow a career in Māori education began in 1987, when I enrolled my two eldest children (twins), Rongomai and Rua, in *te kōhanga reo* (elementary language nest). Immediately I loved the interaction with the other new mothers and the *kuia* (elderly woman). It wasn't long before I became a parent helper, eventually transitioning into the role as a *kaiako* (teacher).

My desire to learn more about the Māori language inspired me to take my children to kōhanga reo every day. I felt it was an enormous opportunity to give my children the chance to be immersed in our language, something I unfortunately did not have as an integral part of my schooling and education. As a child, I heard the Māori language spoken around me by my parents and Elders, but they did not address me or my siblings in Māori. This was not unusual during the mid-20th century, because the Māori language had been severely undermined since the mid-19th century and banned in mainstream schools till the latter years of the 20th century. I therefore wanted to give my children the opportunity for an education in the Māori language that was not available to me.

In 1991 I was encouraged by one of the kuia to enroll in a teaching degree, and in 1994 I graduated with both a bachelor's degree in education and a Diploma in Kura Kaupapa Māori Teaching (Dip KKMT). Launched by founding members of Te Komiti o Ngā Kura Kaupapa Māori o Tamaki Makaurau (The Committee for Māori Foundation School of Auckland), the Dip KKMT course was the first established kura kaupapa Māori teacher training program to be offered in Aotearoa, designed specifically for the kura kaupapa Māori school sector.

I am therefore in a unique position of being a second-generation advocate and campaigner for kaupapa Māori-based learning as a major part of an educational "intervention system" (Nepe 1991). The kaupapa Māori intervention system of education was first initiated with the introduction of kōhanga reo, followed by the development of kura kaupapa Māori, *wharekura* (secondary school), and *whare wānanga* (house of research and learning [university]).

At university I realized why I wasn't able to speak Māori, which made me feel angry and bitter. I learned that as a result of colonial rule and Pākeha dominance, my language and culture was forcibly abolished from the education system, with dire consequences. This included my feeling an acute sense of loss, a loss shared by many other Māori of my generation.

On reflection I began to understand why my parents protected our whānau from further distress by setting safety barriers in place. My grandparents had been reared in an era where Pākeha suppression resulted in cultural deprivation that occurred on a daily basis, and their sense of loss was even more prominent and pronounced.

My grandparents attended Māori Native Schools and they were physically abused and punished by their teachers for speaking the Māori language at school. I still remember my grandmother showing me a scar on her leg from the many strikes of the whip she received for speaking Māori in the playground. The memory of the pain was still real, and she was adamant her grandchildren would never have to suffer or experience this level of violent abuse.

Learning and speaking Māori became my passion. It continues to be my passion, stirred by the awful knowledge of what my grandparents had endured, making it even more important for me to advocate for my language. I wanted to reclaim Māori language as a right for me and for my children's children, my *mokopuna* (grandchildren). Thus, the aspirations I carry with me are not only my own, but are also those of many who have gone on before me. I acknowledge my parents, grandparents, whānau, teachers, and educators, who have contributed to my knowledge bank, my values and idealistic views, and, more importantly, to my Māoriness.

As an educator with long experience teaching in kura kaupapa Māori, my passion now extends to preparing teachers for working in kura kaupapa Māori. This is through a total-immersion Māori initial teacher education program specifically designed for the kura kaupapa Māori movement, and underpinned by *Te Aho Matua* (a philosophical document, "The Parent Thread"; see the appendix to this chapter), the only philosophy of education from New Zealand.

Te Rūnanga Nui o Ngā Kura Kaupapa Māori o Aotearoa (The Executive council for Māori Based Schooling in Aotearoa) are the *kaitiaki* (guardians) of the *Te Aho Matua* document that ensures Māori epistemologies, theories, and practices are transmitted through the medium of the Māori language. As Tuki Nepe argued, it takes the Māori language to transmit this knowledge (Nepe 1991).

Growing Up Māori

My tribal affiliations derive from my mother, who is of Ngāpuhi descent, one of the Northern tribes; and my father, who is of Te Ati Awa, Ngāti Toa Rangatira, and Ngāti Huia ki Ngāti Raukawa, descended from the Southwestern tribes of the North Island.

I was born in the Auckland suburb of Glen Innes, in a state house rented by my maternal grandparents, Kato Kauwhata and Piwara (Beatrice) Poka. I was named Beatrice after my grandmother, using her English colonial name rather than her Māori name, Piwara. I was later told there were too many negative attachments to her Māori name that she did not want to burden me with. All but one of my siblings, in fact, have English first names, which I believe was a deliberate act of protection by our parents and grandparents to shield us from any backlash or blatant acts of racism, such as mispronouncing our Māori names.

My birth was an eventful one for both my mother and me, and as each birthday is celebrated, the story of how I came into this world is inevitably retold.

It happened that while my mother was scrubbing the kitchen floor she felt a singular but almighty pain in her lower back. Her immediate thoughts were to first finish cleaning the floor before making her way to the bedroom to lie down. Apparently I had other ideas. Before my mother could think, and without any effort on her part, I suddenly burst into this world, sliding headfirst across the wet floor towards the old fridge. My mother quickly scooped me up in her apron, pressing her thumb on where my umbilical cord had been attached to stem any flow of blood, and headed straight to the bedroom. My older sister, who was only four at the time, witnessed it all and, terrified, raced down the road to our aunt's home crying hysterically, "Mummy is dying!"

What can I make of my entry into the world? At the moment of my birth, the bucket my mother was using overturned, spilling water all over the kitchen floor, which helped cushion my hasty arrival and sent me skidding the length of our kitchen. Water was everywhere. People who know me will tell you I absolutely love the water and swimming is my favourite sport and pastime. It is interesting that the Western astrological sign for my birth is Scorpio, with the zodiac element of water. The fast pace of my arrival seemed to foreshadow the pace of my very busy and full life, and being late is something I absolutely loathe.

I am the sixth child in a family of eight children; I have three older brothers and I am the third daughter of five girls. I was raised with many cousins and friends of families, and an extended whānau that easily swelled to 30 or more people on special occasions. Holidays and weekends were spent at my grandparents' home in suburban Glen Innes, where I was born. Their home was always a special place and, as they lived close to the sea, summer months were most often spent food gathering, swimming, and picnicking.

During school breaks and holidays, our whānau would leave our urban existence, swapping it for camping at Whatipu Beach at the tip of the Manukau Harbour in Auckland. These were exceptional times: swimming, hiking, fishing, and learning how to live off the land and how to appreciate each other as a whānau.

My love of water includes the sea, where my appreciation for its bounty deepened as a result of these holiday excursions and my father teaching us how to dive for seafood. By the time I was 12 years of age, our father would send my younger sister and me out to swim to Paratutae Rock, renowned for its abundance of shellfish, where we would fill our sack with mussels. Meanwhile, he and my brother would walk one to two hours further along the beach and around the coves of the bay to gather pāua (sea abalone). I knew how to read the tidal water, so when the tide turned this was the sign for my sister and me to turn back towards shore and get out of the water. We understood our father's teaching and heeded his warnings that, should the water get too deep, we would be swept further out to sea. Our father was a quiet man but was forthright in matters that involved anything around our experiences with, and in, nature. We never specifically learned who Tangaroa (God of the Sea) was, or even spoke his name, but my father taught us to respect the sea, take only what you needed and no more, and look intently to when and how the waves move and turn to warn you of any dangers. Our father trusted my sister and me that we could do this on our own, and knowing this I was left in charge of my younger sister to ensure our safety and that nothing went wrong. At 12 years of age my sense of responsibility was huge; failure was simply not an option because others depended on everyone's full participation and success to be able to have a meal that night. This type of learning for the greater well-being of all concerned is something I continue to carry with me.

I remember our whānau camping trips with great joy, as they were days full of fun and excitement. My parents always encouraged us to be very active and to develop a greater sense of awareness and appreciation for the environment around us, to never be complacent about its awe and beauty but to always have respect for our surroundings.

I acknowledge my grandmother for my love of arts and crafts. She taught me how to bake cakes, make homemade sweets and biscuits, and cook a roast dinner, as well as make *rewana* (sourdough) bread. When I was about eight years old, she also taught me how to knit and crochet. The first item I made was a scarf, then a pair of slippers, and eventually as I got older I taught myself how to knit jerseys with complex and intricate patterns.

My grandmother taught me many things, not only the methods related to the skills learned but also the understanding of what was happening with my thought processes while baking or creating something. These were lessons within lessons, skillfully crafted to instill life's learning underpinned by the principles and values she lived by, to ensure that I would have the drive to complete things to the best of my ability. She did this by asking probing questions: "What can you see? Where to next? Why does the pattern look like that?" It is no coincidence that she has influenced my pedagogical practice, because I do exactly what my grandmother taught me to do when trying to teach something new to someone else. For example, if I made a mistake while knitting, my grandmother would make me undo all my knitting back to that missed stitch and then I'd have to start all over again. She taught me the value of being persistent and focused, being resourceful, saving items for re-use and not being wasteful, not wasting time, and making the effort to do something once and do it properly. Her motto was that if you made a mistake, that was fine, but you needed to be sure you learned from it—that it wasn't a mistake for no good reason—and that time was of the essence, to be used to its fullest potential.

I remember that when my grandmother was teaching me how to knit, my grandfather would be in the background saying to her, "you're just wasting your time; she's not going to get it you know." His words had the opposite effect on me, and I was determined to prove him wrong. First, I did not want to disappoint my grandmother, who would focus her attention on whatever I wanted or tried to do. Her words always encouraged me. Second, I didn't want my grandfather's words to beat me down or for him to see that I felt hurt or angst about his comments. Perhaps this was a strategic and clever ploy by my grandfather, but I don't know and can't ask him now.

Both my grandparents were avid gardeners, and their connection to the *whenua* (land) was remarkable. They knew when rain threatened, when to plant, when not to plant, and other information about the land and the seasons derived from ancestral knowledge handed down through many generations. My grandfather's *kumara* (sweet potato) gardens were amazing and many people at the *marae* (ancestral home) o Piritahi on Waiheke Island would attest to how bountiful the gardens were. Much learning took place between weeding and watering rows upon rows of plants, right up to the time of harvesting the kumara. My grandfather shared his food preservation methods, long-learned traditions handed down to him through the generations.

Offering food, making a meal, and showing hospitality are values I know well and treasure dearly, having learned what such values meant in practice from my grandmother. Many times she would say, "Even if it's a glass of water and a piece of bread, offer them something, show your hospitality." These are traits expressed on the marae, and tenets my parents and grandparents were raised with and which they instilled in their children. The value of *manaakitanga* (care), of caring for and sharing with others, is a core value in Māori customary traditions. Understanding the importance of manaakitanga as a reciprocal relationship demands constant vigilance and dedication. As Tuki Nepe (1991, 40) so succinctly explains, manaakitanga is the basis of a "co-operative whānau, *hapū* [sub-tribe], *iwi* [tribe] framework of understanding."

I learned many values from my grandparents and believe that over time I have acquired many traits from my grandmother. I would like to think that, like my grandmother, I have been imbued with independence, courage, responsibility, and, more importantly, unconditional *aroha* (love), which has given me motivation and determination in life.

As the holders of our family knowledge my grandparents were my guide, my teachers. They helped me to understand the intricacies of retaining good whānau relationships. As siblings there were the inevitable fights and squabbles, and if it was over something trivial our grandfather would send the culprits to the boxing corner and were told to go for it. My grandfather was an amateur New Zealand champion boxer, so boxing skills for everyone, even us girls, were taught without question. Though most of the time I never wanted to be in that corner boxing, I learned that if I was determined enough to want something, I still needed to fight for it, both physically (usually with my brothers), but also mentally striving to find other solutions. I think I may have only stood in that corner twice, which taught me that no small squabble is worth an ear bashing.

What I did learn from my grandmother, however, were the skills of diplomacy. Being the peacemaker was more to my liking, ensuring that everyone came out with a win-win situation, which was more appealing and met everyone's needs.

Working together and being connected to each other, the lands, waterways, flora, and fauna, both physically and spiritually, were vital for the survival of our tūpuna. Our parents and grandparents always urged us to support and encourage one another, something I have tried to instill and nurture in my own children. I was brought up in an environment that acknowledged my whole being as a person within a Māori family but without the Māori language.

As Tuki Nepe (1991, 78) argues, "The whānau as a reproductive unit validates collective consciousness and collective reaffirmations of their cooperative and reciprocal commitments to each other."

As a child I didn't really understand the full implication of what it is to be Māori, why my parents wouldn't allow me to go to some homes to play or stay over, and why the children from these homes were not welcome at our home. Upon reflection these were mainly the non-Māori, non-Indigenous children in my class. Racism was something I was not aware of or even understood, but my parents and grandparents were only too cognizant of the ugly face of racism, which is why they did as much as they could to shield us from racist situations and potential conflict. Education was always very important to our grandparents; although their own educational experiences were not always pleasant, they understood the importance of what a good education could bring you.

We were told that we had to ensure our conduct was not disrespectful towards authority. We were constantly reminded that we needed to go to school and listen, not annoy our teachers, and not answer back to them—or anyone else of authority, for that matter. We were expected to be compliant, civilized, and submissive. These were traits they considered important for us to learn and that would hold us in good stead, in order to make our way successfully in the world.

I don't in any way blame my parents and grandparents for what they were trying to instill in us and why, because I recognize the terrible effects of their own education, which meant they saw conformity as the only solution for survival. As a result I became a habitual conformist without understanding and realizing why. That is, until I had children of my own and the changing face of Māori education was on the horizon, and I needed to be part of that. Values and practices instilled by my ancestors are aspirations that I hope I can recreate in my current teaching and learning practices in the tertiary sector.

Kaupapa Māori Education

My passion for kura kaupapa Māori has spanned 25 years, and I am now involved in a new direction in education by creating an alternative space for a new generation of kaiako who will stand tikanga-proud in front of my mokopuna, my grandchildren. I want them to have everything I had and more: more Māori language and culture within a kaupapa Māori schooling environment where they are nurtured and accepted for who they are and where they are from.

When I think of the bigger picture I try to envision the future of a kaupapa Māori schooling system and what such a system will look like for my grandchildren and great grandchildren in the future.

I began my teaching career in kura kaupapa Māori after graduating from Te Kura Takiura o Ngā Kura Kaupapa Māori o Tamaki Makaurau (Te Kura Takiura) under the guidance of then-Senior Lecturer and Academic Program Coordinator Tuki Nepe. The program was very new at that time; in 1991 when I entered it was in its second year of operation. I did not fully appreciate the political impact Te Kura Takiura was having on a national scale in regards to Māori education and meeting a critical demand for Māori-speaking teachers.

The provision of this kaupapa Māori teacher preparation program on the Auckland campus of a mainstream institution (Auckland University) was fraught with challenges for Tuki Nepe and her team, as well as the students in our cohort. Such challenges included constantly having to explain, negotiate, and navigate kaupapa Māori teacher training activities against the formidable tide of Eurocentric institutional policies and practices. *Whaea* (Mother/Aunty) Tuki encouraged her students to study and learn kaupapa Māori-specific curriculum in ways that did not suit the institution. She was a formidable and courageous person whose passion for kaupapa Māori education was evident in everything she did. She was always accessible and supportive of her students. She ran many wānanga (forums for learning) on the principles of *Te Aho Matua*, the only philosophy of education to emerge out of Aotearoa, and taught particularly how to implement it in every aspect of our daily lives rather than to limit the principles and values to classroom praxis only. Learning and teaching in the Māori language and being exponents of the language were taken for granted. Whaea Tuki held high expectations of all her students, expecting that under her tutelage we would progress with excellence and as quality practitioners in the field.

She instilled a sense of urgency in her students by emphasizing how rapidly the kaupapa Māori schooling system was moving and that we needed to move speedily, too, in order to be ahead of the game. Moreover, we had to be willing to take risks and understand that whatever decisions we made, the outcomes must always benefit the *tamariki* (children) in our care.

As students we sensed her dissatisfaction and frustration that our course was located in a Eurocentric institutional framework and we bore witness to the daily struggles she endured to keep the course authentic and relevant. I have the utmost respect and admiration for her decision to pull the Kura Takiura out and away from under the governance of the mainstream institution and out on its own. This was a tremendously risky act; yet 25 years later the course continues to operate as a private, tertiary education provider of kaupapa Māori initial teacher education (ITE) because of a clear demand for Māori speaking and Māori pedagogical practitioners for the Māori medium sector.

At that time the demand for trained teachers fluent in Māori language was high in order to meet the needs of kōhanga reo graduates who had nowhere else to go but to mainstream schools for their elementary schooling. The results were Māori children conversant in their Indigenous language who were now faced with the effects of root shock, the traumatic stress reaction to the loss of one's emotional ecosystem (Fullilove 2005), a syndrome not dissimilar to that felt by my grandparents two generations earlier. Forced into mainstream schooling, the kōhanga children may not have experienced the physical effects of corporal punishment once meted out to their ancestors for speaking Māori, but they definitely felt the spiritual and psychological loss of being nurtured in their language and culture in kōhanga reo. Moving into mainstream schools was traumatic.

Most mainstream schools were unprepared for the speed at which the kōhanga graduates were entering their classrooms, as well as the need to tackle the onslaught of parents demanding to know who would continue to teach their children in the Māori language. Many of these parents could not speak Māori, but they saw the effects of the transition to mainstream and how quickly the demise of the Māori language took effect among their tamariki. A small and determined group of parents felt they had little choice and therefore sought to establish a new Māori educational system whereby the Māori child would be continually nurtured in the Māori language from the early years of kōhanga reo to kura kaupapa Māori—elementary school.

With the establishment of kura kaupapa Māori, the demand for Māori teachers fluent in the Māori language accelerated. Teacher training programs were established to address the serious issue of Māori-speaking teacher supply for kura kaupapa Māori schools, as well as bilingual units and immersion Māori classes that were proliferating in mainstream schools and also demanded Māori-speaking teachers.

As the founding philosophical document for kura kaupapa Māori schools, *Te Aho Matua* was written by key experts and members of Te Rūnanga Nui o Ngā Kura Kaupapa Māori o Aotearoa. As such, *Te Aho Matua* is the mechanism for implementing Māori pedagogical practice and values in kura kaupapa Māori classrooms.

Once I graduated from Te Kura Takiura I completed another year at Auckland University, and it was then that the kura kaupapa Māori whānau in my hometown of Ōtaki asked me to return there and teach. I was ecstatic with the prospect of moving to my father's tribal area, and also living closer to my mother. More importantly, I knew that in this small town my children would have the benefit of socializing among their tribal kin, thereby consolidating their identity by learning about who they are and where they are from, within a nurturing and rich Māori language environment.

The kura which my children attend has developed learning experiences within a kaupapa Māori approach, establishing and recreating

Māori pedagogical practices within an environment that acknowledges fully all tribal affiliations both of the child and the area where we are located.

When the kura was first established, a *noho-kura* (school stay over) was introduced where every second week the children and their whānau stayed overnight to sleep, eat, and learn together in an immersive Māori-language setting.

Teaching *mōteatea* (ancient folk song) as an important way to transmit mātauranga Māori such as tribal stories, history, and *whakapapa* (ancestral tree) took place in the early hours of the morning. This practice was initiated as a learning and teaching environment aimed at replicating the customary wānanga (forum for learning) of our ancestors, which were held well before daybreak. Within the oral culture the belief was that the early hours before dawn provided the optimum time for learning and committing to memory large bodies of knowledge without distraction. The early morning wānanga would be used by the ancestors to invoke the spiritual guidance of those who have passed on, praying that their spiritual presence would assist in deeper learning and retention, and ensure that the right practices were being maintained.

Within kura kaupapa Māori, developing, learning and teaching experiences for the whole child through these types of spiritual practices, physical exercises, and inclusive methods extorting Māori metaphysics is an integral part of the pedagogical practices outlined in the *Te Aho Matua* document.

For example, our strong spiritual connection to the natural environment supports the view that our children should experience these occurrences on customary learning grounds and that eventually they will become the warriors for the preservation of Papatūānuku (Mother Earth).

Although I never encountered these experiences and opportunities in my own schooling, as a teacher I have continuously drawn upon the values and practices that my parents and grandparents have instilled in me.

What I was experiencing and observing among the children I taught, including my own children, was a fundamental growth pattern of learning and a deeper understanding about being Māori in a tribal community where profound transformations were underway. These changes were the result of a larger tribal initiative, the implementation of Whakatupuranga Rua Mano (Generation Two Thousand—Tribal Educational Programme). As a specific 25-year tribal development plan, Whakatupuranga focused on the revitalization of the Māori language and knowledge of three adjoining tribes with the foresight of what the Generation 2000 would need to ensure the survival of Māori as a whole.

This plan specified that the founding base would derive from the ones still knowledgeable and surviving, the *kaumātua* (Elders), as the reciprocators of knowledge. The importance of these kaumātua and the role they played in the establishment of Whakatupuranga Rua Mano is evident in the success that now flourishes in our community. As a small community, Ōtaki is nevertheless considered to be at the forefront of established Māori educational options with three kōhanga reo, a kura kaupapa Māori, a *kura-ā-iwi* (Tribal School), a Māori Immersion Unit in the local Primary school, as well as Te Wānanga o Raukawa (The University of Raukawa), the first Māori tertiary institution in Aotearoa.

My decision to move south to my hometown of Ōtaki was made to satisfy my aspiration that my children be raised speaking Māori in an immersive context and within our tribal area. I was determined to reclaim a Māori speaking space that had been so willfully removed from my grandparents and parents and denied me in my schooling. As a result of our relocation, my own language skills developed rapidly along with my children's.

Challenging the Contested Spaces

Pākeha institutional frameworks are not aligned with a Māori epistemology and pedagogy of learning and teaching. In my present position as the program coordinator of a mainstream, university-based total immersion teacher training program, the consistent challenge I face is on the one hand how to work within a Pākeha environment, and on the other hand how to maintain our tikanga Māori, te reo Māori, and traditional whānau kinships.

My role is multifaceted. It includes ensuring that the adjunct teaching associates, most of whom are practising teachers and/or principals in kura kaupapa Māori, are able to deliver their part of the program in accordance with Te Aho Matua as well as the obligations set by the members of their organization, Te Rūnanga Nui. There is also the institution's processes and procedures to be met in delivering the program where the challenge is constantly at the nexus of trying to uphold our *Māoritanga* (Māori culture) within a deeply Pākeha institutional framework that is at odds with a Māori/Indigenous sensibility.

The question this conundrum raises, and one I am constantly encountering among Māori practitioners, is whether this type of teaching environment compromises tikanga Māori. How is it possible to express the metaphysical base that is distinctively Māori, for instance in an online environment where we are separated from people by a computer screen? Do we constantly contest the importance of maintaining this space within a Pākeha institutional framework?

I say yes to all of the above. Yes, I believe this learning and teaching environment is not completely conducive to being able to express our Māoriness. When tikanga Māori and te reo Māori acquisition are removed from their natural habitat, then developing new strategies is imperative to ensure students experience the closest possible parallel to a natural face-to-face environment.

I see a huge gap in the technological capabilities of both tutors and students and implementing Māori pedagogical practices within an ever-developing and changing environment that requires us to persevere. Students are having to prioritize between maintaining significant cultural practices on the one hand and the imperative of financial security on the other. Sometimes there is no time or money to be able to meet the demands for reciprocating Māori cultural commitments, so we constantly compromise what can be done as opposed to what should be done under the bounds of tikanga Māori.

There is a proverbial saying: "*Ka takahia taku tikanga kia ora anō ai taku tikanga.*" Translated, it means: "I negate my cultural customs so that my customs culturally survive," and this is a constant challenge that Māori face in our ever-changing global environment.

The validity of tikanga Māori in the provision of a Māori immersion ITE program is constantly being questioned as to whether or not it should articulate a practice within a context that is similar to the marae. Discussing and trying to find clarity around the use of tikanga Māori in this new age and in a Pākeha institution creates situations that are either exemplary or problematic. This is because sometimes those who understand the significance of tikanga and conduct it with integrity are able to do so without any consequences. On the other hand, problems occur when the opposite is evident and these practices are not only examined by Pākeha within the institution but also by some Māori who are constrained by institutional requirements, or worse, have the same Western mindset as their Pākeha counterparts.

The majority of courses in Te Aho Tātairangi are offered online; therefore, one strategy we adopt to deliver within an expression of manaakitanga Māori is having a week-long contact course or wānanga. There are three such courses during the year, where students travel from various parts of the country to the university and are immersed in language, culture, and transmission of knowledge through the principles of *Te Aho Matua*. In holding courses this way we have replicated the wānanga or house of learning within a Pākeha institution. However, our attempt to deliver this program in an authentic kaupapa Māori way is not without its limitations, both internally and externally.

Catering and accommodation are two areas of manaakitanga that are paramount when students arrive. The adjunct faculty requirements are met with the full understanding that their expertise in the field is imperative to the core of this program. Time allocation for each adjunct lecturer is negotiated around their own working lives. Many are full-time teaching *tumuaki* (principals) in the kura located within their communities, so wānanga are delivered during school holidays to accommodate their participation in the program. They give us their time, their expertise, and their passion for the kaupapa (program) at hand. If not for their contributions, the program wouldn't hold its credibility within the wider Māori-medium community.

The importance of the week-long wānanga is that it allows many opportunities for inquiry learning, physical interactions, and contextual relations between student-teacher and teacher-student that would otherwise be difficult to appreciate in an online learning environment. It is also an opportunity for an open wānanga space for experiencing metaphysical learning and spiritual connections that many of the guest speakers at these wānanga bring with them.

The inclusion of a political paper in the course is a learning area that we incorporate to inform our students of the historical and political struggles faced by their ancestors and how teacher training programs such as this one have come about through the many efforts of Māori educators in the past.

Online learning is now a global method for teaching and learning, but it has been a huge learning curve for our students and tutors to come to grips with within a kaupapa Māori environment. For many of them, online teaching and learning is seen as an impersonal imposition where teacher/student face-to-face interaction has been removed and replaced with a computer screen.

An internal survey of our program revealed that many of our students were unable to interact and engage fully with our teaching and learning program online. Some struggled with the lack of interactive teaching and missed nuances that are only gained from having a teacher physically standing in front of them. Unfortunately, this has affected the progress of some students, which has led to staff developing methods of communicating a range of Māori practices and pedagogies that encourage greater levels of engagement for Māori students.

Students are provided with many opportunities to go out into kura and other areas to work and develop their practices. Most students choose to remain in their own communities, working in local kura, because the online learning environment offers them the opportunity to do so. They are not bound to travelling daily or moving to the institution in order to enter the program.

Māori students lead full and demanding lives with whānau and iwi commitments. For most, a major concern is maintaining and upholding their reciprocal commitments to their whānau and meeting the daily financial needs of being able to put food on their tables. So sometimes completing a degree is not a priority, and studying at home within their communities can serve to undermine study responsibilities when whānau and community imperatives take priority.

Despite this, committing to four years of study is important and the nature of such a commitment needs to be constantly communicated to students, their whānau, and their respective communities. The urgent demand for qualified teachers nationally has led to some kura taking desperate actions by placing non-graduated students as relieving teachers, which, besides being unlawful, serves to place them at an even greater risk of not completing their studies.

Validating university-based wānanga three times a year can become complicated, such as when fiscal issues constrain our ability to fully express the principle of manaakitanga. University management has different aspirations and assumptions as to what they envision an initial teacher education program to be and how it should be delivered. So drawing on a supportive management within a Pākeha institution that understands the importance and significance of maintaining wānanga as a multi-layered and meaningful learning and teaching environment is critical.

Rationalizing fiscal spending for nourishing students and providing sleeping arrangements is most often seen as problematic. On the whole, university courses do not provide the same services as a wānanga; students are expected to provide their own meals and accommodation for the duration of their contact course. So why should students in the kaupapa Māori immersion program be treated any differently?

The fact is that when the program was redesigned, great thought and care was given to how students would benefit fully in a total Māori immersion program and experience the full expression of mātauranga Māori within a kaupapa Māori environment. Wānanga was considered the most appropriate and suitable method. Manaakitanga in the context of wānanga is an essential value and an expression of tikanga Māori in practice. Providing pastoral care at wānanga exemplifies manaakitanga. It is a core value that was reflected during my teacher training experiences at Te Kura Takiura, and what I consistently experienced with my grandmother, my mother, and with Whaea Tuki Nepe. Manaakitanga was instilled in me by these *wahine toa* (strong, assertive women).

During wānanga, Māori exponents of mātauranga Māori share their expertise with students who, in turn, are privileged to engage with leading authorities of kaupapa Māori, such as Pita Sharples, Tamati Reedy, Cathy Dewes, the late Amster Reedy, and Neria and Katarina Mataira, daughters of the late Katarina Mataira. After engaging with these exponents, student responses confirm that intergenerational layers of teaching and learning enrich and enhance their own theories and beliefs about being Māori.

Conclusion

The preservation of the link between a university-based, immersive Māori teacher education program in a community partnership with the kaupapa Māori schooling sector, through Te Rūnanga Nui o Ngā Kura Kaupapa Māori o Aotearoa schools and its members, is dependent on many factors.

My position is twofold, observing the requirements of the university as well as the aspirations and expectations of Te Rūnanga o Ngā Kura Kaupapa Māori o Aotearoa and its members. I am fortunate, because prior to entering the Te Aho Tātairangi program I had already established many ties and connections with all external teachers on the program and also with many of the kura communities.

My long-confirmed relations through many years of working in a kura and being a school tumuaki has enabled me to call upon friends and colleagues, find prospective students for this program, and ask for assistance from my community when necessary. I feel confident that I am able to communicate sufficiently to maintain good relationships with all stakeholders. Being aware of the expectations of my kura community and having had firsthand experiences of its hardships, demands, and priorities enables me to work effectively in a teacher preparation program.

The Māori immersion program, Te Aho Tātairangi, with all its challenges, offers an important platform to continue my exploration in applying Māori pedagogical practices at the university level. Despite feeling exhausted, frustrated, or exasperated with situations within the academy that are most often out of my control, it is my inherent values, principles, and ethics acquired over my lifetime that guide me, ensuring that I carry out my work with integrity, reliability, and consistency.

Validating what it is to be Māori is an ongoing challenge, not only in the institution but nationally, because invariably Māori culture and knowledge is still undervalued. Knowing that speaking your language and living and breathing your culture continues to be unappreciated remains a constant disappointment.

However, I now have grandchildren who are entering into the Māori educational arena, so my focus for them is ensuring that their future aspirations are met.

This space within the academy will always be contested as long as the Eurocentric faction claiming it demands its control, its management, and the learning content within it. Therefore, it is required that we be relentless, insistent, powerful, and self-determining in such spaces within the academy, and that the content within remains kaupapa Māori focused within the parameters of tikanga Māori and te reo Māori.

Appendix

Te Aho Matua consists of six principles (Minister of Education 2008):

1. *Te Ira Tangata* (the human essence) affirms the nature of the child as a human being with spiritual, physical, and emotional requirements.
2. *Te Reo* (language) deals with language policy and how the schools can "best advance the language learning of their children."
3. *Ngā Iwi* (people) focuses on "the social agencies which influence the development of children, in short, all those people with whom they interact as they make sense of their world and find their rightful place within it."
4. *Te Ao* (the world) deals with "the world which surrounds children and about which there are fundamental truths which affect their lives."
5. *Ahuatanga Ako* (circumstances of learning) "provides for every aspect of good learning which the whānau feel is important for their children, as well as the requirements of a national curriculum."
6. *Ngā Tino Uaratanga* (essential values) "focuses on what the outcome might be for children who graduate from Kura Kaupapa Māori" and "defines the characteristics which Kura Kaupapa Māori aim to develop in their children."

Note

1. My thoughts return to you who have gone beyond the veil, you have inspired me, farewell.

    To those of you who have set the pathway for our tribal self-determination, we acknowledge your contribution and you will always be remembered.

    For those of us who remain to face the many challenges, let us be strong, brave and steadfast so that we may achieve this aspirational journey.

    Thank you.

References

Fullilove, Mindy. 2005. *Root Shock: How Tearing Up City Neighbourhoods Hurts America, and What We Can Do about It*. London: Oneworld.

Minister of Education. 2008. "Official Version of Te Aho Matua o Ngā Kura Kaupapa Māori." *New Zealand Gazette* 32, February 22, 2008: 733–46. Wellington, NZ: Department of Internal Affairs.

Nepe, Tuakana Mate. 1991. *Te Toi Huarewa Tipuna: Kaupapa Māori, an Educational Intervention System*. Auckland, NZ: University of Auckland.

IV Action
New Directions in Indigenous Education

16 | Improving Special Needs Education for Māori Children

Concepts, Principles, and a Promising Program

JILL BEVAN-BROWN

Introduction

Every country has Indigenous children with special education needs; however, these needs are usually defined and provided for from a majority culture perspective. At best, this results in provisions that are not as effective as they could be. At worst, it contributes to disproportionate representation and special education programs and services that Indigenous and other minority-group students find meaningless and alienating (Blanchett 2006; Graham 2012; Meyer et al. 2013).

While the importance of providing a culturally responsive education is receiving increased international attention and research support (Codrington 2014; Idrus 2014; McCarty and Lee 2014; Owens 2014), limited attention has been paid to what this means for students with special education needs from Indigenous and minority groups. Obviously, these students will benefit from any general initiatives that provide a more culturally responsive education. Beyond this, however, there is also a need to focus on issues and approaches specific to

Indigenous and minority students with special education needs (Bevan-Brown 2009; Bruce and Venkatesh 2014; Gay 2002; Klingner et al. 2005). Similarly, the inclusion movement, which celebrates diversity and advocates for the removal of exclusionary practices and policies (UNESCO 2005) has been criticized for remaining relatively silent on disproportionate representation and other issues pertaining to Indigenous and minority-group students (Artiles 2000). Despite some progress being made since Artiles voiced his initial concerns, the predominant focus on disability and a narrow approach to professional training have resulted in the powerful influence of culture remaining unrecognized and unrepresented (Waitoller and Artiles 2013).

A Way Forward

A suggested first step is an examination of the concept of special education needs and what this means, if anything, to Indigenous and minority groups. In fact, I took this initial step as part of my doctoral research (Bevan-Brown 2002, 2009). I consulted with over 90 Māori parents and *whānau* (extended family) to gather their views on what constitutes a special need. However, before I present their answers, a caveat must be noted. Māori, like other people, are a diverse group. We differ in lifestyle, beliefs, values, socio-economic circumstances, religious and tribal affiliation, geographic location, degree of acculturation and Māori identification, knowledge and practice of Māori culture, and in many other ways. As Durie (1995) reminds us, Māori experience diverse realities; consequently, there can never be a single Māori viewpoint on special education needs. Lynch and Hanson (1992, xiii, 359) also offer pertinent advice:

> Each individual and each family is different and culture-specific information cannot be assumed to apply in every situation. Its value is that it raises issues that should be considered, poses questions that may need to be answered and underscores the interventionist's desire to

respond sensitively to each family and each family member... Although [families and individuals] are influenced by their ethnic, cultural and language backgrounds, they are not fully defined by them. Therefore differences in these areas should be used to enhance our interactions rather than to stereotype or to serve as the sole determiner of our approach to intervention.

A number of participants in my research did not like the term "special needs" because it could be interpreted as meaning some children are more "special" than others, or that some children's needs are more important than other children's needs. As all children are special and all have important needs, it was felt a different term was preferable. One participant questioned the whole concept of "special education," saying that it was not based on Māori values. She pointed out that as the needs of all children were important, there should not be any separate system of funding for "special" education. This opinion aligns with Tau's (1999) objection to "massaging" one culture's perceptions into another culture's framework.

Notwithstanding these objections, participants described a wide variety of special needs, which can be grouped into the following 10 categories:

1. *Physical and Health Needs*: Children with significantly restricted mobility or physical function due to some type of physical impairment, condition, or health-related problem.
2. *Sensory Needs*: For example, children with vision and hearing impairments.
3. *Communication Needs*: Children who have difficulty communicating because of delayed language development or some type of disorder or speech impediment.
4. *Learning Needs*: Children whose learning is significantly impaired for a variety of reasons, such as those with intellectual disability associated with Down's syndrome or brain damage, as well as those with more school-specific learning problems such as attention deficit hyperactivity disorder (ADHD) and dyslexia.

5. *Social and Emotional Needs*: Children who have difficulty relating to others, such as children with autism, Asperger's Syndrome, or long-term depression or unhappiness; abused and neglected children; and those affected by family violence, discord, or specific trauma.
6. *Behavioural Needs*: Children with extreme disruptive, aggressive, non-compliant, and anti-social behaviour.
7. *Needs Associated with Giftedness*: These are a result of the lack/absence of the processes, services, expertise, and resources needed to challenge and extend gifted children.
8. *Needs Associated with Socio-Economic Circumstances and Geographic Location*: Poverty and rural location can potentially create special education needs for many Māori children. The common denominator is the absence of resources and services that impacts negatively on children's progress and development. This can be a primary or secondary influence. Examples of the former are children who fail to progress at school because they cannot afford books, calculators, lunches, school trips, and other necessities to facilitate and support learning. Examples of the latter are children with glue ear whose language development is further delayed because of the time and cost involved in accessing the required support (e.g., getting grommets fitted).
9. *Needs Associated with Perceptions, Attitudes, and Treatment of People with Disability*: Special education needs arising from a child's disability, condition, or circumstances can be exacerbated by people's reactions. For example, low expectations and demands can result in fewer learning opportunities, which in turn limit a child's developmental progress and compound their special education need.
10. *Needs Associated with "Being Māori"*: These needs stem from three principal causes, namely:
    i. *Societal and Individual Practices and Attitudes that Disadvantage Māori Learners*. At the societal level, Māori learners are disadvantaged by assimilative policies and practices and the limited acknowledgement their cultural capital receives within

a Pākehā-dominated education system. At an individual level, a wide range of negative, stereotypical attitudes and behaviours were cited as disadvantaging Māori children. These were mainly associated with the consequent impact of ignoring parents' concerns, and low teacher expectations.

ii. *Certain Cultural Traits and Behaviours that Put Māori at a Disadvantage.* Participants gave examples of the unwillingness of many Māori to "speak up"; a tendency to "go with the flow"; be *whakamā* (shy) in unfamiliar or uncomfortable situations; and a lack of confidence or ability to "hassle" Pākehā institutions to receive services. While it can be debated whether these traits and behaviours are, in fact, "cultural" in nature, they were certainly evident in participants' experiences, as for example with children who were "too whakamā" to ask for clarification when lessons were not understood.

iii. *Te Reo Māori-Related Needs.* Some participants viewed the inability of Māori to speak their own language as being a special need. Others believed that special education needs could be exacerbated by involvement in total immersion education. Examples include children with special education needs who are unable to receive extra assistance because of the shortage of professionals with the cultural and Māori language expertise needed to work in *kōhanga reo* and *kura kaupapa Māori*. Other examples are children without a "special education label" who struggle to learn te reo Māori but are not eligible for additional support because problems associated with learning a second language do not meet special education funding criteria.

The broad, inclusive concept of special needs described by the research participants is in accord with Kingi and Bray's (2000) Māori concepts of disability and Durie's (1985) *whare tapa whā* model, which explains well-being as encompassing the physical dimension (*te taha tinana*), the spiritual dimension (*te taha wairua*), the thinking, emotional dimension (*te taha hinengaro*), and the family dimension (*te taha whānau*).

Principle-Based Provisions

Having determined what special education needs mean for the Māori child and their whānau, the next step for professionals is to provide culturally responsive and effective assessments, programs, services, and resources focused on identifying and meeting these needs. My research (Bevan-Brown 2002, 2009) identified a number of principles foundational to these provisions. These principles are explained below.

1. *Kaupapa Māori*: All assessments, programs, services, and resources should represent a Māori worldview by incorporating Māori concepts, knowledge, skills, attitudes, language, practices, customs, values, and beliefs. Such provisions fulfill the Treaty of Waitangi obligation to actively protect Māori language as a *taonga* (treasured possession). As Ratima et al. (1995, 48) state, "There is an added onus on providers of services to Māori, that not only shall clients be equipped to participate in mainstream New Zealand society, but they should have the opportunity to participate in Māori society, to belong to Māori institutions, and importantly, remain Māori. The costs of disability are high; they should not include cultural alienation."

2. *Importance, Relevance, and Beneficence*: Provisions should focus on matters of importance, concern, and benefit to Māori. Such provisions should be relevant and address needs and aspirations identified by parents, whānau, the Māori community, and the children themselves. Two areas of potential conflict arise when putting this principle into practice. The first relates to general disagreements about what is considered important, relevant, and beneficial, and the second relates to incompatible cultural concepts, expectations, beliefs, procedures, values, norms, and practices.

3. *Participation*: This involves the consultative, collaborative participation of parents, whānau, the Māori community, and the children themselves in all stages of special education provision to the extent that they choose and feel comfortable. Participation is a two-way street. Professionals should be involved in the lives of their students and the Māori community to a degree that is considered appropriate by all concerned. By interacting with students, parents, and whānau outside of the school context and by becoming involved in the activities of the Māori community, professionals can gain an understanding and appreciation of Māori perspectives and increase their knowledge of factors that influence the lives of the students and families with whom they work. This two-way interaction fulfills Treaty of Waitangi obligations of partnership and participation.
4. *Empowerment, Tino Rangatiratanga, and Māori Control*: Special education provisions should result in the empowerment of Māori at multiple levels by offering parents, whānau, children with special needs, and the Māori community the skills, knowledge, means, opportunity, and authority to act for themselves and to make their own decisions. Inherent in the principle of empowerment is the provision of meaningful choices about what decisions can be made. Empowerment requires those who presently hold power to provide space for Māori to participate, opportunities to make their own decisions, and resources to implement these decisions. It involves shared understandings, mutual respect, and valuing diversity.
5. *Accountability*: Professionals should be accountable to children, parents, whānau, and the Māori community for the cultural and general effectiveness of programs and services they provide. Such accountability can be achieved through transparent, specific, ongoing checks and measures developed with stakeholder input into their design, development, implementation, and regular monitoring.
6. *High Quality*: As well as being culturally responsive, special education provisions need to be evidence-based, include accurate and

ongoing assessment, be well-planned and coordinated, employ effective teaching strategies, be pitched at the correct ability level, utilize quality equipment and resources, be positively focused, build on students' strengths, provide for all areas of development, and involve efficient administration and coordination of services. In short, special education provisions should incorporate all the components that have been identified as "best practice" in the field.

7. *Appropriate Personnel*: Educators and service providers should have the personal, professional, and cultural expertise required. They should value and be supportive of Māori culture and the children, parents, and whānau with whom they work.[1]

8. *Equality and Accessibility*: Special education provisions should be readily accessible to Māori children with special needs and their parents and whānau. They should have the same rights and privileges as other learners and experience equitable access, use, and outcomes. Article Three of the Treaty of Waitangi promises Māori the "rights and privileges of British subjects." This constitutes a guarantee of legal equality between Māori and other New Zealanders. The government acknowledges that implicit in legal equality is the assurance of actual enjoyment of social benefits: "Where serious and persistent imbalances exist between groups, in their actual enjoyment of social benefits such as health, education and housing, the Government will consider measures to assist in redressing the balance" (Department of Justice 1989, 13).

The implication of this Treaty provision is that professionals may need to take proactive measures to ensure their Māori students are able to take full advantage of the programs and services they offer. Affordable cost, convenient time and location, friendly personnel, barrier-free and safe environments, and readily available and understandable advertising information are all important accessibility factors that must consequently be taken into consideration.

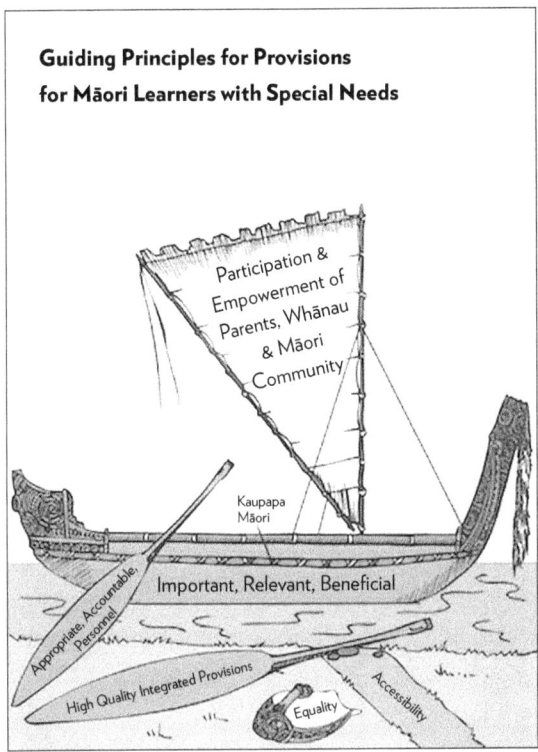

FIGURE 16.1 *He waka tino whakarawea: A well-equipped canoe.*
[Jill Bevan-Brown (2002)]

New Metaphors

The principles above are illustrated in Figure 16.1.

Bishop and Glynn (1999) maintain that teachers develop principles and practices that reflect the imagery and metaphors they hold. In the past, special education in Aotearoa New Zealand has been dominated by the medical model. Similarly, Māori education has been governed by a deficit mentality. Thankfully, these paradigms are changing. To support this change and facilitate progress for Māori students both with and without special education needs, assessments, programs, services, and resources are likened to a *waka tino whakarawea*—a well-equipped canoe on which they travel at one stage of their life's journey. The *kaunoti* (hull) represents the requirements of importance, relevance, and beneficence, while the *hoe* (paddles) represent high quality, integrated provisions, and appropriate, accountable personnel. These components allow the waka to travel smoothly and surely. If a hoe is missing, the waka will travel in circles, making only limited progress. Traditionally, even small waka had *rā* (sails). These assisted the rowers and hastened progress. In this analogy the participation of parents, whānau, and the Māori community provides the rā. The more empowered they are, the greater the rate of progress made. The kaupapa Māori requirement can be likened to the *harakeke* (flax) lashings that bind the various parts of the waka together. As these lashings provide strength and cohesiveness to the waka, Māori input achieves the same task for provisions for Māori students. The *tatā* (bailer) represents equality. If water enters, the tatā is used to enable the waka to remain balanced and afloat. Finally, the path to the waka represents accessibility. If this is blocked, the Māori learner will be forced to make the journey on foot. Progress by this means will be much slower and more laborious.

Improving Professionals' Cultural Competence

While the previous discussion outlines the ways culture impacts the conception and management of special education needs, the challenge remains to make professionals aware of this information so that they can develop culturally responsive and effective assessments, programs, services, and resources for Māori students with special education needs.

In a critical review of a decade of professional development research in inclusive education, Waitoller and Artiles (2013) note that the vast majority of professional training concentrates on a single form of difference, usually ability. This unitary approach assumes that students' exclusion is based on one factor, and so does not equip professionals to "address the needs of students that live with complex and intersecting forms of exclusion" (338). Like Crenshaw (1991) and Hancock (2007), Waitoller and Artiles (2013) advocate for multifocal, intersectional professional education that acknowledges the importance and influence of all forms of difference and the complexity and compounding nature of their interactions:

> PD efforts for inclusive education thus should focus on nurturing teachers that understand complex forms of exclusion and are able to collaborate with other professionals and families to dismantle intersecting barriers that keep certain groups of students from accessing and participating in meaningful learning experiences. (322)

Massey University, in collaboration with the University of Canterbury, has taken up this challenge in the development and delivery of the Post Graduate Diploma (Specialist Teaching), or PGDIP (ST).[2] In 2010, these universities won a Ministry of Education contract to design and administer a national post-graduate course for professionals who work with students who have special education needs in the areas of learning and behaviour, deafness and hearing impairment, blindness and low vision, and autism spectrum disorder, and students requiring early intervention. Subsequently, gifted and talented students and those with high and complex needs have been added as specialty areas in this post-graduate qualification.

Course Structure and Delivery

The qualification is a two-year, four-paper, part-time course that most students complete while continuing in their usual employment.[3] Students attend two compulsory three-day face-to-face contact courses each year, participate in two optional geographically based whānau group meetings, and study online using a variety of e-learning tools, including Moodle, Mahara ePortfolio, Wikipedia, Adobe Connect and Presenter, and Peerwise. The course also has a blog and a Facebook page. Ministry of Education study awards cover most students' course fees, contact course expenses, and a specified number of study leave days. The structure of the program is shown in Figure 16.2.

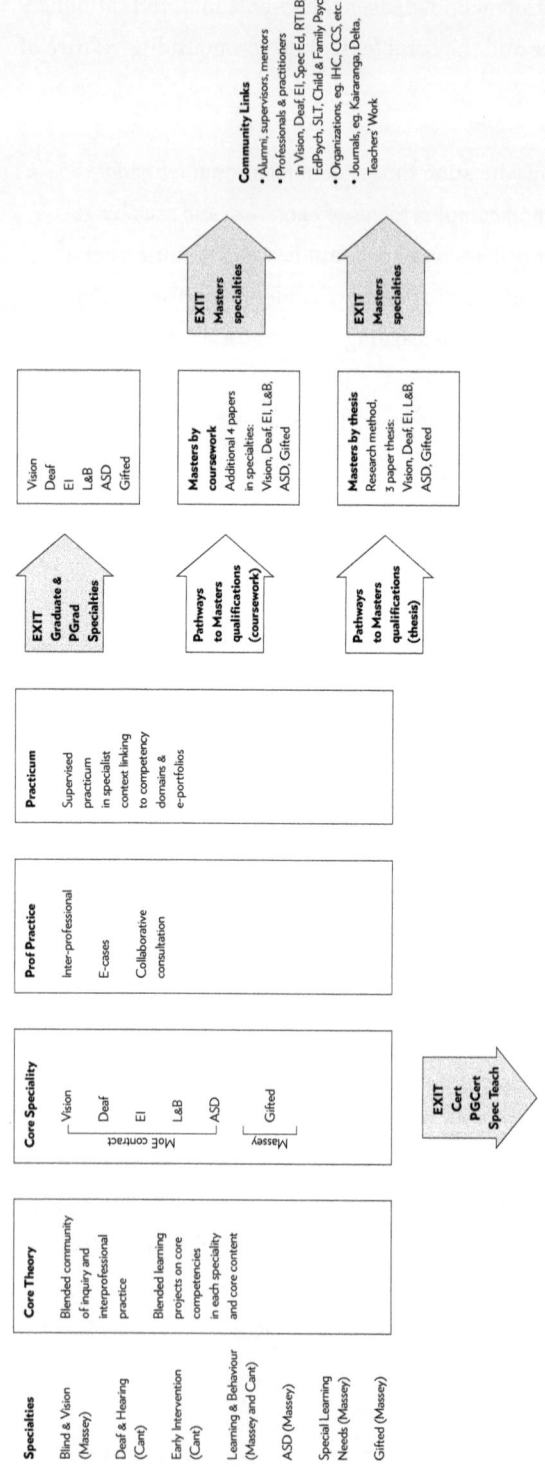

FIGURE 16.2 Structure of the post-graduate diploma (specialist teaching). [Courtesy of Mandia Mentis]

FIGURE 16.3 *Māwhai model showing overall survey data for Cohort one.*
[Data analysis and diagram by Philippa Butler, research officer for the PGDIP (ST)]

The PGDIP (ST) utilizes an inquiry-based, inter-professional, blended learning approach known as the "māwhai model." *Māwhai*, the Māori word for "web" and "net," provides an appropriate metaphor for how students "weave" their professional identity by connecting the competency domains of specialist teaching practice in a networked learning environment. As students progress through the qualification they chart their growth in the various competency areas as illustrated in Figure 16.3.

Cultural responsiveness is modelled in course delivery and practices. Each year both contact courses are opened with a formal *pōwhiri* (welcome ceremony) where staff introduce themselves using a traditional *mihi* (greeting) format. The courses are closed with a *poroporoaki* (leave-taking). Māori students have a dedicated online forum and meetings at contact courses, and are able to submit their assignments in te reo Māori. *Tuakana-tēina* (senior-junior) relationships are facilitated through cross-year whānau groups and the provision of graduate practicum advisors and cultural mentors.

Course Content

In the first year, students study two papers (papers are equivalent to courses in the North American system). The first, "Core Theory and Foundations of Specialist Teaching," is taken by all students and covers common knowledge and skills required by specialist teachers to facilitate a shared understanding and collaborative approach. The second paper covers theory and foundational knowledge in one of the seven specialist areas of study. In the second year, all students take an evidence-based inter-professional paper that requires them to work together in inter-professional groups to examine the nature and application of evidence-based practice for the first two thirds of the paper, while the last third focuses on evidence-based practice in their selected specialization area. The final paper enables them to apply their learning in a practicum situation.

Cultural Content

While the PGDIP (ST) considers culture broadly, particular emphasis is placed on ethnic culture and developing knowledge and skills to work with ethnic minority groups in a culturally responsive manner. In developing the qualification, writers drew on their own expertise, far-reaching stakeholder consultation, the results of a national survey, and the guidance of a variety of advisory groups including a Māori, Pasifika, and multiethnic (MPM) advisory group. Members of the MPM advisory group have extensive cultural knowledge and experience. They contribute to initial course content and processes and play an ongoing role in updating and monitoring cultural input. Each university has a Māori staff member on the MPM advisory group. They are responsible for working with advisory group members and overseeing the cultural content and responsiveness of the qualification. The PGDIP (ST) also has an official *kaumātua* (Elder) who provides hands-on and advisory input, particularly in respect to correct *kawa* (ceremony) and *tikanga* (customs) Māori.

Core Paper

In the core paper all students examine the concept and role of culture and reflect on their own cultural, spiritual, and philosophical beliefs, values, and practices. The rationale behind these requirements is that in order for professionals to work in a culturally responsive manner, they first need to be aware of their own culture and how it influences their practice and impacts on those with whom they interact (Howard 2010). The core paper has six competency domains. Domain two is dedicated to culturally responsive practice. It consists of an initial quiz, Māori and Pasifika books that contain relevant readings and activities, an inter-professional inquiry forum, a specialist inquiry forum, and a resource bank where students and lecturers share a wide range of culturally relevant teaching resources, evaluation templates, video clips, web pages, book reviews, policy documents, and so forth.

The learning outcomes for the culturally responsive practice domain are to demonstrate an understanding of the concept and role of culture; to reflect on one's own cultural values, practices, and beliefs; and to demonstrate an understanding of the concepts of biculturalism and multiculturalism. The Māori book, for example, includes chapters titled "Te Ao Māori," "The Treaty of Waitangi," "Majority Culture, Power and Education," "Māori and Education," and "Working with Whānau: A Partnership Approach."

In their assignments, students set their own learning goals and complete a range of activities to achieve these goals. These activities are recorded in an e-portfolio and must include, among the various postings, completion of the quiz with at least 70% accuracy, contributions in the inquiry and specialist fora, and a resource bank entry.

The inquiry forum enables students to explore, with others in their inter-professional group, their response to the domain's overarching question: "How can I improve competence as a culturally responsive practitioner?" Instructions are as follows:[4]

Based on the knowledge that you have obtained within this domain, what issues, questions, observations, understanding do you now have around what it means to be a culturally responsive and effective practitioner? Pose your inquiry question, statement, view or dilemma in this forum in order to open up a conversation with others in your interprofessional group. Please make sure that you also respond to others forum posts. Use this opportunity to clarify any issues you have around this domain and explore concepts more deeply with your peers. You can pose a question or statement—however small or large, share a video clip, photo, quote, article, case study or just your own thoughts and questions. You might like to consider or comment on:

- Historical and current policy documents;
- Current culturally responsive practice frameworks and guidelines;
- Your own cultural identity;
- Your awareness of diverse cultural beliefs and values;
- Your understanding of resources (including the literature) that describes different perspectives on disability.

Similarly, in the specialist forum students are required to co-construct, with others in their specialist group, what culturally responsive and effective practice means for their particular specialist area and to share examples of the ways they maintain culturally responsive and effective practice within their specialist group. They are asked to consider:

- Examples of ways in which cultural diversity and responsivity is reflected within their workplace environment or those environments that they are a part of;
- Their interactions with children, family/whānau and other professionals;
- The policies, frameworks, and practice guidelines that are adhered to within their workplace context.

Specialist Papers

Each specialist paper has cultural content integrated throughout. All papers also include fora, activities, and assignments with specific cultural content. The autism spectrum disorder (ASD) paper, for example, considers cultural influences on the perception and management of ASD and on the manifestation and interpretation of ASD characteristics; culturally appropriate assessment, programs, interventions, teaching strategies, and service provision; involvement of whānau; and culture-specific research. The paper contains a wide variety of culturally focused readings, video clips, and activities. For instance, following a reading on Māori research into ASD, activity two states:

> As you read through this material, think about what issues and experiences are specific to Māori children and parents and what would be generally applicable. Are you aware of any issues and experiences that would be specific to other cultures? Share your thoughts and experiences in the forum for this activity.

Evidence-Based Interprofessional Paper (EBIP)

In this paper, students work towards achieving the learning outcome of demonstrating an understanding of Māori and multicultural concepts and practices as they relate to professional practice in general and to their area of specialization in particular. Cultural material is integrated into a book on evidence-based practice and another on inter-professional practice. Their content includes material on immersion and bilingual education, working in partnership, whānau, kaupapa Māori frameworks, and culturally responsive teaching and research. The major assignment involves the critical appraisal of a self-selected teaching or assessment practice, resource, program, or tool. This task includes the requirement to appraise cultural appropriateness and to signal any adaptations needed to provide for Māori or other cultural groups. In this paper, students work in self-selected inter-professional groups in areas of particular interest to them. This includes Māori and Māori-medium groups.

TABLE 16.1 *Competencies in culturally responsive practice*

Students are asked to demonstrate growing confidence and competence to work in culturally responsive ways with learners, professionals, parents, families, and whānau within the ASD area. The self-reflective review begins with a score of 1–10, where 1 indicates a novice, and 10 indicates confidence and competence.

Competencies	Self-Reflective Review
a. Demonstrate cultural responsiveness when working with professionals, parents, family, whanau, and learners with ASD.	*Score:* 3 *Comments:* Although I firmly believe in the value of diversity and the importance of cultural input, my knowledge and confidence in this area is sadly lacking.
b. Demonstrate an understanding of the implications of cultural diversity on the care and education of learners with ASD by modelling and promoting bicultural and multicultural values in practicum situations.	*Score:* 3 *Comments:* In my own school and classroom I have relied on others to provide the lead in bicultural and multicultural matters so I am very nervous about having to include bicultural and multicultural input in my practicum.
c. Model and promote the use of te reo and encourage the use of words from the various languages of the school's/centre's/ organization's community.	*Score:* 3 *Comments:* The spirit is willing but the pronunciation is weak! Rather than risk making a fool of myself I avoid using words from other languages but can understand many Māori words when they are written down.

Learning Goals	Planned Activities
To develop my bicultural and multicultural competence and confidence.	Interview an RTLB with Māori expertise, a resource teacher of Māori or other person with cultural expertise about culturally responsive ways of working with Māori students and whānau. Write up recommendations from interview.
	Look for, record & reflect on examples of bicultural and multicultural practices in my own workplace and practicum school.
To increase bicultural and multicultural content in my practice.	Incorporate cultural considerations/input in planning, interventions, assessment, reporting, and resources associated with case study work.
	Provide relevant cultural course readings to interested colleagues associated with the practicum and invite them to discuss the readings.
To increase my knowledge of basic words from some of the cultures represented at my school.	Research, practice and deliver my own mihi on an appropriate occasion.
To increase my knowledge, use of, and confidence in te reo Māori.	Undertake an online or face-to-face course in basic te reo.
	Find out what cultural groups my students come from and research basic words from the cultures represented. Compile a dictionary of commonly used words from the various ethnic groups represented.

Practicum

The practicum paper requires students to apply the knowledge and skills gained from the core, specialist, and EBIP papers in a practicum context. The practicum has culture-specific outcomes, a handbook that contains a Māori-focused chapter, and a discussion forum dedicated to culturally responsive practice. Particular practicum requirements differ between the seven specialist areas, but each includes a cultural responsiveness section containing cultural skills and knowledge specific to the specialist area. In order to pass their practicum every student must plan and implement relevant cultural goals. Table 16.1 shows an example of the cultural responsiveness section in an ASD practicum plan.

Contact Courses

The two face-to-face contact courses contain a number of culturally specific workshops, presentations, and guest speakers with expertise in Māori, Pasifika, and multiethnic education. Examples include presentations on:

- The cultural self-review, a process for identifying and improving cultural responsiveness across a school or early childhood centre;
- An Ohomairangi Trust workshop on a kaupapa Māori early intervention and parenting support program, Mellow Parenting: Hoki Ki te Rito, which supports Māori whānau to help *tamariki* (children) reach their full potential;
- Mana Potential, a strengths-based tool for behaviour change;
- Te Kura Kaupapa Māori o Whānau Tahi's WAI program to promote Māori students' success in reading and learning;
- The work of Ngāti Kapo, a national Māori health and disability service provider run by and for Māori who are vision impaired; and
- Parenting Māori children with autism spectrum disorder (ASD).

The PGDIP (ST) is premised on the *whakatauaki* (proverb) *"he kura te tangata,"* which means "humans are precious." This refers to the intrinsic value and contribution each person makes to the well-being of others. This sentiment is echoed in the course mantra of "learning with, from and about each other" and exemplified in interactions with children, families, and whānau. Students are encouraged to value themselves and others and to appreciate that every person has something worthwhile to contribute.

Effectiveness of the Post-Graduate Diploma (Specialist Teaching)

Proving the effectiveness of the PGDIP (ST) program in increasing students' cultural competence and responsivity is a difficult task, as the evidence available is mainly based on self reports. Notwithstanding this, an analysis of relevant evaluation survey data from two cohorts and an examination of forum posts, course activities, assignment tasks, practicum involvement, and post-course activities indicates many positive changes. Following is a selection of data from these various sources from different endorsement areas. They provide a snapshot of the nature and extent of students' cultural competence and an indication of progress made in this area.

Evaluation Surveys
Autism Spectrum Endorsement
Students complete a survey prior to beginning the course and at the end of years one and two. This survey contains 16 questions pertaining to culture. In the pre-course survey, students are asked about their preparedness to engage in culturally responsive practice both individually and inter-professionally. They are also asked how prepared they are to learn more about pupils from ethnic minority groups, and about how culture impacts special education needs and provisions.

In relation to their specific endorsement area, students are asked about their preparedness to demonstrate an understanding of Māori, Pasifika, and multicultural concepts and practices and how important they consider these to be.

They are also asked how important it is for teaching staff to value diverse cultures and respect the cultural background of the professionals they work with; how important it is for their study to include working in a culturally responsive way, both at an individual and inter-professional level; how important it is to learn more about students from ethnic minority groups; and about the impact of culture. Surveys at the end of the first year and at the end of the program contain the same questions as the initial survey, but with adjustments to probe what students have actually achieved (as opposed to their preparedness in various areas).

To date, two cohorts have graduated from the PGDIP(ST): cohort one (2011-12) and cohort two (2012-13). Tables 16.2 and 16.3 show a sample of evaluation data collected from cohort one in this period. Means have been calculated over a four-point Likert scale, with 1 indicating "very important/prepared/very well achieved" and 4 indicating "not important/prepared/achieved."

TABLE 16.2 *Cohort one: Importance of cultural responsiveness*

Importance of:	2011-pre	2011-post	2012-end
Teaching staff valuing diverse cultures	1.43	1.34	1.12
Teaching staff respecting students' cultural background	1.59	1.65	1.65
Engaging in culturally responsive practice	1.24	1.23	1.15
Demonstrating an understanding of Māori concepts and practices as they relate to specialist area	1.37	1.28	1.32
Demonstrating an understanding of Pasifika concepts and practices as they relate to specialist area	1.46	1.40	1.48
Demonstrating an understanding of multicultural concepts and practices as they relate to specialist area	1.39	1.37	1.32
Learning about working in a culturally responsive way	1.25	1.25	1.15
Learning more about students from ethnic minority groups and how this impacts on their special needs	1.41	1.24	1.32

TABLE 16.3 *Cohort one: Achieved cultural responsiveness*

Preparedness/Achievement	2011-pre	2011-post	2012-end
Teaching staff valuing diverse cultures		1.50	1.29
Teaching staff respecting cultural background		1.75	1.41
Engaging in culturally responsive practice	2.33	1.89	1.56
Demonstrating an understanding of Māori concepts and practices as they relate to specialist area	2.61	2.11	1.79
Demonstrating an understanding of Pasifika concepts and practices as they relate to specialist area	2.96	2.46	2.41
Demonstrating an understanding of multicultural concepts and practices as they relate to specialist area	2.74	2.09	1.91
Learning about working in a culturally responsive way	2.40	1.94	1.59
Learning more about students from ethnic minority groups and how their culture impacts on their special needs and provisions for them	2.47	2.36	2.26

Figures 16.4–16.7 represent the data above for selected questions.

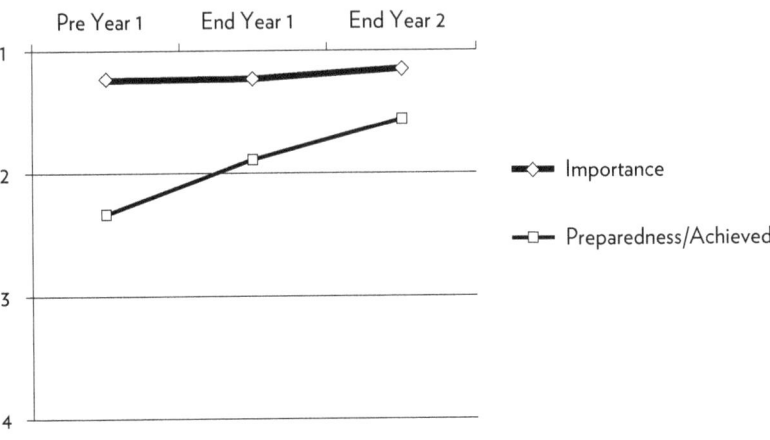

FIGURE 16.4 *Cohort one: Engaging in culturally responsive practice.*

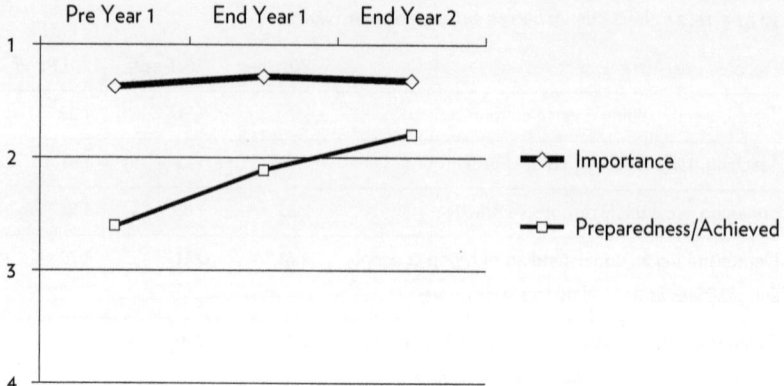

FIGURE 16.5 *Cohort one: Demonstrating an understanding of Māori concepts and practices as they relate to specialist area.*

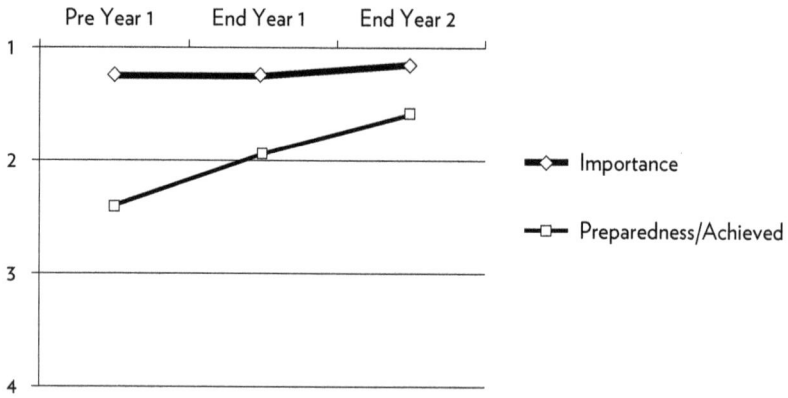

FIGURE 16.6 *Cohort one: Learning about working in a culturally responsive way.*

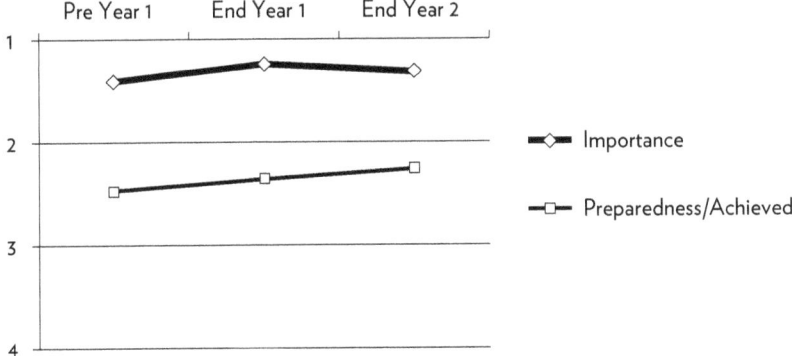

FIGURE 16.7 *Cohort one: Learning about students from ethnic minority groups and the impact of their culture.*

Figure 16.8 contains a summary of all 16 culture questions from students in the first cohort of the program.

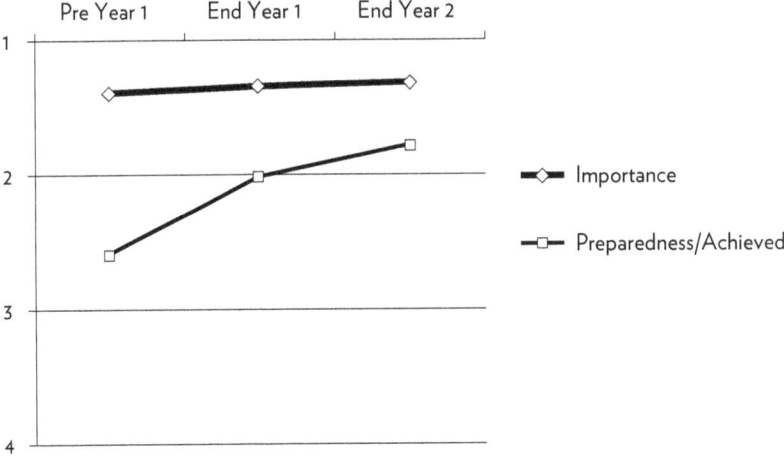

FIGURE 16.8 *Cohort one: Summary of mean responses to cultural responsiveness questions.*

Tables 16.4 and 16.5 present data collected from cohort two.

TABLE 16.4 *Cohort two: Importance of cultural responsiveness*

Importance of:	2012-pre	2012-post	2013-end
Teaching staff valuing diverse cultures	1.34	1.26	1.23
Teaching staff respecting students' cultural background	1.54	1.50	1.49
Engaging in culturally responsive practice	1.23	1.17	1.21
Demonstrating an understanding of Māori concepts and practices as they relate to specialist area	1.39	1.41	1.24
Demonstrating an understanding of Pasifika concepts and practices as they relate to specialist area	1.41	1.54	1.31
Demonstrating an understanding of multicultural concepts and practices as they relate to specialist area	1.36	1.35	1.29
Learning about working in a culturally responsive way	1.27	1.23	1.18
Learning more about students from ethnic minority groups and how their culture impacts on their special needs and provisions for them	1.28	1.32	1.32

TABLE 16.5 *Cohort two: Achieved cultural responsiveness*

Preparedness/Achievement	2012-pre	2012-post	2013-end
Teaching staff valuing diverse cultures		1.58	1.53
Teaching staff respecting cultural background		1.71	1.67
Engaging in culturally responsive practice	2.52	1.94	1.71
Demonstrating an understanding of Māori concepts and practices as they relate to specialist area	2.61	2.17	1.93
Demonstrating an understanding of Pasifika concepts and practices as they relate to specialist area	2.98	2.77	2.58
Demonstrating an understanding of multicultural concepts and practices as they relate to specialist area	2.69	2.27	2.20
Learning about working in a culturally responsive way concepts and practices as they relate to specialist area	2.28	1.89	1.74
Learning more about students from ethnic minority groups and how their culture impacts on their special needs and provisions for them	2.38	2.30	2.16

Figures 16.9 to 16.12 represent the data above for selected questions.

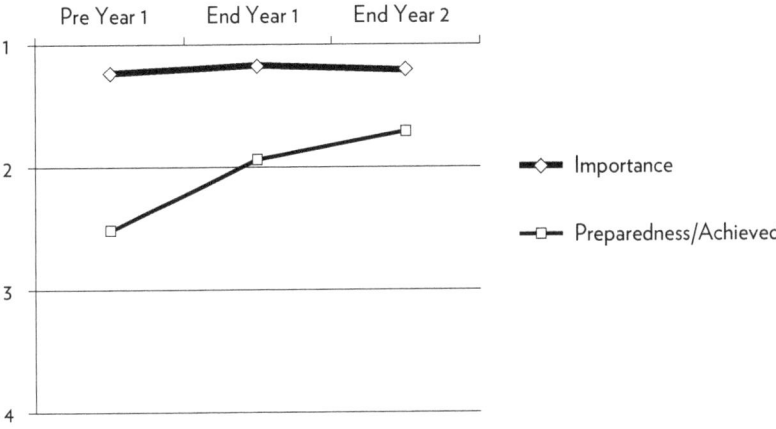

FIGURE 16.9 *Cohort two: Engaging in culturally responsive practice.*

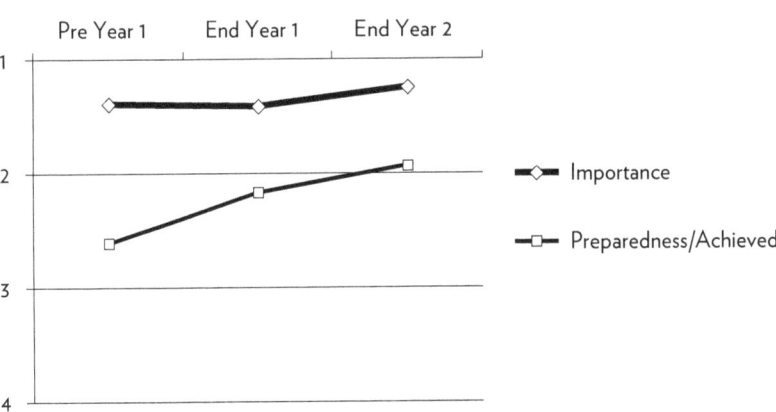

FIGURE 16.10 *Cohort two: Demonstrating an understanding of Māori concepts and practices as they relate to specialist area.*

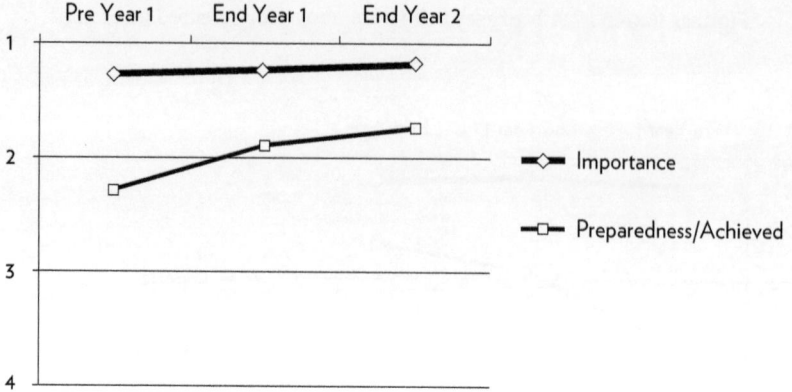

FIGURE 16.11 *Cohort two: Learning about working in a culturally responsive way.*

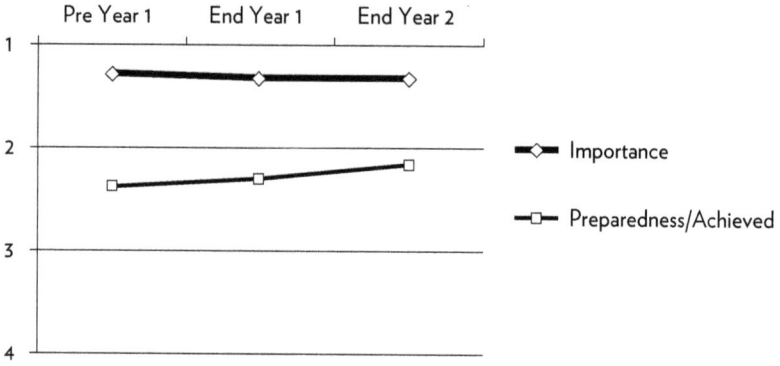

FIGURE 16.12 *Cohort two: Learning about students from ethnic minority groups and the impact of their culture.*

Figure 16.13 contains a summary of all 16 culture questions from students in the second cohort of the program.

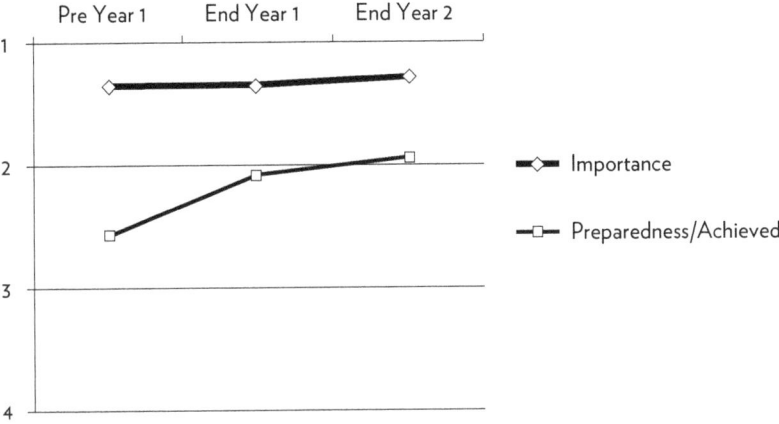

FIGURE 16.13 *Cohort two: Summary of all 16 culture questions.*

A consideration of the mean summary data of the cultural responsiveness questions for both cohorts shows that (1) students entered the course already placing a very high value on cultural responsiveness, which increased slightly over the duration of the program, and (2) in their two years of study there was a considerable increase in students' overall cultural competence score. T-tests comparing the means of students' responses at the beginning of year one and at the end of year two for both cohorts one and two showed that the increases were statistically significant with a probability value of value of $p = .001$—that is, there is a less than 0.1% likelihood that the improvements are due to chance. Interestingly, students' achieved cultural competence score is still not as high as the importance they attribute to this area, which may indicate that they could make further improvements in cultural competence in the future.

When considering individual questions over the two years in both cohorts one and two, importance scores increased in all but three areas: namely the importance placed on Pasifika concepts and practices as they related to their specialist area, and on teaching staff respecting professionals' cultural background (cohort one); and the importance placed on learning more about students from ethnic minority groups and how their culture impacts their special needs and provisions for them (cohort two). However, it should be noted that these areas were all scored highly from the outset.

In respect to what students achieved, in both cohorts all 32 questions showed increases over the two years. T-test scores showed that these increases were statistically significant for questions relating to engaging in culturally responsive practice, demonstrating an understanding of Māori concepts and practices as they relate to the student's specialist area, demonstrating an understanding of Pasifika concepts and practices as they relate to the student's specialist area, demonstrating an understanding of multicultural concepts and practices as they relate to the student's specialist area, and learning about working in a culturally responsive way.

Deaf and Hearing Impairment Endorsement (D & HI)

> Imagine you are at the *tangi* of a loved one. The *kuia* calls you on; the old men address the visitors; and all around you, the people grieve and cry. Now imagine you see all that is going on—but you cannot hear. This is how it feels to be one of New Zealand's...Māori Deaf, born into a culture that is oral and aural at its core. (Cohort two, student 19)[5]

This quote is the introduction to a set task in the D & HI endorsement. In 2012 the cultural responsiveness domain contained activities and associated resources relating to deaf Māori children and those from other ethnic minority cultures. Informed by supplied readings and video clips, students were required to post reflections on and discussion of key issues for deaf Māori; how, as teachers of the Deaf, they could uphold the rights and dignity of Māori in their work; key issues for deaf children from other cultural groups; and what was needed to ensure the availability of culturally appropriate education and support for these children.

An analysis of all D & HI fora posts showed:

- In-depth discussion of a wide range of issues and culturally relevant strategies for working with Māori, Pasifika, and multiethnic deaf students;
- Sharing of personal experiences of working with deaf Māori and their whānau and with deaf children and parents from other cultural groups;
- analysis of key education documents and policies and their relevance to deaf Māori (e.g., *The Teachers Council Code of Ethics, Tātaiako: Cultural Competencies for Teachers of Māori Learners*, and *Ka Hikitia: The Māori Education Strategy*);
- Discussion of historic events and their impact on deaf Māori;
- Sharing of a wide variety of resources including culturally relevant journal articles, reports, TV documentaries, YouTube and other video clips, trilingual resources, a dictionary with Māori/English/New Zealand Sign Language (NZSL), and useful websites including interactive sites for learning te reo Māori;
- Sharing of information from relevant interviews, observations, and visits;
- Explanation of NZSL and its inclusion of Māori terminology;
- Sharing of a signed mihi used when working with Māori students and whānau.

However, the single most impressive aspect of the students' posts was the extent to which they had used the multitude of resources identified to develop their understanding of the importance and complexity of providing a culturally responsive education to Māori and multicultural deaf students and the formulation of their own personal plans to do so.

Learning and Behaviour

This endorsement has a range of voluntary activities in each domain. Students set their own learning goals and then complete activities that will assist them to achieve these goals. In 2012, although cultural content was included in all domains, two domains were dedicated specifically to Māori and general cultural influences. They contained eight activities. The 38 students in this cohort contributed 162 posts in response to the tasks set.

The first activity in the Māori domain was related to professional and Māori-specific standards. Students were asked to locate a Māori-specific standard within one of the seven professional standards in the Resource Teacher: Learning and Behaviour (RTLB) toolkit. They were then required to reflect on what the selected standard meant to them professionally and to compose a reflective question that they would use when trying to achieve that standard. Nineteen students completed this activity. Table 16.6 presents the post from student 101 in cohort two.

The other four activities in the Māori domain were related to the following:

- Differing cultural perceptions: Based on a set reading that discussed culturally linked ways of thinking, students were asked to think of an example where their perception was different from that of a family they had worked with and to reflect on how it made them feel and act. An example given was when a child avoided eye contact—the whānau view was that he or she was being respectful; the specialist view was that he or she was being defiant.
- The impact of Māori worldviews: Students were asked to consider how Māori worldviews impacted how they might approach the Māori family of a child with learning and/or behavioural challenges. They were required to identify three specific examples using Durie's (1985) whare tapa whā model as a guide. The role of grandparents or extended whānau was cited as one example that could be included in te taha whānau.

TABLE 16.6 *Reflections from a student in cohort two*

Relationship Management Standard

RTLB Professional Standard	Māori-Specific Standard	Reflective Questions
consultation collaboration, facilitation responsiveness	cultural sensitivity and an understanding of Treaty of Waitangi culturally responsive	Am I committed to the Māori Education Strategy: Ka Hikitia and focusing on realizing potential, identifying opportunities, collaborating, and co-constructing when working with students and whānau?
		Am I helping to develop and strengthen relationships based on mutual trust between student/whānau and teachers/school?
		Am I valuing the culture of the students and seeing it as a cultural advantage? Am I listening to their voice?

- *He tikanga whakaaro* and key competencies: Thinking of a specific child they had worked with, students were asked to select one of the tikanga whakaaro competencies listed and to describe what they had done to promote the chosen competency for the child.
- Applicability of Treaty of Waitangi principles: Students were asked to reflect on and record how Treaty of Waitangi principles might guide and inform their practice. They were also asked to consider

the different meanings of "equality" and "equity" and why the latter had been preferred in a particular piece of writing.

Answers to the activities above were posted in open fora. Not only was the quality of shared work very high, but the discussion that ensued was evidence of in-depth reflection and clarity of understanding.

Practicum Involvement

Blind and Low Vision (B & LV)

The students' practicum experience provided them with the opportunity to learn from practitioners in the field, put their own learning into practice, and try various resources they had discovered and/or developed. A good example of the latter is the booklet written by student 22 in cohort one of the B & LV endorsement. Not only was it used in her practicum but it was also shared with, and is being used by, her fellow students and Resource Teachers: Vision (RTV) throughout Aotearoa New Zealand.

In their practicum, students in this cohort also reported:

- Working with Māori children with vision impairments;
- Interviews with whānau to discuss ways of making the IEP process more user-friendly;
- Interviewing a resource teacher of Māori;
- Observations of a bilingual functional vision assessment by an experienced practitioner;
- Observations at Te Kura Kaupapa Māori o Ngāti Kahungunu o te Wairoa;
- Discussion of the Tātaiako document;
- Identifying resources to use in Māori Immersion education, including a Braille tactile book in Māori;
- A visit to the Gisborne Visual Resource Centre;
- Compilation of *karakia* and language ideas.

Such experiences and activities all contributed to building students' cultural confidence and competence.

All Endorsements

Similarly, across all endorsements students reported a range of activities that were evidence of their increased cultural responsiveness. These included adapting programs to include cultural content, accompanying host schools on *marae* visits, developing a Makaton sign dictionary in Māori, lobbying for the development and sharing of Māori resources, and contributing to Māori-focused professional workshops. An excellent example of the latter was reported by a student who was a speech language therapist. She went out of her "comfort zone" by seeking a practicum experience in a kura kaupapa Māori. Her request was initially met with suspicion and reluctance. However, she persevered and ended up working in the kura (school), assisting teachers with children with speech language difficulties, and running a workshop for Māori immersion teachers. The approval and respect she earned were evidenced in the glowing feedback included in her practicum portfolio.

This portfolio is the final practicum assignment. It outlines what students did on their practicum, and contains reflections on the experience and supporting evidence such as resources developed, colleagues' feedback sheets, journal notes, photo artifacts, observation sheets, and so forth. Feedback from assignment markers frequently includes comments about the strength of cultural content and the effectiveness of students' culturally responsive practices across a wide range of cultures.

Post-Course Activities

A strong measure of the effectiveness of the PGDIP (ST) is the degree to which students put their increased cultural competence into practice in their own work situations, both during the course and once they have qualified. Unfortunately, there is presently no research or other formal means of gauging this input. However, PGDIP (ST) staff regularly receive incidental reports from past students and people with whom they are associated about their successful practice. Apart from their own culturally responsive practice, there is anecdotal evidence of past students' further achievements:

- Enrolling in Māori language courses;
- Enrolling in master's level courses that include cultural content;
- Publishing culture-specific material from their studies;
- Providing cultural guidance and resources as field/practicum advisors;
- Providing cultural guidance and resources to their colleagues;
- Delivering culture-specific conference presentations and workshops in Aotearoa New Zealand and overseas;
- Joining the Māori, Pasifika, and multiethnic advisory committee for the PGDIP (ST).

Conclusion

Waitoller and Artiles (2013) advocate for a multifocal, intersectional approach to professional development that equips professionals to identify, understand, and dismantle the multiple barriers to learning and participation experienced by students. This chapter supports their stance and describes the role the PGDIP (ST) is playing in equipping professionals to understand the multidimensional nature of exclusion. Going one step further, it also helps students to provide a culturally responsive, strengths-based education that celebrates cultural diversity.

For Māori children with special education needs, professionals must consider these needs from a Māori perspective and base assessments, programs, services, and resources on the underlying principles of kaupapa Māori, importance, relevance and beneficence, participation, empowerment, tino rangatiratanga and Māori control, accountability, high quality, appropriate personnel, equality, and accessibility. When this is done, Māori children with special education needs will experience a smooth, successful, and enjoyable ride on a well-equipped waka.

Notes

1. For a list and discussion of the personal, professional, and cultural expertise required, see chapter 9 of Bevan-Brown (2002).
2. The author would like to acknowledge all those involved in developing and delivering the PGDIP (ST) reported in this section. This qualification is truly a collaborative endeavour and its success is attributed to all those who have and are still contributing to it—Julia Budd, Philippa Butler, Vijaya Dharan, Maggie Hefer, Wendy Holley-Boen, Garry Hornby, Alison Kearney, Jude MacArthur, Sonja Macfarlane, Helen Mataiti, Laurie McLay, Mandia Mentis, Marcia Pilgrim, Denise Powell, Tracy Riley, Dean Sutherland, Desley Tucker, and Anne van Bysterveldt. In particular, acknowledgement must go to Associate Professor Mandia Mentis whose inspiration and ideas are foundational to the structure of the qualification and whose continuing input drives its evolution and success; Dr. Alison Kearney for her unwavering leadership as director of the program; and Dr. Sonja Macfarlane, who has provided strong and consistent Māori input and support.
3. More information about the PGDIP (ST) can be found by clicking on the "about" button on the course website, http://masseyuniversity.mrooms.net/.
4. Quotations from PGDIP (ST) instructions are from the original version of the online study material available to enrolled students.
5. Permission to include this quote has been given by the student concerned, as is the case for all student work included in this chapter.

References

Artiles, Alfredo J. 2000. "The Inclusive Education Movement and Minority Representation in Special Education: Trends, Paradoxes and Dilemmas." Keynote address to the International Special Education Conference, Manchester, UK, July 2000.

Bevan-Brown, Jill M. 2002. "Culturally Appropriate, Effective Provision for Māori Learners with Special Education Needs: He Waka Tino Whakarawea." PHD diss., Massey University.

———. 2009. *Māori Learners with Special Needs*. Saarbrucken, Germany: Lambert Academic Publishing.

Bishop, Russell, and Ted Glynn. 1999. *Culture Counts: Changing Power Relations in Education*. Palmerston North, NZ: Dunmore Press.

Blanchett, Wanda J. 2006. "Disproportionate Representation of African American Students in Special Education: Acknowledging the Role of White Privilege and Racism." *Educational Researcher* 35 (6): 24-8. https://doi.org/10.3102%2F0013189X035006024

Bruce, Susan M., and Kavita Venkatesh. 2014. "Special Education Disproportionality in the United States, Germany, Kenya, and India." *Disability and Society* 29 (6): 908-21. https://doi.org/10.1080/09687599.2014.880330

Codrington, Jamila. 2014. "Sharpening the Lens of Culturally Responsive Science Teaching: A Call for Liberatory Education for Oppressed Student Groups." *Cultural Studies of Science Education* 9 (4): 1015-24. https://doi.org/10.1007/s11422-013-9543-2

Crenshaw, Kimberle. 1991. "Mapping the Margins: Intersectionality, Identity Politics, and Violence Against Women of Color." *Stanford Law Review* 43 (6): 1241-99. http://doi.org/10.2307/1229039

Department of Justice. 1989. *Principles of Crown Action on the Treaty of Waitangi*. Wellington, NZ: Author.

Durie, Mason H. 1985. "A Māori Perspective of Health." *Social Science & Medicine* 20 (5): 483-6. http://doi.org/10.1016/0277-9536(85)90363-6

———. 1995. *Ngā Matatini Māori: Diverse Māori Realities*. Report to the Ministry of Health. Palmerston North, NZ: Massey University, Te Pūmanawa Hauora, Department of Māori Studies.

Gay, Geneva. 2002. "Culturally Responsive Teaching in Special Education for Ethnically Diverse Students: Setting the Stage." *International Journal of Qualitative Studies in Education* 15 (6): 613-29. https://doi.org/10.1080/0951839022000014349

Graham, Linda J. 2012. "Disproportionate Over-Representation of Indigenous Students in New South Wales Government Special Schools." *Cambridge Journal of Education* 42 (2): 163-76. https://doi.org/10.1080/0305764X.2012.676625

Hancock, Ange-Marie. 2007. "When Multiplication Doesn't Equal Quick Addition: Examining Intersectionality as a Research Paradigm." *Perspectives on Politics* 5: 63-79. https://doi.org/10.1017/S1537592707070065

Howard, Tyrone C. 2010. "Developing Cultural Competence and Racial Awareness in Classroom Teachers." In *Why Race and Culture Matter in Schools: Closing the Achievement Gap in America's Classrooms*, edited by Tyrone C. Howard, 111-28. New York: Teachers College Press.

Idrus, Faizah. 2014. "Initiating Culturally Responsive Teaching for Identity Construction in the Malaysian Classrooms." *English Language Teaching* 7 (4): 53-63. https://doi.org/10.5539/elt.v7n4p53

Kingi, Jo, and Anne Bray. 2000. *Māori Concepts of Disability*. Dunedin, NZ: Donald Beasley Institute.

Klingner, Janette K., Alfredo J. Artiles, Elizabeth Kozleski, Beth Harry, Shelley Zion, William Tate, Grace Zamora Durán, and David Riley. 2005. "Addressing the Disproportionate Representation of Culturally and Linguistically Diverse Students in Special Education through Culturally Responsive Educational Systems." *Education Policy Analysis Archives* 13 (38): 1-40. http://dx.doi.org/10.14507/epaa.v13n38.2005

Lynch, Eleanor, and Marci Hanson, eds. 1992. *Developing Cross-cultural Competence: A Guide for Working with Young Children and Their Families*. Baltimore, MD: Paul H. Brookes.

McCarty, Teresa L., and Tiffany S. Lee. 2014. "Critical Culturally Sustaining/Revitalizing Pedagogy and Indigenous Education Sovereignty." *Harvard Educational Review* 84 (1): 101-24. https://doi.org/10.17763/haer.84.1.q83746nl5pj3421

Meyer, Luanna, Jill Bevan-Brown, Hyun-Sook Park, and Catherine Savage. 2013. "School Inclusion and Multicultural Issues in Special Education." In *Multicultural Education: Issues and Perspectives*, 8th ed., edited by James Banks and Cherry A. McGee Banks, 269-89. Hoboken, NJ: John Wiley & Sons.

Owens, Kay. 2014. "Changing the Teaching of Mathematics for Improved Indigenous Education in a Rural Australian City." *Journal of Mathematics Teacher Education* 18 (1): 53-78. https://doi.org/10.1007/s10857-014-9271-x

Ratima, Mihi M., Mason H. Durie, G.T. Allan, P.S. Morrison, A. Gillies, and J.A. Waldon. 1995. *He Anga Whakamana: A Framework for the Delivery of Disability Support Services for Māori*. Palmerston, NZ: Massey University, Te Pumanawa Hauora, Department of Māori Studies.

Tau, T.M. 1999. "Mātauranga Māori as an Epistemology." *Te Pouhere Kōrero* 1 (1): 10-23. http://doi.org/10.7810/9781877242205_3

UNESCO. 2005. *Guidelines for Inclusion: Ensuring Access to Education for All*. Paris: UNESCO.

Waitoller, Federico R., and Alfredo Artiles. 2013. "A Decade of Professional Development Research for Inclusive Education: A Critical Review and Notes for a Research Program." *Review of Educational Research* 83 (3): 319-56. https://doi.org/10.3102%2F0034654313483905

17 | Maintaining Indigeneity within Education and Broader Contexts

WIREMU DOHERTY

THIS CHAPTER SUPPORTS THE IDEA that context is a critical component that must be understood in a teaching and learning environment. Māori and Tūhoe[1] will be used as the illustrative site for this chapter; it will draw on the cultural elements that have been used to maintain both a physical and a cognitive connection to the space and places that inform the context for Māori. The theoretical methodology is drawn from kaupapa Māori.

Kaupapa Māori

Kaupapa Māori theory is a political instrument that takes account of the unequal power relations that exist between Māori and Pākehā (Europeans). It critically responds to the processes of colonization, which have been embedded in "taken-for-granted" practices and ideas within the schooling and education system. Kaupapa Māori theory attempts to provide a space outside assimilation, acculturation, exploitation, domination of Māori by Pākehā, and Pākehā knowledge hegemony.

Kaupapa Māori theory describes the transformational shifts that are required to respond to unequal power relations. The transformational shifts required and explored under the concept of kaupapa Māori theory are taken from the tradition of critical theory, using Māori and non-Māori theoretical tools (Smith 1997). Critical theory underpins kaupapa Māori theory because it focuses on emancipatory outcomes and provides an approach to a range of challenges facing Māori, including neo-liberal economics, the reification of science over culture, the rise of technological rationality, the pressure to develop a structural analysis rather than only a culturalist one, and the need for social transformation.

In explaining the need for kaupapa Māori theory, Smith (1997) uses the analogy of "shadow paintings" of tools on the garage wall. In the university/academic environment, we have lots of Western tools hanging on the wall at our disposal. From time to time, however, when we are working on specific Māori issues, the available tools do not quite fit. Smith argues for the need to add specific "Māori theoretical tools" to the wall—the best tools to get the job done.

By using specific Māori theoretical tools, kaupapa Māori theory allows the assertion of the validity and legitimacy of Māori knowledge, language, culture, and practice as "taken-for-granted" givens. In this sense, kaupapa Māori theory, both in its theoretical and practical dimensions, is about making legitimate space for *mātauranga Māori* (Māori knowledge; Smith 1997). Kaupapa Māori theory has allowed the creation of total immersion schools using Māori language and culture to emerge onto the New Zealand educational landscape. This introduced the concept of "mainstream" schooling, to distinguish schools different from total immersion schooling.

Māori were outside the mainstream and Pākeha were within the mainstream. Historical accounts in New Zealand have tended to view Māori history from this mainstream perspective, and have tried to understand Māori through Pākeha perspectives or lenses. From this position, Māori are viewed from a non-Māori perspective in an attempt to comprehend the Māori world.

Elsdon Best[2] (1972) described a Māori way of life as a mythological and quaint folklore not to be placed seriously in the same category as Western accounts of history. Best found it difficult to rationalize Tūhoe history from his perspective. During the early stages of his writing he was relying on Pākeha lenses to understand elements of Tūhoe epistemology and, because he was unable to comprehend it, he marginalized it, diminishing it as an absurdity.

Marie Battiste and James (Sákéj) Youngblood Henderson (2003) highlight the dilemma of using a non-Indigenous theoretical base to explain what Indigenous knowledge is: Indigenous knowledge is difficult for non-Europeans to comprehend because Eurocentric thought has created a mysticism around Indigenous knowledge that distances the outsider from Indigenous Peoples and what they know.

Kaupapa Māori theory made it possible to create a series of Māori lenses to view and describe Māori. This perspective clarified and intensified the focus, highlighting that Māori are not a homogeneous group. Māori are an eclectic grouping of tribes that have unique stories and histories. Mātauranga Māori is a summary of tribal knowledge that has been collectively called Māori. Kaupapa Māori theory provided the space to build the lenses required to see mātauranga Māori and *mātauranga-a-iwi* (tribal knowledge). Mātauranga-a-iwi has always been there, and kaupapa Māori theory created the space to allow the transformational shifts that need to occur when moving between these knowledge forms.

Applying the lenses created in kaupapa Māori theory enabled a sharper focus so that mātauranga Māori could "see" mātauranga-a-iwi. Kaupapa Māori theory enabled a Māori understanding of the term Māori. For Māori, the term Māori does not always imply a homogeneous approach; instead, whichever *iwi* (tribe) occupies the district you are in is taken as Māori. Māori operate in a world of diverse realities, and what is taken as Māori differs from iwi to iwi (Rangihau 1975).

Kaupapa Māori theory has made it possible to describe Māori without leaving a Māori context that was not readily applicable from a non-Māori world view. These Māori contexts are described by the terms mātauranga Māori and mātauranga-a-iwi.

Mātauranga Māori

Mātauranga Māori is defined as "Māori knowledge." It is a term that places importance on Māori histories, knowledge, and language; it refers to the Māori way of thinking, doing, and acting (Mead 1997; Smith 1997). Mātauranga Māori bridges both traditional and contemporary Māori knowledge curriculum, pedagogy, and philosophy. It is through mātauranga Māori that histories and knowledge within Māori education are uncompromisingly told.

Educational structures that have developed and evolved under the aegis of mātauranga Māori are the *kura kaupapa Māori* (total immersion schools), *te kōhanga reo* (total immersion preschools), and *wānanga* (universities) that are based on Māori epistemologies. These are sites of learning that hold Māori tradition, customs, and language as the core curriculum validating Māori knowledge. The basis of the Māori curriculum is informed by mātauranga Māori. The curriculum within these Māori educational settings places importance on Māori histories, knowledge, and language; it enables Māori processes of learning and teaching, or *ako*. This term describes both teaching and learning, recognizing the fact that in teaching, one is still learning. Teaching mātauranga Māori removed Māori histories from being labelled merely "myth and legend," repositioning Māori knowledge onto a legitimate epistemological base.

Mātauranga Māori hosts the core values and principles that apply to all Māori. While the core values and principles are located here, their application is not. The application of these values and principles are filtered through mātauranga-a-iwi. Each iwi has their own specific sense and use of these core values and principles that link them with their particular environment. This tribal application cannot be applied to another tribe, as they will have their own application that links them to their environment and iwi. Because the application cannot be located in the broader term mātauranga Māori, it is presented as de-contextual knowledge.

Mātauranga-a-Iwi

Mātauranga-a-iwi is tribal knowledge. Tribal knowledge is defined as the relationship between the tribe and its land base. Mātauranga-a-iwi is knowledge specific to an iwi and its rohe. It is the exchange between the rohe and the iwi that provides the context for mātauranga-a-iwi. As the iwi engages with and describes its environment, the basis for mātauranga-a-iwi is established. The application of the principles and values in mātauranga Māori occurs, though each iwi has its own particular process that links their particular rohe and people together.

Each tribe has its own version of knowledge that defines the application of the values and principles in mātauranga Māori. An in-depth study of mātauranga Māori produces mātauranga-a-iwi. This is not in order to replace or undermine mātauranga Māori; rather it is to provide the depth and wider explanation of mātauranga Māori. Mātauranga Māori is premised on mātauranga-a-iwi; this is where the deeper explanations, meanings, and signposts are found to the many questions raised within mātauranga Māori. The interaction the tribe has with its environment, expressed using its language, shapes and forms the epistemology of that particular tribe. The link that is created here establishes the context for mātauranga-a-iwi to exist.

Examples of Mātauranga-a-Iwi

Examples of mātauranga-a-iwi can be found by analyzing particular terms that have been purposefully used. The following examples have been drawn from my particular background, which is Tūhoe, where the naming of the forest (*ngahere*) and certain plants that grow there has been deliberate. An analysis of the terms provides an insight into the mātauranga-a-iwi that is located there.

Ngahere

Ngahere is the term given to describe the forest. The word has two parts to it: *ngā* (plural) and *here* (connections), drawing out the understanding that ngahere is describing the multitude of connections. In doing so it reminds us we have a connection to the elements that grow there. The name reminds us we have a genealogical connection through the creator of the forests,[3] who later created the first human.

Kauri

Moving into the actual ngahere we see a similar theme occurring in the deliberate naming of trees and vines. In particular the tree, *kauri*, again has two elements to it: *ka* is a sentence particle, and *uri* is "relation," creating the meaning of "to be related." This tree is reminding us that we are indeed related and share a common ancestor through Tane.

Pirita

Pirita (supple jack) is a vine whose name describes its pattern of growth: it spreads out from a central point and takes hold of the neighbouring plants, and continues to spread from each of the plants that have been connected to the central plant, emanating outwards and creating a web whereby everything is connected. This action is described in the name, *piri* (stick) and *ta* (together), which reminds us that as people we must maintain a certain level of contact with each other.

Ahika

The term *ahika* is used to refer to one's occupation over the traditional lands; the name describes burning fires: *ahi* (fire) and *ka* (burning). Where maintaining a claim to the ancestral lands requires a continued presence by the people, the naming of this concept "ahika" was deliberate. The general translation has been explained as maintaining the home fires. From a Tūhoe perspective this concept is derived from the particular use of a fungus, *pukutawai*, that grows on the *tawai* (beech) tree. The pukutawai fungus absorbs water and sap from the tawai until it becomes too heavy for the branches to sustain the weight. Then it drops to the ground, where it is harvested and dried. When dried, it has a consistency similar to polystyrene. This dried fungus is placed into a hole approximately half a metre deep, and a glowing ember is taken from the main fire in the settlement and placed on top of the fungus now located in the hole. After several minutes the ember begins to smoulder and sinks into the fungus, at which point the hole is covered and the fungus with the smouldering ember is buried. This was normally done as the community prepared to relocate to the next site of settlement, largely driven by the availability of certain foods or particular weather conditions. When the community returned to the site the following season, the buried fungus would be unearthed and placed into the fireplace with kindling where, exposed to the air again, it would resume smouldering and eventually flame a fire into life. The fire for this season's occupation was, therefore, begun from an ember taken from last season's fire, and would burn continuously while the site was occupied, hence the term ahika: the continuous burning fires. It is from this position the term ahika is used to describe the occupation of the ancestral lands, in that the people's occupation of ancestral settlements was maintained through the smouldering ember, which waited for the people to return to reignite the fires from previous seasons.

The connection between the iwi and their landscape informs mātauranga-a-iwi, which produces contextual knowledge. This is different from mātauranga Māori, which, as an amalgam of numerous tribes with their numerous land bases, is difficult to link to a particular land base. Such a generic approach, with mātauranga Māori existing outside its tribal context, produces de-contextual knowledge. Proper explanations of Māori processes cannot be given in mātauranga Māori; these are located within mātauranga-a-iwi. An example of this is the formal welcoming principle, *pōwhiri*. All Māori use this principle of action; however, the application of the principle differs markedly from iwi to iwi. This variance cannot be understood within the framework of mātauranga Māori. What is required is an iwi explanation to provide the rationale as to why a particular process was used. Explaining the application of pōwhiri within an iwi context will provide a rationale linked to that iwi and its region. My own iwi, Tūhoe, does not allow pōwhiri to take place after nightfall; other iwi do. This deviation occurred early in Tūhoe history when the tribe was still known as Ngā Pōtiki.[4] A Ngā Pōtiki *marae* was expecting the return of a food-gathering party but, unbeknownst to the expectant marae, the group had been killed. The marauders knew the marae would be expecting the slain group's return, and so waited until the onset of nightfall to enter the marae. The marae, seeing a group returning at nightfall, assumed it was the food-gathering party returning and took no precautions. The marae was attacked and destroyed. As a result, Tūhoe do not allow pōwhiri to occur at night. The relationship with the environment and the people of Tūhoe has shaped and adapted the principle of pōwhiri.

Whakapapa and Tūrangawaewae

The connection between the people and the tribal environment (rohe) is managed through the term *whakapapa* (genealogy). Te Urewera is the territory that Tūhoe occupies, and through whakapapa Tūhoe genealogically connects to Te Urewera. It is the land base that builds the identity for Tūhoe. It was the interaction Tūhoe has with its land base that established Tūhoe as a distinct grouping of people, different from other tribes. It is the connection to the land base that provides the platform for Tūhoe to build its identity; this is the *tūrangawaewae* (place of standing), this is the Tūhoe comfort zone. It is within the space, place, and environment of Te Urewera that Tūhoe gains its identity, which is unique to Tūhoe. This is the context for mātauranga-a-iwi. The rationale behind the application of the principles and values expressed in mātauranga Māori are found here. The rationale is expressed in the relationship that the tribe has with its tribal environment. The applications of the principles and values have their context defined by the rohe. The purpose and reason for the values and principles is defined here as knowledge. Within the context of the tribal lands, this knowledge strand is contextual knowledge; it is expressed within its own environment, as opposed to mātauranga Māori, which is de-contextual, operating outside of its context. Within this strand a more authentic understanding of Māori is reached; it defines Māori as a tribal grouping with subsets of *hapū* (sub-tribes) and *whānau* (families).

The term whakapapa is commonly used to describe genealogical connections between people. However, my argument from a mātauranga-a-iwi base is that whakapapa maps epistemologies (including tribal concepts, principles, ideas, and related practices) and locates them within a particular context. Whakapapa will map the inception of a concept, identify the reason and purpose for the idea, and track its changes that have occurred to date. Whakapapa links people and the landscape together within and through concepts or ideas.

To more fully understand the impact of whakapapa, the relationship of past to present is important. To describe the past is to state *i ngā ra o mua* (the days that hang in front of [me]). Māori are walking backwards into the future; the days that have passed hang in front, and the future is behind. When analyzing a particular concept by reference to whakapapa, the sequential order of events that have occurred to form that concept or meaning are laid out "in front of you" to provide the historical context showing the purpose and reason for the existence of the concept, idea, or principle, and how this relates to the iwi and rohe.

To link a particular practice or concept to an iwi or rohe requires an intimate understanding of the people and land they occupy. If concepts cannot be linked to the iwi and/or rohe it is likely the practice or concept is not Indigenous to the area, but imported.

When the concept of whakapapa is applied to knowledge it creates the connection to the tribal lands (rohe), and to the individual. Whakapapa indicates the rationale behind different tribal practices by showing the sequential order of events required for tribal knowledge. Within this sequential order of events, why the practice was created and how it was established will be shown.

Mauri

The term whakapapa describes the sequential order of events; the component that links these events is *mauri*. Mauri is the component that creates the linkage that is described in whakapapa. Every single object within Tūhoe has a mauri. The clue to the meaning and understanding of the term mauri becomes clear when analyzing the word: from *ma* (by), *uri* (relation), we can extrapolate the meaning as the relationships that occur between objects. To fully understand my perspective of mauri we need to return to the term whakapapa, which, in my view, comes from the term *raupapa*: to lay things out in the sequential order of events that created them. To ensure these elements are linked and do not exist mutually exclusive of each other, it is mauri that links them. Mauri describes the relationship that occurs between every object and aspect in mātauranga-a-iwi. If a connection is not made through whakapapa, it is more than likely an imported idea from another epistemology. It is the linkages expressed in whakapapa and mauri that locate and identify knowledge within the tribal landscape and, ultimately, the people of the tribe. It is through mauri that whakapapa is realized—the stages of physical development and cognitive development that place the individual physically and cognitively on a continuum in relation to the knowledge, culture, and discourse of the tribe. It is through mauri and whakapapa that connections to tribal lands and boundaries become visible, as mātauranga-a-iwi is inextricably connected back to the tribal lands. It is through this connection that identity is made with the tribe. Using the principles of whakapapa to highlight the sequential order of events provides a particular connection to the landscape, the people, and, more broadly, to a tribal epistemology. The links expressed by mauri linking the stages of development described in whakapapa produce a tribal holistic view. People, knowledge, and the landscape must be linked, and mauri and whakapapa map this development.

While whakapapa locates the individual as a member of the tribe, particular attention needs to be maintained to ensure a continued physical connection to the district and people. Continued appearance and presence in the rohe is to maintain the currency of public discourse that takes place on the marae, which in part ensures the existence of knowledge of peers and other members of the tribe. In doing this, iwi are able to continue to draw the whakapapa links that illustrate and maintain a tribal connectivity.

Contextual Knowledge

Whakapapa establishes the sequential order of events for mātauranga-a-iwi, from inception through to the current agreed practice for the iwi. Mātauranga-a-iwi must have a whakapapa that links it to the rohe and the iwi for it to be termed mātauranga-a-iwi. This link not only provides the evidence to support iwi ownership of a particular practice; it also places the learner and knowledge into context. Through whakapapa, three important elements—people, land, and knowledge—are linked together, providing the context for each to exist. This is mātauranga-a-iwi. It is contextual knowledge.

De-Contextual Knowledge

Early recordings of Māori knowledge taken from tribal districts were later confused when sections of differing tribal accounts were combined by Pākehā anthropologists, altering what was once a true tribal component of knowledge. This resulted in a series of muddled stories that became termed "myths and legends of the Māori." These versions had lost their true tribal context; they had become de-contextualized. The explicit link to a particular territory and people occupying the sites these accounts were based on became obscure and confused; they were removed from the people and landscape they were intended for. This "de-contextual" knowledge has significantly contributed to what is now often termed mātauranga Māori. When properly located within their environment, historical accounts form the basis of mātauranga-a-iwi. This is knowledge that is described within its own context and is a lived reality. It has not been confused by unknowingly drawing from other tribal knowledge.

Returning to the notion that context matters, the key terms that have been presented so far are examples highlighting practices that maintain a connection to space and place. While some of these processes may not be immediately visible, they will become clearer when an analysis of the deliberately named elements is undertaken; the deeper meaning and intent becomes clear. The concept of tūrangawaewae (place of standing) is often used to describe the physical place where, through whakapapa, one is able to physically locate themselves, and thus track the sequential order of events that have occurred to the present. While the term has been applied in the physical sense, there is also a cognitive space and place that is referred to here by the term tūrangawaewae. This is the "comfort zone" to which one reverts to cognitively process ideas; the cognitive space is inextricably linked to the physical space and place that is informed by the physical relationship that occurs between people and the environment.

Through the terms of whakapapa—sequential order of events, physical and cognitive, linked through mauri—every element is aware of its physical and cognitive connections when mapped, providing the critical elements to establish the tūrangawaewae.

To briefly summarize what we have covered so far, mātauranga-a-iwi is presented as contextual knowledge. Through the terms whakapapa and mauri, physical and cognitive connections are made to the tūrangawaewae; physically it refers to the rohe land district, and cognitively it refers to mātauranga-a-iwi. It is this process that maps the cognitive and physical context for tribal knowledge that I argue is a critical component that must be understood in the teaching and learning environment. By understanding the context, learners are able to locate themselves in relation to what is being taught, and in doing so draw the relevant connections to learner and content. As a secondary school teacher, I would repeatedly hear students ask, "What does this have to do with me?" as they struggled to understand new ideas and content. Where the process of mapping and contextualizing knowledge occurs through the critical elements of whakapapa and mauri, engaging these concepts through the sequential order of events and understanding the relationship responsibilities required through mauri, the introductions of new content can be managed.

The examples provided earlier in this section have been presented to show how the connection to context is maintained, but it is important to point out they were also the elements required to map the creation or establishment of a "new" context, needed for introducing new content to students. It is important to highlight here that while the elements provided refer to historical points of reference that connect the people and land, there are also processes that establish connections to "new spaces and places"; when taken through a process, the "new" elements are connected to the "old" elements. Mapping the sequential order of events outlines the process of introducing the "old" to the "new," establishing a new addition to the context.

The next section will show how this process occurred with a summarized version of the arrival of the ancestral Mataatua waka into the current township of Whakatane.

Mataatua: Creating the "New" Context

This section will explore the notion of creating a new context by following the key points of engagement that occurred as the ancestral canoe Mataatua made its way here from the outer parts of the Polynesian Triangle in the early part of the 12th century AD.

This version is taken from a Tūhoe perspective; other tribal regions will have their own nuanced version as will have been told to them from the perspective of their ancestors. It is another example of matauranga-a-iwi.

This account starts some 200 years earlier, around 1150 AD, with an ancestor, Toi, and his pregnant partner at the time, Te Kuraimonoa, who are living in a settlement of Oropoā on Taputapu-atea Island, around the Tahiti islands. While here, his grandchildren, Whatonga and Rahui, participate in inter-island racing. Their waka is damaged and they decide to land on Rangiatea to repair it.

Meanwhile back on Taputapu-atea, Toi and a heavily pregnant Te Kuraimonoa are concerned and set sail on their waka, Aratauwhaiti, in search of their grandchildren. The waka Aratauwhaiti eventually makes landfall at Te Aurere in the northland of New Zealand, where Te Kuraimonoa goes into labour; up to this point, Toi had had concerns of the paternity of his partner's child. At the birth of his son, however, the concerns Toi had about paternity are immediately dismissed, and his tears of relief fall like great waters from the sky as he names his son Awanuiārangi. At the birth of Awanuiārangi, Te Kuraimonoa returns to Taputapu-atea and leaves Toi to continue the journey in search of Whatonga and Rahui. Toi departs Te Aurere, at the top of the North Island of New Zealand, leaving the kumara (sweet potato) that he had brought with him from Taputapu-atea.

As Toi makes landfall, he names a part of the coast Kākahoroa; *kākaho* is the plant commonly known as cutty grass (*austroderia*). As it covers the entire stretch of coast, Toi names it the long stretch of kākaho, and the name remains today. From here Toi climbs up onto an escarpment, feeling absolutely disheartened. His partner and child have returned to Taputapu-atea, he has not found his grandchildren, he is feeling his age, and in absolute desperation he stretches his hands to the sky, whereby the name of this site is created: Kāputerangi. The Indigenous Peoples located around Kāputerangi help Toi establish a settlement for him, where he remains until his death.

However, before his passing, his grandchildren, Whatonga and Rahui, accompanied by another grandchild, Rauru, do meet him again. Back in Rangiatea, Whatonga and Rahui repair their waka, Hawai, and return to Oropoā to discover that their grandparents have left in search of them. They immediately attach another hull to their waka, Hawai, renaming it Kurahaupo. Whatonga, accompanied by his son Taraika and his brother Rauru, set off in search of their grandparents, eventually reconnecting at Kāputerangi. Having met again, they remain with their grandfather until his passing, after which Whatonga and his son set sail, heading south until they arrive into a large bay that Whatonga names after his son, Te Whanganui-a-Tara. Today this is where Wellington, the current capital of New Zealand, is located. The brother of Whatonga travels to the west and settles in the Taranaki region.

At this point, the people at Kāputerangi settle into life on the escarpment named from the actions of Toi, and life continues for approximately 200 years. The principal person of the settlement around 1300 AD is Tamakihikurangi.

Around this time, Te Kurawhakaata, the daughter of Tamahikurangi, is walking along the shore below Kāputerangi and happens upon two individuals resting on the shore, having destroyed their waka on landfall. She immediately returns to inform her father, who instantly commands her to return and, in keeping with tradition, invite them to the settlement to be appropriately hosted. Upon her relaying the request, the visitors, Hoaki and Taukata, are introduced to Tamakihikurangi and Te Kurawhakaata. During the introductions a meal is shared, comprised of produce that could be accessed locally. During this interchange Hoaki and Taukata produce a tuberous plant and share it with their hosts. Tamakihikurangi is immediately taken with this product, and inquires about its name and availability. They respond that the plant is kumara, and it is freely accessible on their home of Mauke, an island in the outer Cook Islands. This is the first time Tamakihikurangi and the current community of Kāputerangi have seen kumara, as 200 years earlier Toi had left the kumara in the north as he continued in search of Whatonga and Rauru. Immediately Tamakihikurangi begins to make plans to travel to Mauke, an island he is familiar with, to secure kumara. Tamakihikurangi was introduced to Mauke by Irakewa, a resident of Mauke who travelled to Kāputerangi and fathered a son with Kiwa, who is named Taneatua. Kiwa is the granddaughter of Tamakihikurangi and the daughter of Te Kurawhakaata.

Hoaki and Taukata agree to assist Tamakihikurangi to obtain kumara, as they were sent to visit their sister Kanioro, who was living with Pourangahua in what is now known as the Gisborne region. The father of Hoaki and Taukata was Rongoataua, who was the principal person at Mauke and who had become concerned for his daughter. At the time that Hoaki and Taukata arrive at Kāputerangi, Kanioro is in the throes of labour. Pourangahua delivers the first child and then realizes that Kanioro was in fact carrying twins; the second child is suffering from complications and not expected to survive. Pourangahua conceals the illness of this child from his partner, and decides to take the child to Mauke to save his partner, Kanioro, from the grief of watching her newborn child die. If the child, by some miracle, happened to survive the trip to Mauke, his father-in-law could spend time with his grandchild, albeit briefly. Upon arrival in Mauke, much to the relief of everyone, the child survives, at which point Pourangahua sends word for Kanioro to make sail for Mauke.

Returning now to Hoaki and Taukata—they are at Kāputerangi in the process of making another waka with Tamakihikurangi from the driftwood, called *tawhao*, that littered the coast, as their waka had been destroyed upon landing. The name given to this waka was Te Aratawhao: *ara* meaning pathway, and tawhao being the name for driftwood.

Having completed the waka, Tamakihikurangi and Hoaki set sail for Mauke, leaving Taukata behind at Kāputerangi. They arrive, around the same time as Kanioro, at a community that is busy crafting a waka to head to Aotearoa, a name given by their ancestor Kupe, an earlier traveller. Tamakihikurangi reunites with Irakewa, the father of his granddaughter's child Taneatua, and subsequently meets the other children of Irakewa: Toroa, who is leading the building of the waka with Pikitua, his sister Muriwai, and their youngest brother, Puhi, the principal person of the island of Rongoataua.

Rongoataua was named after the father of Irakewa, the principal person of his generation, who in his time was attacked by a neighbouring island, Rapanui, resulting in his partner being killed. In retaliation, Rongoataua built a waka, travelled to Rapanui, and attacked the island to avenge the killing of his partner, and then returned to Mauke, where he sank the waka into the lagoon to signify the end of the warring with neighbouring islands.

As Toroa begins to complete the work on the hull of the waka, they are all startled by the cries of surprise of a woman in the undergrowth. As the fast-approaching group nears her, Irakewa hears her muttering, "It is the face of a god, it is a face of a god." Following her gaze he also states, "Yes, it is indeed a face of a god." Protruding from the undergrowth is the prow of waka. It is the long-forgotten waka of Rongoataua the first; it is pulled from its resting place and lashed to the nearly complete hull that Toroa was working on and named "the face of a god"—Mataatua.

The waka, now complete with its name, Mataatua; captain, Toroa; and navigator, Tamakihikurangi—returning with his load of kumara—makes sail for Kāputerangi. Prior to the arrival of Tamakihikurangi at Mauke, the community had decided to establish a new settlement at Kāputerangi, largely driven by the descriptions given to them by Irakewa from his recent visits. Having Tamakihikurangi arrive at this time made the return trip to locate Kāputerangi a little easier, as Toroa was working off landmarks his father had given him, such as "There is a waterfall with a cave located nearby that would be a good home for your sister Muriwai; there is a rock in the river entrance that looks a little like me; above this rock on the ridge is the settlement Kāputerangi." These were the landmarks given to Toroa prior to his departure.

The waka Mataatua departs from Ngatangia bay in Mauke, where an altar known as a *tuahu* is established. Placed within this tuahu is a carefully selected stone as a locator beacon for the people, to create a connection to the new home they are about to establish in Aotearoa.

The waka Mataatua eventually makes landfall on the east coast of the North Island. Tamakihikurangi, being familiar with where they are, begins to follow the coastline in a northerly direction, travelling around a point known as Whangaparoa. They see where the Tainui waka has made landfall and decide not to interrupt them and continue to sail on. After a while they are completely engulfed by fog, and with no visible landmarks they are simply left to wait. As time draws on, the crew become unsettled. In an attempt to settle the crew Puhi offers to help, but the offer is publicly and forcibly rejected by Toroa. This action adds more stress to an already tenuous and strained relationship between the two siblings. Shortly after this interchange, Tamakihikurangi spots two birds flying in front of the waka, and he commands, "Follow those birds, they will lead us to the land of our ancestor Kupe." These birds, named

Mumuhau and Takeretau, were living on Repanga Island (Cuvier Island). This island is located some distance away in the outer parts of Waitemata Harbour, where the current city of Auckland is located.

The waka continues its journey around the top of the North Island, travelling down the west coast and entering what is now called Manukau Harbour, where the waka is portaged across the isthmus to continue its journey south along the east coast. As the waka nears the coastline named Te Kākahoroa, they stop to rest by a river outlet, and Wairaka, the daughter of Toroa, returns to the waka. Her father notices that she is menstruating, to which she responds, *"koinei te awa o te atua"* (this is the river of god), which is a name that remains to this day for that particular river.

As the waka nears the river entrance, where the rock resembling the appearance of Irakewa is located, Wairaka becomes seasick, creating the name for the ridgeline: *kohi*, the term for seasickness. The waka turns into the river mouth and finally lands below the escarpment of Kāputerangi. Immediately, people head off in haste and the waka is left unsecured, and as the tide comes in the waka is at risk of being washed away. Muriwai and her niece, Wairaka, rescue the waka, and in doing so utter the statement *"me whakatane au i a ahau"* (give me the strength of a man). The name is still currently used by the now-established town of Whakatane.

Having securely fastened the waka, Toroa and his older sister Muriwai establish a tuahu in Whakatane. They place into the carefully selected location the tuahu and a stone they have brought from Mauke, and ceremonially plant a manuka tree on top of the stone. This is to demonstrate their commitment to this new home they are about to establish, by the example of the manuka tree growing from the sustenance received from this home. This site is called Te Manuka-Tutahi, a name it still carries today, over 700 years later. Another significant function of this tuahu is to reconnect to the tuahu beacon stone located in Ngatangia bay; in doing this the old home is connected to the new home, and Te Manuka-Tutahi becomes a physical link to the old home of Mauke.

With the creation of the tuahu at Te Manuka-Tutahi a physical link was created for the people to connect with. This particular tuahu was connected with the waiting tuahu established at Ngatangia, providing a physical link for the descendants of Mauke to connect to and draw strength from, to guide them through the process of engaging with a new land and experiences. Using the names and examples described here by Toi, and later by Irakewa and Tamakihikurangi, points of reference were created as points of engagement to link and map the sequential order of events that were being created daily as the new arrivals engaged with their new landscape.

Politics to Maintain Contextual Knowledge

The purpose of providing a heavily redacted version of the Mataatua journey to Whakatane is to show that while we must maintain a connection to a particular region (rohe), we can add to this rohe by making new connections to places, and in doing so create a new context for us to operate in by either reconnecting to a history of the area or by establishing new history in a place. This is demonstrated by Toi and the impact he made on the community, resulting in the naming of Kāputerangi, which created the point of reference for his descendant Tamakihikurangi and Irakewa to meet in later years.

The brief overview of the experiences of Toroa and his crew in establishing a new home for them in Whakatane 700 years ago shows how the people created a new context for themselves by connecting to the context that was familiar to them in Mauke. Using this as a point of reference enabled them to create a new context. As the environment would have been very different from that of Mauke, drawing on experiences from Mauke and mapping the fusion of the new elements required in this new territory through whakapapa created a context for "here" that was connected to the old home of Mauke.

Returning to the idea that context is a critical component that must be understood in teaching and learning, for Māori context requires a connection to space and place. This is mapped physically and cognitively through whakapapa, providing the layers that inform the present state; in doing so, it locates the individual in his or her environment and worldview.

The context becomes more important as we begin to move away from the anchor points that were created to guide us in the past and prepare to engage in new environments. Without these reference points, how do we know that what we are practising is not some mutant form of what we were? Returning to my opening statement: context is a critical component that must be understood in the teaching and learning environment. By drawing connections between learner and content, what is being delivered becomes relevant, supporting Maslow's (1943) idea that learning requires a personal connection. By creating the relevant connections students are able to see that they belong, and will subsequently feel safe and secure, motivating them to achieve. By managing this process, the learner is able to "own" and draw on the cultural strengths and examples he or she has to support the learning. By following examples mapped through whakapapa, learners are able to examine the processes used by ancestors in adopting new ideologies and experiences.

While the purpose of presenting my arguments here is to encourage learning new formations of knowledge, I must point out that this is becoming more and more critical for the maintenance of mātauranga-a-iwi. The ability to maintain a connection to space and place for Māori, in my view, becomes increasingly more important as we begin to engage with different forms and formations of Māori knowledge, knowledge we have inherited, and the social construction that occurs in connecting old to new.

If we do not understand the need to locate content for learners and see content as being a key component in the politics of knowledge, then Māori learners are in danger of reproaching mutant forms of language and knowledge and therefore disconnecting from a more authentic iwi base.

If this is to be the case, then the danger is that a less authentic language, knowledge, and cultural base is the likely outcome; while this may be useful in the short term, it will lack the epistemological rigour and social basis to be sustainable over the long term. This precarious, short-sighted approach will also destabilize the societal structures of Māori community, resources, and cultural practice, which in turn are dialectically related to the survival of language and knowledge. One cannot have the language without the culture.

Notes

1. Māori organizational structures are made of different tribes. Each tribe occupies a particular territory, termed *rohe*, that is, linked through occupation. Over many centuries, each tribe will connect to an ancestral canoe (*waka*).
2. Best was an early ethnographer who recorded the Tūhoe histories in the late 1800s.
3. Tane Mahuta, in Tūhoe and Māori epistemologies, is the creator of the forests and also created the first human.
4. Ngā Pōtiki is an early tribe that occupied the territories now occupied by Tūhoe.

References

Battiste, Marie, and James Y. Henderson. 2003. *Protecting Indigenous Knowledge and Heritage*. Saskatoon, SK: Purich Publishing.

Best, Elsdon. 1972. *Tūhoe: The Children of the Mist*. Wellington, NZ: A.H. & A.W. Reed.

Maslow, Abraham H. 1943. "A Theory of Human Motivation." *Psychological Review* 50: 370-96.

Mead, Linda. 1997. "Ngā Aho o te Kakahu Matauranga: The Multiple Layers of Struggle by Māori in Education." PHD diss., University of Auckland.

Rangihau, John. 1975. "Being Māori." In *Te Ao Hurihuri: The World Moves On*, edited by Michael King, 165-75. Wellington, NZ: Hicks Smith.

Smith, Graham. 1997. "The Development of Kaupapa Māori: Theory and Praxis." PHD diss., University of Auckland.

18 | Essentially Māori
A Māori Art Paradigm

ROBERT JAHNKE

Timatanga: Introduction

"Essentially Māori" is a chapter about contesting space for Māori art, not only in relation to New Zealand art but also within the broader context of international art. By its very nature, the ethnic labelling of Māori art is an essentialist act aimed at arguing that Māori art can be different from art created by "other" cultures. This chapter promotes a paradigm called *he tataitanga kaupapa toi*, in which form, content, and the genealogy of the artist are critical determinants of Māori cultural relativity and relevance. Each of these determinants is contextualized in relation to a Māori worldview and pertinent Western theoretical perspectives that intersect in understanding form, content, and genealogy, within a transcultural context of change that occurred as a consequence of European settlement. At the heart of contesting space for Māori art is the naming of form, content, and genealogy in the language of the culture and from a Māori worldview. This is fundamental in establishing a paradigm that is meaningful for Māori in terms of cultural relativity and relevance; that is, for making the art acceptable and accessible for Māori.

He Tataitanga Karanga: A Call to Unite

As an introduction to this chapter I resort to a tribal aphorism reconfigured textually in a painting by Māori woman artist Robyn Kahukiwa, entitled *Ko Hikurangi te maunga ko Waiapu te awa ko Ngati Porou te iwi* (Figure 18.1). This aphorism, "Hikurangi is the mountain, Waiapu is the river, Ngati Porou are the people," which I share with the artist, is conceptualized in the carved panel representing the ancestress Te Aomihia in the tribal house Te Hono ki Rarotonga.[1]

Recourse to this painting of a carved image of our shared ancestor allows me an opportunity to conceptually enact the *"ritual of pae,"* the protocol of Māori social interaction between host and visitor (Jahnke 1966). These images of Māori women become a conceptual *karanga* or call acknowledging the critical role of women in Māori society as the first voice heard on the *marae* (tribal communal space). This acknowledgement of the karanga is pertinent because it anchors the chapter within a paradigm of Māori cultural relativity and relevance, in which *whakapapa* (genealogy) is foundational.[2]

This painting by Robyn Kahukiwa is also appropriate since the image is grounded in whakapapa, references Māori form in the painted representation of carved figurative imagery, and navigates Māori content, which together constitute the three critical indices in the art paradigm for Māori cultural relativity and relevance outlined in Table 18.1.

The karanga is a customary ritualized "performative"[3] act, sanctioned in tradition and culturally empowered in cosmo-genealogy. In a tribal version of cosmo-genesis,[4] the first female entity was shaped from the earth by a male deity[5] who breathed life into her nostrils, resulting in the ensuing "sneeze of life."[6] The enactment of this story is enshrined in karanga and reiterated by male orators in the words *"tihei mauri ora"* (the breath of life), which calls the assembled to attention. Historically, the karanga was reserved for older women (Salmond 1975). The function of the karanga, which is initiated by the *kaikaranga* (caller) of the host group, is to introduce the formal marae protocol.[7] At the heart of the ritual exchange associated with the karanga is the contextualization

FIGURE 18.1 *Left*: Robyn Kahukiwa, Ko Hikurangi te maunga ko Waiapu te awa ko Ngati Porou te iwi. *Alcyd painting, 1985. Auckland, New Zealand. [Collection Robin Scholes] Right*: Te Hono ki Rarotonga, Te Aomihia. *Carved ancestral house panel, 1934. Tokomaru Bay, New Zealand.*

of hosts and visitor in relation to female pre-eminence, the sacred and the profane, and the deceased and the living.[8] These are acknowledged, in a conjunction of past and present, in a holistic continuum of cultural interconnectedness where space and time, people and place are implicated in the cultural context of the occasion.

In her painting *Mo Irihapeti tenei karanga* (Figure 18.2), Robyn Kahukiwa protests non-Māori "performance" of the karanga. As sanctum of customary practice, the ancestral house in the painting is a collage of text of the Treaty of Waitangi, the covenant signed by independent and autonomous chiefs and the British, which gave the latter permission to enter New Zealand in 1840. The text demands respect for the articles of the Treaty, and Article

FIGURE 18.2 Robyn Kahukiwa, Mo Irihapeti tenei karanga. *Alcyd painting, 1988.* Wellington, New Zealand. [Collection of Irihapeti Ramsden Estate]

Two in particular, which promised Māori the control of their treasured possessions, of which Māori language and ritual constitute inalienable cultural elements.[9] The bird-like form signifying the karanga is composed in the stylized tradition of the *manaia*, a cultural signifier for the spiritual essence of the human forms it supports, invoking communication beyond the material world.[10] In *Karanga for Irihapeti Ramsden* the manaia signifies the sacrosanct nature of the karanga, while the blacked kaikaranga (caller) announces Māori women as the rightful heirs and guardians of this treasured possession. The chromatic symbolism intensifies the tenor of Māori women's angst. House, ancestors, and land are blood-red, sanctified in cosmo-genealogical narrative through the separation of earth and sky.[11] The black sky and black-clad caller mourn the infiltration of callers without genealogical sanction. The lament is made more poignant by the caller's role of bidding farewell to the dead and generating a union of ancestors and living. The painted ancestors on the porch wall of the house gesticulate under the advance of a neo-colonial invasion, the appropriation of the karanga by non-Māori women. Even the house appears to partake in the signification process. The porch wall is populated with ancestral images charged in a chromatic code of empowerment in accord with cosmo-genesis.[12] The appearance of carved ancestral images in the porch area was exceptional for 19th-century carved houses but common in storehouses.[13] In this regard the images function to confront the observer, thereby engendering cognition of the sanctity of cultural *taonga* (precious possessions) stored within.[14] The bargeboard that comprises the outstretched hand of welcome is a collage of Treaty text that forewarn *tangata tiriti* (non-Māori signatories of the Treaty of Waitangi) to honour their part of the covenant by respecting Māori *taonga katoa* (all their valued treasures). The Treaty text is black and white in its emphatic statement of tribal sovereignty, while the oppressive white cross of colonialism looms heavy in its attempt to erase the bird-like manaia, the cultural signifier of tradition.

The establishment of the Waitangi Tribunal in 1975, together with the statutory moves to shift Māori identity from a blood quantum system to self-identification as "Māori," were watershed acts of Parliament that fed a stream of Māori consciousness and trans-customary interlocution in contemporary Māori art. Legislation and land protest in the 1970s fed a socio-political current that energized Māori art through the late 1980s and into the new millennium.

Within the context of the post-1980s consciousness, Robyn Kahukiwa emerged as a significant painter of Māori oppression. By contextualizing her work among other Māori artists, this chapter aims to demonstrate how genealogy, form, and content commingle in a current of contemporary Māori art. Robyn Kahukiwa's work straddles customary and non-customary visual form, while its content articulates a Māori worldview that is bathed in genealogical integrity and connection, not only in terms of her identity but also in relation to the form and content in her work. It goes without saying that making the whakapapa of the artist a compulsory condition for what constitutes Māori art is an essentialist strategy. This is a necessary precondition, because artists without a Māori whakapapa can also achieve visual correspondence or visual empathy with prior models within the tradition of Māori visual culture.[15] Within the context of this chapter, taking the artist's whakapapa as a precondition for Māori relativity and resonance is not subscribing to biological determinism as a prerequisite for visual correspondence or visual empathy. Rather, it is a proposal that the art produced by artists with Māori whakapapa will more likely resonate with Māori because Māori would prefer one of their own to create the art.

The painted effigies of carved ancestral figures (Figures 18.1 and 18.2) owe their evolution to Robyn Kahukiwa's ancestor Te Aomihia (Figure 18.1); however, a precedent for painted images of carved ancestors can be found in tribal houses in the late 19th and early 20th centuries. Robyn Kahukiwa's style of painting owes a debt to Cezanne, while the collage of text may be attributed to Picasso. However, text has been part of the fabric of Māori visual culture since the 1840s, and a collage of linoleum was used in a tribal house on the east coast in the 1890s as a substitute for customary lattice patterns.

Genealogy as a critical index in the Māori art paradigm (Table 18.1) is not only related to the whakapapa of the artist but is also aligned with consideration of the genealogy of knowledge, site, form, process, and customary protocols (Table 18.4).[16] Tribal houses of late 19th and early 20th centuries were resplendent with settler-community-influenced naturalistic paintings of subjects such as potted plants, lions, English royalty, and even a goddess of the silent screen, Mary Pickford. What has changed in the paintings of Robyn Kahukiwa is the migration of Māori art from tribal houses to art galleries; that is, the site has changed. The process (encompassing medium, technique, and tools) has switched from the wooden panels in tribal houses to commercial paint on canvas. The Māori art paradigm considers form, not only in terms of its archetypal, transitional, or unconventional manifestation, but also in terms of the genealogy of the artist and the art (Table 18.4). Therefore, the genealogical index analyzes form and content within a historical context, because Māori visual culture has changed as a result of European contact, and further change is inevitable. It is critical that, as Indigenous people, we are able to shift the goal posts in our assessment of what constitutes Indigenous art in order to accommodate a changing worldview that will be the inheritance of new generation of Indigenous artists.

TABLE 18.1 *He tataitanga kaupapa toi (Art paradigm for Māori cultural relativity and relevance)*

He Tataitanga Ahua	He Tataitanga Kōrero	He Tataitanga Whakapapa
Form	Content	Genealogy

TABLE 18.2 *He Tataitanga Ahua (Form)*

Ahua Tuturu	Ahua Whakawhiti	Ahua Rereke
Customary form (Archetypal)	Trans-customary form (Transitional and transcultural)	Non-customary form (Unconventional and transcultural)

TABLE 18.3 *He Tataitanga Kōrero (Content)*

Kaupapa Māori	Western
Māori-centric	Non-Māori-centric

TABLE 18.4 *He Tataitanga Whakapapa (Genealogy)*

Māori	Non-Māori
Whakapapa	Genealogy of the artist
Matauranga	Knowledge framework
Ahua	Visual form
Waihanga	Process (material, tools, technique)
Wahi	Site
Tikanga	Protocol

He Tataitanga Kaupapa Toi: An Essentialist Strategy

He tataitanga kaupapa toi, as an essentialist strategy and an art paradigm for Māori cultural relativity and relevance (Tables 18.1 to 18.4), maintains an ideological relationship with *kaupapa Māori* discourse, which acknowledges "the validity of Māori world views as well as the importance of a Māori critique of social structures" (International Research Institute 2002, 13). As Leonie Pihama (1993) has argued,

> intrinsic to Kaupapa Māori theory is an analysis of existing power structures and social inequalities. Kaupapa Māori theory therefore aligns with critical theory in the act of exposing underlying assumptions that serve to conceal power relations that exist within society and the ways in which dominant groups construct concepts of "common sense" and "facts" to provide ad hoc justification for the maintenance of inequalities and the continued oppression of Māori people. (57)

It is not the intention of this chapter to engage in an extensive analysis of "existing power structures and social inequalities" or to examine "power relations," except at the level of claiming that art created by Māori is an ideological construct that sustains a position of cultural relativity and relevance for those for whom the art generates a sense of cultural empowerment and continuity. This strategy is essentialist. No apology is made for such a position, since art, by nature, is a Western essentialist construct that was transformed over time into a narcissistic concept privileging individuality, innovation, and exclusivity at the expense of collective pursuit of creative endeavour.

In proposing a Māori art paradigm,[17] it is possible to contextualize Gayatri Spivak's notion of "strategic essentialism" (cited in Sarup 1998, 166), since the naming of the art as Māori and making Māori genealogy a condition of an art paradigm is an essentialist proposition.

Ideologically, essentialism is not only about protecting Indigenous knowledge and value systems but also about enforcing a code of ethics in relation to intellectual and cultural property rights of which art is an inseparable component. However, we must acknowledge Spivak's warning to Māori in 2002 when she suggested that we must avoid donning the essentialist yoke, "since cultural fossilisation engenders cultural stagnation and...any perpetuation of a traditional mindset is a sign of an incapacity to translate customary cultural values and beliefs into relevant contemporary codes of practice" (Spivak 2002, n.p.).

While I support the spirit of her caution I would argue that, as Indigenous people, we should not make excuses for exclusionary practices that might be viewed as essentialist, whether strategic or otherwise. As bell hooks (1992, 30) maintains, what is absent from the critique of essentialism "is the way that essentialism informs representations of whiteness. It is always the non-white...who is guilty of essentialism." Western epistemology and ontology are inherently exclusive—or, to express it another way, essentialist. This does not mean that we should abandon Spivak's caution in relation to Indigenous art, since I myself create non-customary art. Also, this chapter navigates both essentialist traditions—Māori and Western. If I were a true essentialist I would write and speak in my mother tongue and become truly exclusive, and ultimately, a recluse. What I am arguing for is the right of Indigenous people to practise their art, whether it is customary, trans-customary, or non-customary (Table 18.2): expressed succinctly, whether the art we create looks like the art created by our ancestors or not. While it may appear that I am making concessions to a postmodernist position, it is really about the right of Indigenous people to determine their own creative practices, which may or may not accommodate other cultural positions.

Transcultural Inflection

For much of the 19th and 20th centuries, there remained two poles of artistic expression within the tribal context: customary and non-customary (archetypal and unconventional); that is, art that looked Māori and art that did not.

Text appeared in Māori visual culture in the 1840s. At this time, it was considered unconventional or non-customary. Māori language, as an exemplary form of transcultural inflection, was incorporated into tribal carving and painting beginning in the 1840s, remained prominent through the 1920s, and resurfaced as a critical dimension of Māori art in the 1980s, welcoming visitors, naming ancestors, and spreading words of good tidings to visitors.[18] At a linguistic level, Māori language has been incorporated into tribal carving (Figure 18.3) and contemporary art (Figure 18.1) as a linguistic referent with mnemonic or polemic intent.

In the semiology of Roland Barthes,[19] the juxtaposition of image and text gives rise to three messages: the linguistic, the coded iconic, and the non-coded iconic (Barthes 1986).[20] Only the linguistic message is relevant in this context. In tribal carving of the 19th century, the names of ancestors were carved in relief to name ancestors in a code of Māori-language. The code served two functions, "anchoring and relaying" (Adams 1996, 154).[21] Māori language anchors by denoting the ancestor in relation to other ancestors, while relaying an ideology of whakapapa as a critical premise for survival as a people. It is this second function of the code that is particularly important for the Māori art paradigm.

Transcultural adaptation should not be viewed as a debasement of Māori visual culture but as a natural consequence of cultures in collision and collusion. A negotiation of transcultural influence is important as new knowledge, because there has been a tendency to undermine change in tribal visual culture as appropriation, assimilation, colonization, or degradation, or to ignore these influences altogether.[22]

FIGURE 18.3 Te Hau ki Turanga, Kahutia. Carved ancestral house panel, 1843. Wellington, New Zealand. [Museum of New Zealand Te Papa Tongarewa]

FIGURE 18.4 Left: Te Hau ki Turanga, Kahutia. Detail, carved ancestral house panel, 1843. Wellington, New Zealand. [Museum of New Zealand Te Papa Tongarewa] Right: Te Mana o Turanga, Agnew Brown. Carved ancestral house panel, 1882. Manutuke, New Zealand.

While there have been attempts to eradicate transcultural adaptation as impure or foreign, it is part of the reality of cultures in conjunction.[23] The examples of tribal house carving (Figure 18.4) demonstrate the influence of a European tradition on Māori art in the 19th century. Within this temporal context, the image of Agnew Brown with his Dalmatian dog was non-customary or unconventional in its use of a European perspective system in place of the tradition of non-perspective representation, albeit naively rendered. Today the carving is considered "customary." In other words, what is non-customary in one context or period may be customary in another. If the temporal index is shifted from the 19th century to the 1970s, the indices for form (Table 18.2) will also shift. However, Māori, like many other Indigenous Peoples, are essentially conservative (or essentially essentialist) when it comes to accepting change—so much so that the trans-customary art of the 1970s is still viewed with apprehension, with many Māori still unwilling to accept the art as customary even after 35 years within the tribal context. As a liberal essentialist, I would like to see the temporal index shifted to the new millennium, making all forms of art created today customary or archetypal; but such a position is untenable, at least into the foreseeable future. For now, most Māori continue to use the 19th century as the temporal benchmark for Māori art.

It was not until 1976 that a distinctive trans-customary or transitional art form appeared within tribal dining halls, exemplified in the multi-media mural by Paratene Matchitt, *Te Kaweketanga o Turongo raua ko Mahinarangi* (1976), which can be seen in the Kimiora Dining Room, Ngaruawahia, New Zealand. This transcultural art practice owes its manifestation to a collusion between a modernist aesthetic and customary tribal tradition in which customary forms were stylized anatomically and customary patterns from the woven arts and painting were reconfigured two- and three-dimensionally using Western mediums and techniques.

TABLE 18.5 *He tataitanga kaupapa toi (Criteria of Māori resonance)*

He Tataitanga Ahua (Form)	He Tataitanga Kōrero (Content)	He Tataitanga Whakapapa (Genealogy)
Ahua Tuturu (Customary form)		
• Visual correspondence with historical models. • Customary modification is minimal or absent, maintaining mimetic relationship with customary form.	• Take (rationale) or mātauranga Māori • Can be implicit	• Māori • Self-identification
Ahua Whakawhiti (Trans-customary form)		
• Visual empathy with historical models. • Transcultural modification retains perceptual relationship with customary form.	• Take (rationale) or mātauranga Māori • Can be implicit	• Māori • Self-identification
Ahua Rereke (Non-customary form)		
• Absence of visual correspondence and empathy. • Transcultural modification obscures perceptual relationship with customary form, making it non-customary.	• Take (rationale) or mātauranga Māori • Can be implicit	• Māori • Self-identification

Division of Form

Visual modification (Table 18.5) to form must have as its goal cultural relevance if art is to resonate with Māori. In other words, what we are concerned with is what the form looks like. Does it look like the art produced in the past? Does it break with tradition?

FIGURE 18.5 Left: Lyonel Grant, Pou maumahara. Carved commemorative post, 1990. Wellington, New Zealand. [Creative NZ Collection] Right: Michael Parekowhai, Roebuck Jones and the Cuniculus Kid. Detail, rabbit and mixed media, 2001. Auckland, New Zealand. [Chartwell Collection, Auckland Art Gallery Toi o Tāmaki]

At one end of the art spectrum, visual modification to form maintains visual correspondence with historical models where a perceptual relationship with customary form is retained. That is, it looks like it could have been created in the past. The *poumaumahara* (commemorative post) by Lyonel Grant (Figure 18.5, left) epitomizes this relationship to customary form because it aligns visually with prior models, particularly those of the 19th century. Māori embrace this form of art because Māori need to see themselves in the art. This form of creative practice is viewed as essentialist because it mimics tradition. However, it is the form of art that most Māori embrace, because it looks Māori, is grounded in the culture, and exists, for the most part, within Māori spaces of communal interaction.

At the other end of the art spectrum, visual modification to form obscures any perceptual relationship with customary form, as exemplified in Michael Parekowhai's *Roebuck Jones* (Figure 18.5, right). Both correspondence and visual empathy with historical models are absent. That is, it looks like mainstream art. This is problematic for Māori, because there are no visual cues that allow Māori to empathize with the art. If form has been subject to visual modification that obscures a perceptual relationship with historical models, the content must be culturally relevant. While Michael Parekowhai's creation appears problematic in terms of content, he often resorts to humour in the art he creates. In this work he revisits childhood games of cowboys and Indians, parodying stereotypes of popular culture that are part of the lived reality of many of the urban youth of his generation. The holstered rabbit, outfitted in Hollywood clichés of the "wild wild West," is a parody of the romanticized visions of how the West was won that flooded our cinema screens in the 1960s and 1970s. The rabbits that have invaded New Zealand shores, pests that cannot be eradicated, become an allegory for colonization.[24] While essentialism is absent from the work at a perceptual level, one is able to locate Māori-centric content through an analysis of imagery. Of course, following Barthes I am at liberty to translate the text in the absence of the author.

In this respect, I am arguing for an essentialist position in the continuum of Māori art, and indeed Indigenous art. Ideologically, this essentialist strategy privileges a Māori worldview and supports *tino rangatiratanga* (sovereignty) relative to art, whether customary, trans-customary, or non-customary.

Ahua Tuturu: Customary Form

As indicated above, visual correspondence (Table 18.5) relates to the conformity between historical models and their visual reiteration. In other words, such art looks like it has been created in the 19th century. In the case of visual correspondence, customary modification is minimal or absent, maintaining a mimetic relationship with prior models. Figure

FIGURE 18.6 *Left: John Taiapa. Porch panel carving, 1980. Auckland, New Zealand. Hoani Waititi marae; Right: Lyonel Grant, Pou maumahara. Detail, 1990. Wellington, New Zealand.* [Creative NZ Collection]

18.6 demonstrates the continuity of customary form in the 1980s and 1990s. Ahua tuturu (customary or archetypal form) maintains a close affinity with forms created during the 19th century. As intimated previously, this form of contemporary Māori art is grounded in tradition both visually and conceptually, embracing both formal and conceptual essentialism.

Ahua Whakawhiti: Trans-Customary Form

Visual empathy (Table 18.5) involves modification to the visual substitute relative to historical models. In its most exemplary form, prior models can be perceived through the retention of visual structures or patterns recontextualized in an ahistorical manner. Visual empathy is a product

FIGURE 18.7 Top: Cliff Whiting, Te Hono ki Hawaiki. 1998. Wellington, New Zealand. [Museum of New Zealand Te Papa Tongarewa] Bottom: John Taiapa, Tukaki tribal house, 1944. Te Kaha, New Zealand. Te Kaha-nui-a-tiki marae.

of trans-customary modification resulting from a collusion of tribal form and subject matter with modernist practice.[25] The historical models are stylized through a design process that retains anatomical associations with prior figurative form, while non-figurative form retains pattern relationships with carved, painted, and woven precedents, in spite of the application of non-customary materials, tools, and technique. *Te Hono ki Hawaiki* (Figure 18.7, top) illustrates the trans-customary form that came to prominence in the 1950s, with its mature template emerging during the 1970s and into the 1990s. Trans-customary form evolved from the engagement of Māori artists who, under the tutelage of inspirational educationist Gordon Tovey in the 1960s, were encouraged to look to their culture for inspiration. Like customary form, trans-customary form has the capacity to embrace both conceptual and formal essentialism.

Trans-cultural modification (or adaptation) is used to capture the notion of change where influence from outside the culture results in either trans-customary or non-customary change to form. As stated above, trans-customary modification results in form that has visual empathy, allowing for a visual relationship between the customary model and its trans-customary modification.

However, trans-cultural modification can also result in non-customary form where no visual relationship exists between the customary model and its non-customary modification. Both visual correspondence and empathy are absent. For all intents and purposes, the final product appears to have been created by an artist from outside the culture. The painting *School Patrol* (Figure 18.8) by Kelcy Taratoa epitomizes non-customary form and aligns with Western models of art using forms, materials, tools, and techniques associated with mainstream art. Unlike the prior models where conceptual and formal essentialism can exist simultaneously, only conceptual essentialism is pertinent as Kelcy Taratoa revisits the sites of his urban upbringing. He is joined by the Hulk, referencing comic book heroes he idealized as a child. For the artist, they epitomize the dilemma faced by many urban Māori of his generation in search of their true identity. These fictitious comic book

FIGURE 18.8 *Kelcy Taratoa*, School Patrol, 2004. Auckland, New Zealand.
[Private collection]

characters face a constant battle with their alter egos in their attempts to conform to the dictates of their human condition while being entrusted with protecting the world or avoiding persecution in their transformed states.

Conclusion

This chapter builds on earlier models associated with the development of an art paradigm for Māori cultural relativity and relevance, first conceived in 1996, refined in 1998, theorized in 2006, and contextualized relative to essentialism in this latest version (see Jahnke 1998, 2006a, 2006b, 2009). The chapter attempts to address a critical question relating to the 2010 Essentially Indigenous Symposium: What makes Native art Native?

In the first instance I reflect on the title of the session I participated in at this symposium: "Indigenous aesthetic paradigms: Community and the artist." The use of the term "aesthetic" to qualify the Indigenous paradigm perpetuates a knowledge platform in which taste and beauty constitute the determinants for making art Native. In other words, it deals with the superficial appearance or form, omitting a consideration of content and genealogy that constitute critical indices in the paradigm discussed in this chapter. Critically, aesthetics is largely concerned with what the art looks like, and whether it is good or bad. It is essential that we as Indigenous commentators choose terms that are more empathetic with our respective worldviews.

The first question to answer in determining what makes Native art Native (depending on the "Natives") is: Does the art look Native or not? If the answer to the question is yes, the second question must be: Is the artist Native? This is necessary, since the paradigm outlined in this chapter argues that a non-Native artist can create work that looks Native. If both questions are answered in the affirmative and the artist acknowledges his or her Native genealogy, then the third question must surely be: Does the content relate to Native concerns or issues? If the answer is yes, then the art is Native.

There is, however, another question that is often asked: Does the Native community recognize the artist as Native? The answer to the question is a perplexing one, and depends on where the Native community is located. In Table 18.5 under "genealogy," self-identification is used as the criteria for determining Māori ethnicity in Aotearoa New Zealand. In the USA, blood quantum complicates the process of identity and tribal membership, and can lead to a hegemonic system of disenfranchisement in terms of the right to call one's work "Native" or to belong to more than one tribal community. In Aotearoa New Zealand it is the individual's right to determine their identity, and tribal affiliation is limitless; it is a right of whakapapa. In the case of community recognition of the artist as Native I personally view it as a bonus and a privilege, but it is not a prerequisite of the paradigm that I have constructed.

What has not been addressed is the quality of the art; that is, is it good art or bad art? This is the aesthetic debate.

If we revisit the first question (Does the art look native or not?) and the answer to the question is no, we have another problem. This is the non-customary or unconventional form discussed in this chapter as trans-cultural inflection. The short answer to the question is: If the artist is Native and the work he or she creates relates to Native concerns and issues, then the art should rightly be regarded as Native. More often than not, this Native artist will have to explain the work either verbally or in written form in order to convince the Native community to whom she or he belongs to extend artistic endorsement, sanction, or membership.

In returning to the aesthetic debate over good or bad art, the community decides—not only the Native community, but also the non-Native community. If your art is good you will have a long career as an artist; if your art is bad you will have a short career, if you have one at all. In the time-honoured words of a Western cliché, there is no accounting for taste, and beauty is inevitably in the eye of the beholder.

Notes

1. Both Robyn Kahukiwa and I are linked genealogically to the ancestress Te Aomihia. The name of the tribal house translates as "the reunion at Rarotonga" in deference to a shared ancestry between Māori and the people of Rarotonga.
2. A distinction can be made between cosmo-genealogical oration and narrative. Oration relates to the form of genealogical recitation in which names are listed sequentially to generate the *tataitanga korero* (meaning). The narrative form explicates Māori cosmology through stories of origin and development. Cosmo-genealogy is used in preference to cosmology because Māori conceived the world as a genealogically integrated universe in which all matter, animate and inanimate, was interconnected, and tataitanga as a genealogical term constitutes

the thematic context for this chapter, in which a whakapapa system regulates the dissemination of *matauranga*. Cosmo-genealogy in the context of this chapter is used as a substitute for the Western term "myth," which undermines the theoretical nature of Indigenous narratives.

3. I resort here to Gayatri Spivak's notion of the performative *within* a cultural context in contradistinction to the performance *outside* the cultural context: "When one is *in* a cultural context one is not thinking *about* a cultural context, one *is* the culture—one is doing, making and moving in it. This is a performative" (Spivak 2002, n.p.).

4. There are tribal variations in the narrative of the origin of the first woman, including her formation out of earth or sound, or a consequence of reflection. In the generic version, she is known alternatively as Hineahuone (woman formed of the earth) or Hinehauone (woman of resuscitated earth).

5. In the Ngati Kahungunu version of Wairarapa, more than one deity was responsible for the creation of the first woman.

6. The "sneeze of life" is expressed in Māori oratory as "tihei mauri ora," which may be translated in George Lucas-speak as "may the life force be with you."

7. "The ritual begins with karanga [of the host woman]...signalling the visitors to enter the marae...the first voice heard on the marae is that of a woman. She has the power of mana wahine to neutralize the tapu of strangers. The manuhiri enter the marae with an answering call from one of their women, while a kaumatua chants a waerea, a protective incantation against local demons" (Walker 1992, 22). See also Karetu (1992).

8. The hosts are *tangata whenua* (people of the land), visitors are *manuhiri*. *Mana wahine* is the term for female pre-eminence, *tapu* is sacred, *noa* is profane, *hunga mate* are the deceased, and *hunga ora* are the living.

9. The Treaty of Waitangi was signed in 1840, and laid the foundation for relationships between the Crown and Māori with respect to citizenship, governance, and issues of sovereignty within New Zealand. Two articles cover Crown authority to govern; tribal authority over cultural, social and economic resources; and royal protection and citizenship rights (Durie 1980).

10. The *manaia* is a figurative form normally associated with Māori carving. It has been variably interpreted as the profile of a human form, reptile, bird, and spiritual or psychic entity. The origin of the manaia has been the subject of constant debate ranging from those that associate its form with the human profile, a vestige of a distant bird cult, reptile, or the mana of the tiki forms with which it is often associated. "Kendall in his early writings mentioned that manaia

were the protective spirits surrounding the chiefly person. Traditionally they represent the aura, charisma, prestige, mana and hereditary power of the chiefs and their antecedents. They also express the spiritual and tapu states of man" (University of Auckland 1988, 19).

11. In generic tribal narratives of cosmo-genesis, the separation of earth and sky is personified as a battle of separation in which the embracing parents were forcibly separated with a lacerating of limbs necessary to achieve the task. The red earth signifies the spilt blood resulting from the separation.

12. In these narratives in which natural phenomena are deified, the red earth is signified as the blood spilt during the separation of earth and sky, and of the earth from the pubic region of the earth mother that was used to create Hineahuone, the first woman formed of the earth.

13. Ruatepupuke (1890s) in the Field Museum in Chicago is an exception to the rule. The porch area is fully carved. This house, which belongs to Te Whanau a Ruataupare in Tokomaru Bay, is also one of Robyn Kahukiwa's ancestral houses.

14. Ruatepupuke (1890s) is the only example of a house with a fully carved porch wall. The function of the carved porch in this instance was to commemorate the Ngati Porou narrative in which the origin of the art of carving was located in the ocean realm of Tangaroa, the deity responsible for the waterways and the creatures within. This house consolidates the Tangaroa theme by using the *mangopare* (hammerhead shark) kowhaiwhai pattern on the ridgepole and the rafters.

15. Several of the contributors to the Taharora Project (the refurbishment of my ancestral house on the east coast) were Pākehā. In spite of this, my role as concept designer and project manager ensured that the form created by Pākehā students was en-framed in *tataitanga kaupapa toi* at the level of content and genealogy.

16. When considering the transcultural framework, whakapapa in this context refers to the genealogy of the artist; matauranga is the knowledge embedded in the art work; *wahi* is the site of presentation; *ahua* is the form in the art work; *waihanga*, which means to build, is used to encompass not only the processes used in its creation but also the tools and materials used; while *tikanga* refers to the protocols applied during the creation of the art work or during its presentation.

17. Paradigm is used in Kuhn's (1979) sense of the term: "a social construct of reality... the entire constellation of beliefs, values, techniques, and so on shared by the members of a given community."

18. This transcultural accession to literacy retained Māori language as a critical notation of cultural relativity and relevance. However, in the late 19th century, this transcultural accession extended to incorporating passages of English language within the marae context as well (Jahnke 2003).
19. Roland Barthes (1915-80) expanded "Saussure's Structuralism by extending the relation between the linguistic signifier and signified to different cultural systems—including imagery" (Adams 1996, 154), hence imagery relies on equivalence as opposed to identity.
20. The second message is also called the literal or the denoted message. The third message is also called the symbolic or connoted message (Barthes 1986).
21. "For Barthes the linguistic message is a link to the image, and it serves two functions: 'anchoring and relaying.' It anchors by denoting…The relaying function is related to connotation, which constitutes Barthes' notion of the 'rhetoric of the image,' and it conveys an ideological message. 'Rhetoric,' he wrote, 'appears as the signifying aspect of ideology'" (Adams 1996, 154).
22. "They [Ngata, and the experts of the Māori School of Arts and Crafts] appropriated Māori Morehu, Christian and Pakeha ideas in a way that made them part of the Morehu architectural whakapapa" (Brown 1997, 161). "Māori art might then be defined as art that looks Māori, feels Māori, is done by Māori following the styles, canons of taste and values of Māori culture. A Māori artist might be defined as a person who identifies as Māori, is Māori by whakapapa and has some proven ability in Māori art" (Mead 1997, 232).
23. See Neich's (2001, 204) discussion of the imposition of a "veil of orthodoxy" by Charles Nelson and Augustus Hamilton on the Rotorua carvers in the 19th century, which led to the carving out of "European-style boots."
24. The rabbit is actually a hare in Aotearoa New Zealand—but "rabbit" sounds so much better in this context.
25. Damian Skinner (2008, 79) labels the work of this period "Māori modernism."

References

Adams, Laurie S. 1996. *The Methodologies of Art: An Introduction*. Boulder, CO: Westview Press.

Barthes, Roland. 1986. *The Responsibility of Forms: Critical Essays on Music, Art and Representation*. Translated by Richard Howard. Oxford: Basil Blackwell.

Brown, Deidre. 1997. "Morehu Architecture." PHD diss., University of Auckland.

Durie, Mason. 1980. *Te Mana Te Kawanatanga: The Politics of Māori Self-Determination*. Auckland, NZ: Oxford University Press.

hooks, bell. 1992. *Black Looks: Race and Representation*. Boston: South End Press.

International Research Institute for Māori and Indigenous Education and Te Ropu Rangahau Hauora a Eru Pomare. 2002. *Iwi Māori Provider Success*. Wellington, NZ: Te Puni Kokiri.

Jahnke, Robert. 1966. "Voices Beyond the Pae." *He Pukenga Korero* 2: 12–19.

———. 1998. "Contemporary Māori Art: Fact or Fiction." In *Māori Art and Culture*, edited by Darota C. Starzecka, 159–79. London: British Museum Press.

———. 2003. "Māori Visual Culture on the Run." Keynote address at Ngā Waka Art Education Conference, Auckland College of Education, Auckland, NZ. Ngā Waka: Anzaae Aotearoa New Zealand Association of Art Educators Refereed Conference Proceedings Vol. 1 (1). CD-ROM.

———. 2006a. "The House That Riwai Built: A Māori Art Continuum." PHD diss., Massey University.

———. 2006b. "Tribal Art and Its Incorporation into Contemporary Art." In *Eye of the Beholder: Reception, Audience, and Practice of Modern Asian Art*, edited by John Clark, Maurizio Peleggi, and T.K. Sabapathy, 2–28. Sydney, Australia: Wild Peony.

———. 2009. "Toioho ki Apiti, The Awakening of Creativity: A Pedagogy for Transnational Art." *International Journal for Arts in Society* 4 (2): 97–112.

Karetu, Timoti. 1992. "Language and Protocol of the Marae." In *Te Ao Hurihuri: The World Moves On: Aspects of Māoritanga*, edited by Michael King, 29–31. Auckland, NZ: Reed.

Kuhn, Thomas S. 1979. *The Structure of Scientific Revolution*. Chicago: University of Chicago Press.

Mead, Sidney M. 1997. *Māori Art on the World Scene*. Wellington, NZ: Ahua Design and Matau Associates.

Neich, Roger. 2001. *Carved Histories Rotorua Ngati Tarawhai Carving*. Auckland, NZ: Auckland University Press.

Pihama, Leoni. 1933. "Tungia te Ururua, Kia Tupu Whakaritorito Te Tupu o te Harakeke: A Critical Analysis of Parents as First Teachers." Master's thesis, University of Auckland.

Salmond, Anne. 1975. *Hui: A Study of Māori Ceremonial Gatherings*. Auckland, NZ: Reed.

Sarup, Madan. 1998. *Identity, Culture and the Postmodern World*. Edinburgh: Edinburgh University Press.

Skinner, Damian. 2008. *The Carver and the Artist: Māori Art in the Twentieth Century*. Auckland, NZ: Auckland University Press.

Spivak, Gayatri Chakravorty. 2002. "Responses to One New Friends & Bits from a Paper." Unpublished keynote address to the Indigenous Art & Heritage and the

Politics of Identity Conference, Palmerston North Convention Centre, Manawatu, New Zealand, July 7–9, 2002.

University of Auckland. 1988. *Tanenuiarangi*. Auckland, NZ: University of Auckland.

Walker, Ranginui. 1992. "Marae: A Place to Stand." In *Te Ao Hurihuri: The World Moves On: Aspects of Māoritanga*, edited by Michael King, 15–28. Auckland, NZ: Reed.

19 | Indigenous Knowledge Systems as the Missing Link in Scientific Worldviews

A Discussion on Western Science as a Contested Space

DANIEL LIPE

I AM A NATIVE AMERICAN SCIENTIST AND EDUCATOR who has been shaped by both Indigenous and Western scientific knowledge systems. Both the formulation of my understanding of science along with the methodology of how I carry out scientific research are embedded in and grow out of the fact that I am a product of two cultures—the American culture in which I was colonized/socialized and a Native American culture that has been, more times than not, muted and treated as a subordinate culture by the Western world. I, like many of my Native American peers, am a bi-product of this duality. We view the world around us, including the phenomenon called "science," through multiple lenses. Differentiation in how we communicate "science" to a predominantly Western scientific world is often a confusing, difficult, and painstaking process. Therefore, this reality of Western scientific domination over Indigenous knowledge has created a contested space, especially for those of us who want to utilize multiple knowledge systems.

Analyzing Foundational Values of Indigenous and Western Science

One way I have been able to begin to make sense of both Western science and Indigenous knowledge systems has been through analyzing each system's core values. Making sense of the complexities of each of the two knowledge systems can be a complex process. Acknowledging that each of these two knowledge systems is sizeable and could not be documented fully in any one piece, I cover a range of topics that have helped inform my work and shape my thought processes about Indigenous and Western science systems of knowledge. Table 19.1 is a summary of some of the components of Indigenous knowledge and Western Euro-American knowledge scientific systems. My goals for presenting this table are threefold. The first is to define and de-mystify each knowledge system. This is important so that we can engage in conversations and praxis that are based on some common understandings. Second is to present the two knowledge systems side by side to illustrate the similar and unique qualities of each. In doing so, we can begin to identify how the knowledge systems can complement each other and thus create a more wholistic approach to science. Third, I purposefully present the two knowledge systems as a way to invite current and future scientists to recognize, embrace, and utilize multiple scientific worldviews, including Indigenous knowledge systems, in this way, inviting dialogue between individuals within Indigenous knowledge systems (IKS) and Western science (WS) to start talking about how both these knowledge systems have much to offer within the scientific world.

This table is a compilation of the research of many, including but not limited to Berkes (1999), Cajete (2000), Knudtson and Suzuki (1992), Lake (2007), and Lévi-Strauss (1973). I have taken the concepts and ideas put forth by such authors, made sense of that information through analysis, research, and reflection, and compiled the information into a concise summary.

TABLE 19.1 *Identifying foundational values of Indigenous knowledge and Western science; a summary of comparisons between Indigenous and Western Euro-American approaches to the world*

Indigenous Science	Western Science
Teaching/Learning Styles and Goals	
High-context approach that includes multi-variables that interact concurrently	Low-context approach that tries to isolate single variable away from outer influence
Wholistic, multisensory, and boundless in scope grounded in thorough observation	Fragmented and restricted in scope through an intellectual and technical toolkit
Information that began with or before humankind itself and has continued to expand through oral traditions and knowledge base, even today	Information beginning in 17th-century European Christianity and natural philosophy; foundational ideas trace back to writings of early Greek philosophers
Goal to comprehend knowledge in a practical manner, knowledge for sake of application	Goal to comprehend the workings of the entire universe, to explain through a finite set of natural laws, knowledge for knowledge's sake
Physical World	
Viewed as sensible qualities that are abstract	Viewed as a set of formal concrete qualities
Nature as holy, sacred, unity, familial	Nature as savage, wild, wasteland, disconnected from
Gift economy based upon reciprocal responsibilities	Commodities to be used and sold

TABLE 19.1 *continued*

Indigenous Science	Western Science
Humans and Relationships to Nature	
Active participants in and part of as an equal working part of nature	Separate from, superior to, viewed as an inanimate other to nature
Humans have reciprocal responsibilities and relationship with nature, expression of gratitude for benefits provided	Humans seen as dominion above nature to be used as seen fit, extraction of resources
Maintaining relationship with nature is required, viewed as a daily lifelong practice	Relationships with nature viewed as admirable but not required every day
Spiritual Component	
Spiritual energy or lifeline dispersed throughout all living and non-living things	Spiritual understanding comes only through one supreme, monolithic being

The following sections elaborate on the information provided in Table 19.1.

Indigenous Science and "Indigenous Knowledge Systems"

The Indigenous Peoples of North America have developed, expanded, and utilized their own ontological understandings of the world (Foley 2003; Lake 2007; Cajete 2000; Wilson 2008). Different researchers have utilized different terms to describe Indigenous ways of knowing. A few examples include Native American sciences (Cajete 2000), Indigenous knowledge systems (IKS; Grenier 1998), traditional ecological knowledge (TEK; Alexander et al. 2011; Berkes, Colding, and Folke 2000; Lake 2007; Prober, O'Connor, and Walsh 2011; Tallmadge 2011), and traditional environmental knowledge (Johnson 1992). The definition of each of these terms is similar. Grenier (1998, 1) describes Indigenous knowledge systems as "covering all aspects of life, including management of the natural environment...a matter of survival to the peoples who generated the systems. Such knowledge systems are cumulative, representing observations of experiences, careful observations, and trial-and-error experiments." Grenier begins to illustrate the level of information found within Indigenous knowledge systems. Wholistic in approach, IKS are viewed as high-context ways of knowing, in which knowledge is gained through the understanding of many different variables at many different levels simultaneously (Cajete 2008). IKS are not stagnant systems of the past but are very dynamic, co-evolving over time along with the environment's ecological processes that have shaped them. Knowledge found within the IKS is much more than just scientific information and includes Indigenous ontological understandings. Traditional environmental knowledge (TEK) is defined by Johnson (1992, 4) as "a body of knowledge built up by a group of people through generations of living in close contact with nature...With its roots firmly in the past, traditional environmental knowledge is both cumulative and dynamic, building upon the experience of earlier generations and adapting to the new technology and socioeconomic changes of the present."

Native American science is very dynamic, with multilevel dimensions and definitions (Bohensky and Maru 2011). For example, Cajete (2008) describes Native American science this way:

> Indigenous science is a category of Traditional Ecological Knowledge that includes everything from metaphysical to philosophy... At its most inclusive definition, Indigenous science may also be said to include practically all of human invention...these include areas such as astronomy, healing, agriculture, study of plants, animals, and natural phenomena. Yet, Indigenous science extends beyond these areas to also include a focus on spirituality, community, creativity, appropriate technology that sustains environments, and other essential aspects of human life. (490)

Therefore, though the terms vary among scholars, the definitions are very similar. Consequently, for the purposes of this article, "Native American science" and "Indigenous knowledge systems (IKS)" will be the two terms used interchangeably to describe scientific knowledge systems of the Indigenous Peoples of North America. I have chosen to use the term Indigenous knowledge systems because I believe it better illustrates the wholistic perspectives found within Indigenous scientific understandings. At the same time, many of the Indigenous authors whom I have studied have defined the Indigenous scientific perspectives found within the people of North America as Native American scientific understandings.

Western Science

Western science (ws) can and has been defined in a variety of ways. Depending upon what definition or the spatial and temporal range looked at, the term "Western science" encompasses everything from the phenomena found within the natural world to the social and cultural understandings and knowledge found within each of these areas (Patterson 2006). According to *Webster's New Collegiate Dictionary*, the definition of science is "knowledge attained through study or practice," or "knowledge covering general truths of the operation of general laws, esp. as obtained and tested through scientific method [and] concerned with the physical world" (cited in UCSB ScienceLine 2007). Today's modern science is much more focused and restrictive of the type of knowledge allowed to be called scientific knowledge, allowing only naturalistic or materialistic explanations and causes. Modern science's viewpoint limits the depth of understanding that science can have to ideas that are testable, repeatable, observable, and falsifiable (Shuttleworth 2009). In this manner modern Western science can be viewed as a very restricted, methodological way of obtaining information about the natural world. Western science removes any supernatural claims that cannot be tested or repeated.

The History of Western Science

Nordgren (1998) provides an overview of the history of Western science. The 17th century was the beginning of modern science. Through modern science the world was beginning to be viewed as a set of natural rules that could be identified and solved through mathematical models. In 1620 Francis Bacon published *Novum Organum*, a philosophical work in which he interpreted nature through an inductive method of reasoning. Bacon believed that all aspects of nature could be understood and illustrated through natural laws (not a supernatural being) that were derived through a methodology. In 1637 René Descartes published *Discourse on Method*, further expressing science as a method that could be used to understand and create knowledge. Descartes, through the creation of geometry and geometric expression, believed that knowledge was best explained through reason as opposed to experience. Nordgren (1998, par. 3) describes Descartes's method as a four-step process: "(1) accepting as 'truth' only clear, distinct ideas that could not be doubted, (2) breaking a problem down into parts, (3) deducing one conclusion from another, and (4) conducting a systematic synthesis of all things. Descartes based his entire philosophical approach to science on this deductive method of reasoning."

Through Descartes's methodology, modern Western science began the practice of seeing the natural world as a set of truths best examined through a geometric, mechanistic approach of breaking down the complex into simple elements. According to Tallmadge (2011, 50), Linnaeus took Descartes's research a step further and "based his classification system on a mechanical structure combined with a hierarchy modeled on feudal society with its kingdoms, classes, orders, and families, and Darwin added the final temporal dimension necessary to link them all in a grand narrative." Since its conception, modern Western science has become the dominating perspective of scientific viewpoints, excluding many other ways of knowing as untruthful. "The notion that science is authoritative, neutral and universal privileges science. It gives science the status of a standard measure against which all other realities may be evaluated and judged to be either rational or otherwise" (Rigney 2001, 3). Science as defined through a Western lens has become so powerful that it is the only perspective used in finding solutions to the issues we face in Western society today.

Teaching and Learning Styles and Goals

Both Indigenous knowledge systems and Western science utilize a variety of pedagogies.[1] However, IKS's and WS's approaches to teaching and learning are from opposite sides of the spectrum. Indigenous knowledge systems have been identified as high-context wholistic information systems (Cajete 2008). Teaching and learning are focused on a wholistic approach of looking at the entire system (Berkes 1999; Cajete 2008). Since all things are connected, there is no separating out individual components.

The foundations of Western science teaching and learning styles have been based on isolating individual parts (Bohensky and Maru 2011; Lévi-Strauss 1973; Mazzochi 2006). Recently, WS has begun to approach science from more wholistic perspectives. However, WS does not acknowledge and recognize the generations of wholistic knowledge and pedagogies that IKS bring to science. Because WS is so dominant, important IKS pedagogies are not utilized in scientific endeavours. However, as I will present below, pedagogies from both IKS and WS are unique and, if used together, can add greatly to scientific understandings and practice.

Application Through Oral Traditions

Indigenous knowledge systems are older than any other knowledge systems and are considered to extend back to a time before humans (Mooney 1992). For example, in the Cherokee creation story, the earth is formed by the Water Beetle who dives down into the sea to find mud. When the Water Beetle brings the mud to the surface, it spreads out the mud and the mud turns into the earth. Later, the Great Buzzard flies down to the earth to see if it is dry enough so the sky animals can come and live on it. When the Great Buzzard flies too close to the earth, his great wings touch down and form the mountains and valleys where the Cherokee people later come to live (Mooney 1992).

Wholistic approaches like IKS find understanding through the complexities, relationships, and interactions between all parts of the world as demonstrated in the Cherokee creation story. IKS are adaptive and have been described as high-context dynamic knowledge systems encompassing multilevel variables and processes at the same time (Berkes 1999; Cajete 2008). Although colonization, exploitation of resources, and subjugation of Indigenous Peoples have reduced the volume of IKS available globally, the knowledge found within Indigenous cultures around the world is as valuable today as it was in the past. Barnhardt and Kawagley (2005, 9) state, "The depth of Indigenous knowledge rooted in the long inhabitation of a particular place offers lessons that can benefit everyone, from educator to scientist, as we search for a more satisfying and sustainable way to live on this planet." Just as our environments do not remain static and are ever changing and adapting to different conditions, so too are Indigenous knowledge systems adapting (Cajete 2008). IKS continue to be utilized by Indigenous Peoples to seek understanding for practical and applicable reasons today. In this way, IKS are not static systems of the past.

Although IKS have very deep theoretical foundations, they include much more than a methodology used in finding knowledge for knowledge's sake. Rather, IKS are a way of life that have been developed through hands-on observation and scientific applications (Berkes, Colding, and Folke 2000; Bohensky and Maru 2011; Cajete 1999; Lake 2007; Tallmadge 2011). According to Cajete (2000, 66), "The perspective of Native science goes beyond objective measurement, honoring the primacy of direct experience, interconnectedness, relationship, holism, quality, and value." Indigenous knowledge systems are participatory and have been created through lived and practised applications with nature; they also require knowledge in order to have an application and use. Without application via human relationships with environments, IKS lose their meaning.

Teaching and Learning Through Stories

Indigenous knowledge systems derive from lived experiences that have been explained and passed on through oral traditions from generation to generation (Barnhardt 2007; Berkes, Colding, and Folke 2000; Cajete 1999; Lake 2007; Martinez, Salmón, and Nelson 2008; Prober, O'Connor, and Walsh 2011). The telling of stories, according to Tallmadge (2011, 50), "is the oldest and most enduring technology that humans have devised for constructing, preserving, and transmitting knowledge." Indigenous knowledge systems are taught through encoded stories that incorporate thousands of years of knowledge and understanding. However, such oral traditions are not merely stories for story's sake. Instead, Indigenous stories are super-saturated with information and knowledge, teaching everything from cultural norms and practices. These stories are communicated at many different levels of understanding, requiring the learner, through participation, to create understanding at multiple cognitive levels (Cajete 2000).

However, for those outside the cultural context of the story, Indigenous oral traditions have been interpreted as nothing more than entertainment. Therefore, the dominance of ws has created a contested space in which IKS, through oral traditions, have been ignored for their scientific value. To counter this master narrative, I demonstrate below the value of Indigenous oral traditions as scientific knowledge systems.

Oral traditions were used to teach all ages. At the most basic level, oral traditions taught learners the necessary life skills and societal norms and values required in order to maintain a sense of community and balance within the universe (Cajete 2008). Oral traditions gave the student the ability to build cognitive skills and the ability to understand and process information at a higher level (D.F. Lake, personal communication, March 22, 2012). Often stories do not offer direct answers for resolving issues. Cognition is expected at a level in which the student (or reader) deciphers understanding of the knowledge through their ability to identify, translate, and internalize the expressed meanings (Wilson 2008).

Over time, Indigenous stories have been encoded with knowledge. Many stories hold multiple understandings that are learned over time. In this way, understanding the lessons found within stories is a lifelong process. Lessons are learned and remembered from hearing the same story over and over (Happynook 2004). In addition, stories like the one below, from the Karuk of northwest California, teach everything from cultural norms to species identification and habits and much more.

A2. Kingfisher Snitches Food

a. Kingfisher (shahkunishamman) grew across-river from Ti't, 15 miles above mouth of the salmon. He thought, "I will marry." So he married. Soon he had plenty of children, two little girls and two little boys. He said, "I am going to fish downstream across the river." He went into his boat, crossed and went downstream. There he started to fish with his dip net, after dancing a little, he caught a large salmon. He thought, "I will cut off its tail." He threw the tail away. Then he thought "I will eat it by myself." He cooked it ate and was satisfied. Then he went up river again in his boat. When he came near his house, he shouted from the river, "Children, a tail! (ahichip ipumnish)." The children cried, goody, goody, goody! (yutwi)." He came and said, "Too many persons came to where I was fishing. I gave them all some. So I have only the tail left." Soon they ate their supper. "Here, take a piece of the salmon," said his wife. "No, the children will get hungry. I will eat acorns. That will be enough," he said.

b. Not long after he went fishing again. (With the same result!). This time his wife began to be suspicious of her husband's actions.

c. Next morning he said, "I will go fish." He went downriver, sang, "tanimuuh," and danced. Then he caught a salmon, and, throwing the tail away, cooked and ate the fish. But his wife had said to the children, "go and see. Perhaps he eats it alone. Go down and watch from the side of the river what he does." The children went and saw him catch the fish, cook it, and eat it. Then they ran to the house. The woman said, "Let us leave him. We will go somewhere. Make a fire there upriver and make another up the hill." So the children made a fire by the river and one on the hill. Then they all went off.

d. When Kingfisher called "Ahichip ipumnish," no one answered. He went to the house; he saw nobody. Soon he noticed smoke upriver. He went up, far, but saw nobody. There was only a fire. Looking uphill, he saw smoke there. He thought, "Maybe they went uphill," and went, but he did not see them, even though he shouted. He was still carrying the salmon tail. He went back to his house and shouted again. A mouse tittered. When it laughed again, he caught it and said, "I will kill you unless you tell me where they went." The mouse said, "do not kill me. I know; I will tell you. They took up this acorn-pounding slab and went in underneath." Kingfisher took it up. He saw tracks going into the ground. They led uphill and came out again somewhere. There he shouted again. The woman said to the children, "do not look back. Leave him." He was still carrying the salmon tail, shouting, "Ahichip ipumnish!"

e. Then he overtook them. He wanted to throw the tail into her pack basket. She threw it out again. Picking it up, he tried to throw it back in. Then, becoming angry, he said "well, then, I let you go." He threw her up and she turned into a yellow pine, and he threw away the children. The woman said to him, "You will eat no more salmon. You will fly up and downriver and eat anything you can. As long as people live they will use me. I will be for their good, and so will my children be. They will be hazel (sharip) and Xeroyphllum (panyurar) and five-finger fern (kiritapkir) and Woodwardia fern (tiptip). As long as people live, they will use us (for baskets)." She herself was the yellow pine (whose roots make wefts). (Kroeber and Gifford 1980, 5–6)[2]

Stories like this one can be found throughout Indigenous cultures. Children hear these stories from the time they are born, teaching them culturally important norms such as the need to share and not be greedy. As children grow older and develop the ability to pick out different understandings and lessons, the same story teaches them about culturally important plant species that can be used as basketry materials, and how to identify species like the water wren in given areas. Later, the story provides learners with a familial relationship to the plants used as basketry materials and the reciprocal relationships between humans and other species. There are genealogical connections between plants and animals as the wife and children of Kingfisher turn into plant materials. Stories can also teach skills. For example, this story teaches what fishing techniques work best at the place it describes and the protocols that go along with fishing there. Every tribe has stories like this that help build upon the relationships between humans and local environments, which in turn help to teach science as well as the accompanying ethical lessons like the responsibilities of taking care of one another and the environments that sustained us. As demonstrated, there is much scientific knowledge to be gleaned from such stories. Therefore, I presented one story as an invitation to begin to re-evaluate what "science" looks like and the sources we draw from it. When we begin to include Indigenous Peoples and their stories in our education systems as "science," then we begin to grow a new generation who can recognize and utilize a variety of scientific perspectives. This movement can aid in eliminating the contested space.

Western Science: Low Context, Fragmentation
Western science has been identified as a low-context knowledge system that tries to identify how the world works through fragmenting the whole into individually defined and operable pieces (Cajete 2000). Western science seeks to understand the entire universe and beyond, not for any purposeful necessity but as a means to control the world.

Based on a methodological approach developed in the 17th century, Western science utilizes a set of natural laws and rules to identify the truth of the natural world (Moore 1993). Through this methodology, Western science breaks down systems into fragmented individual pieces.

The term "Western science" is a process for obtaining knowledge as well as obtaining knowledge of the natural world (University of California Museum of Paleontology, n.d.). Moore (1993, 3) emphasizes this process: "Science is a way of knowing by accumulating data from observations and experiments, seeking relationships of the data with other natural phenomena, and excluding supernatural explanations and personal wishes. It has proved a powerful procedure for understanding nature." Therefore, the scientific methodology is the means by which science achieves its findings. Fundamentally, then, science can be characterized as a method of obtaining reliable, though not infallible, knowledge about the universe around us. According to Knudtson and Suzuki (1992, 11), "The [Western] scientist seeks nothing less than eventually to comprehend the workings of the whole universe, to 'explain' it rationally by somehow reducing all of its seemingly unfathomable mysteries to a finite set of natural laws that grant order to the cosmos."

The Physical World

Both IKS and WS have relationships to the physical world that help to create the foundational views to how one treats environments. For IKS, these relationships are ones of familial connection in which the environment is treated with respect and all things both great and small are important (Lake 2011). For WS, relationships are much different in that environments and environmental goods are seen as commodities to be owned and dealt with as possessions (Taylor 1999). These two relationships with the physical world are clearly opposing. The dominance of Western science then creates a contested space for IKS in which relationships to the natural world are not recognized. I define each of these relationships to the physical world below.

Indigenous Knowledge Systems: Founded on Relationships

Indigenous knowledge systems are founded upon familial, respectful, reciprocal relationships with the environment (Happynook 2004; Martinez, Salmón, and Nelson 2008). Through relationships, Native Americans are connected to and value all things. According to Kudtson and Suzuki (2006, 15), "Native minds reveal a profound sense of empathy and kinship with other forms of life... Each species is seen as richly endowed with its own singular array of gifts and powers." Native American belief systems and familial ties extend beyond local environments and into the global. According to Cajete (2000, 70), "Particular places are endowed with special energy that may be used but must be protected. This sentiment extends from the notion of sacred space and the understanding that the Earth itself is sacred." Therefore, anything received from the environment is viewed as a gift, but it can also be taken away if not respected appropriately. In IKS, a gift is not considered a possession to be owned but is seen as something that has to be returned or passed on. This relationship is what guides scientific ethics within Indigenous knowledge systems.

Western Science: A Commodity Economy

From a Western science perspective, nature is a set of formal qualities that can be described through a set of concrete mathematical rules. According to Knudtson and Suzuki (1992, 121), "In the spiritually detached Western view of nature, land is lifeless. It is inert, a two-dimensional physical surface to be surveyed, subdivided, and zoned. It is a commodity valuable but no more sacred than a stack of cedar logs, a heap of coal, or any other economic resource."

The Western perception of land and resources as lifeless and a commodity began to develop, according to Hayward (1997), in the late 10th and early 11th centuries. At this time there was a shift in perspective when the Greek philosopher Aristotle's work was rediscovered. Aristotle's writings were reflected in the Roman Catholic Church's perspective that the earth and nature were one realm and the heavens a separate realm. However, according to Aristotle, the heavenly realm was not a perfect place where God could be found but a separate realm made up and controlled by outer forces. Nature and the world were not directly controlled by God, who overlooked it from the heavenly realm; rather, they had their own modes of functioning that were separate from God and the heavens.

In the 13th century, Thomas Aquinas took the scientific philosophies of Aristotle and the Greeks a step further by stating that the earth was the centre of the world and that there were nine additional realms (planets) that moved around the earth (Peat 2002). Aquinas also stated that everything could be understood and explained as being made up of matter. Matter itself was made up of four different elements or combinations of elements, the earth being the central element, with fire, water, and air being the other three. This philosophy tried to reconnect Aristotle's writings with Church doctrine through the belief that human souls travel through the nine realms until they reach the outer tenth heavenly realm. Since matter was believed to be lifeless, and if everything within nature was made of lifeless matter, then separation from any relationship or responsibility to care for nature was possible. Furthermore, if humans could better understand matter, then they could learn to control nature and the world around them.

The concept of matter further separated humans from nature in Euro-American scientific philosophy. Today, Western science has further separated society from nature. Berkes (1999, 3) points out, "Surrounded by the built landscape, it has become difficult for people to relate to the environment. This alienation from nature has contributed to the many environmental issues of the contemporary world." In today's fast-paced world, even the on-the-ground biologists find themselves working more within their offices and spending less time out in the field. More often than not Western scientists today are using a variety of data, including statistics, in order to run computer simulation programs in hope of recreating what is taking place within ecosystems and projecting what will take place in the future. One of the issues with this type of virtual management, as pointed out by Lichatowich (1999) in his discussion of salmon management, is that the management takes place in offices where scientists look through reams and reams of data. In this virtual model, the biologists lose contact with the natural world, and when they talk about salmon, they are talking about lifeless, virtual representations of the real thing. Lichatowich states, "In the 'reality' of the conference rooms, the numbers are abstracted from the living salmon, the salmon are abstracted from their habitat, the habitat is abstracted from the river, and the river is abstracted from the ecosystem" (3). While computers, numbers, and meetings can be helpful in today's salmon management, the real-life connections to the rivers and the salmon are equally important.

Humans and Their Relationship to Nature

Indigenous Knowledge Systems: Active Participation

Indigenous knowledge systems require active participation between humans and their environments (Lévi-Strauss 1973; Happynook 2004). Participation is a lifelong process that is carried out daily. At the core of IKS are relationships established through hands-on learned experiences, based upon respect and reciprocity between humans and their environments. According to Happynook (2004, 1), "At the root of Indigenous self-determination are duties, responsibilities, philosophies, jurisdictions, and authorities that have evolved over millennia into unwritten Indigenous laws." Through these unwritten laws, relationships, and sustainable cultural management practices, Indigenous Peoples have shaped and continue to shape their local environments because they live as integrated members of the natural world (Happynook 2004). According to Cajete (2008, 491), "Humans are co-creators with the higher powers of nature so that everything that we do has importance for the rest of the world...It is a map of reality drawn from the experiences of thousands of human generations that gave rise to technologies for hunting, fishing, gathering, making art, building, communicating, visioning, healing and being."

The above belief that everything humans do affects the world is an important lesson in Indigenous knowledge systems. Through the teachings in IKS, society is taught that humans need to understand how we affect our surroundings. Sustaining ecosystems and the functions, products, and values they provide for future generations is at the core of these teachings. What we learn from IKS is that humans need to re-establish relationships with nature.

Familial Relationships to Land

Many of the stories connect humans through a familial relationship to the world at different levels. It is through familial relationship to place that IKS have developed sustainable environmental land ethics and understandings of the importance of all things in nature. Many lessons have been learned along the way that have shaped the environmental ethics found within IKS, including the importance of a familial relationship to the land. When people share a familial relationship to the earth they become more conscientious about management decisions. One such example of a familial relationship can be found between the Cherokee and the cedar tree, which is described in "The Legend of the Cedar Tree" as told by Jim Fox (n.d.):

> A long time ago when the Cherokee people were new upon the earth, they thought that life would be much better if there was never any night. They beseeched the Ouga (Creator) that it might be day all the time and that there would be no darkness.
>
> The Creator heard their voices and made the night cease and it was day all the time. Soon, the forest was thick with heavy growth. It became difficult to walk and to find the path. The people toiled in the gardens many long hours trying to keep the weeds pulled from among the corn and other food plants. It got hot, very hot, and continued that way day after long day. The people began to find it difficult to sleep and became short tempered and argued among themselves.
>
> Not many days had passed before the people realized they had made a mistake and, once again, they beseeched the Creator. "Please," they said, "we have made a mistake in asking that it be day all the time. Now we think that it should be night all the time." The Creator paused at this new request and thought that perhaps the people may be right even though all things were created in twos...representing to us day and night, life and death, good and evil, times of plenty and those times of famine. The Creator loved the people and decided to make it night all the time as they had asked.

The day ceased and night fell upon the earth. Soon, the crops stopped growing and it became very cold. The people spent much of their time gathering wood for the fires. They could not see to hunt meat and with no crops growing it was not long before the people were cold, weak, and very hungry. Many of the people died.

Those that remained still living gathered once again to beseech the Creator. "Help us Creator," they cried! "We have made a terrible mistake. You had made the day and the night perfect, and as it should be, from the beginning. We ask that you forgive us and make the day and night as it was before."

Once again the Creator listened to the request of the people. The day and the night became, as the people had asked, as it had been in the beginning. Each day was divided between light and darkness. The weather became more pleasant, and the crops began to grow again. Game was plentiful and the hunting was good. The people had plenty to eat and there was not much sickness. The people treated each other with compassion and respect. It was good to be alive. The people thanked the Creator for their life and for the food they had to eat.

The Creator accepted the gratitude of the people and was glad to see them smiling again. However, during the time of the long days of night, many of the people had died, and the Creator was sorry that they had perished because of the night. The Creator placed their spirits in a newly created tree. This tree was named *a-tsi-na tlu-gv* {ah-see-na loo-guh} cedar tree.

When you smell the aroma of the cedar tree or gaze upon it standing in the forest, remember that if you are Tsalagi (Cherokee), you are looking upon your ancestor.

Tradition holds that the wood of the cedar tree holds powerful protective spirits for the Cherokee. Many carry a small piece of cedar wood in their medicine bags worn around the neck. It is also placed above the entrances to the house to protect against the entry of evil spirits. A traditional drum would be made from cedar wood. (paras. 1–9)[3]

This story connects the Cherokee to the cedar tree, which is one of the most important and sacred trees found within their territories. Similar stories can be found throughout the IKS. At the foundational level, Indigenous stories link the people to the world around them through familial relationships (Mooney 1992). It is a relationship in which humans treat the earth with the same respect they treat their parents and grandparents.

Western Science: Control over Nature

Western science is rooted in the need to control nature. Cajete (2000, 16) highlights this point: "Western science is committed to increasing human mastery over nature, to go on conquering until everything natural is under absolute human control." According to Callicott (1997), humans were put on this earth by God in order to control and dominate their surroundings and all the plants and animals have been placed on this earth to serve God's people. In this manner humans are superior to all that God has created and may use it as they see fit.

This type of thinking has led to a knowledge system that values land as a commodity as opposed to being connected to or a part of the earth (Taylor 1999). Furthermore, Western science views nature as an object, an inanimate other (Knudtson and Suzuki 1992). Consequently, Western science does not connect people to place. Instead, there is a great distance placed between humans and their environments in which familial relationships, respect, and connection are lost.

An example of the contested space that this disconnect causes was shared with me by an Indigenous colleague. While performing research on Indigenous cultural management practices of plants and environments, including burning and cutting of cultural basketry materials, he found that the management practices resulted in the regrowth of high-quality plants and materials. Specifically, he followed Indigenous management practices as carried out in that area for generations in which prescribed[4] fire is used but not to the detriment of plants.

Upon completion of his experiments he was told by a Western science mentor that in order to be a truly respected scientist he had to perform multiple prescriptions. First, he had to have a control group of plants in which no fire or harvesting was applied. Then he had to apply multiple prescriptions, from short periods of fire to very long periods of fire in an area, in order to test the reaction and regrowth of the plants. The extreme prescription would leave the plants completely dead. This expectation by the dominant Western science world left my Indigenous colleague trapped in a contested space. He was forced to choose between being recognized by the larger Western science community and following his familial responsibilities to the plants and environments. If he did not manage the plants at all, he would be neglecting his responsibilities to care for those resources. If he inappropriately burned the area until the plants were completely dead, then he again would be neglecting his familial responsibilities. In the end, he chose not to conform to the Western scientific paradigm of environmental management. Consequently, my Indigenous colleague and his IKS continue to be questioned by the Western scientific world.

Spiritual Components

One of the major differences between IKS and WS is spirituality. For IKS, spirituality cannot be removed without losing meaning. Spiritual life forces are found in all things. In modern WS, spiritual events and processes cannot be measured, tested, or proven and are therefore not science (Patterson 2006). Western science utilizes a methodology that removes all spiritual and super natural events out of what is defined as science. However, in many cases, Indigenous knowledge systems' definition of spiritual is much different from Western science's definitions of spiritual.

Indigenous Knowledge Systems: Spirit in All Things

Everything found within IKS has a purpose, including spiritual beliefs. Spiritual beliefs and ceremonies are used as a way of respecting and honouring the relationships humans have to their world. For Indigenous Peoples, all things have life energies, forces, or spirit (Cajete 1999; D.F.

Lake, personal communication, March 22, 2011). These energies or spirits are considered "power." Many Indigenous people consider sacred places or ceremonial objects as powerful.

The way in which life energies or forces are honoured is through ceremonies. Ceremonies are used not only as a means to carry out and honour spiritual energies and forces but also as a means to learn from the forces and energies found within all living and non-living things. Ceremonial objects include placed-based environmental objects, species, and tools that can be found within the lands that each tribal group maintains (Berkes 1999). To prepare for ceremony, many Indigenous people visit "power[full]"[5] places to acquire sacred knowledge, as well as collect animals, plants, rocks or other materials having "power" to assemble what they need for ceremonies. Indigenous spirituality is a way of understanding the inter-relatedness of forces and elements found in the world. It is the foundation of Indigenous science.

When the Indigenous spiritual component is removed, so is a part of the understanding of how that place works. It is like having a definition without all of the defining parts. Knudtson and Suzuki (1992, 16) highlight an important point: "It is important to emphasize that this inherent spiritual dimension does not mean that Native nature-wisdom is somehow naively romantic, ethereal, or disconnected from ordinary keen personal observation, interaction, and thought, sharpened by the daily rigors of uncertain survival."

Indeed, Indigenous spirituality is one way that Indigenous Peoples explore and come to understand and teach about the elements, forces, energies, and science found within the world. Spirituality is yet another connection to place creating yet another level of respect and way to learn from the many environments that sustain all living things.

Western Science: Spirituality Is Separate from Science
Western science views spirituality through a different lens. Spirituality is defined through the influences of the Church and its religious beliefs. Over the years Western science has tried with different levels of success

to remove religious beliefs from the realms of science. Religion is seen as something to be separated from science. Still science has been heavily influenced by religion and church beliefs. One such influence has been through the connection of the first humans to the environment (Callicot 1997). Modern science believes that understanding can only be found through natural laws. Therefore, super natural phenomena and religion, which could not be fully explained through natural laws, were removed from modern scientific fields. Regarding the relationship between super natural phenomena and science, Miller (2007) states,

> Super natural phenomena are always possible, but they are above the capacity of science to analyze and interpret. Saying that something has a super natural cause is always possible, but saying that the super natural can be investigated by science, which always has to work by natural tools and mechanisms, is simply incorrect. Matters of opinion, morality, and spiritual beliefs that cannot be tested with empirical evidence are not within the domain of science. "Natural" means explainable and understandable, capable of being explained, whereas "supernatural" means unexplainable—beyond human understanding. Thus, supernatural beliefs are excluded from science because they deny the very essence of science. (1)

Whether or not spirituality is labelled as "science," it is an interconnected and necessary component of Indigenous knowledge systems. However, as described above, ws refuses to accept any sense of spirituality in its realm, thus creating a contested space for anyone who wants to include spirituality in their scientific practices.

An example of such contested space for Indigenous scientists was shared with me by an Indigenous graduate student who was studying science. The student engaged in the culturally appropriate practice of introducing oneself to a new environment by offering a prayer. Later the student was approached by a Western professor and questioned regarding the practice of prayer. Upon explanation, the professor told the student that prayer was a waste of time and it made the professor feel uncomfortable. Further, the professor told the student to stop the practice of prayer while engaging in fieldwork. Later, other professors in the department heard of the student's cultural and spiritual practice and thus refused to be a member of the student's dissertation committee. As a result, the student was forced out of that department and had to find a new department in which to continue this doctoral work.

Building Multiple Perspectives

This chapter has illustrated the contested space in which IKS is forced to exist within the dominant WS world. As described, one of the main reasons WS currently dominates is because it comes from an ideology that argues there can only be one scientific truth. Further, WS dominance has been perpetuated as the only scientific perspective utilized in North American education systems. This has led to a total lack of understanding of any other scientific perspectives, including Indigenous knowledge systems. This chapter has focused on IKS and on the foundations of Western science. In doing so, it has recognized the contributions of each that can help us find ways to use these multiple scientific perspectives for the benefit of our world.

As described in this chapter, both IKS and WS have their own scientific methodologies to acquiring knowledge. Because of the major differences between IKS and WS, it seems impossible to merge the two systems into one. However, differences do not mean that IKS and WS cannot work together or alongside one another, thus eliminating the current contested space. Research has shown that indeed IKS and WS can be complementary to each other if utilized in the correct manner. Moller et al. (2004) identify four complementary aspects of IKS and WS:

1. While Western science is good at collecting synchronic data over large areas for short terms of time, IKS are based upon diachronic data over relatively small local areas for long amounts of time.

2. While most Western science information is based upon averages, IKS identify extreme events.
3. Science relies strictly on the quantitative while IKS utilize a holistic qualitative approach.
4. While IKS provide answers to relativity, they often do not try to look at the mechanisms behind questions like Western science does. (12)

Utilizing IKS and WS as a means to develop more in-depth and comprehensive understandings of the very complex and multilevel issues associated with environmental management can benefit all peoples and environments. This is why it is imperative that we explore ways to eliminate the current contested space and move towards utilizing diverse scientific perspectives.

There is a movement of Indigenous scientists and non-Indigenous supporters of IKS who are trying to make a change not only for themselves but also for their families, communities, cultures, and local and global environments. This change is taking place through individuals who are making efforts to learn from both IKS and WS. In addition, these individuals are also learning facilitation and communication skills to assist the transition between IKS and WS and each of their communities.

As this movement begins, an integral first step is to learn the foundational core values and beliefs of both IKS and WS. Once these foundations and histories are learned, then individuals can better grasp how these two systems can begin to work together. Otherwise, our world will continue to suffer as important scientific understandings and methodologies are ignored, such as those found in Indigenous knowledge systems.

Notes

1. Pedagogies are defined as the styles of teaching that are used by educators to teach (Collins and O'Brien 2003).

2. Alfred L. Kroeber and E.W. Gifford, *Karok Myths*, ©1980, University of California Press. Used with permission.
3. "The Legend of the Cedar Tree" is used with permission of the © Cherokees Of California, Inc., http://www.powersource.com/cocinc/articles/cedar.htm. All rights reserved.
4. Prescriptions are the type of treatment applied to an area. In this particular case, prescriptions refer to burning and harvesting at different levels (from no fire to extreme fire use).
5. I use the word "power" to describe the spirit and sanctity of people, places, and things as understood in Indigenous worldviews.

References

Alexander, Clarence, Nora Bynum, Elizabeth Johnson, Ursula King, Tero Mustonen, Peter Neofotis, Noel Oettlé, Cynthia Rosenzweig, Chie Sakakibara, Vyacheslav Shadrin, Marta Vicarelli, Jon Waterhouse, and Brian Weeks. 2011. "Linking Indigenous and Scientific Knowledge of Climate Change." *BioScience* 61 (6): 477-84. doi:10.1525/bio.2011.61.6.10

Barnhardt, Ray. 2007. "Creating a Place for Indigenous Knowledge in Education: The Alaska Native Knowledge Network." In *Place Based Education in the Global Age: Local Diversity*, edited by Gregory A. Smith and David A. Gruenewald, 113-34. Hillsdale, NJ: Lawrence Erlbaum Associates.

Barnhardt, Ray, and Angayuqaq Oscar Kawagley. 2005. "Indigenous Knowledge Systems and Alaska Native Ways of Knowing." *Anthropology and Education Quarterly* 36 (1): 8-23.

Berkes, Fikret. 1999. *Sacred Ecology: Traditional Ecological Knowledge and Resource Management*. Philadelphia: Taylor & Francis.

Berkes, Fikret, Johan Colding, and Carl Folke, C. 2000. "Rediscovery of Traditional Ecological Knowledge as Adaptive Management." *Ecological Applications* 10 (5): 1251-62.

Bohensky, Erin L., and Yiheyis Maru. 2011. "Indigenous Knowledge, Science, and Resilience: What Have We Learned from a Decade of International Literature on 'Integration'?" *Ecology and Society* 16 (4): 6. doi:10.5751/ES-04342-160406

Cajete, Gregory. 2000. *Native Science: Natural Laws of Interdependence*. Santa Fe: Clear Light Publishers.

———. 2008. "Seven Orientations for Developing an Indigenous Science Education." In *Handbook of Critical and Indigenous Methodologies*, edited by Norman K. Denzin, Yvonne S. Lincoln, and Linda Tuhiwai Smith, 487-96. Thousand Oaks, CA: Sage.

Callicott, J. Baird. 1997. *Earth's Insights: A Multicultural Survey of Ecological Ethics from the Mediterranean Basin to the Australian Outback.* Berkeley: University of California Press.

Collins, John W., and Nancy Patricia O'Brien, eds. 2003. *The Greenwood Dictionary of Education.* Westport, CT: Greenwood Press.

Foley, Dennis. 2003. "Indigenous Epistemologies and Indigenous Standpoint Theory." *Journal of Social Alternatives* 22 (1): 44–52.

Fox, Jim. n.d. "The Legend of the Cedar Tree." *Cherokees of California.* http://www.powersource.com/cocinc/articles/cedar.htm. Accessed January 15, 2019.

Grenier, Louise. 1998. *Working with Indigenous Knowledge: A Guide for Researchers.* Ottawa: International Development Research Centre. https://www.idrc.ca/en/book/working-indigenous-knowledge-guide-researchers

Happynook, Tom. 2004. "Securing Food, Health and Traditional Values Through the Sustainable Use of Marine Resources." Brentwood Bay, BC: World Council of Whalers. https://ilja-herb.squarespace.com/s/Happynook_Securing-Food-Health-Traditional-Values_Whaling20022.pdf

Hayward, Jeremy W. 1997. *Letters to Vanessa: On Love, Science, and Awareness in an Enchanted World.* Boston: Shambhala.

Johnson, Martha, ed. 1992. *Lore: Capturing Traditional Environmental Knowledge.* Dene Cultural Institute: International Development Research Centre. https://www.idrc.ca/en/book/lore-capturing-traditional-environmental-knowledge

Knudtson, Peter, and David Suzuki. 1992. *Wisdom of the Elders.* New York: Bantam Books.

Kroeber, Alfred L., and E.W. Gifford. 1980. *Karok Myths.* Berkeley: University of California Press.

Lake, Frank K. 2007. "Traditional Ecological Knowledge to Develop and Maintain Fire Regimes in Northwestern California, Klamath-Siskiyou Bioregion: Management and Restoration of Culturally Significant Habitats." PHD diss., Oregon State University.

Lévi-Strauss, Claude. 1973. *The Savage Mind.* Chicago: University of Chicago Press.

Lichatowich, James A. 1999. *Salmon Without Rivers: A History of the Pacific Salmon Crisis.* Washington, DC: Island Press.

Martinez, Dennis, Enrique Salmón, and Melissa K. Nelson. 2008. "Restoring Indigenous History and Culture to Nature." In *Original Instructions: Indigenous Teachings for a Sustainable Future,* edited by Melissa K. Nelson, 88–115. Rochester, VT: Bear and Company.

Mazzochi, Fulvio, 2006. "Western Science and Traditional Knowledge: Despite Their Variations, Different Forms of Knowledge Can Learn From Each Other." *EMBO Reports*, 7 (5): 463–6.

Miller, Kenneth. 2007. "In Defense of Evolution." *NOVA PBS*. http://www.pbs.org/wgbh/nova/evolution/defense-evolution.html

Moller, Henrik, Fikret Berkes, O'Brian Lyver, and Mina Kislalioglu. 2004. "Combining Science and Traditional Ecological Knowledge: Monitoring Populations for Co-management." *Ecology and Society* 9 (3): 2. https://www.ecologyandsociety.org/vol9/iss3/art2/

Mooney, James. 1992. *James Mooney's History, Myths, and Sacred Formulas of the Cherokees*. Asheville, NC: Historical Images.

Moore, John A. 1993. *Science as a Way of Knowing: The Foundations of Modern Biology*. Cambridge, MA: Harvard University Press.

Nordgren, Tim. 1998. "The Scientific Methods of Rene Descartes and Francis Bacon." *Things Revealed*. http://www.thingsrevealed.net/dscrtbacn.htm

Patterson, Roger T. 2006. *Evolution Exposed: Your Evolution Answer Book for the Classroom*. Hebron, KY: Answers in Genesis.

Peat, F. David. 2002. *From Certainty to Uncertainty: The Story of Science and Ideas in the Twentieth Century*. Washington, DC: Joseph Henry Press.

Prober, Suzanne M., Michael H. O'Connor, and Fiona J. Walsh. 2011. "Australian Aboriginal Peoples' Seasonal Knowledge: A Potential Basis for Shared Understanding in Environmental Management." *Journal of Ecology and Society* 16 (2): 12. https://www.ecologyandsociety.org/vol16/iss2/art12/

Rigney, Lester-Irabinna. 2001. "A First Perspective of Indigenous Australian Participation in Science: Framing Indigenous Research Towards Indigenous Australian Intellectual Sovereignty." *Kauma Higher Education Journal* 7: 1–13.

Shuttleworth, Martyn. 2009. "The History of the Scientific Method Is a Fascinating and Long One, Covering Thousands of Years of History." *Explorable*. http://explorable.com/history-of-the-scientific-method.html

Tallmadge, John. 2011. "Linked Through Story: Natural Science, Nature Writing, and Traditional Ecological Knowledge." *Journal of Natural History Education and Experience* 5: 49–54.

Taylor, Joseph E. 1999. *Making Salmon: An Environmental History of the Northwest Fisheries Crisis*. Seattle: University of Washington Press.

University of California Museum of Paleontology. n.d. "What Is Science?" *Understanding Science: How Science Really Works*. https://undsci.berkeley.edu/article/whatisscience_01.

UCSB ScienceLine. 2007. "What Is Science?" University of California at Santa Barbara. http://scienceline.ucsb.edu/getkey.php?key=1408

Wilson, Shawn. 2008. *Research Is Ceremony: Indigenous Research Methods*. Black Point, NS: Fernwood.

20 | Is "Space" the Final Frontier?
Talking Forward Indigenous Frameworks in Education

PATRICIA MARINGI G. JOHNSTON

Introduction

In 1999, at the Australian Association for Research in Education (AARE) Conference, a colleague and I suggested in our presentation that the best space for Indigenous educators to build and develop Indigenous education programs was a space where members of the colonizing groups were not present (Waitere-Ang and Johnston 1999a). Several people in the audience stood and left the room. While our critique and "hard-hitting" message was directed mainly at those members of dominant groups who had attempted to create space for Indigenous education in their own institutions (and then promptly filled those spaces themselves), we took the opportunity to dialogue about what an Indigenous space might look like and the multiple "frontiers" that existed in relation to those spaces. We spoke directly about an Indigenous frontier where the decision-making relating to education and the strategies for development would reside with Indigenous Peoples and not members of the dominant group.

That dialogue in 1999 was about challenging how dominant groups responded to Indigenous aspirations for self-determination, and to the subsequent representations of those aspirations in a number of spaces like research, curriculum, and the education system. While the notion of creating space for Indigenous education is not new, Indigenous academics continue to argue that creating space for Indigenous education involves far more than simply allocating positions or creating "a space" for those who identify as Indigenous within education settings (L.T. Smith 1999; Johnston and McLeod 2001; Johnston 2003, 2004, 2012). Nor does it simply mean adding cultural or ethnic additives to education programs, the curriculum, or education policies (Johnston 2010; Waitere-Ang and Johnston 1999). Creating space includes the active recognition and practice of worldviews and knowledge bases that are distinctly Indigenous, which encompass the ways in which Indigenous Peoples think about the world, articulate their relationships with it (Waitere-Ang and Johnston 1999), and aspire to their own self-determinations and developments (G. Smith 2015). The creation of such "spaces" is not only physical, but theoretical and conceptual as well, and that has the potential to "push back" and "disrupt the hegemonic spaces" of dominant groups (Johnston 2003).

Initially our 1999 reflections were based on the experiences and critiques of Indigenous academics working within dominant frameworks and institutions, as that was the space I found myself in. I wondered, however, if the dominant framework and institution were an Indigenous one if that would make a difference for Indigenous education. In addressing this question, this chapter examines explicitly the creation of an Indigenous higher education tertiary institution, Te Whare Wānanga o Awanuiārangi (TWOA), in Aotearoa New Zealand. I joined TWOA in March 2003 to establish post-graduate programs. The chapter examines how that educational setting generated a transformative context for Indigenous self-determination, while also acknowledging ongoing challenges and issues created by colonial views about what education for Māori should look like.

A Theoretical Discussion about "Space"

In 1999, Waitere-Ang and I discussed some of the difficulties associated with "Indigenous space," in terms of how Māori (the Indigenous group of New Zealand)[1] were accounted for within an education system that was controlled by and that supported the interests of the dominant group, Pākehā.[2] That discussion drew from specific examples of Māori attempts to negotiate within and around terrain that positioned Māori knowledge and culture as ethnic additives to education programs and curriculum subjects. We discussed a strategy employed by Māori academic staff within one specific mainstream[3] teacher training institution that attempted to create change by moving our involvement in Māori education beyond being just merely additive "window dressing" to an already prescribed "real curriculum." We identified and named a number of spaces where this was occurring; these spaces are outlined in Figure 20.1 and are named as follows: Indigenous; colonial; "un-named"; occupied; breathing; positional; disruptive; and supportive spaces.

In the context of this chapter, *Indigenous space* refers to the recognition, theory, and practice of worldviews that draw from knowledge bases that encompass the ways in which Indigenous Peoples think about their world and articulate their relationships within their world. *Colonial space* refers to the taken-for-granted normality represented by the actions, beliefs, and views of the dominant group, as the points for comparison with and for "Indigenous education."

The point at which the Indigenous and colonial spaces meet in higher education is where Indigenous programs (represented generally as ethnic studies, cultural studies, and Māori studies, for example) operate. In that meeting place, the colonial space tends to dominate what gets to count as Māori education because of the very rules and regulations that control what counts (Johnston 1998). The colonial space contains *occupational* and *un-named* "space": the occupational space represents areas in which non-Indigenous educators reside and we recognize that much of the decision-making relating to Māori education sits with those who are not Māori. Furthermore, this space is filled with "gatekeepers" who control,

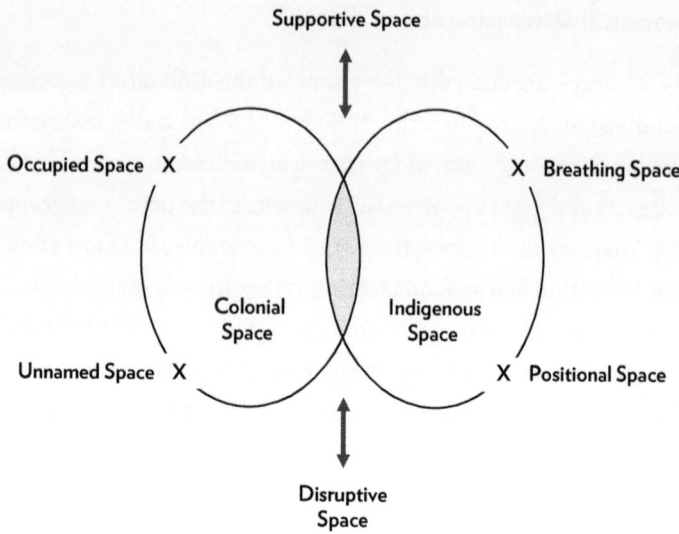

FIGURE 20.1 *The identification and creation of space, adapted from Waitere-Ang and Johnston (1999). [Patricia Maringi G. Johnston]*

subvert, and sabotage our endeavours for "the right of education" (Dei 1996, 17) by occupying (through employment) those spaces. Their role can become one of interfering in Māori assertions for decision-making by Māori for Māori (G. Smith 1991) and they are able to do so merely because of the places of authority that they occupy.

The un-named space is one that supports the legitimacy and validity afforded to Pākehā worldviews and English language as the norm against which Māori knowledge is compared. That legitimacy is based on un-stated, unwritten dominant normality (Waitere-Ang and Johnston 1999). This can be seen through the curriculum in which the focus is on Māori culture as cultural diversity (to the norm) rather than as an integrated aspect of the everyday operation of curriculum subjects. The un-named space, however, needs to be recognized for what it is—monoculturalism; the assertion of dominant worldviews and practices as the only legitimate forms of education.

"Breathing space" is a space without outsider/settler voices or presence that enables Indigenous Peoples to discuss and contest things

Indigenous in relative safety; a space where there is an understanding that Indigenous languages and cultures are taken for granted. In this space, autonomy over our own decision-making, goals, and objectives occurs. It is a space that enables us to disengage from the politics of dominance if we so choose.

"Positional space" is the recognition of decision-making relating to Indigenous knowledge and worldviews that resides with academics and educators in positions of authority. Indigenous participation becomes central to decision-making forums like committees, or in university processes that hear our "voice" as a right and not by default. Those positions afford to us the ability to implement our ideas and plans. Positional space also acknowledges those who are Māori in key decision-making positions, in positions of seniority throughout academic institutions, in schools, and in the education system.

Perspectives of history are those of the dominant group, culture is often represented through an anthropological lens, and Māori knowledge/language is not accorded any status except as a curriculum subject. However, where the colonial and Indigenous spaces meet is where contestation and challenges to Western hegemony occur. Thus we find disrupted and supportive spaces—the points at which we as Indigenous academics challenge others to think and act outside of the colonial space. This also includes Indigenous Peoples who may need to move through processes of "decolonization" or disruption from the hegemonic assimilative processes that have led them to think of their own language, knowledge, and culture as inferior.

Within the New Zealand context in particular, the right side of Figure 20.1 represents the support that is afforded to the Indigenous space by both Māori and Pākehā. Ultimately, we would like to facilitate Pākehā to be active disrupters and "decolonizers" of other Pākehā students, teachers, and lecturers. The goal is to teach them and help them see their own complicity in colonization through theoretical dialogues that challenge students' thoughts about Māori education and Māori children in terms of Indigenous frameworks and not colonial ones. However, if we don't provide others with the ability to move forward, then what is created is a reactionary space in which Pākehā react in negative ways, reinforcing the stereotypes and prejudices that they hold about Māori (Waitere-Ang and Johnston 1999). They then tend to move back into their Pākehā centred comfort spaces that endorse Pākehā culture as privileged and normal (demonstrated on the left-hand side of Figure 20.1). It is important, then, that we provide those who engage with the means to move forward while supporting them to be able to do so.

The left side of Figure 20.1 also represents the spaces within the colonial space in which Māori educators engage, as do Pākehā who support movements towards an inclusive education and schooling system. Through contestation and challenges to hegemony in our teaching, research, and publications, those un-named spaces and the spaces that non-Indigenous educators occupy can be challenged. Our engagement is as equally important as our occupancy within our own "breathing space," as it is through the engagement and contestation that we can create structural changes that result in spaces that can become "captured" and therefore changed.

What this chapter has outlined thus far is that although issues and representations of space may vary, few are detached from struggling with conceptions of power and how power affects the creation and interpretations of those spaces. For instance, because the power to define education continues to be debated within contexts that we have no control over (Waitere-Ang and Johnston 1999b), definitions of inclusion in terms of who is occupying what space are not necessarily those that are in the best interests of Māori educators. One such example of power and control relates to the distinction to be drawn here between those who work in the area of Indigenous education (within the occupational space) and Indigenous educators.

I claim to be an Indigenous educator, not because my field of research or teaching is in the area of Indigenous studies, but because I have a *whakapapa* (genealogy) that links me to a specific place in Aotearoa. That link positions me as *tangata whenua*—a person of that *whenua* (land). Other Indigenous Peoples have referred to themselves as First Nations,

People of the Land, Pacific Nations, Pacific Peoples, and so on. Outside of Aotearoa (my land context), I am not tangata whenua but certainly I can draw connections, links, and affiliations to those who are Indigenous within their own lands, because issues like colonization and exploitation are relevant to Indigenous Peoples more globally.

Some of those who teach and research in the area of Indigenous education are not necessarily Indigenous in the context within which they teach. This is one of the areas in which Indigenous analysis and critique is currently engaging, as the meeting ground between Indigenous and colonial spaces is a territory fought and struggled over at the academic level as Indigenous People vie to be heard, seen, and represented within academia, and as members of dominant groups assert their right to be located and included in those spaces. The struggle is one that contests dominant ways of knowing and representing the world (L.T. Smith 1999), in which academic terrain is up for negotiation and in which dominant worldviews are contested as not being the only legitimate forms of methodologies, pedagogy, and knowledge.

The challenge, then, is one of "creating space" for Indigenous knowledge, beliefs, cultural perspectives, methodologies, philosophies, and worldviews within academic, research, teaching, and policy archives. Without that space, the possibility of providing a "safe space" is lessened considerably. Creating space is also, then, about the "vacating of space" by members of dominant groups, about accepting Indigenous Peoples' rights to ownership of their own knowledge, culture, and worldviews. Vacating space is recognizing that those referred to in the "walk" (research), the "talk" (policy), and the "chalk" (teaching) might like to occupy those spaces themselves.

At times academia has accused us of being "precious" or exclusionary, of employing separatist methods and processes that "shut out" those who are not "insider"' and who wish to engage. And yet the exclusionary forces of scientific and Western methodologies of academics, of research archives, and of the right of Western forms of knowledge to describe, label, and categorize us has never, until very recently, been put "on the table" for discussion. Inclusion and its relationship to space are multi-positional, complex, and context specific, and often couched within uncertainty.

The next section of this chapter examines an Indigenous higher education institution established in New Zealand named Te Whare Wānanga o Awanuiārangi (Awanuiārangi). Incorporated in 1992 by the local tribe Ngāti Awa, Awanuiārangi was confirmed as one of three "official" state-funded *wānanga* (Indigenous higher education institutions) in 1997. Wānanga are tertiary institutions charged through legislation to promulgate teaching and research embedded with *mātauranga Māori* (Māori knowledge) and within the context of *tikanga* (culturally ethical practice), and te kura kaupapa Māori primary (Māori culture and practice). The name Awanuiārangi is linked to the whakapapa (genealogy) of the ancestral canoe—Mataatua—that landed at Whakatāne in the Bay of Plenty. Many tribal groups claim descent from the Mataatua canoe and the ancestor Awanuiārangi. Among these tribal groups are Ngāti Awa, Te Whānau-ā-Apanui, Whakatōhea, Tūhoe, Ngāti Manawa, Ngāti Whare, and Ngāi Te Rangi.

Background: Te Whare Wānanga o Awanuiārangi

The general perception of wānanga is one of being a "Māori institution," interested in offering only "Māori things" to a largely "Māori audience." However, section 162(4)(b)(iv) of the 1989 Education Act provides a broader definition:

> A wānanga is characterised by teaching and research that maintains, advances and disseminates knowledge and develops intellectual independence, and assists the application of knowledge regarding āhuatanga Māori (Māori tradition) according to tikanga Māori (Māori custom).

The distinctive characteristics and contributions that Awanuiārangi makes to education should not be underestimated. Wānanga are expected to perform to *iwi* (tribal) criteria and iwi benchmarks, and are subjected to intense iwi evaluation, monitoring, and moderation—sometimes very publicly on tribal marae (meeting place), which other tertiary institutions are not. The duality for Awanuiārangi is accountability both to government *and* to iwi. While other tertiary institutions enjoy measures of autonomy and decision-making, Awanuiārangi must always consider the desires, visions, and views of those iwi that it works with and the Māori communities that it serves—to build educational capability, to disseminate Māori language and knowledge, and to teach and to research.

As a result of the educational challenges presented by our communities, Awanuiārangi has developed a range of educational opportunities designed to meet the needs of Māori and of all students who are seeking excellent qualifications and skills for employment, for cultural competencies, for professional, for long-term careers, and as contributors to both New Zealand society and the world. Awanuiārangi has established ways of allowing education to provide positive pathways for Māori development. It operates according to Māori philosophy and seeks to establish and reinforce links with other Indigenous Peoples. Although Awanuiārangi has strong links to the people of Mataatua, its doors of learning have always been open to all iwi and all New Zealanders. Awanuiārangi has always been mindful of its mission expressed in the proverbial saying, "*Rukuhia te mātauranga ki tōna hōhonutanga me tōna whānuitanga*"—to pursue knowledge to its greatest depths and broadest horizons.[4]

This institution is a *whare wānanga* (house of higher learning). The term *whare* in our title is distinctive within the wānanga sector: it embraces the original founding aspiration to provide high-quality educational opportunities at all levels within the tertiary arena. The breadth of our learning provision is necessarily expansive given the needs of our communities of interest and therefore extends from community-based learning programs to graduate programs at master's and doctoral levels. The focus of our graduate programs is on the theme of Māori and Indigenous knowledge—in turn benchmarked to a wider body of international Indigenous research activity and qualifications—as a basis for transformative development and advancement.

The wānanga does not offer a large number of programs but rather provides programs from Level One to Level Ten of the New Zealand Qualification Authority Framework[5] within a select area of disciplines that have been identified as key to meeting the needs of Māori. Awanuiārangi is concerned with ensuring that education through our academic pursuits is enabled via a culturally affirming pedagogy and learning environment and is, to this end, involved in research, teaching, and publication. Tertiary study at Awanuiārangi is supported by a vibrant academic community led by an impressive number of Māori PHD-qualified staff and supported by an adjunct faculty of national and international experts, all of whom are committed to assisting students to successfully fulfill their learning aspirations while simultaneously developing Awanuiārangi as an outstanding site for Māori scholarship.

Focusing on maintaining the unique characteristic elements of the wānanga is a continual key priority as we grow culturally appropriate networks of provision with other like-minded tertiary organizations. This includes relationships with other international Indigenous institutions as well as Indigenous entities in less Indigenous spaces. We believe that educational success for Māori and other Indigenous Peoples, wherever it can be attained, is vital and that it is an important prerequisite for a sustainable social and economic revolution within our communities. Decisions about what and how Awanuiārangi teaches are not simply made around vocational outcomes. The aim is to improve academic achievement and to also create Māori citizens who have the language and cultural skills to participate more fully in Māori cultural life. Too often our students are offered a narrow education in which academic achievement is often at the expense of their Māori cultural capital. Māori students need and must have both elements to experience success—this is not an either/or choice.

Education Challenges for Māori

The need for wānanga-type education and environments has arisen from the need to address decades of Māori educational underachievement, in which policies and practices have consistently failed to improve the position of Māori. The main factors contributing to educational underachievement were a curriculum and practices that sought to separate Māori from their traditional knowledge bases, language, and culture. The result of these practices was the decimation of Māori knowledge, the loss of language and culture, fragmented identities, disenfranchised communities, and overall poor quality of life.

Statistically, the demonstration of poor performance was first identified by the 1960 Hunn Report (Department of Māori Affairs), although the roots of underdevelopment can be traced well back into the era of the Mission and Native Schools of the 1800s (Simon 1990). In the 1960s, a rash of practices in schools were implemented to address the "Māori educational problem," which unfortunately for Māori continued to focus on their language and way of life as being the central problem. These deficit-based practices continued to erode the fabric of Māori society to such a point that many believed the Māori language would die out (Benton 1979).

During the 1980s and 1990s, Māori responded by developing their own educational answers to underdevelopment. We saw the rise of Māori educational initiatives like te kohanga reo preschools established in 1981, te kura kaupapa Māori primary schooling established in 1986, and the seeding of wānanga as fledgling tertiary institutions. These developments were a result of what G. Smith (2015) refers to as a "revolution of the mind," during which Māori took control of their own destinies and futures by building their own answers to educational underachievement. At the core of these initiatives was the focus on restoring Māori language, culture, and knowledge.

Contradictory beliefs about what the education system should be delivering to Māori, how, and why, have existed for a number of years. Disparities between what Māori wanted from the education system and what the government and educationalists wanted for Māori were due to different points of view as to what was needed, and the result was policies that did not address the preciseness of the problems. As Hekia Parata (1994) has noted,

> Good policy analysis relies on precise problem definition. It appears that the policy analysis of successive governments has been at fault with its inaccurate diagnosis of the problem. The "Māori problem" (in accordance with popular tendencies to lay fault with the victim) has been variously attributed; to dispassion or alienation from resources, poor housing, poor location, inadequate or inappropriate education, mistimed or misdirected training, insensitive or incorrect health treatment, and so on. (45)

Past educational policies and programs implemented for Māori have been based upon some notion of "difference," but a difference that recognized Māori in terms of deficits. It also appeared that these deficit-based theoretical beliefs underpinned why Māori were not developing to their full potential and were in fact signalling "difference" as negative or inferior and therefore undesirable (Johnston 1998). This was because, as Iris Marion Young (1990) stated:

> [There were] the positions of [a] norm, against which all others are measured. The attempt to reduce all persons to the unity of common measure constructs as deviant those whose attributes differ from the group-specific attributes implicitly presumed in the norm. The drive to unify the particularity and multiplicity of practices, cultural symbols, and ways of relating in clear and distinct categories turns "difference" into exclusion. (169)

As a result of that normalization process, Māori knowledge, language, and culture (even Māori themselves) were seen as inferior and so the intent of policies (and practices) became one of excluding "Māori" from the curriculum and the educational environment.

Elizabeth Grosz (1994) has suggested, however, that "difference" does not have to represent inferiority. Rather, it is those who have control over the context of defining "difference" (and the representations that these definitions take) who ultimately have control over how difference is perceived. The aforementioned Māori education initiatives te kohanga reo and te kura kaupapa Māori (and subsequently whare kura and wānanga) initially evolved out of a necessity to protect Māori knowledge, language, and culture, to rejuvenate and grow what educational processes had decimated. But a common factor for all of these institutions is that they have taken the perceived "differences" of Māori (the perceived inferiorities) and "normalized" those differences within their own educational context. Thus Māori language, culture, and knowledge (which reinforces Māori identity) contributes to providing an environment that facilitates educational achievement because of the normalization element. Māori recognize themselves in the education curriculum and environment and, as a result, are more likely to experience success.

These points are supported by Jessica Lai (2010), who is associated with the International Trade of Indigenous Cultural Heritage in Switzerland and who states that "there is a strong Māori view that knowledge and use of Māori cultural practices are important for a Māori person's sense of identity and connectedness to other Māori and important Māori institutions like marae" (14). Outside of those environments, the inconsistency for many Māori students is that, first, the places provided for them to study and engage in have been driven by a normalization focus that is not Māori. If a Māori context exists, it is predominantly an addendum to the mainstream norm, which means that all things Māori still have to compete or be accommodated within a non-Māori norm.

Second, those contexts have also focused on what goes wrong in education for Māori, instead of building on what goes right.[6] Thus Māori students' experiences in education have tended to differ according to the institution and grade levels into which they gain emtry. This is where the wānanga sector plays an important role in the education of Māori, because the normalization of those contexts is Māori and the educational ethic focus is on what works. As a result, Te Whare Wānanga o Awanuiārangi provides a unique and specific niche education for Māori, and it does so by recognizing a number of aspects that run counter to past (and present) views about the validity and worth of an education "by Māori for Māori" (G. Smith 1986). History is always at the forefront of our pathways and journeys, because in order to understand where we are moving to in the future, we need to understand where we have come from. While we cannot undo the past, we can certainly learn from it.

Within that niche, Awanuiārangi developed a range of programs that are uniquely positioned to enable Māori participation through to higher-end credentials. These programs were developed through the application of innovative pedagogy and curriculum design based on transforming praxis and the application of kaupapa Māori critically informed practices.

These approaches build on and extend the theoretical work of kaupapa Māori scholars (many of whom are employed at Awanuiārangi), whose approaches put the validity and legitimacy of Māori language, knowledge, culture, and practice in the curriculum as a central component of their transforming intention. Furthermore, culture, language, and knowledge practices are "wrapped around" the learning, teaching, and living environment within Awanuiārangi so that students are completely immersed within "Māori as the norm." Thus positive cultural reinforcement and success is seen as an important conduit to facilitating success more broadly. This matches the Ministry of Education's current policy emphasis on Māori being able to succeed as Māori and also connects to the legislated requirement on the wānanga sector embedded in the Education Amendment Act (1990).

Te Whare Wānanga o Awanuiārangi builds on kaupapa Māori models of transforming praxis. G. Smith (2015) outlines mechanisms for testing whether or not kaupapa Māori is operating, as summarized briefly here:

1. Criticality (ensuring that students are enabled to engage with critical theory as a means to be able to analyze the problems/what is going wrong in order to get solutions right);
2. Structuralist/Culturalist (which is about developing strategies to address Māori educational underdevelopment. It is not just about focusing on culture or people. It is also about focusing on changing societal structures to facilitate policy and economic development—not an either/or situation);
3. Transformation (moving beyond the status quo and engaging in meaning change within a climate of disadvantage and inequalities);
4. Praxis (the engagement of theory and practise and understanding the logic of what is being done. This, in a sense, is the "walking of the talk," the enactment/implementation of the theory into real outcomes); and
5. Positionality (which is the understanding of where we are speaking from, that includes an understanding of constraints and challenges, understanding our own complexities and that there is not just one struggle but multiple struggles occurring simultaneously). (64–76)

While the intervention elements remain important and central, additional factors that underpin Māori success are emerging from wānanga work with iwi and communities. The "Roderick Report" (The Adult Community Education Evaluation Research Project [Roderick 2010]), for example, quantified the "value add" of marae-based education programs. This model is described as one of *transforming praxis* as the "360 Māori Education Development Model," a holistic model that engages in transforming approaches within multiple sites using multiple strategies that are often simultaneously applied. The approach requires a change of mindset and practice and it challenges the current government funding emphasis of developing policy and practice that are "singular," "one-off," "project-based" initiatives. These are some of the challenges that Awanuiārangi currently faces, as examined in the next sections.

Policy Challenges

The unilateral development of policy by the government continues to create tensions for Awanuiārangi. There has been a clear move away from "rights-driven" policy to "needs-driven" policy, which Parata (1994) defines as follows:

> A rights-driven policy would require the State to recognise, in concert with its international commitments, the status of indigenous people, plus domestic obligations it has entered into (legislation) or inherited (the Treaty of Waitangi). This approach has much wider implications for the nature of the State's responsibilities and duties, and the way in which these are carried out. (45–6)

The position of Māori as having "rights" within the context of the Treaty Settlement was positioned to one of Māori being an interest group, which has subsequently seen Māori repositioned as a group who has a set of grievances to be addressed (Johnston 1998). This subtle shift in policy thinking and framing is how groups in power, according to Lukes (1974), convince minorities to buy into "playing the game." It shifts the focus from inequality and equity to one of equality of opportunity by producing mechanisms to address inequalities so that all are treated the same. As Parata (1994) notes:

> A needs-driven policy reduces the role of the State to dealing with issues of income. Policy then is focused on eliminating barriers—legislative, regulatory, structural and administrative—to individuals securing adequate income to sustain their chosen lifestyle. (45)

So, a needs-based policy tends to treat all New Zealanders as the same, which results in dealing with the symptoms rather than the problems themselves (Parata 1994, 46). Thus, inequalities are addressed through the offer of "neutralizers" like student loans, which is a mechanism to "address financial inequalities," without changing the circumstances that result in Māori students having to take up student loans in the first place.

Anomalies to the policy and practices are tweaked to accommodate differences. Te Whare Wānanga o Awanuiārangi has been let down by some of this "tweaking" and subjected to inequalities because of the "university sector as the norm" perception that has resulted in misalignment of policy direction for the perceived "wānanga sector is different" practices. For example, changes to funding across the tertiary sector in Aotearoa saw universities funded at a higher rate for post-graduate programs even though wānanga and universities were subjected to the same rules and regulations of compliancy and standards. Policy on international students excludes the wānanga from offering domestic fees to international students because of an original perception that wānanga are not "internationally" focused (because they are Māori institutions), even though Awanuiārangi has operated in the international (Indigenous) arena for a number of years, has numerous memorandum of understanding with Indigenous and traditional universities globally, and a cohort of First Nation students in Washington State.

Transforming/Intervention Strategies

Current policy and strategies are limited. Policy cannot facilitate success for overcoming the "learning gap" that affects large numbers of Māori, because they are designed to "fill a gap" rather than to "transform it"; they focus on what is wrong rather than on what is right and what works. Awanuiārangi recognizes the need to do things differently and to *not* keep on with the same strategies and practices that have proven to be ineffective. Awanuiārangi has therefore moved to deliberately reshape the institution's approach to intervention based on two key understandings:

1. That there will not be a sustainable socio-economic revolution for Māori without a prior or simultaneous educational revolution, and

2. That the potential for intervention must move beyond singular, one-off project strategies. (G. Smith 2015)

This multi-strategic approach to intervention is an innovative and unique approach, which has emerged out of the context of the experiences at Te Whare Wānanga o Awanuiārangi. It is an approach that is concerned with responding to cultural, iwi, rural, socio-economic, learning, marae, and vocational aspirations of Māori. This approach is an important educational contribution that will more urgently and more broadly advance Māori social and economic development based on some fundamental principles. These principles accentuate the well-being of Māori individuals, groups, and communities, which is a focus well beyond just an educational one (G. Smith 2015).

These ideas are captured by the Treasury Living Standards Framework, which was emphasized in the report entitled *Wānanga Ringahora: The Economic Contribution of the Wananga Sector* (Business and Economic Research Ltd. [BERL] 2014, 5). This framework designed a tool to "assist policy analyst to consider the key elements of the living standards framework" (The Treasury 2012). The framework highlights five dimensions (outcomes) for real and/or perceived policy changes on living standards, which The Treasury (2012) believes are important for overall living standards. They are economic growth; sustainability for the future; increasing equity; social infrastructure; and managing risks, all of which contribute to producing higher living standards. Furthermore, the framework highlights four types of capital: financial and physical; natural; social; and human capital. As outlined in the report, the wānanga sector is "focused on the development of human and cultural capital as part of the investment in education and well-being." The BERL report (2014) further argues:

> The Treasury Framework...could provide an additional means of measuring government investment in the Wananga sector, as the framework indicates that the various elements of social capital, such

as language and culture, have a value that can conceptually be quantified. This framework also indicates that investment by the Wananga sector in the revival of Māori language and culture increases social infrastructure and living standards. (5)

Lai (2010, 14) adds that as cultural identity affects overall well-being, "the loss of the Māori cultural identity impacts negatively on this. In a philosophical sense, well-being is what is ultimately good for a person. This includes health, economic, social and cultural aspects... From this it is clear that cultural identity is closely related to culture well-being." Awanuiārangi is committed to developing and building health, economic, social, and cultural elements, which we believe are necessary for the forward development and advancement of Māori individuals and communities. As education has been signalled as a primary contributor to economic development, it makes sense to take note—as both Lai (2010) and BERL (2014) highlight—of those aspects that reinforce identity and cultural well-being within the curriculum and the teaching and learning environment of Awanuiārangi. These elements are constantly being infused throughout the everyday practices within the wānanga, in the programs with students, staff, and external communities. Awanuiārangi as a "different from the normal university sector" institution does have a number of challenges to address.

The new direction in policy and practice from the Tertiary Education Commission will require realignment by the wānanga to facilitate internal growth in our own prioritized areas as well as those set by the Tertiary Education Commission in the *Tertiary Education Strategy: 2014-2019* (Ministry of Education and the Ministry of Business, Innovation and Employment 2014). While the operation of Awanuiārangi as an Indigenous space and context occurs, the shape or compromises that the wānanga has to take or make is influenced by external dominant policy factors controlled by government. They occupy our Indigenous space.

Te Whare Wānanga o Awanuiārangi is an Indigenous space: 96% of our students are Māori (or Indigenous) and undertake a range of

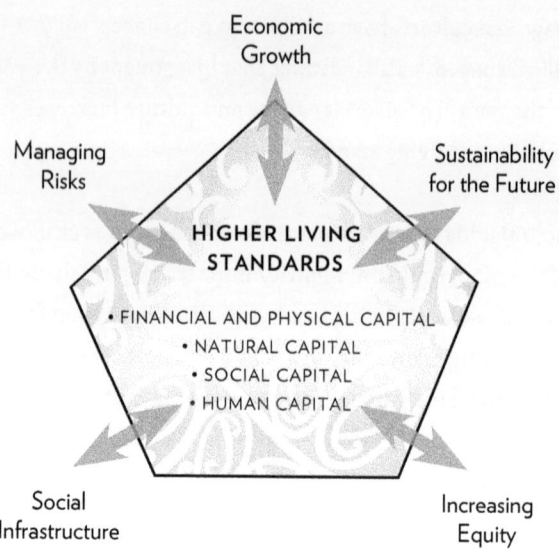

FIGURE 20.2 *Assess the impact of policy across key living standards.*

programs and degrees from certificates to PHDs; our student body represents an extremely broad cross section of Māori communities, including grandparents, parents, children, and grandchildren; we own our buildings and properties and, unlike most other institutions, have not acquired these through government sources.

We reflect on and transform our programs and practices in a continual struggle to achieve excellence and to offer the type of culturally informed education that Māori deserve, but more importantly, that they are entitled to: an education that reinforces Māori knowledge, cultural identity, and language as valid; an education experience that is a central component of teaching and learning at Awanuiārangi. We see the intergenerational educational experiences and transformation that occurs when parents and their children enroll in tertiary programs, and we have witnessed, over the years, up to three generations of students from single families being enrolled. Grandparents (and parents) are role models for their children. The concepts around culture and identity are practised in the classroom, in student/staff engagements, on the *marae atea* (open space), in the kitchen, everywhere. Our students often tell us that one of the factors that brings them to Awanuiārangi is that they see "themselves" reflected in the environment—not on the walls or through the visuals, but in the staff, in other students, in the pedagogy, in the *wairua* (soul), and in the *manaakitanga* (care of people) that is Awanuiārangi.

There are many unique aspects and ways of thinking that drive Awanuiārangi and the type of institution it is today.

a. **Our student demographics are not the same as the universities or polytechnics.** Our audience is predominantly a mature one. At pre-degree and bachelor level, our students are likely to have had "broken educational opportunities" and as second-chance learners, they start well back from the tertiary education starting line.

b. **Students under 25 are a rarity in the wānanga.** Those who are able to succeed in the secondary system are more likely to want to advance to a university or a polytechnic for their education. We support their endeavours, but in doing so, Awanuiārangi is likely to attract different types of students who require that extra time be given to them to first support them in their studies and, second, to support them as they continue through their studies. While this is one of the unique facets of Awanuiārangi, the "value add," it is also a result of social injustices that cannot be accounted for in the number-crunching activities that make up the ways in which government "measures" our performance as an institution.

These are also difficult performance indicators to measure. We have our work cut out for us in not just trying to provide a tertiary education but also in most instances trying to make up for the lack of a primary or secondary education that Māori students did not receive.

Some of the students noted above return to us at a master's or a PHD level (note that 90% of the graduate students at Awanuiārangi come through other institutions of learning). This results in a huge diversity within the wānanga in terms of the student population. Some of the unique aspects, however, relate to intergenerational, knowledge, experience, and the rural experience (rurality), which require a diversity of learning methods and models of teaching practice: a one-size-fits-all scenario does not fit!

c. We aspire to change educational opportunities so community members can be productive and equal citizens.
The ways in which education is shaped for the future is as a business, meeting specific government targets that are predominantly aligned at this point with science, technology, engineering, and mathematics (STEM), and that's okay if everyone starts at the same place. But as Parata (1994) has noted,

> In the case of Māori, their downward spiral to the bottom of the socio-economic heap is not going to be eliminated (although it may be alleviated) simply by addressing income issues. If the marketplace in which these individuals were operating was totally value free, then perhaps overcoming income disparity would be sufficient. But the reality of the New Zealand market place is that it is imperfect in its monocultural orientation. (46)

And so, for our students, focusing on government priorities for employment and building a labour force becomes more difficult if you are poor, live in an economic "dead-zone" (where the wānanga is located), have failed at primary and secondary school, and have failed to meet the basic requirements for entry into a tertiary institution. This is where Awanuiārangi steps in. We aspire to change the educational situation for our communities, iwi and *hapū*, so members can be productive members of society and equal citizens of this country; citizens who count in different ways than is normal today.

The extra that we bring to the education sector is one of being able to understand the complexity of the situations and to implement (quickly) the changes that need to occur to support our students. Education is more than a business; it is a social and moral right that all communities should be able to enjoy and benefit from.

d. We are concerned with a holistic approach to addressing educational development for Māori.
As noted in previous sections, educational success and development for Māori is linked to cultural identity and well-being (Lai 2010). Cultural identity is linked to the investment in financial and physical, natural, social, and human capital as a means to lift living standards and enable Māori to participate more fully in the economy (BERL 2014).

e. Education is about opportunities and, for Māori, these opportunities mean being able to be Māori.
While āhuatanga and tikanga Māori are necessary in the thinking and operational aspects of the wānanga, the right for Māori to an education that is Māori is also a taken-for-granted "given" within Awanuiārangi. While the processes and systems might be articulated in ways that are not necessarily understood by some, the expectations of outcomes and outputs are the same as for other tertiary institutions: quality and academic excellence, and for Awanuiārangi, being confident and capable of moving through two worlds: "te ao Pākehā and te ao Māori."

f. Education is about investing in human and cultural capital.
While the primary focus within the tertiary sector is on the contributions that education can make to the workforce, the economy, science, technology, engineering, and mathematics (including the contributions that Māori can make in these areas), a wānanga education further entails multiple complex levels of focus that start with the well-being of individuals, groups, and communities. As an institution, we have contributed to New Zealand society through the following ways:

1. Lifting educational outcomes by producing students with a degree;
2. Elevating students through education to acquire skills that are relevant to the workforce and society;
3. Applying new knowledge through research that has a positive impact on issues of significance to the iwi, hapū, and whanau of New Zealand and to Indigenous communities around the world;
4. Being involved in the Māori public good (service to the community) by providing scholarly or professional expertise that contributes to external communities.

Te Whare Wānanga o Awanuiārangi is focused on working collaboratively to support the emergence of effective Māori citizens of the world. Our graduates will be well equipped with the skills and knowledge to advance and develop their communities, which in turn will make a contribution to wider society in a post-Treaty Settlement era. In particular, the role of the Māori economy as a significant contributor to the wider New Zealand economy provides a necessary focus for programme development within the Whare Wānanga.

g. We are an institution that upholds āhuatanga and tikanga Māori. Āhuatanga, tikanga, and te reo Māori are embedded in the very structures and frameworks that are Te Whare Wānanga o Awanuiārangi. In our everyday practices, behaviours, teaching, and administration, āhuatanga and tikanga prevail. This is one of the "norms" for Awanuiārangi that is "unspoken" and central to this institution. It is recognized by those who come with the same normality (identity, culture, etc.), found to be congruent by those of other ethnic groups who embrace different but similar normalities, and able to be "walked through" by those who don't.

h. Our models of intervention are not "conventional" nor necessarily recognized by current educational institutions and organizations. Awanuiārangi operates within a number of models that are based on Māori cultural aspects that students recognize in the institution and in their programs. These models are the key for our students to experience success. There is much evidence that highlights that Māori students fail when they are subjected to "conventional" models of teaching and learning, so our models are as much about success as they are about learning and teaching. Our models for intervention are as follows:

1. A "360 degree" intervention model that acknowledges the intergenerational educational experiences and transformation that occurs when parents and their children enroll in tertiary programs. Our observations have been that the most significant indicator for a child gaining a bachelor's degree is whether or not one of the parents has a degree. A further observation is that in the wānanga programs there can be three generations enrolled across the wānanga: child, parents, and grandparents. There is a particular need for ongoing support being given to Māori parents by Awanuiārangi, as a much larger proportion of them left school with minimal qualifications. Parents in tertiary study are role models for their children. Awanuiārangi is committed through its strategies, as noted within this chapter, to assist young people (under 25) to achieve at Level Four and above so they can enter into the fields of Indigenous business/management and science.
2. Our teaching within the learning environment is based on the normalization of āhuatanga and tikanga Māori that incorporates cultural frameworks and cultural protocols that extend cultural familiarity for Māori students. For example, our teaching incorporates noho marae (overnight stay), which entails students staying at one of our sites or marae (communal meeting place) for a specified number of days to cover the curriculum aspect of their programs. We recognize that learning and teaching occur not only within the timetable for the delivery of the program (9:00 am to 5:00 pm) but also at meal times where students and lecturers continue conversations; or during after-dinner activities that include one-on-one discussions or a lecturer holding group discussions with students;

or group discussions that carry on well into the early hours of the morning. The noho provides the framework while the cultural aspects are incorporated through formal learning (between nine and five) and the formal discussions that are related to the practices of wānanga or hui (meeting, discussion).

Conclusion

I asked the following question in the introduction to this chapter: If the dominant framework of an institution were an Indigenous one, would that make a difference for Indigenous education? In terms of Te Whare Wananga o Awanuiārangi, the answer is yes...BUT.

The "yes" relates to being able to operate and practise in ways that are Indigenous, which reinforce identity, language, cultural spaces, and our Indigenous space. This is clearly the right-hand side of Figure 20.1. Māori aspirations are noted, and they impact on our program developments. The cultural operations of the institution and the ways of thinking and doing that uniquely reflect Māori knowledge and practices (as discussed in this chapter) operate. However, our future still hinges on our ability as an institution to be able to adapt, be reflective of change, and develop quickly with the expectations of policy directives and strategic priorities of government. That is the space of the intersections outlined in Figure 20.1, the space where the colonial and the Indigenous worlds meet. That is the space of contestation, challenges, and issues for Awanuiārangi if policy makers do not grasp and understand what a wānanga is about.

The "BUT," however, recognizes those relationships of power, wherein the wānanga is still accountable to the funder—the government, the taxpayer. The inequities in funding, and the drive to have the wānanga conform to current government thinking and policies, is the "disruptive space" referred to in Figure 20.1. Our direction as an institution currently fits within the government's agenda for Māori, and so this can create tensions between what our communities ask of us and what the government expects from us. Therefore, the challenge for

Awanuiārangi is one of resisting that pull towards that colonial space, which would result in Indigenous assimilation and conformity. Our struggle is to be Indigenous. Our struggle is for our own self-determination. Our struggle continues.

Notes

1. The term Māori refers to the Indigenous population of Aotearoa New Zealand. I use the term Māori in recognition of the relations between Māori and Pākehā, but my use of the term *does not imply homogeneity* of Māori ideas, desires, or expectations.
2. The term Pākehā is an equally difficult term. What Pākehā means and represents is a relational one with Māori. Neither term can be discussed in isolation, as their existence relies on the presence of the other. In this context, Pākehā refers to European settler New Zealanders.
3. Mainstream is the term used to refer to the dominant education system.
4. This is a *whakatauaki*, a traditional proverb from antiquity.
5. The New Zealand Qualification Authority Framework is the government's national body that approves degrees and programs in New Zealand offered at the tertiary level.
6. See, for example, Johnston (1998) who, in examining the Māori Affairs Select Committee Inquiry of 1997 for Māori Educational Underachievement, noted that the committee focused on what worked in the education system for Māori, instead of the usual focus on what is wrong.

References

Benton, Richard.1979. *Policy Implications for English-Māori Bilingual Education in New Zealand*. Wellington, NZ: New Zealand Centre for Educational Research.

Business and Economic Research Ltd. 2014. *Wananga Ringahora: The Economic Contribution of the Wananga Sector*. Wellington, NZ: BERL.

Dei, George. 1996. *Anti-Racism Education: Theory and Practice*. Halifax, NS: Fernwood Publishing.

Education Act. 1989. Section 162. https://www.nzqa.govt.nz/audience-pages/wananga/

Grosz, Elizabeth. 1994. "Identity and Difference: A Response." In *Critical Politics*, edited by P. James, 29-33. Melbourne, Australia: Arena Publications.

Hunn, Jack. 1960. *Report on the Department of Māori Affairs.* Wellington, NZ: Government Printer.

Johnston, Patricia. 1998. "He Ao Rereke: Education Policy and Māori Underachievement: Mechanisms of Power and Difference." PHD diss., Auckland University.

———. 2003. "Disrupting/Contesting/Creating Space: Challenging Students to Think Māori Education." DELTA 55 (1/2): 43-60.

———. 2004. "When Indigenous Knowledge Questions the Limits: A Lesson about Wisdom." Keynote address to the HERDSA Conference, Curtin University, July 5-7, 2004.

———. 2010. "Towards Culturally Appropriate Assessment? A Contribution to the Debates." *Higher Education Quarterly* 63 (3). https://doi.org/10.1111/j.1468-2273.2010.00463.x

———. 2012. "Talking Back to the Colonial Experience: Creating an Indigenous Framework for Education." In *As the World Turns: Implications of Global Shifts in Higher Education for Theory, Research and Practice*, edited by W.R. Allen, R.T. Teranishi, and M. Bonous-Hammarth, 261-83. Bingley, England: Emerald Group Publishing.

Johnston, Patricia, and Jennifer McLeod. 2001. "Disrupting Hegemonic Spaces: Challenging Teachers to Think Indigenised." Paper presented at the CINSA Conference, University of Saskatchewan, Regina, SK, May 31-June 3, 2001.

Lai, Jessica. 2010. "Māori Culture in the Modern World: Its Creation, Appropriation and Trade." International Communications and Art Law Lucerne Working Paper No. 2. Lucerne, Switzerland: University of Lucerne.

Lukes, Steven. 1974. *Power: A Radical View.* London: Macmillan.

Ministry of Education and the Ministry of Business, Innovation and Employment. (2014). *Tertiary Education Strategy: 2014-2019.* Auckland, NZ: Government of New Zealand. https://www.education.govt.nz/assets/Documents/Further-education/Tertiary-Education-Strategy.pdf

Parata, Hekia. 1994. "Mainstreaming: A Māori Affairs Policy?" *Social Policy Journal of New Zealand* 3: 40-51.

Roderick, Miki. 2010. "Report of the Adult Community Education Evaluation Research Project / Te Whare Wananga o Awanuiārangi," Internal Report / Te Whare Wananga o Awanuiārangi. Unpublished document.

Smith, Graham. 1986. "Taha Māori: A Pākehā Privilege." DELTA 37: 10-23.

———. 1991. "Reform and Māori Educational Crisis: A Grand Illusion." Monograph No. 3. Auckland, NZ: Research Unit for Māori Education, Education Department, University of Auckland.

———. 2015. "Equity as Critical Praxis: The Self Development of Te Whare Wananga o Awanuiārangi." In *Paulo Freire: The Global Legacy*, edited by M. Peters and T. Besley, 55–78. New York: Peter Lang Publishers.

Smith, Linda Tuhiwai 1999. *Decolonising Methodologies: Research and Indigenous Peoples*. London: Zed Books.

Simon, Judith. 1990. "The Place of Schooling in Māori-Pākehā Relations." PHD diss., University of Auckland.

The Treasury (New Zealand). 2012. "Improving the Living Standards of New Zealanders: Moving from a Framework to Implementation." Auckland, NZ: The Treasury. https://treasury.govt.nz/publications/speech/improving-living-standards-new-zealanders-moving-framework-implementation

Waitere-Ang, Hine, and Patricia Johnston. 1999a. "If All Inclusion in Research Means Is the Addition of Researchers That Look Different, Have You Really Included Me At All?" Paper presented at AARE-NZARE Conference, "Global Issues and Local Effects: The Challenge for Educational Research," Melbourne, Australia, December 1999.

———. 1999b. "In Absentia: Mana Wahine in Institutional Contexts." Paper presented at the Women's Studies Association Conference, Hui Raranga Wahine, Victoria University, Wellington, NZ, November 5–7, 1999.

Young, Iris. 1990. *Justice and the Politics of Difference*. Princeton, NJ: Princeton University Press.

Closing

Drawing the Threads of Contested Spaces

SPENCER LILLEY, HUIA TOMLINS-JAHNKE,
SANDRA STYRES, & DAWN ZINGA

IN COUNTRIES THAT HAVE GONE THROUGH colonization and the hegemonic violence associated with it, Indigenous Peoples have continuously struggled to ensure that their histories, values, traditional knowledge, and languages are not only included within Western academies but are taught from an Indigenous perspective. It is evident from the chapters in this book that the struggle is encountered on every campus and across different faculties and disciplines. The contestations that take place are never over but are merely postponed for future engagement, at another faculty or committee meeting. Similarly, contestation can take many forms and be on several different fronts concurrently. It might always seem that the contestations are "treading water," as the same issues are litigated by different contestants who have not been involved in previous iterations of the academic discourse. This contestation has meant that for Indigenous academics it has not always been possible to make progress or to advance research and scholarship within institutions, as the structures within them are geared towards rewarding individual rather than collective efforts.

The space that Indigenous knowledge seeks to occupy within these institutions might be seen to be on what Smith (2005) calls "tricky ground," as they could be viewed as intruders or imposters inside a Western construct, and unwelcome by the guardians of the academic tradition. If this space is so "tricky" and the contestations are forever endless, does this make these institutions unsafe grounds for the inclusion of Indigenous knowledge? Potentially, yes. However, the absence of Indigenous knowledge in these places would see a return to academic environments where Western knowledge would remain supreme and unchallenged by Indigenous thought and cultural traditions.

As several of the authors have pointed out, historical research has been an academic tradition whereby Indigenous Peoples were studied from a Western observer's perspective; where Indigenous Peoples were the subject of research; where they were studied and analyzed using a lens steeped in ideas about Western intellectual superiority and Indigenous intellectual inferiority. Throughout the latter half of the 20th century, and continuing today, there has been a push back and increasing resistance against this form of research. This has led to more collaborative research and the recognition of the importance of Indigenous scholars exploring Indigenous issues, which has been taken up to some extent within the academy and within granting agencies that support research. Many of the authors remind us of the importance of remembering that such approaches have not been extinguished and that the attitudes and belief systems that gave rise to these approaches to research linger beneath the veneer of advancement in the academy, continuing to fuel many of the points of contestation.

Do we live in more enlightened times? In some ways, yes, we do. In other ways, possibly not. What has emerged from the chapters in each of the sections of this book is that Indigenous academics have to be forever watchful and prepared to engage in the varied and complex contestations. It is evident that the unique positionalities of the authors and their connections to places and stories have informed and shaped this book. While each author has engaged in the concept of contestation, narratives of place have shaped that engagement. The individual authors are also connected by their shared stories of the legacy of colonization, leading to clusters of salience as well as themes unique to some places. For example, Bevan-Brown illustrates the importance of including cultural understandings of exceptional learning needs among Indigenous students when providing culturally responsive education. Furthermore, Doherty highlights the importance of context as critical, both in how we understand the contexts within which contestation occurs and in the creation of new contexts from which learning can be built. If we are to successfully navigate these contestations as Indigenous scholars, we quite literally have to walk in two worlds—we have to know the rules of engagement that frame the disparate systems that constitute and underpin Western academies. Pidgeon explores the discourse framing what it means to be Indigenous in the academy and the challenge of acting as a cultural broker to create a bridge between Indigenous students and Western academia while negotiating these contested places and spaces. As Pihama reminds us, contested places and spaces for Indigenous academics are experienced in multiple ways, including at the level of the physical, cultural, spiritual, spatial, and temporal, as well as at the level of curriculum, theory, and disciplines. What this means in practice is disrupting the colonial mindset, debunking colonial mythologies through the art of simmering resistance, usurping our hidden anger and frustration by understanding the debilitating patterns of colonizing influences, and diverting our energies and efforts towards hope, to the reclamation of our languages, our lands, and our souls through transformative praxis.

At every turn this requires a high level of stoic contemplation and critical analysis of the various dimensions of schooling, the institutional workplace, state policies, and systems that are manifest in imposed legislation, political rhetoric, state-sanctioned curriculum documents, and co-option of Indigenous thought by the non-Indigenous "expert," to name a few examples. Indigenous academics, by the very nature of the work that they do, inevitably raise the kinds of questions that are not always well received or even understood by the academy or by society in general, creating a disconnect that allows misunderstanding and contestation to flourish. Maaka, for example, questions the role of democracy as mob rule, and the tyranny of the majority in perpetuating a level of systemic violence of the Indigenous schooling experience that is cruel, dislocating, remote, detached, and separate from reality but nevertheless considered necessary preparation for the "ideal citizen."

Donald argues that the ontological violence perpetuated by the state simply affirms ideological mythologies. What is required, he suggests, are ethical rationalities that interconnect the sacred ecologies of life with Indigenous Peoples, in opposition to the Western view that sees humankind as having control over nature. The notion of ethical rationalities as a strategic response to the global crisis of Indigenous education is possible within what Willie Ermine refers to as an "ethical space of engagement" (Ermine 2007). Several authors implicitly explore ideas that Ermine associates with ethical space, while others explicitly discuss the concept of ethical space and how is can be applied to understanding contestation in the academy.

According to Ermine (2007, 194), ethical space is the space between two entities, an imagined meeting place or neutral zone between "the Indigenous and Western thought worlds," a kind of "schismatic ambience...created between peoples and cultures...wherever the physical and philosophical encounter of Indigenous and Western world's takes place" (195). It is at the deeper level where thoughts, interests, and assumptions—which largely remain concealed as epistemologies of ignorance—need to be acknowledged and illuminated if complex encounters and relationships within the ethical space are to be understood transculturally. It would mean traversing what Penetito argues are the contested spaces and denialism of the historical, political, theoretical, and empirical issues and the impact these have had at the convergence of Western-colonial–Indigenous relations. Deer highlights the importance of Indigenous identity within mainstream schools where these convergences come to bear on the formation of young people's understandings of themselves in cultural and societal contexts. Restoule and Nardozi also engage the collision of Western-colonial ideas and Indigenous knowledges within mainstream educational settings that they have had to navigate when designing resources to embed Indigeneity within teacher education. Similar but distinct, Hohepa and Hawera focus on the critical need for training teachers to teach in Māori classrooms and the implications this has for teacher education and the success of Indigenous learners. In other chapters, authors directly explore how networks and relations of power exert influence over the inclusion of Indigenous philosophies within multiple levels of education and explore the tangled interconnections between initiatives to Indigenize teacher education and state and national initiatives. State initiatives across lands such as Canada, New Zealand, and Hawai'i, will continue to remain flawed without an understanding of social justice issues and the denialism that normalizes inequality. These include the effects of cultural oppression and the priority of individualism promoted by the dominant society on the psyche of multiple generations of Indigenous Peoples.

In the Canadian context, November 2016 marked the 20-year anniversary of the publication of the report by the Royal Commission on Aboriginal Peoples (RCAP). In this five-volume, 4,000-page document, the Commission acknowledged the legacy of colonialism, covering a wide range of issues. The report contained 440 recommendations and set out an ambitious 20-year agenda for implementing changes to better the lives of Indigenous people across Canada and revitalize nation-to-nation relationships. The two decades of that agenda have now come to an end. The Commission's main conclusion can be summarized by this one statement: "The main policy direction, pursued for more than 150 years, first by colonial then by Canadian governments, has been wrong" (RCAP 1996, n.p.). Once completed and released, the RCAP was largely ignored and subsequently forgotten by the government. In an interview with CBC News in March 2016, Paul Chartrand, one of the original RCAP commissioners, stated "There is a very powerful lesson there, which is that today still, I don't think it's changed much" (Troian 2016). Twenty-three years after the 1996 RCAP report and four years after the release of the 2015 Truth and Reconciliation Commission's report, it is long past time for Canada as a whole and for individual provinces to deliver on the TRC's Calls to Action.

In New Zealand, it has been 44 years since the Waitangi Tribunal was established as a commission of inquiry to hear claims by Māori tribes around laws, policies, actions, or omissions of the Crown that have breached the promises made in the Treaty of Waitangi. What has followed includes, among other things, the development of a *kaupapa Māori* system of education from early years to tertiary education; Māori language recognized as an official language of New Zealand; the establishment of tribal radio stations and a Māori television network; and an increase in Māori representation in Parliament, all of which serve to affirm Māori people as the *tangata whenua* or first peoples of the land. In an international context, it is this failure of many colonized countries to address the historical and contemporary realities of colonization that has led to the development of the 2007 United Nations Declaration on the Rights of Indigenous Peoples. While the majority of states initially signed the Declaration, what is most notable is that New Zealand, the United States (claiming Hawai'i as one of its states), and Canada refused to sign the document. Eventually, on the heels of political pressure, New Zealand signed in April 2010, the United States signed in December 2010, and, finally, Canada signed in May 2016.

Many authors called our attention to the multiple ways cultural oppression is expressed in the suppression of certain aspects of language and thus one's worldview, as well as the tensions and challenges of naming and mapping practices that reframe and re-represent the traditional understandings of our places. Several authors make the point that the questions that Indigenous scholars bring into conversations about various contestations are not well received, not just because they are not often well understood but frequently because they make Western listeners uncomfortable. Wong explores an area of language not often seen as relevant or even appropriate in academic conversations about language reclamation and revitalization, largely because from a Western viewpoint these aspects of language are seen to be impolite, leading to discomfort such that the Western viewpoint oppresses the cultural understanding of these words and their use in everyday life. Correspondingly, other authors such as Oliveira discuss cultural oppression associated with mainstream mapping practices and the naming and renaming of places. Johnson, in similar fashion, brings issues of social and systemic oppression to the fore by exploring Indigeneity and metaphysical spaces in higher educational contexts and the ways these spaces have the potential to disrupt colonial relations of power and privilege within the academy.

This book set out to demonstrate the possibilities of collective hope—that when given the space, Indigenous scholars have the potential to be highly innovative and add significantly to the curricula in established Western disciplines. This creates multiple points of difference that open up opportunities for advancing scholarship and learning in these areas. This is strongly illustrated by the educational initiatives discussed in Lipe's chapter on Indigenous science and Jahnke's on Māori art. Ropata-Te Hei demonstrates that not only is Indigenous knowledge important, but it has so much more substance and relevance when the pedagogical context is immersed within the language that the knowledge has been created in.

The contestation that takes place from institution to institution needs to be responded to, in large part due to the desire to have Indigenous knowledge take its rightful place in the academy. This makes the contestations, no matter how frequently they occur, worth the effort. Indigenous agency of speaking for ourselves; maximizing Indigenous languages' independence from English; seeing the world through our ancestors' eyes by reinscribing the land, place, and environment through cultural wisdom maps and reclaiming original names for places; and daring to theorize our own experiences and knowledge of the universe are among some of the powerful efforts of Indigenous academics in institutions across the globe that are taking place today, and that are discussed in the chapters of this book.

References

Ermine, Willie. 2007. "The Ethical Space of Engagement." *Indigenous Law Journal* 6 (1): 193–203.

Royal Commission on Aboriginal Peoples (RCAP). 1996. "A Word from Commissioners." In *Highlights from the Report of the Royal Commission on Aboriginal Peoples*. Ottawa: Indigenous and Northern Affairs Canada. http://www.aadnc-aandc.gc.ca/eng/1100100014597/1100100014637#chp2

Smith, Linda Tuhiwai. 2005. "On Tricky Ground: Researching the Native in the Age of Uncertainty." In *The Sage Handbook of Qualitative Research*, 3rd ed., edited by Norman Denzin and Yvonna Lincoln, 85–107. Thousand Oaks, CA: Sage.

Troian, Martha. 2016. "20 Years since Royal Commission on Aboriginal Peoples, Still Waiting for Change." *CBC News*, March 3, 2016. http://www.cbc.ca/news/indigenous/20-year-anniversary-of-rcap-report-1.3469759

Truth and Reconciliation Commission of Canada. 2015. *The Final Report of the Truth and Reconciliation Commission of Canada*. 6 vols. Montreal: McGill-Queen's University Press.

Contributors

Jill Bevan-Brown (Ngāti Raukawa, Ngāti Wehiwehi, Ngāti Awa, Ngāi Te Rangi) is an Adjunct Professor at Massey University. She is a long-standing scholar, researcher, teacher, leader, colleague, and policy advocate. She was the inaugural director of the Massey University Centre for Research Excellence in Inclusive Education, and is a foundation fellow of the Massey University Academy for Māori Research and Scholarship, Te Mata o Te Tau. Jill received the inaugural Te Manu Kotuku Award for her work into understanding gifted and talented Māori learners. She is well published internationally and is passionate about her work, which has made a significant and positive difference to the lives of many children, young people and their whanau, in particular those with special needs.

Frank Deer is Canada Research Chair in Indigenous Education and Associate Professor in the Faculty of Education at the University of Manitoba. Frank is Kanienkeha'ka from Kahnawake, Quebec. He graduated from the University of Saskatchewan in 2008 with a PHD in Educational Administration, and has served as a classroom teacher in the Frontier School Division and the Winnipeg School Division. Frank studies Indigenous language education, Indigenous religion and spirituality, and philosophy of education.

Wiremu Doherty is the Chief Executive (CE) of Te Whare Wānanga o Awanuiārangi. Prior to this appointment, he was Deputy CE Academic Provost Executive Dean and Head of School. His whakapapa/geneological connections are Tūhoe and Ngāti Awa, and he is an active participant in governance and iwi development issues. Wiremu comes from a background in secondary school and kura kaupapa Māori teaching and tertiary education. He is the Chair of Ngā Kaitūhono, the body established by New Zealand Qualifications Authority to ensure Māori content is used appropriately.

Dwayne Donald is a descendant of the amiskwaciwiyiniwak (Beaver Hills people) and the Papaschase Cree. He is an Associate Professor in the Faculty of Education at the University of Alberta. His work focuses on ways in which Indigenous philosophies can expand and enhance our understandings of curriculum and pedagogy.

Ngarewa Hawera is a Senior Lecturer and the Program Leader of Māori Education at Te Kura Toi Tangata, Faculty of Education, University of Waikato. Her research and publications focus largely on mathematics education for learners in Māori and English medium settings. Ngārewa's experience as a lecturer at the university includes coordination and promotion of the Kākano Rua program, a pathway for Māori medium initial teacher education.

Margie Hohepa is the Associate Dean Māori and Associate Professor at Te Kura Toi Tangata Faculty of Education, University of Waikato. Margie has extensive research and publication experience within Māori education. Her research is framed by kaupapa Māori principles and theory. Her research interests focus on Māori medium education and have included the study of Māori educational leadership, assessing and reporting student achievement in Māori medium settings, Māori medium initial teacher education, and transitions in Māori medium education.

Robert Jahnke (Ngai Taharora, Te Whanau a Iritekura, Te Whanau a Rakairo o Ngati Porou) is an artist, writer, and curator working principally as a sculptor, although trained as a designer and animator. His work focuses on the dynamics of intercultural exchange and the politics of identity. Robert is a Professor of Māori visual arts and the architect of the Māori Visual Arts program's Toi Oho Ki Āpiti in the Whiti o Rehua School of Art at Massey University. He is widely published and has works in public and private collections in New Zealand and internationally. In 2016 Robert was made an Officer of the New Zealand Order of Merit for services to Māori art and education.

Patricia Maringi G. Johnston was the inaugural Head of Post-Graduate Studies and Research at Te Whare Wānanga o Awanuiārangi, a tribal university in Aotearoa New Zealand. Her move to the whare wānanga was based on a growing concern at how the mainstream continues to marginalize and fail Māori students because of an emphasis on cultural norms that are inherently non-Māori. Her research interests include anti-racist education, policy, educational administration, Māori education, and the politics associated with representation and difference. She has published extensively.

Spencer Lilley is a Senior Lecturer at Te Pūtahi a Toi at Massey University. His Māori tribal affiliations are to Te Atiawa, Muaūpoko, and Ngāpuhi. He has published widely on Indigenous transformation of the library and information professions. Before assuming his academic position, Spencer held leadership positions in the university and special library sectors, specializing in the development and delivery of library and information services to Māori clients. He is an Honorary Life Member of Te Rōpū Whakahau (Māori in libraries and information management) and is a fellow and former president of the Library and Information Association of New Zealand Aotearoa.

Daniel Lipe is Western Band Cherokee. He grew up in the Pacific Northwest in the woods and alongside the rivers of Oregon. He lives with his wife and two children in Hawai'i, where he continues to learn traditional ecological knowledge and teach at the University of West Oahu in the Sustainable Community and Food Systems Program. Daniel has worked in STEM education for over 20 years developing programs for under-represented minorities and educating students and educators alike about the need for including diversity, specifically Indigenous knowledge systems in STEM and STEM education. When not in the classroom, he is teaching his children about the outdoors. He is an avid bow hunter and steelhead fly-fisherman.

Margaret J. Maaka (Ngāti Kahungunu, Ngāti Awa, and Ngāi Tahu) holds a PHD in Educational Psychology from the University of Hawai'i at Mānoa where she is a professor in the College of Education. She is co-founder of the American Educational Research Association's Indigenous Peoples of the Pacific Special Interest Group (SIG) and a former member of the Ngā Pae o te Māramatanga International Research Advisory Board. She is also the former co-chair of the Sovereign Councils of the Hawaiian Homelands Assembly Committee on Education. Currently, she serves as the Chair of the AERA SIGS Executive Committee and as a member of the AERA Council. Margaret's research interests include educational psychology, Indigenous development and advancement, Indigenous leadership, educational policy, multi-literacies, and language and cognitive development.

Angela Nardozi is a Settler/guest on Turtle Island, with both sides of her family originating in Italy. She is a sessional lecturer in OISE/UT's Master of Teaching program and the author of a blog on Indigenous education.

Katrina-Ann R. Kapāʻanaokalāokeola Nākoa Oliveira is a Native Hawaiian. She was born on the island of Oʻahu and raised on the islands of Maui and Oʻahu. She earned dual Bachelor of Arts degrees in Hawaiian Language and Hawaiian Studies; a Master of Business Administration; a Master of Arts and a PHD in Geography from the University of Hawaiʻi at Mānoa. She is a Professor of Hawaiian and the Principal Investigator and Co-Executive Director of the Noʻeau Program, a multi-million dollar multi-year grant to advance Native Hawaiians and revitalize the Hawaiian language. Her research includes Kanaka geographies, epistemologies, language acquisition methodologies, and place-based experiential learning curriculum development.

Wally Penetito is a Professor Emeritus of the University of Wellington in Victoria. He is author of the first book on Māori education written by a Māori educationalist, entitled *What's Māori About Māori Education*. His research interests include anything related to Māori education. Other interests include sociology of education, Indigenous education, management of educational change, contexts for learning, pedagogy, teacher education, and philosophy of education.

Michelle Pidgeon is an Associate Professor in the Faculty of Education at Simon Fraser University. Her research agenda is located within the areas of higher education and Indigeneity. In particular, she is interested in the intersections between the curricular and co-curricular in holistically supporting Indigenous understandings of success throughout post-secondary education. She is also passionate about expanding the understanding of Indigenous research ethical protocols and processes. Theoretically, her work is influenced by Indigenous theory, social reproduction theory, and retention theories. This research agenda with the goal of empowering Indigenous success focuses on university and college responsibility and accountability to Aboriginal higher education from policy to practice.

Associate Professor **Leonie Pihama** is a mother of six and a grandmother of five. Leonie is the Director of Te Kotahi Research Institute at the

University of Waikato. She is a leading kaupapa Māori educator and researcher and was a recipient of the Hohua Tūtengaehe Post-Doctoral Research Fellowship (Health Research Council). Leonie completed a Fulbright Scholarship with the University of Washington, and in 2015, was awarded the New Zealand Association for Research in Education's (NZARE) Te Tohu Pae Tāwhiti Award for excellence in Māori Educational Research. Leonie is Principal Investigator on the Health Research Council projects Honour Project Aotearoa, exploring the well-being of Takatāpui (Māori LGBTIQ); He Oranga Ngākau: Māori Approaches to Trauma Informed Care, and He Waka Eke Noa: Maori Cultural Frameworks for Violence Prevention and Intervention, funded by the Ministry of Business, Innovation, and Enterprise (MBIE). In 2018, Te Kotahi Research Institute was the recipient of the inaugural Te Tohu Rapuora Award for Māori Health Research Leadership.

Jean-Paul Restoule is Anishinaabe and a member of the Dokis First Nation. He is Professor and Chair of Indigenous Education at the University of Victoria. Jean-Paul's research includes Indigenous pedagogy in online learning environments and looking at how teachers feel best supported when learning to bring Indigenous perspectives into their classrooms.

Mari Ropata-Te Hei is a Senior Lecturer at Te Putahi-a-Toi of Massey University. She is of Ngāpuhi, Ngāti Raukawa ki te Tonga, Te Ati Awa me Ngāti Toa Rangatira descent. She is the Programme Coordinator of Te Aho Tātairangi and Te Aho Paerewa that are total immersion kaupapa Māori initial teacher education programs. She has taught for many years in the Kura Kaupapa Māori system of education and has been a Principal of Te Kura Kaupapa Māori o Te Rito. She holds a BED in Kura Kaupapa Māori and degrees in Māori Visual Arts.

Sandra Styres is of Kanien'kehá:ka, English, and French descent, and is an Assistant Professor with the Department of Curriculum, Teaching, and Learning at OISE/University of Toronto. Sandra's research interests specifically focus on various aspects of Indigenous education that include decolonizing Land-centred approaches to Indigenous pedagogies and teaching practices; pre-service and in-service teacher development; Indigenous philosophies and knowledges; Indigenous research methodologies; and issues relating to the ethics and protocols that guide the work between Indigenous Peoples, communities, and universities.

Huia Tomlins-Jahnke (Ngāti Kahungunu, Ngāti Toa Rangātira, Ngāi Tahu, Ngāti Hine) is Professor of Māori and Indigenous Education at Massey University. She was the Director of the Te Mata o Te Tau Academy for Māori Research and Scholarship. She is Massey University's inaugural Toi Wānanga Research Fellow. Huia is Co-Chair of the American Education Research Association Indigenous Peoples of the Pacific special interest group and currently the Chair of the Research Committee of Ngā Pae o Te Māramatanga, hosted at the University of Auckland, New Zealand. Her research interests include Māori and Indigenous development, Indigenous research methodologies, the ethics of knowledge production, and Māori education.

Sam L. Noʻeau Warner (Native Hawaiian) held a PHD in Educational Psychology from the University of Hawaiʻi at Mānoa where he was an Associate Professor with the Kawaihuelani Center for Hawaiian Language in the Hawaiʻinuiākea School of Hawaiian Knowledge. He was a humanistic educator who made significant contributions to Hawaiian education, particularly in the areas of language revitalization and immersion schooling. He was deeply committed to promoting the survival of the Hawaiian language through improving the standard of teaching at the pre-school through to adult education levels. Warner was also dedicated to encouraging only the finest students to become Hawaiian immersion teachers. His research areas were language learning and teaching, teacher education for Hawaiian immersion contexts, teacher education, children's literature, and language structures and world view. His passing in 2016 heralded a significant loss to the Hawaiian language revitalization movement.

K. Laiana Wong (Native Hawaiian) holds a PHD in Linguistics, specializing in the Hawaiian worldview, from the University of Hawai'i at Mānoa where he is a Professor with the Kawaihuelani Center for Hawaiian Language in the Hawai'inuiākea School of Hawaiian Knowledge. His is the first dissertation written in the Hawaiian language. He has three children, all of whom have been raised speaking Hawaiian, and three grandchildren who are also being raised speaking Hawaiian. For over 30 years, he has devoted his personal and professional life to the advancement of Hawaiian people through Hawaiian language education and research. He is particularly interested in researching Hawaiian ways of speaking and thinking that diverge from those of English in order to curb the heavy influence English has on contemporary Hawaiian.

Dawn Zinga is a Canadian of several-generations-removed European descent. She is Professor in the Department of Child and Youth Studies at Brock University. Dawn has had the privilege of working with a number of Indigenous scholars, communities, and youth. Her research interests include Indigenous pedagogies and practices, integration of Indigenous approaches to teaching and learning in higher education, and cultural accommodation in schools.

Other Titles from University of Alberta Press

Wisdom Engaged
Traditional Knowledge for Northern Community Well-being
LESLIE MAIN JOHNSON, Editor
Collaboration between traditional knowledge and Western bio-medicine aims to improve health care in Northern communities.
Patterns of Northern Traditional Healing Series

Keetsahnak / Our Missing and Murdered Indigenous Sisters
KIM ANDERSON, MARIA CAMPBELL & CHRISTI BELCOURT, Editors
A powerful collection of voices that speak to antiviolence work from a cross-generational Indigenous perspective.

The rose that grew from concrete
Teaching and Learning with Disenfranchised Youth
DIANE WISHART
Qualitative research with interviews of at-risk inner-city students reveal the humanity behind the statistics.

More information at uap.ualberta.ca

www.ingramcontent.com/pod-product-compliance
Ingram Content Group UK Ltd.
Pitfield, Milton Keynes, MK11 3LW, UK
UKHW020125110825
461745UK00003B/221